AF361591

DANTE'S LYRIC POETRY

Poems of Youth and of the *Vita Nuova*

(1283–1292)

The first comprehensive English translation and commentary on Dante's early verse to be published in almost fifty years, *Dante's Lyric Poetry* includes all of the poems written by the young Dante Alighieri between c. 1283 and c. 1292. Introductory essays by Teodolinda Barolini guide the reader through the new verse translations by Richard Lansing, illuminating Dante's transformation from a young courtly poet into the writer of the vast and visionary *Commedia*.

Barolini argues that Dante's lyric poems are early articulations of many of the ideas and themes in the *Commedia*, including the philosophy and psychology of desire and its role as motor of all human activity, the quest for vision and transcendence, the search for justice on earth, and the transgression of boundaries in society and in poetry. With splendid new English translations and commentary, this edition brings Dante's early poems to a wider audience, while providing important literary and historical context.

(The Lorenzo Da Ponte Italian Library)

TEODOLINDA BAROLINI is the Lorenzo Da Ponte Professor of Italian at Columbia University.

RICHARD LANSING is a Professor Emeritus of Italian Studies and Comparative Literature at Brandeis University.

ANDREW FRISARDI is a writer, editor, and translator who lives near Orvieto, Italy.

THE LORENZO DA PONTE ITALIAN LIBRARY

General Editors

Luigi Ballerini and Massimo Ciavolella
University of California at Los Angeles

Honorary Chairs

Mr Joseph Del Raso Esq
Ambassador Gianfranco Facco Bonetti
Honorable Anthony J. Scirica

Advisory Board

Remo Bodei, Università di Pisa
Lina Bolzoni, Scuola Normale Superiore di Pisa
Francesco Bruni, Università di Venezia
Cesare De Michelis, Università di Padova
Giorgio Ficara, Università di Torino
Giuseppe Mazzotta, Yale University
Gilberto Pizzamiglio, Università di Venezia
Margaret Rosenthal, University of Southern California
John Scott, University of Western Australia
Elissa Weaver, University of Chicago

Dante Alighieri

DANTE'S LYRIC POETRY
Poems of Youth and of the *Vita Nuova*
(1283–1292)

Edited with a general introduction and introductory essays
by TEODOLINDA BAROLINI
With new verse translations by Richard Lansing

Commentary translated into English by Andrew Frisardi

UNIVERSITY OF TORONTO PRESS
Toronto Buffalo London

© University of Toronto Press 2014
Toronto Buffalo London
www.utppublishing.com
Printed in the U.S.A.

ISBN 978-1-4426-4840-1 (cloth)
ISBN 978-1-4426-2619-5 (paper)

Printed on acid-free, 100% post-consumer recycled paper.

The Lorenzo Da Ponte Italian Library

Publication cataloguing information is available from Library and Archives Canada.

Publication of this book has been assisted by the Istituto Italiano di Cultura, Toronto.

This book has been published under the aegis and with financial assistance of:
Fondazione Cassamarca, Treviso; the National Italian-American Foundation; Ministero
degli Affari Esteri, Direzione Generale per la Promozione e la Cooperazione Culturale;
Ministero degli Affari Esteri, Direzione Generale per i Beni e le Attività Culturali,
Direzione Generale per i Beni Librari e gli Istituti Culturali, Servizio per la Promozione
del Libro e della Lettura.

This book has been published with the assistance of a grant from the Modern Language
Association.

University of Toronto Press acknowledges the financial assistance to its publishing
program of the Canada Council for the Arts and the Ontario Arts Council.

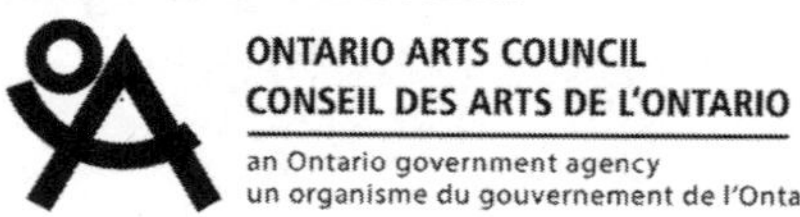

University of Toronto Press acknowledges the financial support of the Government of
Canada through the Canada Book Fund for its publishing activities.

Contents

DANTE'S LYRIC POETRY

Poems of Youth and of the *Vita Nuova*

(1283–1292)

Dante's Lyric Poetry: From Editorial History to Hermeneutic Future

This commentary offers critical readings of Dante's youthful lyrics (*rime* in Italian), spanning the years circa 1283 – circa 1292, and including the poems eventually inserted by Dante in the *Vita Nuova*. My aim is to illuminate the conceptual itinerary that led a young courtly poet of the final decades of the thirteenth century to become the writer of the vast and visionary *Commedia*. My readings of the poems work to shed light on the relationship of the *rime* to the *Commedia,* to show how the first inklings of the *poema sacro* can be found in the lyrics. Indeed, my commentary is the first systematically to connect Dante's early poetry to his later masterpiece. The importance of the early poems to understanding the *Commedia* is the overarching theme of this work.

Dante's lyric poetry has traditionally been the province of philologists, and it has remained to some degree virgin territory for critics. My commentary reads critically, rather than merely glossing, bringing to bear critical approaches (for instance, an interest in gender) that have never before been employed in discussing Dante's lyric poetry. Throughout this commentary I look more forward than back, in terms of Dante's own trajectory. Along with the traditional work of showing echoes of this troubadour or that Sicilian precursor, I work to illuminate the ideological wellsprings of the *Commedia*, the early presence of many of the core issues that we associate with the later Dante: the philosophy and psychology of desire and its role as motor of all human activity, the quest for vision and transcendence, the frustrating search for justice on earth, and the transgressing of boundaries in society and in poetry, along with an abiding interest in gender issues and social anxiety.

Stylistic and Ideological Experimentation

The extraordinary texts – canzoni, *ballate*, and sonnets – to which we refer when we talk about Dante's lyrics (this is not a unitary work: there is no collection identified and entitled by the author), consists, according to tradition, of eighty-eight poems whose attribution to Dante is certain. Domenico De Robertis recently increased this number by eight poems; we will return to the issue of poems of uncertain attribution later in this Introduction. Written over a period of approximately twenty-five years, the lyrics offer us access to the poet's workbench, allowing us to glimpse the process through which Dante became Dante. These poems on the one hand testify to the paths not taken, and on the other allow us to identify with greater clarity when, how, and by what incremental and gradual steps Dante ventured along the path that would ultimately become his.

Dante started to compose his lyrics sometime before 1283 (the date of the sonnet *A ciascun'alma,* the first poem in the *Vita Nuova*) and continued to write them for about a quarter of a century: throughout the time – from the condemnations of January and March 1302 onward – of his exile from Florence (witnessed by the canzone *Tre donne*) and lasting to approximately 1307 (the presumed date of the canzone *Amor, da che convien*). Dante's lyrics manifest enormous variety, beginning with early compositions written in the Guittonian manner (for example, the *tenzoni,* or poetic dialogues, with Dante da Maiano), and as evidenced in other youthful poems that explore various styles: the Sicilian style of the canzone *La dispietata mente*; the courtly brio associated with Folgore da San Gimignano that we see, for example, in the sonnet *Sonar bracchetti*; the Cavalcantian delicacy that infuses the *ballata Per una ghirlandetta*; and the style (found quintessentially in sonnets like *Tanto gentile e tanto onesta pare*) that Dante in *Purgatorio* 24 will retroactively christen *dolce stil novo* (sweet new style), a style that we find not only in many poems of the *Vita Nuova* but also in the love poems that the *Convivio* dedicates to Lady Philosophy.

After a phase of stylistic and lexical contraction, aimed at achieving the refined purity of the *stil novo,* the restricting of lexicon and rhetoric gives way to a phase of expansion, which then characterizes all of Dante's subsequent poetic production. This centrifugal push is already foreshadowed in the lyrics that make up the *tenzone* with Forese Donati, written before the latter's death in 1296, as well as in the *rime petrose* (stony lyrics), dedicated to a cold and unresponsive woman, whose heart is "petrified" and who is called accordingly *la pietra* (the stone) – lyrics datable to about December 1296, the date indicated by the astronomical periphrasis in the *petrosa* canzone *Io son venuto.* There are also moral and philosophical poems, as for example the canzone on true nobility, *Le dolci rime,* in which Dante is likely the first poet who incorporates a translation of Aristotle's *Ethics* into verse;[1] the socially engaged canzone dedicated to the courtly quality of *leggiadria* (the grace or refinement of the courtly lover), *Poscia ch'Amor*; the canzone *Doglia mi reca,* a meditation on desire, and the canzone of exile, *Tre donne*; and finally the last poems that have love as their subject, such as the sonnets exchanged with Cino da Pistoia and the late canzone with a clearly Cavalcantian affect and tonality, *Amor, da che convien.* Although Dante's lyrics have often been undervalued compared to the more cohesive and monotonal production of a Cavalcanti or a Petrarch, it is in fact precisely this variety that determines their greatness. They constitute – together with

---

1 See Teodolinda Barolini, "Aristotle's *Mezzo,* Courtly *Misura,* and Dante's Canzone *Le dolci rime*: Humanism, Ethics, and Social Anxiety," in *Dante and the Greeks,* ed. Jan M. Ziolkowski (Washington: Dumbarton Oaks, 2014), pp. 163–79.

the prose works of the early exilic years, *De vulgari eloquentia* and *Convivio* – the linguistic, stylistic, and ideological prerequisites of the *Commedia*.

The lyrics document Dante's stylistic and ideological experimentation and help us connect the dots between the youthful courtly Dante and the mature poet-philosopher. For instance, the *tenzone* in rapid-fire scurrilous sonnets battled out between Dante and his friend Forese Donati helps us construe the passage from the narrow, circumscribed world of the *Vita Nuova* to the philosophically inclusive and socially differentiated universe of the *Commedia*. From a stylistic point of view, the lyrics reveal many features that will converge in the *Commedia*: for instance, the *tenzone* with Forese contains the germs of what will be the low back-and-forth style of the brawl between Sinon and Master Adam in *Inferno 30*. From an ideological point of view, the lyrics may also reveal features that Dante will later abandon: thus the early canzoni *E'm'incresce di me* and *Lo doloroso amor* bear witness to the presence of a Beatrice who presages not life but death. In *Lo doloroso amor* Dante affirms that "per quella moro c'ha nome Beatrice [I die for/on account of her whose name is Beatrice]" (14), a decidedly perverse statement for a poet who constructed his mature ideology on the concept that "I live for/on account of her whose name is Beatrice." *Lo doloroso amor* provides in this way an interstice – a fissure – through which we can glimpse the deviations in Dante's thought, the shifts of ideological orientation, shedding light on the not always linear path that Dante travelled. We learn that Dante's arrival at the mature notion of Beatrice and salvific love was far from preordained.

That arrival is so far from preordained that, in the sonnet *Io sono stato con Amore insieme*, datable to between 1303 and 1306 (thus about a decade after the theologizing of love that had taken place in the *Vita Nuova*), love is characterized in antithetical terms as an irresistible force capable of dominating reason and free will: "Però nel cerchio della sua palestra / libero albitrio già mai non fu franco [So in the sphere of its authority / free will has never been completely free]" (9–10). Still more surprising, the poet claims to have experienced this passion for the first time in his ninth year, that is, toward Beatrice:

> Io sono stato con Amore insieme
> dalla circulazion del sol mia nona,
> e so com'egli afrena e come sprona
> e come sotto lui si ride e geme.
> Chi ragione o virtù contra gli sprieme
> fa come que' che ['n] la tempesta suona ...
>   (*Io sono stato*, 1–6)

> [I've dwelled together with the god of Love
> from when the sun had circled back nine times,
> and I know how he checks and how he prods
> and how one laughs and cries beneath his rule.
> Opposing him with force or reason
> is like sounding the alarm within a storm ...]

Here the lover finds himself literally at the mercy of love, completely subordinated, to use a word that in *Inferno* 5 characterizes the lustful, those "che la ragion sommettono al talento [who subordinate reason to desire]" (*Inf.* 5.39). Foster-Boyde comment: "This is the more remarkable in that Dante is now about forty years old and has behind him not only the *Vita Nuova* with its story of an entirely sublimated 'heavenly' love, but also the series of canzoni that more or less directly celebrated a love that had its seat in the mind or intellect."[2]

In short, Dante cannot be pigeonholed, not even by Dante himself. His lyrics are a salutary reminder of the dialectical progress of his evolution as a poet and offer the reader the opportunity to confront the radical shifts in his development, and to witness how far from predetermined his journey really was.

The Future of Interpretation

The lyrics highlight, sometimes implicitly and sometimes explicitly, themes of great topicality for Dante and for his audience.

Among the themes that run throughout Dante's work, one of the most important is the great ethical theme of desire: is desire a compulsion that controls reason? Dante will explain clearly in the *Commedia* that "lume v'è dato a bene e a malizia, / e libero voler [a light is given to you on good and on evil, and free will]" (*Purg.* 16.75–6), but such an assertion is a conquest; we just saw that the sonnet *Io sono stato* asserts the opposite: "Però nel cerchio della sua palestra / libero albitrio già mai non fu franco [So in the sphere of its authority / free will has never been completely free]" (*Io sono stato,* 9–10). The early sonnet *Savere e cortesia,* addressed to Dante da Maiano, already posits the problem of compulsion and demonstrates the fatalistic solution that will recur later in *Io sono stato*, in the declaration that there is no power that can impede love: "ché nulla cosa gli è incontro possente [for nothing has the power to take him on]" (*Savere e cortesia,* 13). A version of the mature solution of the *Commedia*, in which desire can and must be governed by reason, is found instead in the post-exilic canzone *Doglia mi reca.*[3] The theme of friendship, considered a subset of love within the ethical context provided by Aristotle's *Ethics* and Cicero's *De Amicitia*, is glimpsed in the sonnets *Deh ragioniamo, Sonar bracchetti, Volgete gli occhi, Guido, i' vorrei,* and *Amore e monna Lagia,* where the concepts inherited from antiquity assume a new physiognomy against the courtly background.

The theme of friendship is not only philosophical/ethical but also social/historical, given the theoretical treatment of courtly life in a canzone like *Poscia ch'Amor* and

2 *Dante's Lyric Poetry,* ed. Kenelm Foster and Patrick Boyde (Oxford: Oxford University Press, 1967), 2:323 (hereafter cited as Foster-Boyde).

3 On *Doglia mi reca,* see Barolini, "Guittone's *Ora parrà,* Dante's *Doglia mi reca,* and the *Commedia*'s Anatomy of Desire," 1997, now in Barolini, *Dante and the Origins of Italian Literary Culture* (New York: Fordham University Press, 2006), pp. 47–69; and Barolini, "*Sotto benda*: Gender in the Lyrics of Dante and Guittone d'Arezzo," in *Dante and the Origins of Italian Literary Culture*, pp. 333–59.

the evocation in these sonnets of the life of the group. The exclusively male groups (*brigate*) glimpsed in certain texts (*Sonar bracchetti, Volgete gli occhi*) should be compared with the exclusively female *brigate* present for example in the sonnets *Vede perfettamente* and *Di donne io vidi una gentil schiera*. Taken together, these texts suggest the existence of a "sociology of the *brigata*" that can be extrapolated from the lyrics. The unusual mixed-gender company of men and women made famous by the *Decameron* is already present in the enchanted vessel of *Guido, i' vorrei*.[4]

There is still much historical material to extract from Dante's lyrics, above all in the areas of gender and social behaviour. The sonnets cited above as exemplars of the way in which Dante treats the theme of friendship are useful also for opening a window onto social relationships among men. The *tenzoni* with Dante da Maiano offer a glimpse of the behavioural codes that govern such relationships, from the veiled rivalry that runs through sonnets that are superficially friendly ("che di saver ver' voi ho men d'un moco [compared to yours my learning is but scant]," writes Dante Alighieri in *Qual che voi siate, amico*, a sonnet in which the word *amico* pertains less to the lexical sphere of friendship than to that of professional interactions between poet-rivals), to the open aggression of Dante da Maiano in *Di ciò che stato sè dimandatore*. Many texts that until now have been read exclusively in terms of an ideology of love also document distant and stylized – but not irrecoverable – moments of social life. For example, the sonnets *Voi che portate la sembianza umile* and *Se' tu colui c' hai trattato sovente* tell the story of a poet who does not respect the boundaries established by his society with regard to the rituals of public mourning. The poet wants to participate in weeping, an activity that belongs to the women, who reaffirm their role and re-establish the boundaries dictated by social norms: "Lascia piangere noi e triste andare [Leave weeping and unhappiness to us]" (*Se' tu colui*, 9). Exploring the transgressive impulses of the poet, the sonnets also end up offering a description (tenuous but nevertheless present) of female activity around mourning. There is no doubt that these sonnets and many others merit future in-depth analysis of their historical and anthropological background.[5]

The historical and civic realities of Dante's world are visible as well in sonnets such as *No me poriano*, which refers to the famous "Garisenda / torre [Garisenda tower]" in Bologna, and *Di donne io vidi*, where reference is made to the feast of "Ognissanti [All Saints' Day]." In both we can sense the daily life of the commune;

---

4 See Barolini, "Sociology of the *Brigata*: Gendered Groups in Dante, Forese, Folgore, Boccaccio – From *Guido, i' vorrei* to Griselda," *Italian Studies* 67, no. 1 (2012): 4–22.

5 As I noted in *Dante and the Origins of Italian Literary Culture*, p. 17, the anthropological material that can be extrapolated even from two unheralded sonnets like *Voi che portate* and *Se' tu colui* suggests the massive work of historical contextualization that awaits us. See too my "'Only Historicize': History, Material Culture (Food, Clothes, Books), and the Future of Dante Studies," *Dante Studies* 127 (2009): 37–54.

the tower itself is emblematic of the internal factions in Italian cities, and in this sense of the politics of the era.[6] The relationship between the social classes is touched upon in *La dispietata mente*, as is the exquisitely social question of honour, featured in the comparison in which the duty of the lady to satisfy the need of her lover is equated with the duty of a "buon signor [good lord]" who does not withhold help from his servant who calls on him, since by defending the servant he is also defending his own honour:

> ché buon signor già non ristringe freno
> per soccorrer lo servo quando 'l chiama,
> ché non pur lui, ma 'l suo onor difende.
> (La dispietata mente, 17–19)

> [an honest lord will never hesitate
> to aid his servant when he calls for help,
> since he defends his honour, not just him.]

Present for the first time in *La dispietata mente*, the master-servant trope is one that Dante will frequently use in the treatises *De vulgari eloquentia* and *Convivio* as well as in the *Commedia*; it opens an unexplored window onto contemporary society.

Dante's lifelong meditation on the craft of writing poetry is much in evidence in the lyrics, as is his intellectual engagement with the phenomenology of visions. The motif of Dante as visionary emerges very early in *A ciascun'alma presa* and in *Ciò che m'incontra*, and a very Dantean metatextual awareness may be found in many of the lyrics, for example in *Se Lippo amico*, *Piangete, amanti*, and *Sonetto, se Meuccio*. Dante's characteristic strategies in the *Commedia*, such as the use of direct discourse for creating the illusion of immediacy and the textual *contaminatio* between various stylistic registers, are amply attested in the lyrics: one thinks, for instance, of the fusion of courtly and biblical registers in the sonnets *O voi che per la via* and *Ne le man vostre*.

The lyrics also boast philosophical themes that we associate with *Paradiso*: already present in the early sonnet *Guido, i' vorrei* is the great theme of the dialectic between the one and the many, between the irreducible self in its individuality and ontological differentiation on the one hand and the enchantment of non-differentiation – of the "gran mar de l'essere [great sea of being]" – on the other. In the canzone *Donne ch'avete intelletto d'amore* we witness the *coniugatio* of intellect and love that will be one of the principal themes of *Paradiso*. One instance among many is the fusion of the faculties of intellect and will in the verse that describes Saint

---

6 For the tower in *No me poriano* see H. Wayne Storey, *Transcription and Visual Poetics in the Early Italian Lyric* (New York: Garland, 1993), pp. 143–55; and for the towers as signs of internal factions see Edward Coleman, "Cities and Communes," in *Italy in the Central Middle Ages*, ed. David Abulafia (Oxford: Oxford University Press, 2004), p. 48.

Bernard, "Affetto al suo piacer, quel contemplante [Rapt in his pleasure, that contemplative]" (*Par.* 32.1), where the first clause corresponds to will and the second to the intellect. Another stunning testament to the links between *Paradiso* and Dante's earliest poetry is the word *leggiadria*. Present in early courtly lyrics such as *Morte villana* and *Per una ghirlandetta*, it appears in the *Commedia* only at the summit of paradise, where it is used to describe the archangel Gabriel: "Baldezza e leggiadria / quant'esser puote in angelo e in alma, / tutta è in lui [All confidence and grace, as much as there can be in angel or in soul, is in him]" (*Par.* 32.109–11).[7]

Editorial History

In the absence of the author's own ordering of the *rime*, various editorial viewpoints have prevailed over centuries of commentary and editorial history. The great editors of the twentieth century turned to a chronological ordering of the poems. Traditionally, in the manuscript collections, the lyrics were divided by genre, canzoni isolated from sonnets and from *ballate*. This, the editorial choice of the manuscript tradition, was recently restored by Domenico De Robertis in his monumental 2002 critical edition.

Each of the major editions over the span of the twentieth century and into the twenty-first is in its own way magisterial. The 1921 edition of the *Rime* edited by Michele Barbi, for the Società Dantesca Italiana,[8] without commentary, establishes the textual nucleus from which his posthumous edition with commentary will take shape, carried to its completion by two disciples designated by Barbi himself, Francesco Maggini and Vincenzo Pernicone. Working with Barbi's notes and integrating his material, published and unpublished, with their own research, Maggini and Pernicone published their respective volumes, *Rime della "Vita Nuova" e della giovinezza* in 1956 and *Rime della maturità e dell'esilio* in 1969.[9] Their efforts were scooped by the edition of the *Rime* with commentary published by Gianfranco Contini in 1939; this edition, immediately praised for its lapidary elegance, was subsequently reprinted with revisions and new materials in 1946 and 1965.[10] The British scholars Kenelm Foster and Patrick Boyde published their translation with commentary in

---

7 On the co-penetration of codes – the theologizing of *courtoisie* and "courtoisification" of theology – see Teodolinda Barolini, "Toward a Dantean Theology of Eros: From Dante's Lyrics to the *Paradiso*," in *Discourse Boundary Creation*, ed. Peter Carravetta (New York: Bordighera, 2013), pp. 1–18.

8 *Rime*, ed. Michele Barbi, in *Le opere di Dante*, critical text by Società Dantesca Italiana (Florence: Bemporad, 1921).

9 *Rime della "Vita Nuova" e della giovinezza*, ed. Michele Barbi and Francesco Maggini (Florence: Le Monnier, 1956) (hereafter cited as Barbi-Maggini); *Rime della maturità e dell'esilio*, ed. Michele Barbi and Vincenzo Pernicone (Florence: Le Monnier, 1969) (hereafter cited as Barbi-Pernicone).

10 *Rime*, ed. Gianfranco Contini (Turin: Einaudi, 1946 [rpt. 1965]) (hereafter cited as Contini). For the history of the edition, see "Postilla del curatore," p. xxv.

1967.[11] Lastly, in 2002 the critical edition edited by Domenico De Robertis came out, followed by his commentary in 2005.[12] Already heralded by Contini in his just cited edition of 1965 (in the "Postilla del curatore"), De Robertis' edition has supplanted Barbi's as the official authoritative edition.

The unusual complexity of the editorial history of Dante's lyrics is rooted in a problem that is structural in nature. Since Dante considered his own lyrics as texts that are independent or complete in themselves rather than as parts of a whole (although he eventually decided to make the lyrics included in the *Vita Nuova* and *Convivio* into parts of a whole, those poems too were originally conceived independently of a macrotext), each poem has an independent and individual editorial history. Hence the disheartening challenge for the editor, who must deal with the dispersion of the texts throughout a very high number of manuscripts and follow the course of transmission of every poem and of every group of poems in the various anthologies assembled by copyists.[13] Pernicone, who had himself received the symbolic investiture from Barbi, entrusted to De Robertis in his turn the task of reconstructing the manuscript tradition of each poem: De Robertis' 2002 edition is therefore the direct geneological successor of Barbi's 1921 edition, completing the enormous undertaking of the *recensio* of the manuscripts that Barbi had projected.

Dante and Boccaccio, First Editors of Dante's Lyrics

The most important editor-copyist in the editorial history of Dante's lyrics is Dante himself, who includes some of his poems, and not others, in the *Vita Nuova* and *Convivio*. These choices had important consequences both for the ensuing transmission of the texts and for their literary fortune. Dante's primal intervention and its ripple effects through time are thus a crucial part of the history I am recounting, and we must take into consideration the historical mechanisms of compensation and misrepresentation that developed in response to Dante's choice to include some of his poems and not others in new macrotexts, which in turn developed their own editorial traditions and their own literary genealogies.[14] With regard to literary history, I refer

---

11 *Dante's Lyric Poetry*; see note 2.

12 *Dante Alighieri: Rime*, in *Le Opere di Dante Alighieri*, Edizione Nazionale of the Società Dantesca Italiana, ed. Domenico De Robertis (Florence: Le Lettere, 2002), 5 vols. (hereafter cited as DR, critical ed.). The numbering of the pages of the five volumes (more precisely, five *tomi* constituting three *volumi*) is not consecutive from one to the other. A first unit is composed by the two tomes that comprise volume 1, *I documenti*; a second unit is composed by the two tomes that comprise volume 2, *Introduzione*; the third and final unit is composed of a single tome that corresponds to volume 3, *Testi*. Three years later, *Rime* was issued, De Robertis' edition with commentary (Florence: Edizioni del Galluzzo, 2005) (hereafter cited as DR, comm. ed.).

13 "The tradition is represented by over five hundred manuscripts" (De Robertis, *I documenti*, tome 1, xviii).

14 For an analysis of these mechanisms of compensation, see Barolini, "Editing Dante's *Rime* and Italian Cultural History," *Lettere Italiane* 56 (2004): 509–42; rpt. in *Dante and the Origins of Italian Literary Culture*, pp. 245–78.

in particular to the line that carries from Dante's *Vita Nuova* to Petrarch's *Rerum vulgarium fragmenta,* a genealogy that bypasses and marginalizes Dante's independent lyrics yet will have a decisive impact on the decisions of their editors.[15]

Second only to Dante himself in importance in the editorial history of the *rime* is Boccaccio, because of his transcription of fifteen canzoni that came to be known, from his notation, as the *canzoni distese*. Boccaccio transcribed the same fifteen canzoni in the same order on three occasions in three different codices (Toledano 104.6, Chigiano L.V.176, Riccardiano 1035). Recently it has been hypothesized that the anthology of fifteen canzoni existed before Boccaccio – that Boccaccio took the sequence from an unknown source preceding him.[16] Even if this hypothesis could be verified, it would not change the fact that we possess the *canzoni distese* only through Boccaccio's transcription, which had the effect of creating a homogeneous block of Dante's lyrics (all canzoni) destined to become canonical: the fifteen canzoni that Boccaccio called "le canzoni distese di Dante [Dante's extended, i.e., pluristrophic, or non-monostrophic, canzoni]." For ease of visualization, I list the fifteen *canzoni distese* in the order in which they appear in Boccaccio's transcription:

Così nel mio parlar vogli'esser aspro
Voi che 'ntendendo il terzo ciel movete
Amor che nella mente mi ragiona
Le dolci rime d'amor ch'io solea
Amor che movi tua vertù dal cielo
Io sento sì d'Amor la gran possanza
Al poco giorno ed al gran cerchio d'ombra
Amor, tu vedi ben che questa donna
Io son venuto al punto della rota
E'm'incresce di me sì duramente
Poscia ch'Amor del tutto m'ha lasciato

---

15 In my "Editing Dante's *Rime*" I show how critics implicitly fault Dante's uncollected lyrics for being "dispersed," considering them in some way deficient because of exclusion from an "organic" and "unified" macrotext: the very label devised for these poems by philologists – "estravaganti," which literally means "wandering outside ones" – declares their insufficiency. At the same time De Robertis also exaggerates their dispersedness, refusing to implement a chronological order because he wanted to protect them from any contamination with the Petrarchan model of unified *canzoniere*.

16 Giuliano Tanturli proposes that the anthology of fifteen canzoni existed before Boccaccio in "L'edizione critica delle *Rime* e il libro delle canzoni di Dante," *Studi Danteschi* 68 (2003): 250–66. Tanturli recognizes, however, that his hypothesis is based exclusively on philological reconstruction and not on material evidence – that is, we do not actually possess a codex earlier than Boccaccio that contains the sequence of *canzoni distese*. It is dismaying, given the lack of material evidence, that in following Tanturli others have gone so far as to claim that the author of the *canzoni distese* is Dante himself. On the logical fallacies of this line of argument, see my "From Boccaccio's *canzoni distese* to Dante's *libro delle canzoni*: *Convivio*, *Rime*, and the Practice of Critical Philology," forthcoming.

La dispietata mente che pur mira
Tre donne intorno al cor mi son venute
Doglia mi reca nello core ardire
Amor, da che convien pur ch'io mi doglia

Later anthologists copied Boccaccio, faithfully reproducing the fifteen *canzoni distese* as he transcribed them.

The First Printed Edition: Giuntina

Of the first printed lyric anthologies, none is more important than *Sonetti e canzoni di diversi antichi autori toscani* (*Sonnets and canzoni of diverse ancient Tuscan authors*), published in 1527 by the Florentine Giunti brothers, and hence more commonly known as the "Giuntina."[17] The Giuntina exercised authority both with respect to the text of Dante's lyrics and with respect to the ordering of the poems, since it offers "the first proposal for systematizing and organizing Dante's lyrics."[18] Dante has pride of place in the Giuntina. The Giunti brothers dedicate the first four books of their lyric anthology to Dante's lyrical production, organized according to the following headings:

Sonetti e canzoni di Dante Alaghieri ne la sua Vita Nuova. Libro primo
Sonetti e canzoni di Dante Alaghieri. Libro secondo
Canzoni amorose e morali di Dante Alaghieri. Libro terzo
Canzoni morali di Dante Alaghieri. Libro quarto

The criteria of classification adopted by the Giuntina are various. A formal criterion – traditionally, copyists grouped poems by genre, according to the hierarchical order canzoni-*ballate*-sonnets – is traceable in the decision to segregate only canzoni into books 3 and 4. A newer thematic criterion can be discerned, instead, in the selection of only what the compiler labels "moral canzoni" in book 4, which begins with the three canzoni from the *Convivio* (showing us that the error of categorizing all three *Convivio* canzoni as "canzoni morali" begins early), in the order adopted by Dante in the treatise, while book 3 groups amorous and moral canzoni together: "Canzoni amorose e morali." Note the dependence of the printed edition on the editorial decisions of Dante himself: book 1 gathers the thirty-one mixed compositions (canzoni, sonnets, and *ballate*) selected by Dante for the *Vita Nuova,* respecting the order in

---

17 See *Sonetti e canzoni di diversi antichi autori toscani*, introduced and edited by Domenico De Robertis (Florence: Le Lettere, 1977), 2 vols. (hereafter cited as Giuntina). The first printed edition of any of Dante's lyrics is the first edition of the *Convivio*: *Convivio di Dante Alighieri fiorentino* (Florence: Bonaccorsi, 1490).
18 De Robertis, *Rime, Introduzione*, 2:1141.

which those poems are found in the *libello*, and respecting as well Dante's innovation in mixing lyric genres. Moreover, there is an embryonic principle of chronological order at work in the Giuntina's placement of the early *Vita Nuova* poems at the opening of its Dante sequence and his later canzoni at its end.[19]

Twentieth-Century Editions: Barbi, Contini, and Foster-Boyde

In the twentieth century the implicit chronological criterion of the Giuntina became the explicit basis for the ordering of Dante's lyrics. Barbi, and after him, Contini – who takes up, without alterations, the sequence of compositions proposed by Barbi, which he calls an "ideal chronology" (Contini, 67) – insert the available empirical evidence into the overall chronological framework provided by Dante's artistic career.

Barbi divides the eighty-eight poems published by him (to which he adds an appendix, "Rime di dubbia attribuzione" (Lyrics of doubtful attribution), which contains twenty-six poems) into seven books (as they had been called in the 1921 edition) or parts (as they were renamed in the later volumes of commentary), each of which is given a title. Barbi's titles provide precise categories, analysing and anchoring the compositions according to a wide array of overlapping criteria. The first of these criteria is authorial-editorial in nature, with implications as well for issues of chronology and biography: by making "Rime della *Vita Nuova*" (*Rime* of the *Vita Nuova*) the first book of his edition, Barbi places himself in the editorial wake of the Giuntina, which in its turn followed Dante. Barbi continues with the chronological-biographical thread in his second book, "Rime del tempo della *Vita Nuova*" (*Rime* of the time of the *Vita Nuova*), and the same principle is applied to the seventh book, "Rime varie del tempo dell'esilio" (Various *rime* from the time of exile). Biographical-chronological criteria combined with formal and thematic considerations underlie the third book, "Tenzone con Forese Donati" (*Tenzone* with Forese Donati), while formally and biographically defined thematic principles sustain the fourth, fifth, and sixth books, respectively: "Rime allegoriche e dottrinali" (Allegorical and doctrinal *rime*; this section contains the canzoni in the *Convivio*), "Altre rime d'amore e di corrispondenza" (Other *rime* of love and correspondence), and "Rime per la Donna Pietra" (*Rime* for the Stone Lady). The seven books are arranged in an order that, on the whole, aims at being chronological.

Barbi's multiply-subdivided and rather cluttered index, informed by a nineteenth-century positivist spirit, seems rather antiquated to us, above all if it is compared

---

19 Book 2 is less cohesive: its thirty compositions mainly consist of sonnets and *ballate* no longer attributed to Dante (for example, *Fresca rosa novella*), with only two canzoni, one of which has been removed from Dante's oeuvre, while the other is the trilingual *descort* that De Robertis has recently restored to Dante's canon. In book 11 of the Giuntina the poetic exchange between Dante Alighieri and Dante da Maiano makes its first appearance in history, under the heading "Sonetti dei sopradetti autori mandati l'uno a l'altro [Sonnets by the above-mentioned authors sent to each other]."

to the slender alphabetical list of texts devised by Contini, whose index emanates a modernist purity: the lack of subdivisions, the change from roman numerals to arabic ones, and the general concision of the volume combine to create a format that even typographically announces itself as new and modern. To understand the enormous impact of Contini's work we must recall that when it came out, first in 1939 and then in 1946, Barbi-Maggini's and Barbi-Pernicone's volumes had not yet been published, with the result that Barbi's writings on Dante's lyrics were fragmentary and had to be consulted piecemeal. Contini's volume, with its fifty-four poems attributed to Dante, followed by twenty-six "Rime dubbie" (Doubtful *rime*), offered both texts and commentary in a single compact and elegant graphic-editorial product. Moreover, his commentary brings a new level of literary analysis and interpretation to a corpus that has been underinterpreted.

Contini follows Barbi's sequence exactly, a fact that is not apparent from his index, which is alphabetical rather than chronological. But then, how is it that Contini's volume contains only fifty-four poems? Recalling the eighty-eight poems of Barbi's edition, of which thirty-four were lyrics that Dante had put in the *Vita Nuova* (thirty-one poems) and in the *Convivio* (three poems), we realize that it is precisely by omitting these thirty-four poems that Contini came to a total of fifty-four texts. Because of his exclusion of the *Vita Nuova*'s poems – Barbi's book 1 – Contini begins his own edition with Barbi's book 2: "*Rime* of the time of the *Vita Nuova*." Thus, by eliminating the *Vita Nuova* poems, Contini is the first editor to begin his edition of the *rime* with Dante Alighieri's poetic exchanges with Dante da Maiano, placed by Barbi at the start of his second section.

There is another chronological model, proposed by Foster-Boyde, which might be described as faithful on the one hand to Barbi's inclusive spirit but updated, on the other hand, by Contini's uncluttered approach in favour of doing away with subdivisions. The Foster-Boyde edition, which contains eighty-nine compositions rather than the eighty-eight of Barbi (the editors reverse, in my opinion not convincingly, the order of attribution of the five sonnets exchanged between Dante Alighieri and Dante da Maiano, thus assigning an extra sonnet to Alighieri),[20] follows Barbi's inclusive and chronological model. However, Foster-Boyde push further than Barbi in the application of his principles of inclusion and chronology, in a way that is bold and truly innovative: they are the first fully to integrate the poems of the *Vita Nuova* into the canon of Dante's lyrics. The English edition of Foster-Boyde, rather than an Italian edition, is the first to include the poems from the *Vita Nuova* not in a separate block – as did the Giuntina and Barbi – but mixed in with the other poems, in a move that lends further depth and rigour to the tracing of Dante's chronological and stylistic progression.

---

20 For the question of attribution, see the introductory essay to the "tenzone del duol d'amore" (which includes, by Dante Alighieri, the sonnets *Qual che voi siate, amico, vostro manto* and *Non canoscendo, amico, vostro nomo*).

We must always remember, however, not to reify any editorial order of the *rime*, for none is authorial: none is Dante's.

De Robertis' Edition

De Robertis' massive critical edition of 2002 is truly anomalous with respect to the modern tradition, because he rejects altogether the chronological criterion for order that became visible in the sixteenth-century Giuntina and that dominates the great twentieth-century editions. De Robertis chooses a radically different criterion from the one chosen by previous editors; he chooses to follow where possible the traces of the editorial history that he tracked so assiduously in his decades of manuscript review. In other words, as an ordering principle for his edition he substitutes the history of the transmission of the poems for the history of Dante's development as a poet.

De Robertis outlines the two choices that confront an editor of the *rime* – the choice of attempting to follow in Dante's footsteps or the choice of following in the footsteps of previous editors – and he chooses to follow the editors: "Either we trace the history of Dante's work as a poet, the history that the *Vita Nova* adumbrates and that the nineteeth and twentieth centuries worked to recover; or we propose a form, a form that the manuscript tradition, the tradition of the text of Dante's lyrics, has gradually coagulated and seems to authorize ... with the secret hope, perhaps, that the tradition reflects the history of the poet's work or will restore (betray) his own principle of organization" (*Introduzione*, 2:1144). De Robertis' edition therefore chooses to reject the attempt to reconstruct "the history of Dante's work as a poet" and offers us instead "the tradition of the text of Dante's lyrics," in the "secret hope" that this second course of investigation will ultimately lead us to the first.[21]

The ordering of the lyrics that results from this methodological choice is one that grafts the Giuntina onto Boccaccio's transcription of the *canzoni distese*. De Robertis' order opens with the canzoni: first the fifteen *canzoni distese* copied by Boccaccio, then the canzone not copied by Boccaccio (*Lo doloroso amor*), then the incipit of the lost canzone mentioned in *De vulgari eloquentia* (*Trag[g]emi de la mente*), and finally the trilingual *descort* that De Robertis reattributes to Dante (*Aï faus ris*).[22] After the canzoni, De Robertis passes to the other lyrics, the sonnets and *ballate*.

De Robertis' order preserves the Giuntina's partitions by genre, while reversing the Giuntina's sequence: we recall that in the Giuntina book 2 consists mainly of son-

---

21 It seems possible that the "secret hope" expressed by the master has nourished the impetuosity with which his disciples have turned the abstract hypothesis, without material evidence, that the *canzoni distese* existed before Boccaccio into the claim that the author of the *canzoni distese* is Dante himself. See note 16 above.

22 The poems numbered 1–18 in De Robertis' index of poems ("Indice delle rime del volume III") are therefore all canzoni (the fifteen *canzoni distese* copied by Boccaccio and three others). But the total of eighteen is misleading, given that De Robertis' number seventeen, *Trag[g]emi de la mente*, does not exist, and that the five canzoni of the *Vita Nuova* are not included.

nets and *ballate*, while books 3 and 4 are dedicated to canzoni. De Robertis rejects the Giuntina's partial adoption of a thematic criterion of organization for the canzoni ("canzoni morali" versus "canzoni amorose"), instead keeping intact the Boccaccian canon of the fifteen *canzoni distese*.

De Robertis reassigns to Dante a certain number of those compositions that Barbi had placed among the lyrics of doubtful attribution ("Rime dubbie"). As we have seen, Barbi assigns a total of eighty-eight compositions to Dante, including the thirty-one of the *Vita Nuova* and the three of the *Convivio*; he places twenty-six more lyrics in the category of lyrics of uncertain attribution. In contrast, De Robertis' edition has seventy-nine poems attributed to Dante and sixteen of uncertain attribution. Starting with Barbi's total of eighty-eight poems, I have reconstructed De Robertis' unexplained total of seventy-nine *rime*, which is obtained as follows: (1) by subtracting the thirty-one *Vita Nuova* poems from eighty-eight, he reaches a total of fifty-seven; (2) by adding back fourteen *Vita Nuova* poems to the base of fifty-seven, he gets a new total of seventy-one; (3) by adding to these seventy-one the eight uncertain lyrics that he restores to Dante, De Robertis reaches a final total of seventy-nine.

The *Vita Nuova* poems De Robertis includes in his edition are the thirteen that exist materially in a redaction that precedes the *Vita Nuova*, plus the first sonnet *A ciascun'alma* (for which he makes an exception that he does not explain). In other words, with regard to the poems of the *Vita Nuova*, De Robertis imposes a criterion of selection that is based on the vicissitudes of historical transmission: if the redaction of the *Vita Nuova* is the first redaction of a poem that happens to have materially survived, if it is the first transmitted by history, then the poem is not included in his edition.[23] It thus occurs that De Robertis' edition does not contain any of the canzoni in the *Vita Nuova*, and that the critical edition of Dante's *rime* sanctioned by the Società Dantesca Italiana ends up including the trilingual canzone *Aï faus ris*, "restored to Dante" by De Robertis, while excluding *Donne ch'avete intelletto d'amore*, Dante's favorite canzone, whose paternity has never been in question and whose separate codicological transmission as a poem presupposes an editorial history independent from that of the *Vita Nuova*.

The present commentary includes all lyrics attributable with certainty to Dante, thus embracing all thirty-one *Vita Nuova* poems. These are poems with respect to whose paternity there has never been any doubt.

De Robertis reduces the total number of poems of dubious attribution from twenty-six to sixteen, annexing eight compositions to the regular canon and eliminating two altogether (these two are *Deh, piangi meco tu, dogliosa petra* and *Nulla mi parve più crudel cosa*). The eight *rime dubbie* readmitted into the canon are *Aï faus ris, Quando 'l consiglio degli ucce' si tenne, Amore e monna Lagia e Guido ed io, Se 'l viso mio a la terra si china, Questa donna ch'andar mi fa pensoso, Non v'accorgete*

---

23 On the hermeneutic issues implicit in De Robertis' decision to exclude from his edition many of the poems in the *Vita Nuova*, see my essay "Editing Dante's *Rime*."

voi d'un che·ssi more, Io sento pianger l'anima nel core, and *Degli occhi di quella gentil mia dama.*[24]

De Robertis turns to the "documenti antichi" – the manuscripts – through which he hopes to recreate the authentically fragmented and resistant-to-interpretation Duecento experience, as compared to the "organic" Petrarchan collection with its invitation to interpretation. The underlying credo of his edition is in this sense anti-Petrarchan, in that he is committed to opposing what he views as an anachronistic Petrarchan solution to the ordering of lyric poems. The irony of De Robertis' edition is that the eminent editor and philologist puts so much effort into resisting the interpretation that is willy-nilly implicit in any editor's order. He thinks to eschew interpretation by turning to Boccaccio instead of making an order of his own.

Nonetheless, as noted earlier, there *is* interpretation – and of a most imprudent sort – built into De Robertis' edition, because he nurtures the "secret hope," picked up and made no longer "secret" by his disciples, that Boccaccio's ordering of the *canzoni distese* is indeed Dante's and that it represents Dante's own "libro delle canzoni." And there are other cases of unwarranted interpretive licence in De Robertis' edition: examples include his choice of "Lippo" over "Lapo" in *Guido, i' vorrei*, for which he gives no strong philological rationale (see the introductory essay), his lack of transparency in his handling of the *dubbie* (see the introductory essay to *Amore e monna Lagia e Guido ed io*), and his unphilological privileging of allegorical "Licenza" over historicized "Lisetta" in *Per quella via che la Bellezza corre* (see the introductory essay).

We need to bear in mind that interpretation is implicit in any order, Boccaccio's as much as Barbi's. Any editorial order – no matter how ancient – will reify a hermeneusis that is not Dante's.

Interestingly, the most recent Italian commentary on the *rime*, by the philologist Claudio Giunta, does not retain De Robertis' painstakingly "philological" order. Giunta follows Barbi's order while omitting the poems of the *Vita Nuova* and *Convivio*, so that in effect his edition replicates the order of Contini.[25]

The Question of Order and Dante's Implicit Poetry Collections

Every editor of Dante's lyrics must tackle the problem of the order. Although the poetic tradition of which Dante is heir boasts short sonnet groupings by authors like Guittone and Monte Andrea (these groupings, known as *corone* of sonnets, are organized by thematic topics such as the virtues and vices or a dramatic enactment of a dialogue between a lover and his lady), Dante himself never organized his poems into such a mini-collection. He did, however, create what I call "implicit poetry col-

---

24 A further analysis of De Robertis' subclassifications of the readmitted *dubbie* may be found in the introductory essay to *Amore e monna Lagia e Guido ed io*.

25 See Dante Alighieri, *Rime*, ed. Claudio Giunta, in *Opere*, vol. 1 (Milan: Mondadori, 2011).

lections." I am referring to the collections that Dante created in his hybrid texts, his texts that are mixtures of prose and of poetry. These are texts in which the poetry was written before the prose and was later set within the prose: the *Vita Nuova* and the *Convivio*. Given that the *Commedia* contains three autocitations by Dante of the first verses of three of his canzoni, I will add the *Commedia* to this list of implicit poetry collections.[26]

The diegesis of the *Vita Nuova* self-identifies as autobiographical and chronological. The *Vita Nuova* narrates a story that is declared to be autobiographical and that is presented as chronological: the ordering of the story, and so of the poems that serve the story, is defined as chronological by the author. Whether or not the chronology is accurate is in this context not the point. The important point for our purposes here is that from the *Vita Nuova* we can deduce Dante's interest in the idea of a chronological ordering of his lyrics. In fact, De Robertis' decision to adapt Dante's lyrics to the conventional ordering of Duecento and Trecento *canzonieri*, in which the canzoni are placed first, should be scrutinized in the context of the innovations for which Dante is so well known. We know that Dante was not tied to the model of the conventional *canzoniere*, in which the canzoni are placed first, because he unveils in the *Vita Nuova* what is effectively a new kind of Duecento *canzoniere*: one in which the poems are presented *as though in chronological order*. Moreover, in the *Vita Nuova* Dante spearheads another innovation along with chronological order: he does not hesitate to desegregate the various lyrical genres, placing sonnets and even one *ballata* before the first canzone. In the *Vita Nuova* Dante thus reveals a lyric sequence *in nuce*, a lyric sequence however still hemmed in and guarded by the prose frame. What he leaves as a seed later blossomed in the hands of Petrarch, who arrived at the solution of the *Rerum vulgarium fragmenta* – the fully realized *canzoniere* form – by abandoning the prose frame of the *Vita Nuova* and by retaining the idea of an order for the lyrics that is meaningful in and of itself. In the *Rerum vulgarium fragmenta* the lyrical genres are desegregated and mixed together – as in the *Vita Nuova* – and the poet arranges his lyrics in a sequence according to a method devised to exploit the idea of chronological succession.[27]

---

26 I am not, of course, suggesting that the *Commedia* contains prose. On the *contaminatio* of the lyrical impulse with the narrative impulse in Dante's works, including *Il Fiore* (if Dante actually wrote it), see Barolini, "*Cominciandomi dal principio infino a la fine*: Forging Anti-Narrative in the *Vita Nuova*" (1994), rpt. in *Dante and the Origins of Italian Literary Culture*, pp. 175–92, esp. pp. 190–2.

27 Petrarch exploits the idea of chronology, both adopting and violating chronological order. For the hermeneutic implications of Petrarch's choices, see Barolini, "The Making of a Lyric Sequence: Time and Narrative in the *Rerum vulgarium fragmenta*" (1989), rpt. in *Dante and the Origins of Italian Literary Culture*, pp. 193–223; Barolini, "Petrarch at the Crossroads of Hermeneutics and Philology: Editorial Lapses, Narrative Impositions, and Wilkins' Doctrine of the Nine Forms of the *Rerum vulgarium fragmenta*," in *Petrarch and the Textual Origins of Interpretation*, ed. Teodolinda Barolini and H. Wayne Storey (Leiden: Brill, 2007), pp. 21–44; Barolini, "The Self in the Labyrinth of Time: *Rerum vulgarium fragmenta*," in *Petrarch: A Critical Guide to the Complete Works*, ed. Victoria Kirkham and Armando Maggi (Chicago: University of Chicago Press, 2009), pp. 33–62.

The *Convivio* presents an entirely different situation: the lyrical genres are not mixed, as only canzoni are present, and the ordering is not chronological but thematic.

In the philosophical treatise Dante uses his canzoni as pre-texts and points of departure for a philosophical discourse in prose. After the first, introductory book, the remaining three books of the *Convivio* all begin with a canzone, whose interpretation launches the encyclopedic and philosophical material of the treatise. In books 2 and 3 of the *Convivio* the relationship between the canzoni and the prose they launch is far from straightforward, for the poems *Voi che 'ntendendo* and *Amor che nella mente* are love poems. (Placement in the *Convivio* has generated ambiguity about their status; we saw that the editors of the Giuntina labelled all the *Convivio* poems "Canzoni morali.") To refashion the canzoni *Voi che 'ntendendo* and *Amor che nella mente* as the starting points for philosophical discourse requires allegorical interpretation. But in book 4 of the *Convivio* the canzone and the prose converge, since *Le dolci rime* is philosophy in verse: the canzone *Le dolci rime* treats a moral topic, that of nobility, and so does not require an allegorical reading in order to lend itself to a philosophical discussion of the same topic in the prose.

The ordering of the canzoni in the *Convivio* is explicitly tied to the philosophical themes of the treatise. From what can be surmised from the presence of only three canzoni in an unfinished text of only four extant books (of the fifteen that were planned), the ordering is not so much chronological as it is thematic (there is an autobiographical element in the *Convivio,* but it quickly fades in the first books). Thus, the order chosen for the canzoni of the *Convivio* would have had to reflect a process of selection dictated by the thematic need to fit the canzoni to the varying philosophical subjects of the treatise.

Dante states that the *Convivio* would include and comment upon fourteen canzoni: "La vivanda di questo convivio sarà di quattordici maniere ordinata, cioè quattordici canzoni sì d'amor come di vertù materiate [The food of this banquet will be prepared in fourteen ways: that is, in fourteen canzoni, whose subject is both love as well as virtue]" (*Conv.* 1.1.14).[28] The text that we have contains, as we just noted, only three canzoni, two "d'amor" and one "di vertù materiat[a]." The books that are absent but explicitly announced have led to centuries of speculation on the identity of the other canzoni that the *Convivio* would have included. I use the term "speculation" rather than "reconstruction" because the absent books of the *Convivio*, never having been written, cannot be reconstructed.

The speculation about the other eleven canzoni that have been imagined as already chosen and destined for the unwritten books of the *Convivio* is the node at which the reception of the *Convivio* overlaps with that of the *rime*. This speculation has

---

28 This and the following quotations are drawn from Dante Alighieri, *Convivio,* ed. Cesare Vasoli, in *Opere minori,* tome 1, part 2 (Milan-Naples: Ricciardi, 1988). Translations of the *Convivio* throughout this volume are by Richard Lansing, *Convivio* (New York: Garland, 1990).

traditionally been focused on the fifteen *canzoni distese* copied by Boccaccio, the more so because the three canzoni of the existing books of the *Convivio* – namely *Voi che 'ntendendo, Amor che nella mente*, and *Le dolci rime* – form a compact group at the beginning of Boccaccio's anthology (preceded only by *Così nel mio parlar vogli'esser aspro*). This line of argument first took material form in a marginal note of Antonio di Tuccio Manetti in his copy of the *Convivio*, today in MS Riccardiano 1044, a work Manetti transcribed between 1460 and 1470. Beginning with *Voi che 'ntendendo*, Manetti proposes as the fourteen canzoni of the *Convivio* a list that corresponds to Boccaccio's *canzoni distese* minus Boccaccio's number one, *Così nel mio parlar*.[29]

The recent proposal according to which the collection of *canzoni distese* existed before Boccaccio (see notes 16 and 21 above) has renewed the old speculative link between the fifteen *canzoni distese* and the fourteen canzoni of the unwritten but projected *Convivio*. This guessing game has been going on for centuries, and continues because of a profound and understandable urge to recover lost Dantean textuality. However, the new theory that the fifteen canzoni existed before Boccaccio does not mean that the list is necessarily Dante's. Moreover, and most important, we cannot deduce how Dante might have organized his *rime* outside the *Convivio* from how he organized the canzoni he placed within it. In other words, even if we knew (as we emphatically do not) that the fifteen canzoni transcribed by Boccaccio (minus the first, *Così nel mio parlar*) were destined by Dante to be the fourteen canzoni of the *Convivio*, and in the same order, we still do not arrive at insight into the organizational principle of a possible lost Dantean *canzoniere*. The organization of the *rime* within the *Convivio*, all canzoni, does not necessarily mirror the order in which Dante would have arranged his *rime*, not all canzoni, outside of the *Convivio*. The *Convivio* follows its own criterion of order, determined by the philosophical topics treated by the prose.

Finally, we need to consider one further "implicit poetry collection" that Dante makes with his own lyrics. Dante cites himself in the *Commedia*, where he transcribes the incipits of three canzoni, all hendecasyllables: *Amor che nella mente mi ragiona* (*Purg.* 2.112), *Donne ch'avete intelletto d'amore* (*Purg.* 24.51), and *Voi che 'ntendendo il terzo ciel movete* (*Par.* 8.37). The three canzoni cited in the *Commedia*

---

29 Beatrice Arduini describes Manetti's marginal note containing the *canzoni distese* thus: "In precedence, in a note to carta 13r, placed next to the transcription by Marabottino of the first strophe of the canzone *Voi che 'ntendendo*, Antonio copies the fourteen canzoni that Dante supposedly intended to gloss in the treatise. In his note Antonio Manetti writes: 'Each of the verses here below is the beginning, that is the first verse, of each canzone that he [Dante] intended to gloss, which were xiiii.' There follows a column of the incipits of canzoni 2–15 ..." See Arduini, "Il ruolo di Boccaccio e di Marsilio Ficino nella tradizione del *Convivio* di Dante," in *Boccaccio in America: Proceedings of the 2010 International Boccaccio Conference at The University of Massachusetts Amherst*, ed. Michael Papio and Elsa Filosa (Ravenna: Longo, 2012), pp. 95–103; citation p. 101.

are all poems that possess complex histories and deep archeological resonance in terms of Dante's poetic autobiography: *Amor che nella mente mi ragiona*, cited in *Purgatorio* 2, is the second of the three canzoni in the *Convivio* (and the third in Boccaccio's anthology of *canzoni distese*); *Donne ch'avete intelletto d'amore*, cited in *Purgatorio* 24, is the first canzone in the *Vita Nuova*; and *Voi che 'ntendendo il terzo ciel movete*, cited in *Paradiso* 8, is the first canzone of the *Convivio* (and the second in Boccaccio's anthology).[30]

This complex stratification suggests a new and different organizing criterion: no longer the autobiographical and chronological criterion of the *Vita Nuova*, and no longer the thematic criterion of the *Convivio*. The ordering of the autocitations in the *Commedia* is in fact clearly *non*-chronological: if the order were chronological, *Donne ch'avete* would have to lead off the small canon of autocitations, and *Voi che 'ntendendo* would have to come before *Amor che nella mente*. Given the importance of *Donne ch'avete* in the *Vita Nuova*, where the canzone's composition is discussed and its chronological and strategic place in Dante's oeuvre clearly established, the non-chronology of the incipits of the *Commedia* seems quite glaring and intentional. The non-chronological ordering of the canzoni cited in the *Commedia* shows Dante's intention to use his lyrics as stages in the construction of an ideal autobiography, an autobiography dedicated to a poetic "I" detached from historical chronology.[31]

In conclusion, we observe that Dante, as an author who acts as publisher and editor of his own lyrics by means of periodically choosing and assigning a certain lyric to a "new life" in a macrotext (whether the macrotext be *Vita Nuova*, *Convivio*, or *Commedia*), does not follow a single organizing criterion. Of course, none of these implicit hybrid "poetry collections" is a pure collection of lyrics; each has precise aims determined by its respective macrotext. The *rime* collected in the *Vita Nuova* are adapted to the chronological and autobiographical story of the *libello*; the canzoni of the *Convivio* are adapted to the treatise's project of popularizing philosophy; and the autocitations in the *Commedia* are adapted to the ideal poetic autobiography inscribed by Dante into the *poema sacro*.

That said, it is also important to remember that the *Vita Nuova* provides the model for the *canzoniere* of the future, the model that Petrarch will follow and that will have immense influence down to our own day: a collection of lyrics, of mixed genres, that follows a tenuous but unmistakeable chronological itinerary.

---

30 The fact that the *Convivio*, insofar as it is unfinished, was not published by Dante during his lifetime takes nothing away from the complex history of these canzoni. Dante himself knew, when he chose to highlight *Amor che nella mente* and *Voi che 'ntendendo* in the *Commedia*, that he had previously highlighted the same two canzoni in the *Convivio*.

31 For the reconstruction of such an ideal autobiography on the basis of the three autocitations see Barolini, "Autocitation and Autobiography," chap. 1 of *Dante's Poets: Textuality and Truth in the "Comedy"* (Princeton: Princeton University Press, 1984).

Editorial Criteria of the Present Commentary and the Poems of the *Vita Nuova*

I will now review the criteria that inform this volume, starting with my approach to the inclusion and ordering of the poems, and moving on to the editions that I have followed.

I have remained faithful to the attempt to establish an overarching chronological order of Dante's *rime*, albeit one executed in broad strokes that lead to the *Commedia* rather than one that claims capillary knowledge of historical information that we do not possess. I stipulate that mine is an unassuming chronology, consciously hypothetical, undertaken in the awareness that our historical knowledge is full of lacunae, but in the faith that an attempt at a reconstructed poetic itinerary, even if imperfect, is preferable to an a priori renunciation. The readings in this volume represent an attempt to reconstruct the ideological history inherent in the composition of the *rime*. Such a history is the necessary basis for the reader who wants to understand these poems not only as individual experiences but as stages in the journey of Dante's poetic and ideological development.

Although it is not identical to that of any of my predecessors, my order has most in common with Foster-Boyde's, not a surprising result considering my sympathy for their innovative handling of the *Vita Nuova* poems: as noted previously, they are the first to print the *Vita Nuova* poems not as a compact group (as the Giuntina and Barbi do), but dispersed among the other texts. One might surpass Foster-Boyde's model in choosing not to retain the exact sequencing of poems that we find in the *Vita Nuova*. I considered this possibility as well, but did not pursue it because the *Vita Nuova* itself adopts a chronological framework for its disposition of the lyrics, and this framework – Dante's own – is not one upon which we can substantially improve.

As I noted above, in my discussion of De Robertis' decision to include some but not all of the *Vita Nuova* poems in his edition of the *rime*, the present commentary includes all lyrics attributable with certainty to Dante. It thus embraces all thirty-one *Vita Nuova* poems.

In my 2004 essay "Editing Dante's *Rime* and Italian Cultural History," I wrote about the cultural forces that may be factors in Italian editors' resistance to including the *Vita Nuova* poems in their editions of Dante's *rime*: cultural factors that I speculate are related to the enormous cultural capital assigned to the "organic" and "unified" whole that once united by an *auctor* should never again be fragmented and disunified. Emblematic of these cultural forces is the "philological" term used traditionally by Italian philologists for the poems left outside of the *Vita Nuova* and *Convivio*: they are the *estravaganti*, literally "the wandering outside ones." This is a cultural context in which philology is clearly not neutral but freighted by cultural baggage that privileges the "organic" and "unified" macrotext at the expense of the lyrics that, simply because never collected, are experienced as "outsiders" condemned to eternal wandering. These lyrics are subsequently labelled by critics as in some way inferior because excluded.

In this context, one in which removing poems from the *Vita Nuova* is viewed as subjecting that which is organic and unified to a "hermeneutics of fragmentation,"[32] a hermeneutics that should only be applied to poems that are already "outside" and hence always already fragmented, I felt it was important to resist the resistance to including the *Vita Nuova* poems in an edition of the *rime*. It seemed thus imperative to disunify the organic macrotext of the *Vita Nuova* and to print, in material form, alongside their uncollected and contemporary companions, the poems of the *Vita Nuova*: not as a unified block that reflects Dante's editorial choices, like the Giuntina and Barbi, but dispersed, à la Foster and Boyde. My Rizzoli volume, *Rime giovanili e della "Vita Nuova,"* is the first Italian edition of the *rime* to intersperse the *Vita Nuova* poems among the other lyrics.

Italian editors of the *rime* have not only resisted interspersing the *Vita Nuova* poems among the other *rime*; as noted previously, many do not include them at all. The following chart displays the treatment of the *Vita Nuova* poems in the editions discussed in this Introduction, a list to which I have added an Italian commentary to the *rime* that has come out since De Robertis' in 2002 and mine in 2009, the 2011 commentary of Claudio Giunta:

Status of *Vita Nuova* Poems in Editions Discussed in This Introduction

Barbi	Includes all 31 *VN* poems as a block in first book, "Rime della *Vita Nuova*" (this is the Giuntina model)
Contini	Omits *VN* poems altogether
Foster-Boyde	Intersperses all 31 *VN* poems throughout the *rime*; the first edition of Dante's lyrics to do so
De Robertis	Includes, and intersperses, only those 13 *VN* poems that are attested in manuscript prior to the *VN*, plus (for no apparent reason) the first sonnet of the *VN*, *A ciascun'alma*. Hence there are 14 *VN* poems in De Robertis' edition.
Barolini	Intersperses all 31 *VN* poems, following precedent of Foster-Boyde; the first Italian edition to do so
Giunta	Omits *VN* poems altogether – a return to the Contini model

---

32 The citation is from an essay of Michelangelo Picone, explaining why it is better not to reprint the *Vita Nuova* poems in editions of Dante's *rime*: "On the other hand Contini is also right in respecting the independence and the specificity of works like the *Vita nuova* and *Convivio*, and in not considering the poems gathered within them to be removable. He thus applies a hermeneutics of fragmentation [un'ermeneutica del frammento] only to the outsider *rime* [*Rime* extravaganti]"; see Picone, "Dante rimatore," in *Letture Classensi: Le 'Rime' di Dante,* vol. 24, ed. Michelangelo Picone (Ravenna: Longo, 1995), p. 174; this passage is cited in my essay "Editing Dante's *Rime*," in *Dante and the Origins of Italian Literary Culture*, p. 266, where too there are other examples of the inferiority imputed by critics to the uncollected "outsider" lyrics.

My task here was to read the *Vita Nuova* poems as though they were not in the *Vita Nuova*. I learned that this is no easy task. In order to show what each poem does on its own, independent of the *Vita Nuova*, I realized that I had first to acknowledge the meaning that accrues to the poem within the *libello*, and then show the reader how much of that meaning is the work of the prose. The encounter with these texts in their pre–*Vita Nuova* form thus requires two stages: a kind of backing out of the *Vita Nuova* followed by an analysis of the poem as an independent entity. In an interesting practical confirmation of the gravitational pull of the *Vita Nuova* prose on the lyrics, I found it necessary to acknowledge the effect of the prose before being able to set it aside. Emblematic of this critical work is that in the present commentary I refer to "Beatrice" only when Dante does so: he uses the name in the prose of the *Vita Nuova*, in the *Convivio*, in the *Commedia*, and in a handful of lyrics. If the name "Beatrice" is not in the text of the poem – and it usually is not – then I refer more generically to *madonna* (my lady).

I follow De Robertis' *Rime* for the text of all lyric poems that he includes in his edition. However, as we have seen, he does not include all the *Vita Nuova* poems in his edition of the *Rime*. Therefore, the texts of the thirty-one *Vita Nuova* poems are taken from two different editions. With respect to the fourteen *Vita Nuova* poems that De Robertis includes in his edition of the *Rime* (the thirteen poems that exist in an early redaction plus *A ciascun'alma*), I follow his *Rime*. The remaining *Vita Nuova* poems come from his 1980 edition of the *Vita Nuova*, for reasons I discuss below.

Our ability to separate the *Vita Nuova* poems from the prose is immeasureably assisted by De Robertis' laudable decision to print the pre–*Vita Nuova* version of a poem where possible. Just to see such a version of the poem printed on the page has a clarifying effect, helping us to resist Dante's pervasive fiction that the poems in the *Vita Nuova* were written for the occasions described in the prose. If we know incontrovertibly that a poem existed in material form before the *Vita Nuova*, many of the interpretive problems that plagued earlier critics disappear. For instance, the issue of the chronology of the First and Second Beginnings of *Era venuta nella mente mia* is a non-issue once we have the earlier redaction of the sonnet in front of us.

Therefore I follow De Robertis in printing the pre–*Vita Nuova* redaction of those thirteen lyrics where such a redaction exists (in his formula, these lyrics are in their "pre–*Vita Nuova* dress"), making this the first English edition of the *rime* to present these thirteen *Vita Nuova* poems in their original form. In cases where I have printed the early redaction, the reader will find also De Robertis' listing of the most significant variants with respect to the *Vita Nuova* redaction. The variants are most often relatively slight. In the case of *Era venuta nella mente mia*, where there is a particularly notable divergence between the two redactions, both the original redaction and the *Vita Nuova* redaction are printed.

The thirteen lyrics of the *Vita Nuova* that exist in a redaction prior to the *Vita Nuova*, in the order in which they appear in De Robertis' *Rime*, are:

O voi che per la via d'Amor passate	DR 33, *VN* VII (2)
Con l'altre donne mia vista gabbate	DR 52, *VN* XIV (7)
Ciò che m'incontra, nella mente more	DR 57, *VN* XV (8)
Vede perfettamente ogne salute	DR 62, *VN* XXVI (17)
Negli occhi porta la mia donna Amore	DR 63, *VN* XXI (12)
Tanto gentile e tanto onesta pare	DR 64, *VN* XXVI (17)
Venite a 'ntender li sospiri miei	DR 67, *VN* XXXII (21)
Era venuta nella mente mia	DR 68, *VN* XXXIV (23)
Deh pellegrini che pensosi andate	DR 69, *VN* XL (29)
Oltra la spera che più larga gira	DR 70, *VN* XLI (30)
Videro gli occhi miei quanta pietate	DR 71, *VN* XXXV (24)
Color d'amore e di pietà sembianti	DR 72, *VN* XXXVI (25)
Lasso, per forza di molti sospiri	DR 73, *VN* XXXIX (28)

I preferred to place these thirteen lyrics not in the above order used by De Robertis but in the order in which they appear in the *Vita Nuova*. In the index I indicate, for the reader's convenience, which of the lyrics were included by Dante in the *Vita Nuova*, and which of them are presented not in the *Vita Nuova*'s version but in the pre–*Vita Nuova* redaction.

For the eighteen lyrics of the *Vita Nuova* that do not exist in a redaction prior to that of the *Vita Nuova*, and for which we have only the redaction of the *Vita Nuova*, I follow (ironically enough, given his decision to exclude them from his *Rime*) De Robertis' edition of the *Vita Nuova*.[33] I do this because this edition of the *Vita Nuova* is, in my view, superior to the subsequent, more belletristic, edition of Guglielmo Gorni. De Robertis also best does the work of comparing poetry and prose with an openness towards ideological discrepancies. Quotations from the *Vita Nuova* give the chapter number first in roman numerals, according to Barbi's numbering system, adopted also by De Robertis, and then in arabic numerals according to the numbering system in Gorni's edition of the *libello*.[34] For example, in the list given above, the sonnet *Lasso, per forza di molti sospiri* is accompanied by the following information: DR 73, *VN* XXXIX (28). The sonnet, which is number 73 in De Robertis' *Rime*, belongs to chapter XXXIX of the *Vita Nuova* in De Robertis' edition and to chapter 28 in Gorni's.

There are a very few instances in which I have indicated that I do not follow De Robertis' text of the poem. Thus, I explain in the introductory essay to *Guido, i' vorrei* why I do not adopt De Robertis' "Lippo" (see especially note 46). In the case of

---

33 *Vita Nuova*, ed. Domenico De Robertis (Milan-Naples: Ricciardi, 1980) (hereafter cited as *VN*). I use "*Vita Nuova*" instead of "*Vita Nova*" because I am using De Robertis' edition and because I do not find Gorni's case for the variant compelling. In a further twist, De Robertis became a convert to Gorni's usage, "*Vita Nova*."

34 *Vita Nova*, ed. Guglielmo Gorni (Turin: Einaudi, 1996) (hereafter cited as Gorni). Gorni unfortunately focuses on numerological reasons for his chapter divisions.

divergences between De Robertis' edition with commentary of 2005 and his critical edition of 2002, I follow the edition with commentary, insofar as it comes later.

In some cases two redactions are reproduced here: *No me poriano zamai far emenda* is reproduced both in the original Emilian version edited by De Robertis and in the Tuscan version edited by Contini (*Non mi poriano già mai fare ammenda*); *Per quella via che la Bellezza corre* is printed in the two versions that appear in De Robertis' critical edition (but that do not, inexplicably, both appear in his edition with commentary).

Finally, with regard to the lyrics of uncertain attribution, the eight "rime dubbie" that De Robertis has "restored" to the canon are not included here, except for *Amore e monna Lagia e Guido ed io*. On the issue of the *dubbie* in general, and the decision to include this sonnet in particular, see the introductory essay to *Amore e monna Lagia*.

I decided to avoid the use of numbers in referring to the *rime*, instead always using the incipit, or first verse, as per the medieval custom. This decision was dictated by both practical considerations and methodological scruple. From the practical point of view, the use of the incipit minimizes problems arising from the variations in the order (and hence in the numbering) among the various editions. It is, moreover, not customary to refer to Dante's *rime* by a number, as it is customary, for example, in dealing with Petrarch's poems in the *Rerum vulgarium fragmenta*. In referring to the latter work, to use the number "126" to indicate the canzone *Chiare, fresche et dolci acque* is not only force of habit but also correct: Petrarch himself placed the canzone *Chiare, fresche et dolci acque* at position 126 of his sequence and the numbering is therefore the author's own. It is precisely here that my methodological scruple comes into play: in the case of Dante's lyrics, where neither the ordering nor therefore the numbering that communicates the order are the author's, the automatic reification of the *editor's* order that is conferred by the use of numbers should be avoided.

My use of only incipits thus reflects a desire for methodological coherence and of fidelity to the principles on which this work has been based.

The Final Poem

In conclusion, I must note that the present volume is the first stage of Dante's lyric itinerary, and therefore – if the fates are willing – the first stage in my own. The texts included here were written before 1293, and those with which the next volume will begin also belong to the Duecento. I will pick up the discussion again with *Voi che 'ntendendo il terzo ciel movete*, the poem that became the first canzone of the *Convivio*, where it is dated by Dante to August 1293. The connection of *Voi che 'ntendendo* to the material in this volume is very strong, in that its "plot" is sketched in the sonnet *Gentil penser*, placed by Dante in chapter XXXVIII (27) of the *Vita Nuova*.

The last poem of this volume, *Per quella via che la Bellezza corre*, underscores the non-finality of the itinerary charted here. To conclude this volume with the last sonnet of the *Vita Nuova, Oltra la spera,* would give the impression of a coherence and inevitability that is belied by what follows in Dante's life and in his poetry. Although written about the time of the *Vita Nuova,* most likely circa 1292, *Per quella via* throws into relief the conflictual aspects of Dante's thought, dramatizing the vital seductions of life and the difficulties of "keeping the threshold of assent" (*Purg.* 18.63).

After being exiled and before starting to draft the *Inferno,* Dante wrote the marvelous passage on the ladder of desire that we find in the *Convivio*: "Onde vedemo li parvuli desiderare massimamente un pomo; e poi, più procedendo, desiderare uno augellino; e poi, più oltre, desiderare bel vestimento; e poi lo cavallo, e poi una donna; e poi ricchezza non grande, e poi grande, e poi più [Thus we see little children setting their desire first of all on an apple, and then growing older desiring to possess a little bird, and then still later desiring to possess fine clothes, then a horse, and then a woman, and then modest wealth, then greater riches, and then still more]" (*Conv.* 4.12.16). Dante is essentially a poet of desire – much more so than Petrarch, who is essentially a poet not of eros but of the ego fragmented by time, more metaphysical than erotic – and the problem of desire as "moto spiritale [spiritual motion]" (*Purg.* 18.32) never fades for him. Desire is the motor of every human journey, of the voyage to the transcendent and to the stars as much as the voyage to the abyss.

How humans negotiate desire is the perennial question of Dante's thought, and it is a question that is present in this commentary from the very first poem written to Dante da Maiano to the very last, *Per quella via.* Although the fifty-eight introductory essays can be consulted independently of one another, they form a narrative through-line that tells the story of Dante's development in time. Most of all, I want to show how that development, beginning in Dante's youthful lyrics, leads to the *Commedia* and is epistemologically essential to our understanding of the *Commedia.* My commentary essays on the fifty-eight poems move in a teleological direction and form a narrative in which I endeavour to tell a coherent story, one that I hope will reward a reading that moves from beginning to end.

A Note on This Volume

This volume is similar to the original Italian but not identical. *Dante's Lyric Poetry: Poems of Youth and of the "Vita Nuova" (1283–1292)* is a translated, revised, and expanded version of *Rime giovanili e della "Vita Nuova"* (Rizzoli, 2009). I have taken the opportunity provided by the English translation to make necessary corrections and to develop my thinking on these poems, sometimes significantly.

Directed toward the English-speaking world, this volume features new verse translations of Dante's poems by Richard Lansing, who has a gift for making old Italian lyrics sound like English poetry while keeping them indelibly themselves. Lansing has masterfully translated all the Italian lyric poems in this volume into sprightly, fast-paced English verse. All of Dante's lyrics and also all of the quotations from other Italian lyric poets are his contribution.[35] Andrew Frisardi translated my Rizzoli commentary; by putting into English my Introduction to the volume and my introductory essays to the poems, which I originally wrote in Italian, he provided the foundation for the updated and amplified Introduction and essays found here.

All translations of the prose of the *Vita Nuova* are from Frisardi's 2012 translation of the *libello*. Translations of the *Commedia* are by Frisardi and me. Due to constraints of space, this English edition forgoes Manuele Gragnolati's excellent line notes to the poems, which grace the Italian edition; those readers who want more philological and lexical assistance should consult those notes in the Italian version. The metrical annotations that follow each poem were prepared for this edition by Grace Delmolino, as too the glossary of Italian metrical terms that closes this Introduction. Beyond these specific contributions, Grace provided essential and sustaining collaboration throughout the tasks of copy-editing and proofing.

Like so many others, I am deeply grateful to the generosity and vision of Ron Schoeffel, who welcomed this volume to the University of Toronto Press.

My thanks also to Martin Eisner for suggesting the cover illustration, Joseph Noel Paton's "Dante's Dream, or Dante Meditating the Episode of Francesca da Rimini and Paolo Malatesta" (1852). Dante dreaming of the *Commedia* is what this book is about.

Teodolinda Barolini
New York, 2013

---

35 On the occasions when the discussion requires a verse or phrase to be translated literally, the English translation is in parentheses without quotation marks.

Editions Cited in the Introductory Essays and Notes

Authors and titles are listed alphabetically; an author's or title's editions are listed chronologically.

Alighieri, Dante. *La Commedia secondo l'antica vulgata.* Ed. Giorgio Petrocchi. 4 vols. Milan: Mondadori, 1966–7.
- *Opere minori.* 2 vols. Milan-Naples: Ricciardi, 1979–8.
- *Rime.* Ed. Michele Barbi. In *Le opere di Dante*, critical text of the Società Dantesca Italiana. Florence: Bemporad, 1921.
- *Rime.* Ed. Gianfranco Contini. Turin: Einaudi, 1946, 1965.
- *Rime della "Vita Nuova" e della giovinezza.* Ed. Michele Barbi and Francesco Maggini. Florence: Le Monnier, 1956.
- *Dante's Lyric Poetry.* Ed. Kenelm Foster and Patrick Boyde. 2 vols. Oxford: Oxford University Press, 1967.
- *Rime della maturità e dell'esilio.* Ed. Michele Barbi and Vincenzo Pernicone. Florence: Le Monnier, 1969.
- *Rime.* Ed. Domenico De Robertis. In *Le Opere di Dante Alighieri.* Edizione Nazionale under the aegis of the Società Dantesca Italiana. 5 vols. Florence: Le Lettere, 2002.
- *Rime.* Ed. Domenico De Robertis. With commentary. Florence: Edizioni del Galluzzo, 2005.
- *Rime giovanili e della "Vita Nuova."* Ed. and introductory essays by Teodolinda Barolini, with notes by Manuele Gragnolati. Milan: Rizzoli, 2009.
- *Rime.* Ed. Claudio Giunta. In Dante Alighieri, *Opere.* Vol. 1. Milano: Mondadori, 2011.
- *Vita Nuova.* Ed. Michele Barbi. Florence: Bemporad, 1932.
- *Vita Nuova.* Ed. Domenico De Robertis. Milan-Napoli: Ricciardi, 1980.
- *Vita Nova.* Ed. Guglielmo Gorni. Turin: Einaudi, 1996.
- *Vita Nova.* Translation, introduction, and notes by Andrew Frisardi. Evanston, IL: Northwestern University Press, 2012.
Angiolieri, Cecco. *Le Rime.* Ed. Antonio Lanza. Rome: Archivio Guido Izzi, 1990.
Boccaccio, Giovanni. *Decameron.* Ed. Vittore Branca. Turin: Einaudi, 1980.
Cavalcanti, Guido. *Rime.* Ed. Domenico De Robertis. Turin: Einaudi, 1986. (Source edition for Cavalcanti's poems, except for *Fresca rosa novella* and *I' vegno 'l giorno a·tte 'nfinite volte,* which are quoted from the text given in the edition with commentary of Dante's *Rime,* ed. Domenico De Robertis)

Cino da Pistoia. *Poeti del Dolce stil nuovo*. Ed. Mario Marti. Florence: Le Monnier, 1969. (Source edition for Cino's poems, except for *Avegna ched el m'aggia*, which is quoted from the text given in the edition with commentary of Dante's *Rime*, ed. Domenico De Robertis.)

Dante da Maiano. *Rime*. Ed. Rosanna Bettarini. Florence: Le Monnier, 1969.

Davanzati, Chiaro. *Rime*. Ed. Aldo Menichetti. Bologna: Commissione per i testi di lingua, 1965.

Folgore da San Gimignano. *Il giuoco della vita bella: Folgore da San Gimignano, studi e testi*. Ed. Michelangelo Picone. San Gimignano: Città di San Gimignano, 1988.

Giacomo da Lentini. Critical edition with commentary. Ed. Roberto Antonelli. Vol. 1 of *I poeti della Scuola siciliana*. Milan: Mondadori, 2008.

Guinizzelli, Guido. *Rime*. Ed. Luciano Rossi. Turin: Einaudi, 2002.

Guittone d'Arezzo. *Le rime di Guittone d'Arezzo*. Ed. Francesco Egidi. Bari: Laterza, 1940.

– *Poeti del Duecento*. Ed. Gianfranco Contini. Vol. 1. Milan-Naples: Ricciardi, 1960.

– *Canzoniere: I sonetti d'amore del codice Laurenziano*. Ed. Lino Leonardi. Turin: Einaudi, 1994. (Edition used for the sonnets, while the canzoni are quoted from Contini's text in *Poeti del Duecento* or, if not present in this volume, from Egidi's edition)

Petrarch, Francesco. *Canzoniere*. Ed. Marco Santagata. Milan: Mondadori, 1996; rev. ed., 2006.

Sordello da Goito. *Le poesie*. Ed. M. Boni. Bologna: Palmaverde, 1954.

Abbreviations

B   Dante Alighieri, *Rime*, ed. Michele Barbi

C   Dante Alighieri, *Rime*, ed. Gianfranco Contini

DR   Dante Alighieri, *Rime*, edition with commentary, ed. Domenico De Robertis

FB   Dante Alighieri, *Dante's Lyric Poetry*, ed. Kenelm Foster and Patrick Boyde

VN   *Vita Nuova*

Note on Italian Versification

Lines

hendecasyllable:
an eleven-syllable line of verse, and the most common metre in Italian poetry. The hendecasyllable is to Italian what iambic pentameter is to English, dactylic hexameter to Latin, etc. In the notation of rhyme schemes, hendecasyllables are represented as upper-case letters, while all verses that are not hendecasyllables are represented as lower-case letters.

novenario:
a nine-syllable line of verse.

settenario:
a seven-syllable line of verse.

Forms

ballata:
a lyric poem composed of one or more metrically identical stanzas, beginning with a *ripresa*. One or more rhymes of the *ripresa* are repeated at the end of each stanza. A *ballata* stanza can be divided into a *fronte* of two *piedi* (also sometimes called *mutazioni*), followed by a single *volta*. *Ballate* may use a variety of metrical lines including hendecasyllables, *settenari*, and *novenari*.

canzone:
a lyric poem composed of one or more metrically identical stanzas. Dante's canzoni are typically of five to seven stanzas, though there are also canzoni of three, two, or even a single stanza. The stanza of a canzone is divided into two parts, the first of which is called a *fronte* and the second a *sirma*. The *fronte* is further divided into two *piedi*; the *sirma* is sometimes an indivisible block and sometimes divided into two *volte*. A canzone is typically concluded with a shorter stanza called a *congedo* (also called *invio* in Italian or "envoy" in English), often following the rhyme scheme of the *sirma*. Canzoni often use both hendecasyllables and *settenari*, and sometimes even shorter metrical lines, though some canzoni may be only hendecasyllables (such as Dante's own *Donne ch'avete*).

sonetto rinterzato: a sonnet whose fourteen hendecasyllables have been "reinforced" or "layered" with *settenari,* so that the poem is longer
than the fourteen lines of the standard sonnet. Also sometimes
called a *sonetto doppio.*

sonnet: the Italian sonnet consists of fourteen hendecasyllables, divided
into an octave (*ottava*) and a sestet (*sestina*). These parts can
be further divided into two quatrains (*quartine*) and two tercets
(*terzine*), respectively. The quatrains may be rhymed either
ABBA (*rima incrociata*) or ABAB (*rima baciata*); the sestet
contains two or three rhymes and its rhyme scheme is variable.

Other Metrical Terms

congedo: a short stanza that concludes a canzone, often addressing the
canzone directly. Its rhyme scheme often follows that of the
sirma.

fronte: the first part of a canzone stanza, followed by the *sirma.* Also
the first part of a *ballata* stanza.

piede: a smaller part into which the *fronte* of a canzone or *ballata*
can be divided. A *fronte* will contain two *piedi* that must be
metrically identical in their disposition of lines of verse and the
relation of rhymes to each other within the *piede.* The presence
of *piedi* is indicated by a space in the notation of the rhyme
scheme.

rimalmezzo: internal rhyme or rhyme that occurs before the end of a line
of verse. *Rimalmezzo* is indicated in the notation of the rhyme
scheme by parentheses and a number representing the number
of syllables at which the rhyme occurs, e.g., "(a5)."

ripresa: a short stanza that opens a *ballata* and some of whose rhymes
will return at the end of each stanza proper. These rhymes are
indicated by the final letters of the alphabet.

sirma: the second part of a canzone stanza, following the *fronte.*

volta: a smaller part into which the *sirma* of a canzone can, in some
cases, be divided. These *volte,* like the *piedi* in the *fronte,* must
be metrically identical in their disposition of lines of verse and
the relation of rhymes to each other within the *volta.* The term
volta may also refer to the second part of a *ballata* stanza, following the *fronte.* The presence of *volte* is indicated by a space
in the notation of the rhyme scheme.

RIME

Tenzone between Dante Alighieri and Dante da Maiano

1a Provedi, saggio, ad esta visïone: Dante da Maiano to various poets
1 Savete giudicar vostra ragione: Dante Alighieri's response

The sonnet *Savete giudicar vostra ragione* is Dante Alighieri's response to a riddle-sonnet, *Provedi, saggio, ad esta visïone*, sent by Dante da Maiano to fellow poets requesting that they provide the "vera sentenza [true significance]" (2) of the vision he recounts.[1] Commonly held to be one of Dante Alighieri's earliest poetic forays, *Savete giudicar* is generally dated to a little before 1283. This is the date indicated by Dante Alighieri in the *Vita Nuova* for his own erotic visionary riddle, *A ciascun'alma presa e gentil core*, a poem that also belongs to the correspondence between the two Dantes: Dante da Maiano was one of the three poets who responded to *A ciascun'alma*.[2] If we accept the *Vita Nuova*'s date of 1283 for *A ciascun'alma*, *Savete giudicar* would most likely precede it by a little, both on stylistic grounds and because it seems improbable that Dante Alighieri would write to Dante da Maiano with the respectful tone that we encounter here *after* having received Dante da Maiano's disrespectful response to *A ciascun'alma* (the sonnet *Di ciò che stato sè dimandatore*). Whatever the case, when we read *Savete giudicar* and the other correspondence poems with Dante da Maiano, we are reading the work of a very young poet, no more than seventeen or eighteen years old.

These very early correspondence poems help us to remember that their author developed in time, that he was not born as the poet of the *Commedia*: even Dante Alighieri wrote early poems of more modest artistic value – frequently sharper and more interesting than the poetry of his peers, however – and experienced a diachronic process of development and change that we can study and map. Moreover, Dante Alighieri lived in a given historical moment, to which these texts bear witness – and part of the witness is that in writing about these poems we need to use his full name in order to avoid confusion. In other words, Dante was not always already Dante.

---

1 The other respondents are Chiaro Davanzati, Guido Orlandi, Salvino Doni, Ricco da Varlungo and ser Cione Baglione. The responses, along with Dante da Maiano's sonnet, are preserved in book 11 of the Giuntina (on the Giuntina, see the Introduction to this volume). For printed texts of the the other responses to Dante da Maiano's *Provedi, saggio*, see Dante da Maiano, *Rime,* ed. Rosanna Bettarini (Florence: Le Monnier, 1969).

2 The two other respondents to *A ciascun'alma* are Guido Cavalcanti and (with less certainty) Terino da Castelfiorentino.

He starts out in a group of poets that includes names many readers of this edition will never have encountered. Moreover, in corresponding with Dante da Maiano, "a member of Guittone's school writing in the Provençal style" (Barbi-Maggini, p. 155), Dante Alighieri reveals that he too started his poetic life as a stylistic follower of Guittone d'Arezzo.

It is interesting that the sonnet to which Dante Alighieri takes the trouble to respond should narrate a "vision" – "Provedi, saggio, ad esta **visïone** [Consider well, wise friend, this dream of mine]" [1]), writes Dante da Maiano in his opening verse – for vision will hold a privileged place in Dante Alighieri's imaginary. Even if a taste for the enigmatic is part of the Occitan rhetorical repertory, we should not discount the fact that here, in one of his earliest poetic forays, we find Dante working to come to terms with a concept that will later mean so much to him, one that he will continue to develop in the *Rime* (see, for instance, the introductory essays to *Ciò che m'incontra* and *Donna pietosa*), in the *Vita Nuova* (where the word "visione" is prominent beginning in chapter III [1]), and above all in the *Commedia*.[3] Not long after receiving Dante da Maiano's visionary riddle Dante Alighieri composed a visionary riddle of his own, *A ciascun'alma*, to which he subsequently gave a high-profile position as the first poetic text of the *Vita Nuova*.

Dante da Maiano narrates his vision in an explicitly diachronic form, with great attention to his speech ("Dico [I say]" [3]) and non-speech ("del più non dico [I'll say no more]" [13]). Dante Alighieri confirms the narrativity of *Provedi, saggio* with the verb "narrate" (8) in his response. (Similarly, Chiaro Davanzati uses "narrasti" in his own reply to *Provedi, saggio*: "Amico, proveduto ha mia intenzione / a ciò che mi narrasti per tua scienza [Friend, my intellect has attentively considered that which you narrated according to your knowledge]").[4] The story that Dante da Maiano narrates, whose explicit eroticism reminds us that unsublimated sexuality is part of the tradition inherited by the stilnovist poets, is the following: first he receives the gift of a garland from a beautiful woman, then he finds himself putting on her shirt,[5] then he embraces her ("dolcemente presila abbracciare [threw my arms around her tenderly]" [10]), then, seeing that "non si contese, ma ridea la bella [she offered no resistance, only laughed]" (11), he kisses her, "molto la basciai [I kissed her many

---

3 Dante represents visionary experience in his *rime* but he thematizes vision in his prose: whereas he never uses the word "visione" in his lyrics, he uses it seven times in the prose of the *Vita Nuova*, beginning with the "maravigliosa visione" of III.3 (1.4). After showing his interest in *visione* in the larger mystical sense in the *Vita Nuova*, Dante retrenches (the *Convivio*'s only use of "visione" is technical, appearing in a discussion of optics in 3.9.9), before the expansive treatment of the *Commedia*. On the concept of vision in the *Commedia*, see Barolini, *The Undivine Comedy: Detheologizing Dante* (Princeton: Princeton University Press, 1992), esp. chap. 7, "Nonfalse Errors and True Dreams of the Evangelist."

4 These are the first two verses of *Amico, proveduto ha mia intenzione*, Chiaro's sonnet of response to Dante da Maiano. We will come back to the significance of Chiaro's use of *amico* in his incipit.

5 As Foster-Boyde note, the point is not that the lady has taken off the shirt she was wearing to give to the poet, but that the shirt she gave him was one of hers.

times]" (12). At this point in his story, Dante da Maiano passes to "più non dico [I'll say no more]" (13), adding only the cryptic information that with the beautiful lady a dead woman also appeared, and that she is "mia madre [my mother]" (14). The words "più non dico" remain in Dante Alighieri's textual memory; a later variant, sharpened by the addition of the repeated personal pronoun *ti*, exemplifies lack of narrative generosity in the *Inferno*: "più non ti dico e più non ti rispondo [I'll say no more to you, respond no more to you]," says Ciacco to Dante in *Inf.* 6.90.

What is most striking – and anomalous with respect to his peers – in Dante Alighieri's response is the seriousness with which he effects a total transposition from the event described to its meaning. (Nor does he respond *per le rime*, repeating only the first rhyme of Dante da Maiano's quatrains – Alighieri's *ragione* rhymes with da Maiano's *visïone* – and he changes the rhyme scheme of the sestet.) The commitment with which the young Dante throws himself into the work of manufacturing significance is confirmed by the presence of the verb *significare*: "**significasse** il don che pria narrate [the gift you spoke of earlier / did signify]" (8). We see here Dante's first use of a verb that he will use rarely and in signature moments,[6] as in the verses of the *Purgatorio* in which he describes the composition of love poems as a process of making significance on the basis of Love's dictation: "a quel modo / ch'e' ditta dentro vo **significando** [in that way that he (Love) dictates within, I signify]" (*Purg.* 24.53–4). Immediately following are the verses in which Dante baptizes the lyric production of his own youth as the "sweet new style" – the "dolce stil novo" (*Purg.* 24.57) – in marked comparison to that of previous influential poets who, along with their followers, did not compose in the *dolce stil novo*: Giacomo da Lentini, Guittone d'Arezzo, and Bonagiunta da Lucca. As Dante wrote the verses of *Purgatorio* 24 that became official Italian historiography, with their signature "vo significando," did his mind go back to his own youthful Guittonian correspondence with a poet who never evolved beyond Occitan and Guittonian mannerisms to reach the sweet new style? We cannot know, but the sheer rareness of the verb *significare* in Dante's poetic lexicon is suggestive: after he composed *Savete giudicar*, Dante never used *significare* in his verse again until he wrote *Purgatorio* 24, and he subsequently distils his entire poetic enterprise in the verses "Trasumanar **significar** *per verba* / non si poria [Going beyond the human cannot be signified in words]" (*Par.* 1.70–1).

Regarding the interpretations of Dante da Maiano's vision offered by the young Dante Alighieri (the garland is the desire sparked by the lady, the garment signifies

---

6 The prose of the *Vita Nuova* contains two uses of the verb *significare* and two of the noun (*significato* and *significazione*), while the *Convivio* contains twenty-six uses of the verb and two of the noun *significanza*. Most strikingly, the *Commedia* contains no uses of the noun and only three of the verb *significare*, which after *Purgatorio* 24 recurs in "Trasumanar **significar** *per verba* / non si poria" (*Par.* 1.70–1) and "e 'l suo voler piacermi / **significava** nel chiarir di fori" (*Par.* 9.14–15). The young Dante may have noticed Cavalcanti's striking one-time use, in a correspondence sonnet to Gianni Alfani: "**Significàstimi**, in un sonetto / rimatetto, / il voler de la giovane donna [You expressed to me, in a rhyming sonnet, / the young lady's wishes]" (*Gianni, quel Guido salute*, 3–5).

her requital of his desire, the dead woman steadiness in love), more important than the specific glosses is his move to psychologize, his pronounced effort to interpret the internal motivations of the soul. This effort is completely absent in the poem of Dante da Maiano, and also from those of the other respondents (Chiaro Davanzati, Guido Orlandi, Salvino Doni, Ricco da Varlungo, and ser Cione Baglione). With respect to the dead mother of the last verse of *Provedi, saggio*, Guido Orlandi interprets in the light of the strong reproof that he issues to Dante da Maiano for revealing a love affair under cover of a dream vision. It is not correct, writes Guido Orlandi, to disclose your love and to use "I dreamed" as an excuse: "non bona convenenza è palesare / amor di gentil donna o di donzella, / e per iscusa dicere: 'io sognai' [It is improper to reveal / a noble lady's or a maiden's love / and then as an excuse to say: 'I dreamed it']." Hence, continues Orlandi, your mother comes to punish you: "dicer: 'Non dico'. Pensa chi t'appella: / màmmata [sì] ti vene a gastigare. / Ama celato, avra'ne gioia assai [Say rather: 'I won't tell.' Think who calls you: / your mother comes to punish you. / Love secretly and you will have much joy]" (*Al motto diredàn prima ragione*, 9–14). While not as critical as Guido Orlandi, Chiaro Davanzati would like Dante da Maiano to avoid thinking of his mother in the context of a love poem: "Di tua madre ti guarda da pensare, / ch'altra tua cosa s'avverrà con ella [Refrain from thinking of your mother, / for other things of yours will take place with her]" (*Amico, proveduto ha mia intenzione*, 13–14).

Only Dante Alighieri deliteralizes and deepens the significance of Dante da Maiano's mother (explicitly called "mia madre" by Dante da Maiano, an identification duly confirmed by Chiaro Davanzati and Guido Orlandi in respectively "tua madre" and "màmmata" [= "tua mamma"]). Dante Alighieri removes the literal biographical quality of the reference by excising "madre" from his reply altogether, replacing it with the more generic and evocative "figura" and thus giving himself the opportunity to manufacture significance: this "figura" now can represent the steadiness of the lady in love, the unwavering firmness of her desire. Dante Alighieri is analysing desire, as the choice of "fermezza" in "è la **fermezza** ch'averà nel core" testifies: this is a word that resonates with the discourse of desire in earlier love poetry. We need only remember that Arnaut Daniel's sestina begins "Lo **ferm** voler qu'el cor m'intra [The firm desire that enters my heart]" and that Dante in *Io son venuto* writes "ch'ïo son **fermo** di portarla sempre [for I'm resolved to bear it (the thorn of love) forever]" (51). Moreover, there is no word of greater thematic importance for Dante's personal trajectory: here the lady is said to be as unwavering as death, and later in his life Dante will require himself to be unwavering even after his lady's death.

In the verses "Disio verace, u' rado fin si pone, / che mosse di valore o di bieltate [A true desire, one rarely satisfied, / inspired by beauty and great worthiness]" (5–6), we can see the great Dantean theme of desire in its role as the motor of human life. Desire that arises from virtue or beauty ("Disio verace ... che mosse di valore o di bieltate"), and to which one can rarely bring an end ("u' rado fin si pone"), is the motor that pushes us along the "path of our life," the "cammin di nostra vita" of the *Commedia*'s first verse. Desire is both lack – "ché nullo desidera quello che ha, ma quello che non ha, che è manifesto difetto [For no one desires what he has but rather what he does not have, which is manifest lack]" (*Conv.* 3.15.3) – and the spiritual movement with which we attempt to fill that lack: "disire, / ch'è moto spiritale [desire, which is a spiritual motion]" (*Purg.* 18.31–2). Thus, desire is a function of time, the medium that signals mortality – movement, change, absence of being – and that condemns us always to desire. These are the principles that, according to Dante, govern the temporal journey of life (and that govern the narrative journey as well, in imitation of the voyage of life):[7] "Omne quod movetur, movetur propter aliquid quod non habet, quod est terminus sui motus. ... Omne quod movetur est in aliquo defectu, et non habet totum suum esse simul [Each thing that moves, moves because of something that it does not have, which is the goal of its motion. ... Each thing that moves exists in some defect and does not possess all its being at once]" (*Epistola* 13.71–2).[8]

In *Savete giudicar*, we can already catch a glimpse of a much more mature Dante, one who will openly tell us that desire is the motor of the spirit, a motor that stops only when the spirit arrives at its goal: "così l'animo preso entra in disire, / ch'è moto spiritale, e mai non posa / fin che la cosa amata il fa gioire [so the captured soul enters into desire, which is a spiritual motion, and it never rests until the beloved thing causes it to rejoice]" (*Purg.* 18.31–3). We are at the beginning of the path, where we are in a position to note how the rich current of Dante's meditation on "disio verace [true desire]" wells up from the small spring of these verses, and how the concept of desire that is "**moto** spiritale" exists *in nuce* in "disio . . . che **mosse** di valore o di bieltate."

The dependent clauses of these verses are not ornamental fillers, but fully functional, contributing to the analysis of the nature of "true desire." The first clause pushes forward, towards the desired end, the goal of the voyage, and therefore poses the question of fulfilment, here defined as rare ("u' rado fin si pone"). If we consider this phrase in the context of the *Purgatorio* verses just cited, we see that it treats the issue of the soul's arrival at "the beloved thing that causes it to rejoice." The second clause instead folds backward, towards the beginning of the journey, the source from which the soul's desire originally flowed, noting that the stimuli that induce the spirit to desire the beloved object – to make it beloved – are virtue or beauty ("che mosse di valore o di bieltate"). We are already in the presence of Dante's core obsession.

---

7 The textual journey imitates the journey of life; see my *The Undivine Comedy*, esp. chap. 2, "Infernal Incipits: The Poetics of the New."

8 *Epistole,* text and Italian translation, ed. Arsenio Frugoni and Giorgio Brugnoli, in *Opere minori,* 2 vols., tome 2 (Milan-Naples: Ricciardi, 1979–88).

1a (B XXXIX; C1; FB 1a; DR 84)
Dante da Maiano to various poets

Provedi, saggio, ad esta visïone,
e per mercé ne trai vera sentenza.
Dico: una donna di bella fazzone,
4 di cui el meo cor gradir molto s'agenza,
mi fé d'una ghirlanda donagione,
verde, fronzuta, con bella accollienza;
appresso mi trovai per vestigione
8 camiscia di suo dosso, a mia parvenza.
Allor di tanto, amico, mi francai
che dolcemente presila abbracciare:
11 non si contese, ma ridea la bella.
Così, ridendo, molto la basciai:
del più non dico, ché mi fé giurare.
14 E morta, ch'è mia madre, era con ella.

Consider well, wise friend, this dream of mine,
and please reveal its true significance.
To wit: a lady who is beautiful,
to do whose pleasure is my heart's delight,
presented me a garland as a gift,
with leaves all green, arranged quite pleasantly.
Then soon I found myself, it seemed to me,
apparelled in a shirt that had her size.
And then, my friend, I got my courage up
and threw my arms around her tenderly:
she offered no resistance, only laughed.
And while she laughed, I kissed her many times:
I'll say no more, on this she made me swear.
Then one who's dead – my mother – was with her.

METRE: sonnet ABAB ABAB CDE CDE.

1 (B XL; C 1a; FB 1; DR 85)
Response by Dante Alighieri

Savete giudicar vostra ragione,
o om che pregio di saver portate;
per che, vitando aver con voi quistione,
4 com so rispondo a le parole ornate.
Disio verace, u' rado fin si pone,
che mosse di valore o di bieltate,
emagina l'amica openïone
8 significasse il don che pria narrate.
Lo vestimento, aggiate vera spene
che fia, da lei cui disïate, amore;
11 e 'n ciò provide vostro spirto bene:
dico, pensando l'ovra sua d'allore.
La figura che già morta sorvene
14 è la fermezza ch'averà nel core.

You're wise enough to explicate your theme,
O man of learning held in high esteem;
so, steering clear of starting a dispute,
as best I can, I'll answer your fine words.
A true desire, one rarely satisfied,
inspired by beauty and great worthiness,
is what the gift you spoke of earlier
did signify, according to your friend.
The shirt, the gift of her whom you desire,
denotes her love, of this you can be sure.
And so your spirit did foresee the truth,
that is, in view of what she then did next.
The figure of the one already dead
is constancy that she'll bear in her heart.

METRE: sonnet ABAB ABAB CDC DCD.

La tenzone del duol d'amore

[2a Per pruova di saper com vale o quanto: Dante da Maiano to Dante Alighieri]
2   Qual che voi siate, amico, vostro manto: Dante Alighieri to Dante da Maiano
[3a Lo vostro fermo dir fino ed orrato: Dante da Maiano to Dante Alighieri]
3   Non canoscendo, amico vostro nomo: Dante Alighieri to Dante da Maiano
[3b Lasso, lo dol che più mi dole e serra: Dante da Maiano to Dante Alighieri]

This exchange of sonnets between Dante Alighieri and Dante da Maiano is known as the "tenzone del duol d'amore [poetic exchange on the suffering of love]," so named by Flaminio Pellegrini in an essay of 1917. This set of sonnets compels us to confront a problem of attribution that arose because of an error in the text that contains them, the collection of *Sonetti e canzoni di diversi antichi autori toscani* (*Sonnets and canzoni of diverse ancient Tuscan authors*), printed by the publishing house of the Giunti brothers in Florence in 1527. The "Giuntina," as it is known, is the first printed edition of the lyrics of Dante and other "antichi autori toscani"; it constitutes our only source of the poetry of Dante da Maiano and a fortiori of the correspondence between Dante da Maiano and Dante Alighieri. The exchange between the two Dantes can be found in book 11 of the Giuntina, where the five sonnets that make up the *tenzone del duol d'amore* appear in the order preserved in modern editions, but with the following headings:

1. "Dante da Maiano a Dante Alaghieri" (*Per pruova di saper*)
2. "Risposta di Dante Alaghieri a D. da Maiano" (*Qual che voi siate*)
3. "Risposta di Dante Alaghieri a D. da Maiano" (*Lo vostro fermo dir*)
4. "Risposta di Dante Alaghieri a D. da Maiano" (*Non canoscendo*)
5. "Risposta di Dante da Maiano a Dante Alaghieri" (*Lasso, lo dol*)

The error is evident: the editors of the Giuntina present three "responses of Dante Alaghieri" one after the other (poems 2–4 in the above sequence), thus abandoning the alternating pattern that an exchange requires. Clearly, the simplest solution is to break the chain, attributing the third sonnet to Dante da Maiano and imagining that the editor intended to write the heading "Risposta di Dante da Maiano a Dante Alaghieri" instead of the opposite. That is the solution endorsed by Barbi:

The order is correct with respect to the meaning of the poems and cannot be changed; but in the attribution of the sonnets an error has evidently occurred, because there are three of Dante Alighieri's sonnets in a row (2, 3, and 4). The correction that seems obvious, and we can even say certain, is to change the rubric for sonnet 3 to *Dante da Maiano* in order to re-establish the alternating order. Modern scholars have accepted this correction, with the exception of S. Santangelo, who proposes exchanging the attributions between the two Dantes in such a way that Dante Alighieri becomes the proposing writer with sonnets 1, 3, and 5 and Dante Da Maiano the respondent with sonnets 2 and 4. (Barbi-Maggini, p. 159)

As for the modern editors of Dante's *Rime*, Contini and De Robertis follow Barbi, while Foster-Boyde accept Santangelo's proposal, thus adding one text to their canon of Dante Alighieri's poems (and so arriving at a total of eighty-nine poems instead of eighty-eight). I find both Santangelo's arguments and those added by Foster-Boyde unconvincing. They are based on the idea that the presumably mature poet, Dante da Maiano, would not have addressed a young unknown poet, Dante Alighieri. But the most recent editor of Dante da Maiano, Rosanna Bettarini, writes that Dante da Maiano "must have been a little younger than Chiaro and Monte and very close in age to Dante Alighieri";[9] in this case, the entire argument based on the mature poet opposed to the younger poet falls apart. De Robertis confirms Bettarini's position, noting, with respect to the presumed difference in the two Dantes' ages, that "we have no proof that Dante da Maiano was the older and more practiced love poet" (*Introduzione,* 2:934).

Above all, there is no justification for countering the evidence of the Giuntina with such poorly supported biographical conjectures, since the Giuntina is the only textual authority that we possess with respect to the *tenzone* between the two Dantes. I follow De Robertis in thinking that the arguments of Santangelo and Foster-Boyde are far from being sufficiently persuasive to justify four corrections of the Giuntina instead of one: "If it were not for that incongruous attribution, would we be debating proper manners and who was older than who? It seems to this editor of the *Rime* that the most economical hypothesis is to leave the Giuntina as it is, with the one correction of the rubric of the third sonnet, and that this is the hypothesis by which interpretation must abide" (*Introduzione,* 2:935).

In the preliminary sonnet, *Per pruova di saper com vale o quanto*, Dante da Maiano's octave is devoted to the true matter of this *tenzone*, which is not the stated question (what is the greatest suffering of love), but the much more socially compelling question of proving one's worth as a man and as a poet, of testing oneself in the poetic agora. As gold is tested by a goldsmith to discover its true value, so this poem will be submitted to the test of an interlocutor. And not just any interlocutor will do: "l'adduco a voi, cui paragone voco / di ciascun c'have in canoscenza loco, / o che di pregio porti loda o vanto [I'm sending it to you, my touchstone for / whoever claims to rank among the wise, / or who is praised and held in high regard]" (6–8). In the

---

9 Dante da Maiano, *Rime,* ed. Rosanna Bettarini (Florence: Le Monnier, 1969), p. xvi.

sestet Dante da Maiano turns to the putative topic of the *tenzone*, asking his interlocutor to name the greatest suffering caused by love: "che mi deggiate il dol maggio d'Amore / qual è, per vostra scienza, nominare [What kind of suffering brought on by Love, / in your experience, is worst of all]" (10–11). But the real *materia* is the question of a man's *valore*, his comparative worth ("che già inver' voi so non avria **valore**" [13]), expressed in the oft-repeated verb *valere* ("to be worth," "to possess value"). Dante da Maiano is motivated by the desire to ascertain his value, present ("vaglio") and future ("varraggio"): "e ciò non movo per quistioneggiare / (che già inver' voi so non avria valore), / ma per saver ciò ch'eo **vaglio** e **varraggio** [and this I ask, though not to stir debate, / (for, with respect to you, I'd be outclassed), / but just to know my worth and future promise]" (12–14). The multiple uses of *valere* echo the great canzone *Ora parrà s'eo saverò cantare*, in which Guittone d'Arezzo addresses the question of his worth as man, poet, and lover.[10]

In his response, *Qual che voi siate, amico, vostro manto*, Dante Alighieri replies to the question posed by Dante da Maiano only in the last two verses, explaining that pain without equal is carried in the heart of "anyone who loves but is not loved": "chi non è amato, s'elli è amadore" (13). In other words, the unrequited lover suffers most of all. But again the true *materia* of the poem is the contest between the two young men, who seem to use flattery as a means of managing the aggression that animates their wary exchange. Dante Alighieri addresses Dante da Maiano in a stylized fashion that suggests contained aggression, with repeated references to the wisdom of his interlocutor and self-deprecating references to his own comparative lack of knowledge: "che di saver ver' voi ho men d'un moco [compared to yours my learning is but scant]" (6).

In this *tenzone* both poets are unstinting in their praise, seeming to sublimate aggression through stylized compliments. But aggression is not always sublimated in these exchanges. Unsublimated aggression comes to the surface in a sonnet written by none other than Dante da Maiano, who, in his mocking response to *A ciascun'alma presa e gentil core*, addresses Dante Alighieri slightingly as "amico meo di poco canoscente [my friend who understands but little]" (*Di ciò che stato sè dimandatore*, 3). Dante da Maiano further disparages Dante Alighieri as delirious, announcing that he will not alter his interpretation of *A ciascun'alma* until he has submitted Dante Alighieri's urine for examination by a medical doctor: "né cangio mai d'esta sentenza mea / finché tua acqua al medico no stendo [nor shall I change my view / till I submit your urine to the doctor]" (*Di ciò che stato sè dimandatore*, 13–14).

---

10 "The poem [*Ora parrà*] is a testing ground; its purpose is to prove that the poet, now that he flees Love, is still worth what he used to be worth: 's'eo varrò quanto valer già soglio' (2). The repeated forms of *valere* (*varrò* [2], *valer* [2], *valer* [6], *valere* [12], *valor* [14]) keep the tension alive; the issue on the table is a man's worth, his moral/poetic measure" (Barolini, "Guittone's *Ora parrà*, Dante's *Doglia mi reca*, and the *Commedia*'s Anatomy of Desire," 1997; rpt. in *Dante and the Origins of Italian Literary Culture* [New York: Fordham University Press, 2006], 47–69, p. 48).

Here we see again the pattern of *Provedi, saggio* and *Savete giudicar*: we see the same divergence between Dante da Maiano, the literalist who yet desires to be interpreted (*Provedi, saggio, ad esta visïone*), and Dante Alighieri, who in his response to *Provedi, saggio* moves markedly farther away from the literal than the other respondents (*Savete giudicar*). In a reversal, now it is Dante Alighieri who proposes a mysterious vision (*A ciascun'alma*) and Dante da Maiano who, as one of three interpreter-respondents, again shows his literalist bent (*Di ciò che stato sè dimandatore*): he refuses to engage in any interpretation of *A ciascun'alma*, a sonnet whose vision of Love holding the poet's sleeping beloved and then awakening her to feed her the poet's heart apparently is too extreme for Dante da Maiano's tastes. Cavalcanti, by contrast, interprets Dante's vision in the key of existential and epistemological fullness and completion: "Vedeste, al mio parere, onne valore / e tutto gioco e quanto bene om sente [You saw, in my opinion, all worth and all happiness and as much good as man feels]" (*Vedeste, al mio parere*, 1–2).

In these exchanges we can see ideological positions carved out as these rival poets debate not so much the greatest suffering of love but the degree of metaphysical access permitted to love poetry. Dante da Maiano's reply to *A ciascun'alma* may well mark the first time that Dante Alighieri is mocked for his spirtualizing tendency – as Guinizzelli was mocked by Bonagiunta, and as Cino da Pistoia will be mocked by Onesto degli Onesti, for this is an ongoing debate in the Italian lyric tradition – but it is not the last. In the sonnet *Dante Alleghier, Cecco, tu' servo amico*, Cecco Angiolieri will take Dante Alighieri to task for what he considers a self-contradiction in the sonnet *Oltra la spera*, engaging in an almost lawyerly parsing of the sonnet, as though he had taken a tip about the value of "quistioneggiare" from Dante da Maiano's *Per pruova di saper*. Cecco objects that in one stanza Dante claims not to understand the speech of the thought that followed Beatrice to heaven and that in another he claims to understand it well:

> Ch'al mio parer ne l'una muta dice
> che non intendi su' sottil parlare,
> di quel che vide la tua Beatrice;
> e poi hai detto a le tue donne care
> che ben lo intendi: e dunque contradice
> a sé medesmo questo tu' trovare.   (*Dante Alleghier, Cecco, tu' servo amico*, 9–14)

> [For in my view in one tercet it says that
> you don't understand the subtle speech
> of him who saw your Beatrice;
> and then you said to your dear ladies that
> you understood it fine; and so it contradicts
> itself, this poem of yours.]

We note that Cecco Angiolieri critiques Dante Alighieri in a sonnet that begins by featuring the word "amico." The prominent use of *amico* in the incipit *Dante Alleghier, Cecco, tu' servo amico* brings us back to the poetic exchange of Dante Alighieri and Dante da Maiano, where too the word *amico* is featured. These men are poetic rivals in the agora of public opinion who call each other "amico" but clearly are not thinking in terms of Cicero's definition of the friend as an "alternate self": "alter idem" (*De Amicitia* 21.80). Dante da Maiano writes that he does not intend to start a dispute, "ciò non movo per quistioneggiare" (*Per pruova di saper*, 12), but that is precisely what he intends to do; he thinks his prestige can be enhanced by a public dispute with Dante Alighieri, and in fact is reluctant to let the matter drop.

In *Lo vostro fermo dir* Dante da Maiano poses his question again. Indicating that Dante Alighieri's first reply is not satisfactory, he notes that many believe there is a greater suffering than unrequited love: "Dite ch'amare e non essere amato / ène lo dol che più d'Amore dole, / e manti dicon che più v' ha dol maggio [You claim that loving without being loved / entails the harshest pain of Love there is, / yet many say there is still greater pain]" (*Lo vostro fermo dir*, 9–11). Despite being flatly contradicted, Dante Alighieri will not play along – one gets the impression that he doesn't think there is any value to be attained by continued disputation with Dante da Maiano – and he reiterates the same response in *Non canoscendo* that he had previously given in *Qual che voi siate*: "sacci bene, chi ama, / se non è amato, lo maggior dol porta [know this full well: whoever loves / but is not loved will bear the greatest pain]" (*Non canoscendo*, 10–11). Dante da Maiano keeps pressing, and requests further documentation in *Lasso, lo dol*. He tries to push Dante Alighieri into a show of learning, requiring that his rival provide an authority to buttress his point of view: "Però pregh'eo ch'argomentiate, saggio, / d'autorità mostrando ciò che porta / di voi la 'mpresa, a ciò che sia più chiara [And so I now request that you, my sage, / cite which authority substantiates / your view, so it can garner more prestige]" (*Lasso, lo dol*, 9–11). But Dante Alighieri will not be drawn, again suggesting that he does not think there is anything to be gained by "proving" himself ("Per pruova di saper") to the likes of Dante da Maiano.

That Dante Alighieri considered Dante da Maiano not his intellectual peer may be inferred from a later use on Dante Alighieri's part of the very verb, *farneticare*, with which Dante da Maiano belittles him – by casting him as not masculine and hence not authoritative – in *Di ciò che stato sè dimandatore*. As we saw previously, Dante da Maiano refuses to engage in interpretation of the visionary sonnet *A ciascun'alma*, in which Love feeds the poet's heart to his beloved. Rather, Dante da Maiano claims that Dante Alighieri is here engaging in a speech act of a fabulous type ("favoleggiar loquendo"), one moreover that he seems to experience as violating gender boundaries. He seems to feel that Dante Alighieri's sonnet is not manly and he essentially advises him to regain his manhood. He does this by suggesting to Dante Alighieri that he wash his testicles, a highly gendered cure for his proclivity to *favoleggiar*: "che lavi la tua collia largamente / a ciò che stinga e passi lo vapore / lo qual ti fa favoleggiar loquendo [you should give your balls a thorough wash / so as to quench and dissipate the fumes / that make you fantasize when you converse]" (*Di ciò che stato sè dimandatore*, 7–9). Having offensively gendered Dante's *favoleggiar* as female, Dante da Maiano reaches the conclusion that the vision related in *A ciascun alma* is nothing but "hysteria" (to substitute an equally gendered nineteenth-century version of *farneticare*), using *farneticare* to classify Dante Alighieri's sonnet negatively: "sol c'hai farneticato, sappie, intendo [I only mean, please know, you were delirious]" (*Di ciò che stato sè dimandatore*, 11).

About a decade later, circa 1292–94, Dante Alighieri will "reply" to this vulgar and anti-intellectual attack when he writes the prose frame of the *Vita Nuova*, a work that features as its first poem precisely the visionary *A ciascun'alma*. The chapter of the *Vita Nuova* that treats the phenomenology of visions, an examination that lays the foundation for all Dante's later thought on visionary experience, boasts Dante Alighieri's only uses of the adjective *farnetico* and the verb *farneticare*: he describes himself, as he foresees Beatrice's death, behaving "as a delirious person" – "sì come farnetica persona" (*VN* XXIII.4 [14.4]) – and then marks the moment when "I left behind this delirium": "poi che io lasciai questo farneticare" (*VN* XXIII.30 [14.30]). The choice of *farneticare* in the prose gloss of the great visionary canzone *Donna pietosa* is a way of reclaiming the term and recontextualizing it within an intellectual tradition that is beyond the ken of Dante da Maiano. Dante Alighieri is rejecting Dante da Maiano's offensive "sol c'hai farneticato, sappie, intendo" and making the point that to behave "sì come farnetica persona" can be completely appropriate and not incompatible with virility, as when Dante in the *Commedia* experiences ecstatic visions and is bent over "a guisa di cui vino o sonno piega [as one whom wine or sleep bends over]" (*Purg.* 15.123). To understand that there can be a legitimate *farneticare* requires greater learning and an erudition that embraces a wider range of authorities: one has to get beyond the intellectual provincialism of Dante da Maiano and his peers.

Coming back to the early 1280s and the milieu of strutting peacock poets showing their feathers (captured by Chiaro Davanzati in his incipit *Di penne di paone e d'altre assai*), there is another intriguing feature of Dante Alighieri's replies to Dante da Maiano, and that is his insistence that he doesn't know his interlocutor's name. Both of Dante Alighieri's replies begin by ostentatiously calling "amico" a man whom he simultaneously claims not to know. In the first reply this lacuna is casually stated, with the emphasis on the learning of the unknown interlocutor: "Qual che voi siate, amico, vostro manto / di scienza parmi tal, che non è gioco [Whoever you may be, my friend, I find the learning you display to be no joke]." In his second reply Dante Alighieri devotes the entire octave to not knowing the name of the man to whom he is writing, beginning the sonnet with this lack of knowledge – "Non canoscendo, amico, vostro nomo, / donde che mova chi con meco parla [Although, my friend, I do not know your name, / whoever it may be that speaks to me]" – and again connects the absence of the name to the presence of great learning: "conosco ben che scienz'à di gran nomo, / sì che di quanti saccio nessun par l'à [I know indeed his learning's such a legend / no one else can claim to be his peer]" (*Non canoscendo*, 3–4). Throughout the octave of *Non canoscendo* Dante Alighieri plays with language clustered around knowledge – not only *canoscere*, but also *scienza*, *sapere*, and *senno* – in order to emphasize his own ability to recognize, assess, and value learning in someone else, even someone he does not know. The verb *canoscere* weaves through the octave: not knowing your name ("Non canoscendo"), Dante Alighieri says, I do nonetheless know you ("conosco ben") to be of great learning, because one can know ("canoscere") such a thing about a man from his speech, "ché si pò ben canoscere d'un omo, / ragionando, se ha senno, che ben par là [for one can recognize intelligence, / in conversation, by the words employed]" (*Non canoscendo*, 5–6).

While Dante da Maiano performs his standing and attainments with his fluent *ragionare*, Dante Alighieri has to do something even more difficult. He will have to cope with the handicap of praising his interlocutor without knowing his name, in a situation that strains his very ability to produce language: "Conven poi voi laudar, sarà for nomo / e forte a lingua mia di ciò com parla [Since I must praise you without naming you, / it's hard to form the words upon my tongue]" (*Non canoscendo*, 7–8). Dante Alighieri's almost provocative continued emphasis on his ignorance of his rival's name is worthy of further analysis in light of the sustained meditation on the relationship between names and glory in the *Commedia*, where "nominanza" is used for "fama" in *Inferno* 4 and *Purgatorio* 11, and where Dante refuses to give his name to Guido del Duca, because he is not yet famous enough:[11] "dirvi ch'i' sia, saria parlare indarno, / ché 'l nome mio ancor molto non suona [To tell you who I am would be to speak in vain, for my name does not yet much resound]" (*Purg.* 14.20–1). It is an ignorance that seems even stranger in the *second* reply – was there really no way, in the time between reply 1 and reply 2, to find out the identity of an interlocutor who possesses legendary learning? – and that seems calculated to offer faint praise at best and to make the point that Dante Alighieri has the harder task. Similarly Dante Alighieri shows he is a strong competitor by reutilizing in *Qual che voi siate* not just one of Dante da Maiano's rhymes but all of them and even reprising a few of his rival's rhyme-words.[12] The studied quality of the diction and the tortuous complexity of the syntax, all massively Guittonian, also become weapons in the young poet's arsenal.

The interest of this *tenzone* has traditionally been considered to reside more in its hyper-Guittonian form than in its content. However, if by content we refer not to the amorous issues discussed but to the performance being staged, then the Guittonian pedigree of the ritualized honorifics allows us to see how content and form are thoroughly intertwined. The formulaic usage of "amico" can be seen in Guittone's incipits, to wit: *Messer Bottaccio amico, ogn'animale*; *Messer Giovanni amico, 'n*

---

11 See Barolini, *The Undivine Comedy*, p. 136.

12 Note too the pronounced use of *rima equivoca* and of *rima composta*, e.g., "par l'à" and "par là" in *Non canoscendo*, verses 4 and 6. This is an artifice of which traces remain in the *Commedia*: see "pur lì" rhymed with "urli" in *Inf.* 7.28, "Oh me" rhymed with "chiome" in *Inf.* 28.123, and "ci ha" rhymed with "sconcia" in *Inf.* 30.87.

vostro amore; *Mastro Bandino amico, el mio preghero*; and *Finfo amico, dire io voi presente*. We saw Chiaro Davanzati's similar use of "amico" in his incipit *Amico, proveduto ha mia intenzione*, responding to Dante da Maiano. In Dante Alighieri's poetry we find the use of "amico" as a form of address not only in the sonnets to Dante da Maiano but also in the early *Se Lippo amico sè tu che mi leggi*, a poem whose genre, *sonetto rinterzato*, testifies, along with the honorific "amico" of the incipit, to Guittone's influence. However, *Se Lippo amico* is non-aggressive in tone, a plea for help: the sonnet asks the friend for protective clothing (most likely a reference to musical accompaniment) for the canzone-stanza that is being sent to him. The word "amico" then disappears from sight, not used in the great meditation on friendship that is the sonnet *Guido, i'vorrei*, and rarely in Dante's lyrics (generic uses may be found in *La dispietata mente*, *Tre donne*, and *Doglia mi reca*).

The fact that Dante writes one of the world's great poems of friendship without using the word "amico" suggests that the word was still redolent to him of rivalry and competition, that – at least when used in lyric poetry, where it had such a clear history – it still betokens a ritualized formula of address used between two men who are rivals, not friends, who indeed may not even know each other. Perhaps *Se Lippo amico*, a rather technical sonnet endowed with the specific task of presenting itself and the canzone-stanza that follows, is a transitional poem, in which the word "amico" can cohabit with a named friend. Certainly, the affectionate highlighting of names of friends and lady friends in *Guido, i'vorrei* seems almost a nod *e contrario* to the provocative insistence on his interlocutor's anonymity in *Qual che voi siate* and *Non canoscendo*. When Dante wrote *Guido, i'vorrei* his Guittonian mannerisms and the exchange with Dante da Maiano were not yet very distant, and – although he had clearly evolved an *idea* of friendship that is consonant with Cicero's *De Amicitia* – he seems not yet prepared to use in poetry a word that he had used in the recent past in a very different manner.

The reclassification of the word "amico" was, however, occurring in Dante's prose, where Dante worked systematically on the concept of *amicitia* over the years. Beginning in the prose of the *Vita Nuova*, Dante makes explicit what is implicit in a sonnet like *Guido, i'vorrei*, namely the link between making poetry and making friends. This is a link expressed in the labelling of Cavalcanti "primo de li miei amici [first among my friends]" (*VN* III.14 [2.1]) and – in confirmation that a friend would have to be (unlike Dante da Maiano) intellectually equipped to understand the curious visionary subject matter of *A ciascun'alma* – it is precisely Guido's reply to *A ciascun'alma* that "was almost the beginning of the friendship between him and me" ("fue quasi lo principio de l'amistà tra lui e me") (*VN* III.14 [2.1]). The prose of the *Vita Nuova* thematizes and theorizes friendship, just as it thematizes and theorizes vision. Hence we find Beatrice's brother ranked as "uno, lo quale, secondo li gradi de l'amistade, è amico a me immediatamente dopo lo primo [one who, according to the grades of friendship, is friend to me immediately following the first friend]" (*VN* XXXII.1 [21.1]). Dante gradually moves from the Guittonian formulaic usage of "amico" in his early lyrics towards the full Ciceronian usage of the *Commedia*: an instance of this transition is the *De vulgari eloquentia's* self-identification as "amicus eius," where Dante refers to himself not by the name "Dante" but by the tag "his friend," stipulating that he is the one who is the friend of the poet Cino da Pistoia. In other words, he makes real the Aristotelian and Ciceronian idea of the friend as an "other self" – "alter idem" – by defining his own self as the friend of his friend. That he defines himself as the friend of a friend who is a poet is the final step away from the ritualized rivalries between young male poets of his youth. The *De vulgari eloquentia's* expression "his friend"/"amicus eius" thus embodies both the Dantean symbiosis of poetry and friendship and the Aristotelian/Ciceronian ideal: key to the label is the idea that to be "his" is to be myself. Ultimately "amico" reappears in the *Commedia* in contexts that show that Dante has redeemed it as a term of profound intimacy rather than ritualized rivalry.[13]

The rivalries between magnate lineages were at the root of the political faction that the *Commedia* indicts and deplores; they affected Dante's life profoundly, beginning with his early and complicated friendships with the two magnates Guido Cavalcanti and Forese Donati.[14] Dante's work is steeped throughout in the blood feuds and rivalries of magnate culture, whose ritualized codes of honour find their way into the *Commedia* as well. Dante Alighieri will eventually make clear the heavy burden imposed on men by society's codes of honour. We remember the concept of communal "shame" ("onta") in the episode in which Dante encounters his cousin Geri del Bello in the *Inferno*: Geri is angry that his death has not been avenged "per alcun che de l'onta sia consorte [by anyone who shares the shame of it]" (*Inf.* 29.33), and Dante seems to be refusing to accept the ritual shame that is his lot as Geri's kinsman. From the young man who used the *tenzone* as a tool of professional and social self-promotion, and who was willing to work with the currency of male honour, he has become a man who is capable of shining a hard light on the value of such codes and stepping out of their confines altogether.

---

13 For "amico" in the *Commedia*, see the discussion of *Purgatorio* 22 in the introductory essay to *Deh ragioniamo insieme un poco, Amore*. A similar but accelerated trajectory could be posited for *saggio*: Dante's reference to Guido Guinizzelli in the sonnet *Amore e 'l cor gentil sono una cosa* as "saggio" – "sì come il saggio in suo dittare pone" (2) – is not a ritualized honorific, as in his Guittonian address to Dante da Maiano, "o om che pregio di saver portate" in *Savete giudicar* (2). It is rather a genuine tribute to Guinizzelli, akin to the use of "saggio" for Vergil in the *Commedia*.

14 On the interconnections between these early friendships and Dante's early attachment to the Aristotelian concept of nobility, see Teodolinda Barolini, "Aristotle's *Mezzo*, Courtly *Misura*, and Dante's Canzone *Le dolci rime*: Humanism, Ethics, and Social Anxiety," in *Dante and the Greeks*, ed. Jan Ziolkowski (Washington: Dumbarton Oaks, 2014), 163–79.

2a (B XLI; C 2; FB 2; DR 77)
Dante da Maiano to Dante Alighieri

Per pruova di saper com vale o quanto
lo mastro l'oro, adducelo a lo foco;
e, ciò faccendo, chiara e sa se poco,
4   amico, di pecunia vale o tanto.
Ed eo, per levar prova del meo canto,
l'adduco a voi, cui paragone voco
di ciascun c'have in canoscenza loco,
8   o che di pregio porti loda o vanto.
E chero a voi col meo canto più saggio
che mi deggiate il dol maggio d'Amore
11   qual è, per vostra scienza, nominare:
e ciò non movo per quistioneggiare
(che già inver' voi so non avria valore),
14   ma per saver ciò ch'eo vaglio e varraggio.

To ascertain the worth and weight of gold
a goldsmith places it within a fire;
and doing this, he clarifies and learns,
my friend, if it's of great or little worth.
And so to gauge my poem's worthiness,
I'm sending it to you, my touchstone for
whoever claims to rank among the wise,
or who is praised and held in high regard.
I ask, this being the wisest of my poems,
what kind of suffering brought on by Love,
in your experience, is worst of all:
and this I ask, though not to stir debate,
(for, with respect to you, I'd be outclassed),
but just to know my worth and future promise.

METRE: sonnet ABBA ABBA CDE EDC.

2 (B XLII; C 2a; FB 2a; DR 78)
Dante Alighieri to Dante da Maiano

Qual che voi siate, amico, vostro manto
di scienza parmi tal, che non è gioco;
sì che, per non saver, d'ira mi coco,
4   non che laudarvi, sodisfarvi tanto.
Sacciate ben (ch'io mi conosco alquanto)
che di saver ver' voi ho men d'un moco,
né per via saggia come voi non voco,
8   così parete saggio in ciascun canto.
Poi piacevi saver lo meo coraggio,
ed io ·l vi mostro di menzogna fore,
11   sì come quei ch'a saggio è 'l suo parlare:
certamente a mia coscienza pare,
chi non è amato, s'elli è amadore,
14   che 'n cor porti dolor senza paraggio.

Whoever you may be, my friend, I find
the learning you display to be no joke;
and so I smart for having failed at least
to offer, not to say my praise, some cheer.
Be well assured (I know a thing or two),
compared to yours my learning is but scant,
nor can I row my boat as well as you,
so you seem wise in everything you do.
And since you wish to know my point of view,
I'll tell you openly without deceit,
like one conversing with a man who's wise.
My understanding leads me to believe
that anyone who loves but is not loved
bears in his heart the greatest grief of all.

METRE: sonnet ABBA ABBA CDE EDC. Here Dante Alighieri is following the convention whereby in a poetic exchange (*tenzone*) the respondent will frequently use some or all of the rhymes used by the proponent (*rispondere per le rime*). With great virtuosity, Alighieri reprises all of da Maiano's rhyme scheme and even some of his rhyme words (*tanto, voco, canto*).

3a (B XLIII; C 3; FB 3; DR 79)
Dante da Maiano to Dante Alighieri

Lo vostro fermo dir fino ed orrato
approva ben ciò bon ch' om di voi parla,
ed ancor più, ch'ogni uom fora gravato
4   di vostra loda intera nominarla;
ché 'l vostro pregio in tal loco è poggiato,
che propiamente om no·l poria contar là:
però qual vera loda al vostro stato
8   crede parlando dar, dico disparla.

Dite ch'amare e non essere amato
ène lo dol che più d'Amore dole,
11   e manti dicon che più v' ha dol maggio:
onde umil prego non vi sia disgrato
vostro saver che chiari ancor, se vole,
14   se 'l vero o no di ciò mi mostra saggio.

The sure and graceful manner of your speech
confirms the good that others see in you,
and more as well, for anyone would be
hard pressed to register your praise in full;
now your acclaim has soared to such a height
that no one could appraise it properly:
and so whoever thinks he credits you
with all due praise, I say, speaks foolishly.

You claim that loving without being loved
entails the harshest pain of Love there is,
yet many say there is still greater pain.
So in your wisdom, if you do not mind,
I ask you to shed further light on this,
and if experience can show it's true.

METRE: sonnet ABAB ABAB ACD ACD. Dante da Maiano reprises only the rhyme in *–aggio*. His repetition of the *–ato* rhyme from the quatrains in the tercets is an example of the archaic convention whereby the A rhyme may be carried over from the octave to the tercets, from which it is banned by later poets.

3 (B XLIV; C 3a; FB 3a; DR 80)
Dante Alighieri to Dante da Maiano

Non canoscendo, amico, vostro nomo,
donde che mova chi con meco parla,
conosco ben che scienz'à di gran nomo,
4   sì che di quanti saccio nessun par l'à;
ché si pò ben canoscere d'un omo,
ragionando, se ha senno, che ben par là.
Conven poi voi laudar, sarà for nomo
8   e forte a lingua mia di ciò com parla.

Amico (certo sonde, a ciò ch'amato
per amore aggio), sacci ben, chi ama,
11   se non è amato, lo maggior dol porta;
ché tal dolor ten sotto suo camato
tutti altri, e capo di ciascun si chiama:
14   da ciò vèn quanta pena Amore porta.

Although, my friend, I do not know your name,
whoever it may be that speaks to me,
I know indeed his learning's such a legend
no one else can claim to be his peer:
for one can recognize intelligence,
in conversation, by the words employed.
Since I must praise you without naming you,
it's hard to form the words upon my tongue.

My friend (of this I'm sure, for I have felt
true love), know this full well: whoever loves
but is not loved will bear the greatest pain;
this kind of anguish has the upper hand
on all the rest, and takes the name of chief:
from this comes every pain that Love inflicts.

METRE: sonnet ABAB ABAB CDE CDE. Alighieri reprises the rhymes *–arla* and *–ato*, as well as the rhyme words *parla* and *amato*. This is the only sonnet in the sequence that does not use the rhyme *–aggio*.

3b (B XLV; C 3b; FB 4; DR 81)
Dante da Maiano to Dante Alighieri

Lasso, lo dol che più mi dole e serra
è ringraziar, ben non sapendo como;
per me più saggio converriasi, como
4   vostro saver, ched ogni quistion serra.
Del dol che manta gente dite serra
è tal voler qual voi lor non ha como;
el propio sì disio saver dol, como
8   di ciò sovente dico, essend'a serra.
   Però pregh'eo ch'argomentiate, saggio,
d'autorità mostrando ciò che porta
11 di voi la 'mpresa, a ciò che sia più chiara;
e poi parrà, parlando di ciò, chiara
e qual più chiarirem dol pena porta,
14 d'el[l]o assegnando, amico, prov'e saggio.

Alas, the pain that stings and binds the most
is that of thanking you, not knowing how;
a wiser sort than I should take my place,
a mind like yours, to tie up all loose ends.
The pain that you ascribe to some who love
is yearning you and they feel differently;
I'd like to understand this feeling well,
for often, as I say, I'm gripped by it.
   And so I now request that you, my sage,
cite which authority substantiates
your view, so it can garner more prestige.
Then our discussion will have clarified
which suffering begets the greater pain,
as we resolve, my friend, the pros and cons.

METRE: sonnet ABBA ABBA CDE EDC. Dante da Maiano reprises the rhyme *–omo* and the rhyme-word *porta* from the previous sonnet, as well as the rhyme *–aggio* featured in the first three poems of the exchange.

Tenzone between Dante Alighieri and Dante da Maiano

4a Amor mi fa sì fedelmente amare: Dante da Maiano to Dante Alighieri
4 Savere e cortesia, ingegno ed arte: Dante Alighieri's response

This third and final *tenzone* between the two Dantes poses the question of the ability of the will to withstand love. Although embedded in an exquisitely courtly dialogue, the theme here broached is fundamentally ethical, and is rooted in classical philosophy, in for instance Aristotle's treatment of the will and compulsion (see Aristotle, *Nicomachean Ethics* 3.1, for the distinction between voluntary and involuntary action).

In the sonnet *Amor mi fa sì fedelmente amare* Dante da Maiano wants to get Dante Alighieri to "agree" ("Provedi, amico saggio, se l'*appruovi* [Consider, learned friend, if you agree]" [14]) with the following proposition: it is impossible to oppose love when love grasps us and forces us to desire ("e sì distretto m'have en suo disire [(love) has me bound so tightly in his will]" [2]), because neither strength nor cunning can prevail against love ("'inverso Amor non val forze ned arte [strength and shrewdness cannot rival Love]" [10]), and thus it is better to surrender oneself "and serve loyally" ("e ben servir") (13). This youthful exchange is the courtly variant of an ethical issue on which Dante Alighieri will meditate the length of his life: the problem of free will and of human responsibility. Here we encounter the eros-inflected version of a vast problematic that constitutes the very foundation of the *Commedia*: are we, as agents, responsible for our actions or are we not?

If one concedes, as Dante Alighieri does in these sonnets, that we are *not* responsible in matters of love, because the will does not have the power to resist – "nulla cosa gli è incontro possente [nothing has the power to take him (love) on]" (*Savere e cortesia*, 13) – one ends up also conceding that human will does not have freedom of choice in its actions. In other words, if the mature Dante had remained in agreement with the young poet who here agrees with Dante da Maiano, sustaining in the sonnet *Savere e cortesia* that one must submit to eros, precisely because "nulla cosa gli è incontro possente," there would be no *Commedia*. The *Commedia* is founded on the logic of free will and choice, that is, on the premise that our choices become realized into actions by means of the exercise of a will that is by definition free.

The fascination of Dante's lyrics derives in great part from the fact that they allow us to trace the pathway that leads Dante Alighieri from his assent to Dante da Maiano's proposal – according to which we are incapable of acting voluntarily under the goad of amorous compulsion – to his rejection of it. How does he go from the sonnet *Savere e cortesia* to canto 5 of the *Inferno*? This trajectory is one that, far from being concealed or covert, is readily signaled by a poet who holds that the transition hereby negotiated is fundamental to the creation of his mature philosophical identity. Precisely in order to indicate this fundamental philosophical shift, Dante takes the iconic and technical verb of the erotic lyric, *stringere*, used by Dante da Maiano when he writes that Love "sì **distretto** m'have en suo disire [has me bound tightly to his will]," and has it echo in Francesca's words, when she announces having read "di Lancialotto come amor lo **strinse** [of Lancelot, how love bound him]" (*Inf.* 5.128).

Dante ends by condemning erotic passion, if it dominates reason, and by insisting that the subordination of reason to desire is sinful: "carnal sinners" are defined precisely as those "who subordinate reason to desire" ("che la ragion sommettono al talento" [*Inf.* 5.39]). How does Dante arrive at such a formulation, when in *Savere e cortesia* he maintains exactly the opposite, holding rather that it is not possible to resist passion? The road is long, complex, and signposted by texts that belong to our highest celebrations of erotic passion. From this first youthful formulation, rather insipid and conventional ("Onde se voli, amico, che ti vagli / vertute naturale od accidente, / con lealtà in piacer d'Amor l'adovra, / e non a contastar sua graziosa ovra [So if you wish, my friend, to benefit / from inborn worth or accident of chance, / make proper use of it in pleasing Love: / but you must not oppose his gracious work]" [9–12]), Dante will reach remarkable lyrical heights, such as the *rime petrose*, written circa 1296, dedicated to the absolute and indomitable force of eros. All of this before coming to the opposite position – that is, to the triumph of reason. This position, too, makes its first appearance in the lyrics, and will be clearly stated in the post-exilic canzone *Doglia mi reca nello core ardire*.[15]

The first quatrain of the response to Dante da Maiano is composed of a graceful string of nouns that recalls Cavalcanti's sonnet *Biltà di donna*. Looking forward rather than back, we note too the lexical *contaminatio* between a courtly register (for instance, the word "cortesia," which Dante defines in the *Convivio* as deriving from "court," in the incipit *Savere e cortesia*) and the incipient presence of a philosophical-scholastic register (as in verse 10: "vertute natural od accidente"). Such willingness to mix registers is a hallmark of one of the great literary syncretists.

---

15 On Dante's erotic poetry and its relationship to *Inferno* 5, see my essay "Dante and Cavalcanti (On Making Distinctions in Matters of Love): *Inferno* 5 in Its Lyric and Autobiographical Context," 1998, rpt. in *Dante and the Origins of Italian Literary Culture*, pp. 70–101. On *Doglia mi reca*, see also my "Guittone's *Ora parrà*, Dante's *Doglia mi reca*, and the *Commedia*'s Anatomy of Desire," 1997, rpt. in *Dante and the Origins of Italian Literary Culture*, pp. 47–69.

4a (B XLVI; C 4; FB 5a; DR 82)
Dante da Maiano to Dante Alighieri

Amor mi fa sì fedelmente amare
e sì distretto m'have en suo disire,
che solo un'ora non porria partire
4 lo core meo da lo suo pensare.
D'Ovidio ciò mi son miso a provare
che disse per lo mal d'Amor guarire,
e ciò ver' me non val mai che mentire:
8 per ch' eo mi rendo a sol mercé chiamare.
E ben conosco omai veracemente
che 'nverso Amor non val forza ned arte,
11 ingegno né leggenda ch'omo trovi,
mai che merzede ed esser sofferente
e ben servir: così n'have omo parte.
14 Provedi, amico saggio, se l'appruovi.

Love causes me to love so steadfastly
and has me bound so tightly in his will
that even for a single hour my heart
could not take leave of thinking but of him.
I've set my mind to testing Ovid's art
which told how lovesickness is remedied.
But what he said I hold to be a lie;
so I'm resigned to begging just for pity.
And now I fully understand as fact
that strength and shrewdness cannot rival Love,
nor schemes and teachings one might come across,
but only pity, waiting patiently
and serving loyally – this is your role.
Consider, learned friend, if you agree.

METRE: sonnet ABBA ABBA CDE CDE.

4 (B XLVII; C 4a; FB 5; DR 83)
Dante Alighieri to Dante da Maiano

Savere e cortesia, ingegno ed arte,
nobilitate, bellezza e riccore,
fortezza e umiltate e largo core,
4 prodezza ed eccellenza, giunte e sparte,
este grazie e vertuti in onne parte
con lo piacer di lor vincono Amore:
una più ch'altra bene ha più valore
8 inverso lui, ma ciascuna n'ha parte.
Onde se voli, amico, che ti vaglia
vertute naturale od accidente,
11 con lealtà in piacer d'Amor l'adovra,
e non a contastar sua graziosa ovra;
ché nulla cosa gli è incontro possente,
14 volendo prendere om con lui battaglia.

Courtesy and knowledge, wit and skill,
nobility and beauty, worldly wealth,
great strength and kindness, generosity,
renown and valour, joined or separate,
these benefits and virtues everywhere
by their delight can overpower Love:
though one may prove more worthy as its foe
than might another, each one plays a part.
So if you wish, my friend, to benefit
from inborn worth or accident of chance,
make proper use of it in pleasing Love:
but you must not oppose his gracious work,
for nothing has the power to take him on,
if one should want to start a fight with him.

METRE: sonnet ABBA ABBA CDE EDC. Dante Alighieri does not respond *per le rime* and he changes the pattern of the tercets. He reprises the rhymes *-arte* and *-ente* as well as the rhyme-words *arte* and *parte*.

5 A ciascun'alma presa e gentil core

In the sonnet *A ciascun'alma presa e gentil core* Dante addresses two categories of readers: all those who are in love – all the souls "prese," seized, made captive by love – and all hearts that are "gentili," noble. In another sonnet, *Amore 'l cor gentil sono una cosa*, Dante, following Guinizzelli, will explicitly state what here remains implicit: that these two categories are in truth one. If "Love and the noble heart are one sole thing," as stated in the incipit *Amore 'l cor gentil sono una cosa*, it follows then that "every captive soul" is necessarily also a "noble heart." The technical and courtly lexicon used by the poet to cue the restricted group he writes to will remain useful to him much later on. One thinks of Francesca da Rimini in canto 5 of the *Inferno*, who will display similar (ab)uses of the adjective *gentile* and of the verb *prendere* ("Amor, ch'al cor *gentil* ratto s'apprende, / *prese* costui ... [Love, that can quickly grasp the noble heart, seized him ...]" [*Inf.* 5.100–1]), as well as the great definition of love in *Purgatorio* 18, where the "alma presa" of *A ciascun'alma* has become the "animo preso" that achieves its desire (*Purg.* 18.31).

In *A ciascun'alma* Dante addresses himself to all captive souls and noble hearts to ask for the deciphering of a "vision." (Later he will write only to noble women, as in *Donne ch'avete intelletto d'amore* or in *Li occhi dolenti*: "donne gentili, volentier con vui, / non voi parlare altrui, / se non a cor gentil che in donna sia [my gentle ladies, willingly with you / I choose to speak to none / except a lady with a gentle heart]" (*Li occhi dolenti*, 9–11). The word "visione" is used in the prose of *Vita Nuòva* III (1), the chapter in which *A ciascun'alma* is placed as the first poetic composition of the *libello*: "E pensando di lei, mi sopragiunse uno soave sonno, ne lo quale m'apparve una maravigliosa visione [And thinking about her, a sweet sleep came over me, in which appeared a tremendous vision]" (III.3 [1.14]). The word *visione* is not present in *A ciascun'alma* (while it is in Dante da Maiano's riddle sonnet, *Provedi, saggio, ad esta visïone*); this kind of divergence between poem and prose, by which the prose enriches and transforms the poem, is programmatic in the *Vita Nuova*.

As we are now dealing for the first time with a text inserted by Dante into the *Vita Nuova*, the moment has come to emphasize the reflexiveness that is at the origin of the *libello*: a text forged in the reflexive act of returning (between 1292 and 1294 circa) to poems composed quite a while earlier, from early Guittonian efforts to more recent ones of rigorous stilnovist purity, and of choosing some among them to set into the new prose setting. The chosen lyrics undergo not only a passive revision during the selection process, but an active revision as well, thanks to the prose narrative, which moves the poems in a new direction consonant with the ideology of the new life of the poet. The resulting modifications of original intention produce narrative reversals: for example, poems written for other women in other contexts are now presented as written for Beatrice. Thus in this commentary I will refer to "Beatrice" only when she is explicitly named; otherwise, if she is named "Beatrice" in the prose but not in the poetry, I will limit myself to "madonna" (my lady).

Madonna is precisely the word used in the vision described in *A ciascun'alma*: it involves an apparition of Love who, joyful, holds in his hand the poet's heart and in his arms "madonna involta in un drappo dormendo [my Lady wrapped within a cloth, asleep]" (11). Love then wakes the lady and gives her the heart to eat – "Poi la svegliava, e d'esto core ardendo / lei paventosa umilmente pascea [He woke her then, and she, beset by fear, / began to humbly eat my burning heart]" (12–13) – after which Love leaves, in tears ("piangendo" [14]).

The verb *pascere* is rare in Dante's lyrics: we find it only in the sonnet *A ciascun'alma* and then in the sestina *Al poco giorno* ("tutto 'l mio tempo e gir pascendo l'erba [all my time and go around eating grass]" [35]). The "pascea" of *A ciascun'alma* is most likely the first use by Dante of a verb that will have some lexical importance in the *Commedia*, as in the simile of the mother bird at the opening of *Paradiso* 23 ("per trovar lo cibo onde li pasca [to find the food she feeds them with]" [*Par.* 23.5]). Being an aulic synonym of the quotidian *mangiare*, *pascere* is tied to a vast array of human behaviours.[16] The prose of *Vita Nuova* III (1) glosses "pascea" with *mangiare* ("che le facea mangiare questa cosa che in mano li ardea, la quale ella mangiava dubitosamente [that he had her eat the thing burning in his hands, which she anxiously ate]" *VN* III.6 [1.17]), clearly demonstrating the change of register facilitated by the prose. The lightning shifts of register deployed in the *Commedia* are first practised by Dante in the *Vita Nuova*'s shifts from aulic lyric to quotidian prose gloss.

The vision is presented in language and syntax that are relatively straightforward compared to what we saw in the exchange with Dante da Maiano. There were three responses to *A ciascun'alma*. Guido Cavalcanti emphasizes the visionary aspect of *A ciascun'alma* in the first word of his formidable incipit, *Vedeste, al mio parere, onne valore*; he interprets the sonnet in the key of achieved happiness. In the first two lines of his response, "Vedeste, al mio parere, onne valore / e tutto gioco e quanto bene om sente [You saw, it seems to me, all worth, and every joy and all the good man feels]," Guido imagines that Dante has attained precisely that maximum of joy and existential, epistemological completeness ("*onne* valore," "*tutto* gioco," "*quanto* bene") that in his poetry Guido denies to himself. Another response, probably from Terino

---

16 In the lyrics we find the verb *mangiare* only in the sonnet *Messer Brunetto, questa pulzelletta*, where it occurs two times. In the canzone *Così nel mio parlar* the verb *manducare* is used ("co li denti d'Amor già mi manduca [with Love's teeth he already devours me]" [32]), which presages its only use in the *Commedia*, in the Ugolino episode ("e come 'l pan per fame si manduca [and as he who's hungry eats his bread]" [*Inf.* 32.127]).

da Castelfiorentino, interprets the vision in the key of requited love (*Naturalmente chere ogne amadore*).

The response from Dante da Maiano, instead, completely rejects the visionary aspect of *A ciascun'alma* and insists with rough physicality that Dante Alighieri is delirious ("hai farnetico" [11]) and that he won't change his opinion "finché tua acqua al medico no stendo [till I submit your urine to the doctor]" (*Di ciò che stato sè dimandatore*, 14). Perhaps Dante Alighieri has violated a boundary that Dante da Maiano could not or did not want to cross. As discussed in the introductory essay to the *tenzone del duol d'amore*, the gendered aggression of Dante da Maiano's suggestion – "che lavi la tua collia largamente / a ciò che stinga e passi lo vapore / lo qual ti fa favoleggiar loquendo [you should give your balls a thorough wash / so as to quench and dissipate the fumes / that make you fantasize when you converse]" (7–9) – suggests that the boundary is related to gender and that Dante Alighieri's *favoleggiar* had violated some masculine code. When Dante Alighieri then uses precisely the word *farneticare* in the phenomenology of the vision that accompanies the canzone *Donna pietosa*, his lexical choice functions as a rejection of the cultural provincialism and educational limitations of Dante da Maiano and those like him: within Dante Alighieri's larger cultural horizons, visionary behaviour *can* belong to the repertory of a man.

The enigma proposed by *A ciascun'alma presa* is lastly deciphered by Dante himself, in the prose of the *Vita Nuova*, where he indicates in rather baroque fashion that the sonnet was composed by him at the age of eighteen, thus in 1283. According to the *Vita Nuova* the vision described by *A ciascun'alma* occurred the night after Beatrice's first greeting; the greeting took place nine years after their first encounter; and the encounter occurred when Dante was nine years old. The fact that Dante retroactively fit *A ciascun'alma* into a complex autobiographical scheme manufactured years later does not, however, take away from the plausibility of 1283 as the date of the sonnet, given its congruence with other examples of Dante's poetry from this early period.

We note the *Vita Nuova*'s autobiographical energy, which signals a core feature of Dante's art: namely, the conviction that the past is never disposable. Rather, it is to be retrieved, repackaged, reinterpreted. Given the interpretive zeal that Dante had already demonstrated with respect to Dante da Maiano's slight riddle, we can hardly be astonished at the interpretive vigour that he now manifests with regard to his own life experience.

This early sonnet is therefore resemanticized in the context of the *Vita Nuova*, where it is laden with meanings not inferrable from the poetic text. The prose, succulent and rich with details, confers meaning on the comparatively thin poem. We start with a text that does not even authorize us to identify *madonna* with Beatrice, and we finish – by means of the aggressive hermeneutic work of the prose – with a first announcement of Beatrice's death, made possible by adding the further information of her departure for heaven: while the sonnet only says, "appresso gir lo ne vedea piangendo [then I saw him go away in tears]" (14), the prose specifies, "e con essa mi parea che si ne gisse verso lo cielo [and with her he seemed to go off toward the sky]" (*Vita Nuova* III.7 [1.18]). Here we see – and it is but one example among many – how a verse that is ideologically thin undergoes retroactive enrichment by the prose. This early sonnet is used by the author of the *Vita Nuova* as a point of departure for a new ideological adventure.

The shrewdness of the *Vita Nuova* in its construction of a new authorial persona cannot be overstated. This is true despite the fact that Dante himself, in the subsequent archeological layer of his self-creation (the philosophical treatise *Convivio*), dismisses the *Vita Nuova* as juvenilia. An apparently simple but magisterial instance of Dante's authorial shrewdness is his use of spatial design to support his false chronology: by introducing each poem as though written for a given occasion just described in the prose, and placing the poem materially in the book *after* the prose event that supposedly occasions it, Dante reifies the false notion that the poems came into existence after the prose. For discussion of this programmatic "macrotextual deceit," see the essay on *Era venuta nella mente mia*.

This commentary is not the place to undertake a systematic comparison between the prose and the poems of the *libello* – a task that, ideally, should be undertaken by a commentator of the *Vita Nuova*.[17] My task here is to read the *Vita Nuova* poems as though they were not in the *Vita Nuova*. As I note in the Introduction to this volume, this task proved not so easy: I learned that in order to show what each poem does on its own, independent of the *Vita Nuova*, I had first to acknowledge the meaning that accrues to the poem within the *libello* and then show the reader how much of that meaning is the work of the prose. In this way I experienced firsthand the deep imperatives that condition editors to resist removing the poems from the "organic" and "unified" *Vita Nuova* in order to include them materially among the *rime*.[18]

Gathering thirty-one poems and placing them in a prose setting constituted Dante's first great demiurgic act: the act with which the poet, using his past as raw material, remolds himself, remodels himself, reconfigures himself – in effect re-creates himself. Thus a sonnet written at eighteen years of age will serve a much more mature ideology in the *Vita Nuova*, where it illuminates the great archeological project through whose multiple strata Dante becomes Dante.

---

17 The commentary on the *Vita Nuova* that in my opinion best does the work of comparing poetry and prose with an openness towards ideological discrepancies is the 1980 edition of Domenico De Robertis. Dedicated to comparing the poems to the prose with an eye to highlighting and interpreting such divergences is the doctoral dissertation by Carin McLain, "Prose and Poetry and the Making of Beatrice" (Columbia University, 2007).

18 On these cultural imperatives, see my "Editing Dante's *Rime* and Italian Cultural History," 2004, rpt. in *Dante and the Origins of Italian Literary Culture*, pp. 245–78.

5 (B I; FB 6; DR 26; *VN* III.10–12 [1.21–3])

A ciascun'alma presa e gentil core
nel cui cospetto vèn lo dir presente,
in ciò che mi riscrivan suo parvente,
4 salute in lor segnor, cioè Amore.
Già eran quasi che aterzate l'ore
del tempo che omne stella n'è lucente,
quando m'apparve Amor subitamente,
8 cui essenza membrar mi dà orrore.
Allegro mi sembrava Amor tenendo
meo core in mano, e nelle braccia avea
11 madonna involta in un drappo dormendo.
Poi la svegliava, e d'esto core ardendo
lei paventosa umilmente pascea.
14 Apresso gir lo ne vedea piangendo.

To every captive soul and noble heart
before whose eyes my present words appear,
beseeching them the favor of reply,
accept my greeting in the name of Love.
A third of night had almost run its course,
a time that every star is shining bright,
when Love appeared before me suddenly,
the memory of whose manner frightens me.
Jubilant, Love seemed to hold my heart
within his hand, and in his arms he held
my Lady wrapped within a cloth, asleep.
He woke her then, and she, beset by fear,
began to humbly eat my burning heart.
And then I saw him go away in tears.

METRE: sonnet ABBA ABBA CDC CDC.

6 Se Lippo amico sè tu che mi leggi

While on one hand *Se Lippo amico* demonstrates the evident immaturity of the poet, on the other hand it highlights his precocious literary sensibility.

The poet's youth shows in his use of non-Florentine rhymes and forms, such as rhyming the *i* of "scritto" with the *e* of "imprometto" and "metto" (defined by Contini as "Aretine, or better, Guittonian rhymes" [p. 22]), the past participle in the form "cognosciuda" (19), and, above all, in his deployment of the metrical form known as *sonetto rinterzato* (literally "layered sonnet") or *sonetto doppio*. The "layering" of the *sonetto rinterzato* is achieved by inserting *settenario* verses (seven-syllable verses) between a sonnet's fourteen canonical hendecasyllables (eleven-syllable verses). In the same way that the rhyme schemes of sonnets vary, the rhyme schemes of *sonetti rinterzati* vary too; the *rinterzi* – the inserted seven-syllable verses – are added to the base of whichever sonnet rhyme scheme has been adopted by the poet. In the case of *Se Lippo amico*, the base rhyme scheme is ABBA ABBA CDC DCD. The new rhyme scheme is formed by inserting a *settenario* after each odd-numbered verse of the quatrains and after the second (even) hendecasyllable of each tercet. The *settenari* are thus inserted after verses 1, 3, 5, 7 of the quatrains and after verse 2 of each tercet, which are verses 10 and 13 of the whole poem, to yield the following rhyme scheme for *Se Lippo amico*: AaBBbA AaBBbA CDdC DCcD.[19]

The *sonetto rinterzato* was invented by Guittone d'Arezzo, who boasts twenty-one instances of it in his *canzoniere*. There are two other *sonetti rinterzati* among Dante's lyrics, both early works and both later placed in the *Vita Nuova* (*O voi che per la via* and *Morte villana*),[20] where they function as indicators of an early Guittonian poetic

---

19 The odd/even dialectic, fundamental to the "metaphysics of the sonnet" (as in the *Timaeus'* circle of sameness and circle of difference), is thus maintained in the *sonetto rinterzato*.

20 A fourth *sonetto rinterzato* – *Quando 'l consiglio degli ucce' si tenne* – is added to the canon of Dante's lyrics by De Robertis, whose argument for attribution to Dante is entirely stylistic (not philological) and therefore not compelling. *Quando 'l consiglio* is a *sonetto rinterzato* of twenty-four verses, as compared to the twenty-verse format of Dante's three *sonetti rinterzati* of definite attribution, *Se Lippo amico*, *O voi che per la via*, and *Morte villana*. Contini notes of *Quando 'l consiglio* that it has "'degenerated' in the tercets in such a way that the *sirima* cannot be distinguished into two equal *voltae*" (p. 278). De Robertis wants to give *Quando 'l consiglio degli ucce' si tenne* to Dante on the basis of Dante's penchant for stylistic experimentation. Contini more persuasively ascribes *Quando 'l consiglio* to Antonio Pucci, who composed other poems that versify Aesop's fables, and who used this twenty-four-verse type of *sonetto rinterzato* frequently. Following De Robertis, Claudio Giunta in his commentary to Dante's *rime* adds *Quando 'l consiglio* to the canon of authentic Dantean compositions but offers no reasons for doing so (p. 646).

phase – one left behind in order to forge the *dolce stil novo*. One of the tasks that Dante sets himself in the *Vita Nuova* is the systematic reclassification of the stages of his own earlier poetic life, which are put into perspective by the prose and revealed to be in different ways unworthy of the "new" poet that he now aspires to be. The two *sonetti rinterzati* in the *Vita Nuova* thus function as stylistic markers of an outworn poetic phase that Dante can retrospectively place under the rubric, with a not inconsiderable part of his early poetic production, of "Guittone d'Arezzo."[21]

Se Lippo amico certainly belongs under this rubric as well. Even the opening of *Se Lippo amico* is Guittonian, as Barbi and Contini note, who cite Guittone's sonnets *Messer Bottaccio amico, ogn'animale*; *Messer Giovanni amico, 'n vostro amore*; *Mastro Bandino amico, el mio preghero*; and *Finfo amico, dire io voi presente*. And in fact the incipit *Se Lippo amico* recalls the four instances of the word *amico* in the extremely Guittonian sonnets exchanged by Dante Alighieri with Dante da Maiano. See the introductory essays to those *tenzoni* for the evolving significance of the word *amico* in Dante's lexicon.

Not at all Guittonian, however, is the fluid syntax of our *sonetto rinterzato*, which stands in marked contrast to the tortuous syntax of the *tenzoni* with Dante da Maiano. *Se Lippo amico* speaks in the first person, presenting himself to "Lippo amico" (plausibly identified with Lippo Pasci de' Bardi) and defining himself as a "humble sonnet": "io che m'apello umil[e] sonetto [a humble sonnet I am called]" (10). The task of the humble sonnet is to serve as companion to a "naked girl" – "Lo qual ti guido esta pulcella nuda [So I bestow on you this unclothed girl]" (13) – that is, to the single-stanza canzone *Lo meo servente core* (the next poem in this edition). The stanza is "nuda," continues the sonnet, "perch'ella non ha vesta in cui si chiuda [because she hasn't any clothes to wear]" (16), that is, according to the commonly held interpretation, because it is divested of music. Given its nakedness, the *pulcella/ stanza* "vien rieto a me [il sonetto] sì. vergognosa [follows me (the sonnet) with such a sense of shame]" (14) and does not dare to circulate: "ch'atorno gir non osa [she dares not go about]" (15). The sonnet asks Lippo to dress it and to be her friend, so that she may circulate and introduce herself: "e prego il gentil cor che 'n te riposa / che la rivesta e tegnala per druda [Hence I would ask you out of charity / to clothe her and regard her as your friend]" (17–18).

Notable in this poem is its emphatic metatextual lexicon, which offers a glimpse into an already hyperliterary world, one that is no longer, in late thirteenth-century Italy, only oral. Even if the presumed lack of music is considered a serious flaw, the context is self-consciously and unequivocally committed to writing and textuality. The incipit sets off a chain of textual and literary terms – "tu che mi **leggi**" (you who are reading me) (1), "a le **parole**" (to the words) (3), "mi t'ha **scritto**" (wrote to me

---

21 For the denigration of Guittone d'Arezzo in the *Commedia*, along with the notable intertextual presence of the Aretine in the same text, see my book *Dante's Poets: Textuality and Truth in the "Comedy"* (Princeton: Princeton University Press, 1984), chap. 2.

about you) (4), "umil[e] **sonetto** " (humble sonnet) (10) – to say nothing of other terms ("vesta" [clothes] [16], "rivesta" [he may clothe] [18]) with literary associations that harken back to the ancient allegorical tradition.

The young Dante who already shows that he is attracted to literary and textual vocabulary will, as a mature poet, often call our attention to the writerliness of his poetry. Consider, for instance, a verse from the *Inferno* such as "e li altri due che 'l canto suso appella [the other two whom my canto names above]" (*Inf.* 33.90). Here the adverb "suso" indicates that a hypertextual domain has fully absorbed the poet's "canto" (whose origins in an oral tradition are nonetheless clearly revealed in its etymology): Dante refers to Ugolino's sons as those whose names are registered "suso," that is, "above," in the material dimension of a written text.[22]

Noteworthy as well is the careful coding of lyrical genres as sexual beings, characterized according to sexual stereotypes: on the one hand the masculine sonnet, who acts as guide and protector; on the other hand the *pulcella/stanza*, whose feminine nakedness is represented as a sign of vulnerability and need – a topos we will later see elaborated in the great canzone of exile, *Tre donne*. The dynamic between nakedness and being dressed in "colori rettorici" is presented in the *Vita Nuova* – "grande vergogna sarebbe a colui che rimasse cose sotto vesta di figura o di colore rettorico, e poscia, domandato, non sapesse denudare le sue parole da cotale vesta, in guisa che avessero verace intendimento [it would be shameful for one who wrote poetry dressed up with figures or rhetorical color not to know how to strip his words of such dress, upon being asked to do so, showing their true sense]" (*VN* XXV.10 [16.10]) – and will be taken up again by Petrarch: "Se 'l pensier che mi strugge, / com'è pungente et saldo, / così vestisse d'un color conforme [If the thought that destroys me, since it's so sharp and strong, were dressed like this in a similar color]" (*Rerum vulgarium fragmenta*[23] 125.1–3).

In *Se Lippo amico* Dante creates categories that are not only metapoetic but also sexual, a move with interesting ramifications for a poet who belonged to the world of codified eroticism that is the courtly lyric. As we will have occasion to see, Dante's lyrics delineate the development of the poet's thought with regard to many of the ideological categories inherited from the courtly system, including the categories of gender. The issue of gender is central to Dante's lyrics, and so it will be central to this commentary.

What matters is not so much Dante's creation in this early composition of completely conventional – in fact, stereotypical – sexual categories, as his readiness to deal with this material. *Se Lippo amico* gives us a baseline by which we can gauge the development in Dante's thinking about sexual categories. By the time he writes

---

22 For "e li altri due che 'l canto suso appella," see Barolini, *The Undivine Comedy,* p. 96; further examples of the same issue include "nel modo che 'l seguente canto canta" (*Par.* 5.139) and "e però miri a ciò ch'io dissi suso" (*Par.* 13.46), for which see *The Undivine Comedy*, pp. 190 and 204.

23 Hereafter cited as *Rvf.*

the *Commedia,* Dante will enter this same ideological arena in a way that is any-thing but conventional. The case of Beatrice is exemplary: from the Beatrice of the *Vita Nuova,* whose silence is a feature that connects her to the lady of the courtly lyric, she becomes the *Beatrix loquax* – far from silent, naked, or vulnerable – of the *Commedia.*[24]

6 (B XLVIII; C 5; FB 8; DR 31)

Se Lippo amico sè tu che mi leggi,	My dear friend Lippo, if you're reading this,
avanti che proveggi	before you undertake
a le parole che dir t'imprometto,	to scan the gist of what I have to say,
da parte di colui che mi t'ha scritto	by one who's written me on your behalf
in tua balìa mi metto	I yield to your command
6 e rècoti salute quali eleggi.	and send such greetings you'd be glad to have.
Per cortesia audir prego mi deggi	Respectfully I pray you listen now
e co·ll'udir richieggi	and as you do, invite
d[e l]'ascoltar la mente e lo 'ntelletto:	your mind and intellect to listen too.
io che m'apello umil[e] sonetto	A humble sonnet I am called, and join
davanti al tu' conspetto	your present company
12 vegno, perché al non-caler non feggi.	lest you should choose to disregard my plea.
Lo qual ti guido esta pulcella nuda	So I bestow on you this undressed girl
che vien di rieto a me sì vergognosa	who follows me with such a sense of shame
ch'atorno gir non osa	she dares not go about
16 perch'ella non ha vesta in cui si chiuda;	because she hasn't any clothes to wear.
e prego il cor gentil che 'n te riposa	Hence I would ask you out of charity
che la rivesta e tegnala per druda,	to clothe her and then keep her as your own,
sì che sia cognosciuda	so she will then be known
20 e possa andar là 'vunqu'è disïosa.	and go wherever she should wish to go.

METRE: *sonetto rinterzato* of twenty lines with rhyme scheme AaBBbA AaBBbA CDdC DCcD, with a base fourteen-hendecasyllable scheme of ABBA ABBA CDC DCD. Lower-case letters indicate *settenari* or seven-syllable verses. Cf. *O voi che per la via* and *Morte villana.*

---

24 See Barolini, "Notes toward a Gendered History of Italian Literature, with a Discussion of Dante's *Beatrix Loquax,"* in *Dante and the Origins of Italian Literary Culture,* pp. 360–78.

7 Lo meo servente core

This canzone, which consists of a single stanza, is plausibly Dante's first canzone. Dante wrote two other single-strophe canzoni, also early compositions: *Madonna, quel signor che voi portate* and *Sì lungiamente m'ha tenuto Amore*. The latter was placed in *Vita Nuova* XXVII (18). The fact that *Lo meo servente core* is the only canzone in Dante's canon to open with a *settenario* (seven-syllable verse) is another indication of immaturity; later, in the post-exilic treatise *De vulgari eloquentia*, Dante formulates the principle whereby a canzone ought to begin with a hendecasyllable. For Contini, the incipit composed of a *settenario* "is a Guittonianism" (p. 24), but we can go back further, to the Sicilians; Giacomo da Lentini, for example, writes canzoni made entirely of *settenari* (for instance, *Meravigliosamente*). And in fact, given the Provençalisms and the markedly more flowing, breezy style – less bristly and difficult than we find, for example, in the *tenzoni* with Dante da Maiano – we can affirm that *Lo meo servente core* is more notable for its Sicilianizing than for its fidelity to Guittone.

The poet writes a letter in verse to his lady, a letter occasioned by their separation; we think of the great Occitan theme of *amor de lonh*. But in contrast to typical poetry of absence, in this case the poet expresses himself in an optimistic register, saying that the sweet hope of return already comforts him: "mi tien già confortato / di ritornar la mia dolce speranza [a pleasant hope / of soon returning here consoles my mind]" (7–8). The theme of far-off love is lexically dominant: we note "avanti ch'io mi sia guari **allungato**" (before being very far away) (6); "Dëo, quanto fi' poca **adimoranza**" (Ah, how brief will be the sojourn) (9); "per che ne lo meo gire e **adimorando**" (because in my going and staying far away) (13). Also of Occitan derivation is the feudal and courtly lexicon that infuses this canzone: the first verse features the lover's "servente core," literally engaged in love-service to the lady, and in the last verses the lover commends himself to his "gentil mia donna" or noble lady: "**gentil** mia donna, a voi mi **raccomando**" (14).

This same feudal ambience will nourish "la corte del cielo [the court of heaven]" of *Inferno* 2, where one *donna gentile* ("**Donna è gentil** nel ciel che si compiange [A noble woman is in heaven who commiserates]" [*Inf.* 2.94]) commends the lost poet to another *donna gentile,* using the same verb *raccomandare* that harkens back to our youthful monostrophic canzone: "Or ha bisogno il tuo fedele / di te, e io a te lo **raccomando** [Your faithful one needs you now, and I commend him to you]" (*Inf.* 2.98–9).

Of particular interest in *Lo meo servente core* is the insistence on memory and recall, which we see not only in "di me vi rechi alcuna **rimembranza** [bring to you some memory of me]" (4) but also in the poet's memory ("la mente") that frequently turns him back ("mi volge") in longing for his lady: "ché mi **volge** sovente / la mente per mirar vostra sembianza [for memory / now often makes me gaze back on your image]" (11–12). This turning back, with its innuendo of a spiralling curve inscribed within the linearity of the human journey, is very Dantean. Dante *re*-finds himself in the first verses of the *Commedia*: "Nel mezzo del cammin di nostra vita / mi **ri**trovai" (*Inf.* 1.1–2). Here the prefix *ri-* of "mi ritrovai" echoes the form of the spiral, a form made up of many small successive conversions none of which is absolute or final (finality is the jurisdiction not of the spiral, but of the circle). Turning nostalgically and orphically toward the past is a key Dantean trope.[25]

In fact, the verb *volge* in "mi **volge** sovente / la mente" anticipates the great use of the same verb in *Purgatorio* 8, also in a context of voyage and absence: "Era già l'ora che **volge** il disio / ai navicanti [It was already the hour that turns the desire of seafarers]" (*Purg.* 8.1–2). And, while the internal rhyme of "mi volge **sovente** / la **mente** per mirar vostra sembianza" is a technical device that to Contini seems "partly Sicilian and partly Guittonian in taste" (p. 25), I would stress that it is far from an unmotivated formalism. The *rimalmezzo* between *sovente* and *mente* places the accent precisely on the central point of this composition: the mind that turns, the memory that is seized in the moment of its conversion to the past.

7 (B XLIX; C 6; FB 9; DR 32)

    Lo meo servente core
vi raccomando: Amor vi l'ha dato;
e Mercé d'altro lato
4 di me vi rechi alcuna rimembranza;
ché del vostro valore
avanti ch'io mi sia guari allungato,
mi tien già confortato
8 di ritornar la mia dolce speranza.
Dëo, quanto fi' poca adimoranza
secondo il mio parvente!
ché mi volge sovente
12 la mente per mirar vostra sembianza:
per che ne lo meo gire e adimorando,
14 gentil mia donna, a voi mi raccomando.

    Love gave to you
my loyal heart, which I entrust to you;
let Kindness bring
to you besides some memory of me,
for well before
my journey takes me far from your great worth,
a pleasant hope
of soon returning here consoles my mind.
Ah yes, how brief a sojourn this will be,
it seems to me:
for memory
now often makes me gaze back on your image.
My noble lady, while I dwell afar,
it is to you that I commend myself.

---

25 On the properties of the spiral in *terza rima*, see Barolini, *The Undivine Comedy*, chap. 2, esp. pp. 25–6, and on the "nostalgic lapse," see chap. 5, esp. pp. 101–3.

METRE: isolated canzone stanza of fourteen verses (nine hendecasyllables and five *settenari*), with rhyme scheme (a5) b(c5)DdE bDdE Eaa(a3)ECC. The *fronte* is eight verses, divided into two *piedi* of four verses each (4 + 4); the *sirma* is six verses. Internal rhyme (*rimalmezzo*), outmoded in taste like the choice of the opening *settenario*, is a notable feature of this canzone, and is indicated by the notations in parentheses. For example, "(a5)" indicates that an internal rhyme on *–ente* occurs at five syllables in the first line, which will be picked up in verses 10 and 11, as well as in an internal rhyme at three syllables in verse 12, indicated by the notation "(a3)".

8 O voi che per la via d'Amor passate
First Redaction

This *sonetto rinterzato*, judged by Barbi, precisely because a *sonetto rinterzato*, to be "one of Dante's oldest poems" (36), was placed by Dante in chapter VII (2) of the *Vita Nuova*. Here it is printed not in the version of the *Vita Nuova* but in an earlier version written before that work, published by De Robertis in his edition of Dante's lyrics. (See the Introduction to this volume for discussion of the thirteen *Vita Nuova* poems that exist in a first redaction.) It is a "lamentanza," according to the definition of the *libello*, where we are told that the sonnet was written to lament the departure of a woman. In the convoluted context of the *Vita Nuova*, but not of the sonnet, Dante fakes passion for a woman in order to hide his own love for Beatrice: "E pensando che se de la sua partita io non parlasse alquanto dolorosamente, le persone sarebbero accorte più tosto de lo mio nascondere, propuosi di farne alcuna lamentanza in uno sonetto [And realizing that, if I didn't speak about her departure somewhat despondently, people would soon catch on to my cover, I decided to lament it in a sonnet]" (VII.2 [2.13]).

As Foster-Boyde note, there is nothing in the sonnet that connects it necessarily with the story of the *Vita Nuova*. Leaving aside what is recounted in the prose of the *libello*, *O voi che per la via* is a sonnet that laments a love first granted and then taken away. Stylistically and thematically, it is a conventional courtly sonnet – with the exception of the incipit, to which we will return. Underscoring the conventionally courtly nature of the poem is the label *lamentanza*, a technical term that indicates an Occitan poetic genre.

The poet invites the followers of Love, "voi che per la via d'Amor passate [you who walk along the path of Love]" (1), to confirm that there is no suffering equal to his: the line "s'egli è dolor alcun quanto 'l mio grave [if there be any grief as deep as mine]" (3) echoes the *tenzone* on love's suffering with Dante da Maiano, where "il dol maggio d'Amore" (the worst pain of love) (*Per pruova di saper*, 10) was under discussion. In the past Love had granted him the life longed for by every courtly lover, "mi puose in vita sì dolce soave [made my life so pleasant and so sweet]" (9), to the point that he had become an object of envy among people who could be heard saying: "Dio, per qual dignitate / questi così legiadro lo cor have? [Good Lord, what worthiness / confers upon this one so glad a heart?]" (11–12). The interrogative form already indicates the instability of this courtly paradise. The following line both brings us emphatically into the present – "Or [Now]" – and engineers a reversal in the poet's state: "Or ho perduta tutta mia baldanza [Now I have lost my sense of confidence]" (13). From here we proceed to the conclusion: while once he was rich, the lover is now "povero" – poor – ("ond'io pover dimoro [so I find myself in penury]"

[15]), so much that he is ashamed to reveal it, thus putting on an outer appearance of being happy while "dentro da lo cor mi struggo e ploro [deep inside my heart I grieve and weep]" (20).

The lexicon of *O voi che per la via* is thick with Provençalisms; there are also some straightforward Sicilianisms ("have" for "ha [he has]" at line 12). The metrical form of a *sonetto rinterzato* is, as we noted in the commentary on *Se Lippo amico*, of Guittonian pedigree. The placement of this sonnet a short distance from the beginning of the *Vita Nuova*, and near to the only other *sonetto rinterzato* that we encounter in that text (*Morte villana* is in chapter VIII [3]), highlights the wish to trace in the *libello* a metapoetic trajectory that demonstrates how the young poet, having gone through courtly, Guittonian, and Cavalcantian phases, ended up discovering – with the help of the Guinizzellian poetic – his new style. As I wrote in *Dante's Poets*: "As first the *Vita Nuova* depicts the transition from Dante's early Guittonianism to his Cavalcantian stage, it then depicts the transition from his Cavalcantianism to the moment when, in *Donne ch'avete*, he finds his own voice."[26] Dante uses the structure of the *Vita Nuova* to put the label "old style" on this sonnet.

Even though it is used by Dante in the *Vita Nuova* to attest to an outmoded stage, *O voi che per la via* nevertheless advances, as nearly always occurs in Dante's lyrics, various innovative ideas. We have already seen how Dante imagines a paradise of love – a "vita sì dolce soave [life so pleasant and so sweet]" (9) – whose strictly courtly nature is indicated, for example, by the *cor leggiadro* possessed by the lover before love is taken from him: "Dio, per qual dignitate / questi così legiadro lo cor have? [Good Lord, what worthiness / confers upon this one so glad a heart?]" (11–12). Here we find likely Dante's first use of the important lexeme *leggiadr-*, attested in the lyrics by both the noun *leggiadria* and the adjective *leggiadro*.[27]

Leggiadria, from the Provençal *leujairia*, is the courtly virtue of grace, or charm, somewhat akin to Castiglione's later *sprezzatura*, which also prizes lightness over ponderous execution. To *leggiadria* Dante will dedicate the canzone *Poscia ch'Amor*, in which he weds courtly virtues with ethical and moral virtues, thereby preserving courtly values that would otherwise be displaced.[28] Later, the ambivalent ideology of *Poscia ch'Amor* will give way to the ideology of the canzone *Doglia mi reca*, in which courtly values are swept away by moral virtues. But, in the long run, *Poscia ch'Amor*, suspended between *cortesia* and ethics, fascinatingly anticipates *Paradiso*, where courtly values, transformed and reinvigorated, will be reprised.

---

26 Citation p. 129.

27 The adjective *leggiadro* appears four times in Dante's lyrics: once in *O voi che per la via* and three times in the canzone *Poscia ch'amor*, which is dedicated to *leggiadria*. The noun *leggiadria* appears seven times in Dante's lyrics: once in *Morte villana*, once in *Per una ghirlandetta*, once in *Sonar bracchetti*, once in *Due donne in cima della mente mia*, and three times in *Poscia ch'Amor*.

28 On the canzone *Poscia ch'Amor* from this perspective, see my essay "*Sotto benda*: Gender in the Lyrics of Dante and Guittone d'Arezzo," in *Dante and the Origins of Italian Literary Culture*, esp. pp. 338–42.

One testament to the reprising of courtly values in *Paradiso* is the word *leggiadria*, used only once in the entire *Commedia*, to describe the archangel Gabriel: "**Baldezza e leggiadria** / quant' esser puote in angelo e in alma, / tutta è in lui [All confidence and grace, as much as there can be in angel or in soul, is in him]" (*Par.* 32.109–11).[29] The trajectory of the word *leggiadria*, beginning in the courtly paradise of the lyrics and reaching a quite other paradise, goes back to this humble *sonetto rinterzato*, in which we find the same proximity of the word *leggiadro* with the word *baldanza* that in *Paradiso* has mutated into "Baldezza e leggiadria": "Dio, per qual dignitate / questi così **legiadro** lo cor have? / Or ho perduta tutta mia **baldanza** [Good Lord, what worthiness / confers upon this one so glad a heart? / Now I have lost my sense of confidence]" (11–13).

Here, however, we are in an explicitly, unequivocally, and restrictedly courtly setting. But perhaps things are not so simple, even in this simple sonnet. In fact the courtly paradise of *O voi che per la via* is contaminated by a different value system, immediately in its first verse: the incipit is a poetic paraphrase of the Book of Lamentations by the prophet Jeremiah. The biblical text – "O vos omnes qui transitis per viam, attendite et videte si est dolor sicut dolor meus" (Lam. 1:12) – is translated by Dante: "O voi che per la via d'Amor passate, / attendete e guardate / s'egli è dolor alcun quanto 'l mio grave [O you who walk along the path of Love, / behold and see / if there be any grief as deep as mine]" (1–3). The opening of Lamentations will be used later by Dante in the prose of the *Vita Nuova* to announce the death of Beatrice (*VN* XXVIII [19]), and Lam. 1:12 will be cited again by a sinner in the thirtieth canto of the *Inferno*: "guardate e attendete / a la miseria del maestro Adamo [look at and regard the misery of Master Adam]" (*Inf.* 30.60–1).

The history traced by the verses from Lamentations, a biblical text to which Dante was clearly attached, thus stretches from Dante's prehistory – from the version of *O voi che per la via* that existed before the *Vita Nuova* – through the *Vita Nuova*, where it appears both in the poetry and in the prose, to the *Inferno*. From this history we learn not only something about the tenacity of Dante's memory, but above all that Dante was capable of using biblical texts in one of his poetic texts very early on, even before the overt theologizing accomplished by the *Vita Nuova*. The young poet who adds "d'Amor" to the Italian translation of the biblical "O vos omnes qui transitis per viam," thus attaining the remarkable "O voi che per la via d'Amor passate," is already interested in combining various registers and ideologies, in this case the courtly with the biblical.

In the prose of the *Vita Nuova* a slightly more mature Dante emphasizes precisely this combinatory move when he cites Jeramiah's text as source: "ne la prima intendo chiamare li fedeli d'Amore per quelle parole di Geremia profeta che dicono: 'O vos

---

29 The adjective *leggiadro* appears in the *Commedia* only twice, both times in a courtly setting: "L'antico sangue e l'opere leggiadre [The old blood and graceful works]" (*Purg.* 11.61); "rime d'amore usar dolci e leggiadre [using sweet and graceful poems of love]" (*Purg.* 26.99).

omnes qui transitis per viam ...' [in the first I mean to call on Love's faithful, with those words of the prophet Jeremiah: 'O vos omnes qui transitis per viam ...']" (VII.7 [2.18]). The presence in the prose of the original verse from Jeremiah serves to draw the reader's attention to the aspect of the sonnet that the poet considers most important and innovative, and that best suits the new theologizing context. *O voi che per la via* contaminates biblical-theological textuality with secular-courtly textuality and thereby contains in seed a practice – the radical fusion of various textual elements without qualms about respecting the usual rhetorical boundaries – whose systematic exploration will be a distinctive stamp of the *Commedia*.

8 (B V; FB 10; DR 33; *VN* VII.3–6 [2.14–17])
First Redaction

O voi che per la via d'Amor passate,	O you who walk along the path of Love,
attendete e guardate	consider now and say
s'egli è dolor alcun quanto 'l mio grave,	if there be any grief as deep as mine;
e prego sol che d'udir mi soffriate	I only ask you listen patiently
e poscia immaginate	and then see for yourselves
6 s'i' son d'ogni tormento ostale e chiave;	if I'm not key and keeper of all pain.
ch'Amor, non già per mia poca bontate,	For Love, though not because of my slight worth,
ma per sua nobiltate,	but through his charity
mi puose in vita sì dolce soave,	has made my life so pleasant and so sweet
ch'i' mi sentia dir dietro spesse fiate:	that many times I hear it said of me:
"Dio, per qual dignitate	"Good Lord, what worthiness
12 questi così legiadro lo cor have?"	confers upon this one so glad a heart?"
Or ho perduta tutta mia baldanza	Now I have lost my sense of confidence
che m'avenia d'amoroso tesoro,	which came to me from love's own treasury,
ond'io pover dimoro	and so I find myself
16 in guisa che di dir mi vèn dottanza;	in penury, and feel afraid to write.
ma io, volendo far come coloro	But seeking now to do as others do,
che per vergogna celan lor mancanza,	who out of shame conceal their deficit,
di fuor mostro allegranza	I mimic happiness
20 e dentro da lo cor mi struggo e ploro.	while deep inside my heart I grieve and weep.

VN 4. ch(e) audir mi sofferiate – 5. E poi – 7. Amor – 9. dolce e soave – 11. Deh ß (Gorni) – 12. Così leggiadro questi – 14. Che si movea – 17. Sì che volendo

METRE: *sonetto rinterzato* of twenty lines (cf. *Se Lippo amico* and *Morte villana*, but here the rhymes are all alternating) with rhyme scheme AaBAaB AaBAaB CDdC DCcD, with a base fourteen-hendecasyllable scheme of ABAB ABAB CDC DCD.

9 Piangete, amanti, poi che piange Amore

The sonnets *Piangete, amanti* and *Morte villana* are in the same chapter (VIII [3]) of the *Vita Nuova,* where the prose is presented as occasioned by the death of a young woman who had been sometimes in Beatrice's company. The sonnet is a *planctus*: the word "Piangete" initiates the poem and the incipit then repeats the word *piangere,* subsequently reinforced by "plorare" (to cry) (2) and by "lamentare" (to lament) (10). The two poems placed together in *Vita Nuova* VIII (3) are thus closely related to each other: the expression "villana Morte" that Dante uses at line 5 of *Piangete, amanti* becomes the incipit of the following poem, *Morte villana.*

The lament for the death of a deceased person of high social standing is dear to Occitan poetry, which boasts a genre – the *planh* – specifically for this purpose. Very often the lament for the death of a noble lord is tied, in the Occitan *planh,* to the lament for the collapse of a world of courtesy and virtue viewed as embodied in the dead person. If we consider an exemplar of Occitan *planh* that Dante most likely knew, the dirge for Blacatz by the poet Sordello (whose shade we encounter in the sixth canto of *Purgatorio*), we see how smoothly Sordello transitions from weeping in the first strophe – the first word of his *planh* is "Planher," as in our sonnet the first word is "Piangete" – to praising the virtues of the one who has passed away:

> Planher vuelh en Blacatz en aquest leugier so,
> ab cor trist e marrit; et ai en be razo,
> qu'en luy ai mescabat senhor et amic bo,
> e quar tug l'ayp valent en sa mort perdut so.   (1–4; Boni ed.)

> [I want to mourn for Lord Blacatz in this light song,
> with sadness in my grieving heart; and I've good cause,
> since I have lost in him a worthy lord and friend,
> and with his death all virtuousness is gone.]

It is worth noting this characteristic of the Occitan *planh* – the transition from death to praise – in order to better appreciate the presence of the theme of praise in *Piangete, amanti.* In Dante's sonnet there is an explicit cause-effect relationship between death and praise. The poet reproves Death because Death destroys that which is praiseworthy on earth: "ha miso il suo crudele adoperare, / guastando ciò che al mondo è da laudare [carried out her work / to cruel effect within a noble heart, / destroying that which should be praised on earth]" (6–7). Having made the required adjustments from illustrious lord to noble lady, we see here the typical development of a *planh* with its transition from weeping to praise. Dante here emphasizes the theme of praise by means of a word that is especially dear to him: "laudare" (7).

In the *Vita Nuova* praise will be decoupled from lamentation, and will become the basis of Dante's new Beatrician poetics and of what he will call "the style of her praise": "lo stilo de la sua loda" (XXVI.4 [17.4]).

However, the separation of lamentation and praise is far from absolute and the old link between the two is reaffirmed in the *Vita Nuova* through the various deaths that punctuate the plot, culminating in Beatrice's death. In addition, Dante uses the *Vita Nuova*'s prose as an occasion for theorizing the link between praise and awareness of the mortality of the object of praise. In the epiphany by which he learns that Love "ha posto tutta la mia beatitudine in quello che non mi puote venire meno [has placed all my beatitude in that which cannot fail me]" (*VN* XVIII.4 [10.6]), Dante comes to understand that he has to search for his happiness not in the object of praise but in the words that praise the object: "in quelle parole che lodano la donna mia [in those words that praise my lady]" (*VN* XVIII.6–7 [10.8–9]). The poetry of praise is that which will not fail him, which will not die. In this way Dante preserves and renews the old link between lamentation and praise, making his praise a means for avoiding future lamentation.

The Occitan link between lamentation and praise will find its full new, Beatrician expression in the great canzone *Li occhi dolenti per pietà del core*, written both to lament Beatrice's death and to praise her life: not only her earthly life but her new life, in paradise, which can never fail him – "che non mi puote venire meno."

Another notable feature of *Piangete, amanti* is the play on "forma vera [true form]" and "morta imagine [dead image]," an early signpost of Dante's long meditation on representation, on what he views as the poet's trade. In *Piangete, amanti* the poet imagines seeing Amore "lamentare in forma vera / sovra la morta imagine avvenente [in real form / lamenting over her dead lovely image]" (10–11); in other words, Love, "in forma vera," laments the "morta imagine" of the lady. Barbi cites, with regard to Love appearing "in forma vera," the "visible" Love in Cino's *Vedete, donne, bella creatura*: "ch'io veggio Amor visibil che l'adora [I see Love, visible, adoring her]" (13). We recall that in the *Vita Nuova* Dante claims that a poet can talk to inanimate things and can make inanimate things talk among each other.[30] In *Piangete, amanti* Dante plays with the categories that he later theorizes in the *libello*: the inanimate thing, Love, is presented "in true form" ("in person," "visible") over the body of the dead woman who is, because she is dead, only an "image" of what she was. The objective is to probe the boundaries between animate and inanimate, or better, between true and not-true, exchanging the categories and rendering true

---

30 "Dunque, se noi vedemo che li poete hanno parlato a le cose inanimate, sì come se avessero senso e ragione, e fattele parlare insieme; e non solamente cose vere, ma cose non vere [Therefore, if we see that poets have addressed inanimate things as if they had sense and reason, and also have made them talk – and not only real things but imaginary things as well]" (*VN* XXV.8 [16.8]).

the not-true and vice versa: instead of being "accidente in sostanza [an accident in a substance]" (as Love will be defined in *VN* XXV.1 [16.1]), Love here is visible and animated and it is the woman, a true substance, who becomes no longer true but inanimate "image" of her self.

Both the discussion of the link between lamentation and praise and the discussion of the boundaries between true and not-true are fundamental for Dante and show us how *Piangete, amanti* earned its place in the *Vita Nuova*: chapter XXV (16) of the *libello* affirms that the role of poet is that of crossing the boundaries between animate and inanimate, between true and not-true. This is the enterprise that the *Commedia* will call Ulyssean, and it is the enterprise for which the young poet, juxtaposing "forma vera" and "morta imagine," is already preparing. Nor should one forget that Petrarch is thinking of this sonnet and of the same issue when he concludes *Movesi il vecchierel canuto et biancho* (*Rvf* 16) with the line "la disiata vostra forma vera [your desired true form]."

9 (B VI; FB 11; *VN* VIII.4–6 [3.4–6])

Piangete, amanti, poi che piange Amore,	Weep, all lovers, weep, since Love now weeps,
udendo qual cagion lui fa plorare.	as you now hear the reason for his tears.
Amor sente a Pietà donne chiamare,	Love listens on as ladies plead for Pity,
4 mostrando amaro duol per li occhi fore,	with bitter sorrow flowing from their eyes,
perché villana Morte in gentil core	for savage Death has carried out her work
ha miso il suo crudele adoperare,	to cruel effect within a noble heart,
guastando ciò che al mondo è da laudare	destroying that which should be praised on earth
8 in gentil donna sovra de l'onore.	as well as honour in a noble lady.
Audite quanto Amor le fece orranza,	Hear what great honour Love has paid to her,
ch'io 'l vidi lamentare in forma vera	for I did see him in real form
11 sovra la morta imagine avvenente;	lamenting over her dead lovely image;
e riguardava ver lo ciel sovente,	and often he would look up heavenward,
ove l'alma gentil già locata era,	where her kind soul already had a home,
14 che donna fu di sì gaia sembianza.	which once had been a woman of great charm.

METRE: sonnet ABBA ABBA CDE EDC.

10 Morte villana, di pietà nemica

In this *sonetto rinterzato* many of the same motifs that we found in the two preceding poems come together again; the three poems form a compact group within the *Vita Nuova*. *Morte villana*, placed in *Vita Nuova* VIII (3), shares with *O voi che per la via d'Amor passate* (*Vita Nuova* VII [2]) both the metrical form of a *sonetto rinterzato* and the typically courtly lexicon. Symptomatic, from this point of view, is the presence in both poems of the noun *leggiadria*/adjective *leggiadro*. In *O voi che per la via* the "legiadro cor" of the courtly lover is destroyed when he loses his love, while in *Morte villana* "leggiadria" – the courtly virtue par excellence – is destroyed by death, the same "morte villana [savage death]" to which the poet addresses his lament and to whom he then directs his accusation: "distrutta hai l'amorosa leggiadria [you have destroyed the grace that love creates]" (16).

The subject of *Morte villana* is the savagery of death that has abducted from the world a young woman who embodies "ciò ch'è in donna da pregiar vertute [what in woman is revered as worth]" (14). It is therefore the same argument as that of *Piangete, amanti*, the sonnet with which it shares chapter VIII (3) of the *libello* and which directly anticipates the incipit of its companion-sonnet in the "villana Morte" of its fifth verse.

Morte villana uses the moment of grieving over a dead person who is the incarnation of every virtue in order to create the same link between lamentation and praise that we noted in *Piangete, amanti*. Again, with a move formerly seen in the Occitan *planh*, death is an occasion to celebrate the gifts of a person who becomes emblematic of the whole courtly world: "Dal secolo hai partita cortesia / e ciò ch'è in donna da pregiar vertute: / in gaia gioventute / distrutta hai l'amorosa leggiadria [You have deprived this world of courtesy / and what in woman is revered as worth: / in cheerful youthfulness / you have destroyed the grace that love creates]" (13–16).

Although they treat the same subjects, *Piangete, amanti* and *Morte villana* arrive at notably different results. *Morte villana* is a less innovative and more conventional poem than *Piangete, amanti*. Barbi notes among its antecedents the canzone *Morte, perché m'hai fatta sì gran guerra* by Giacomino Pugliese, which has the line "Villana Morte, che non ha' pietanza [Savage Death, who has no pity]" (5). The metrical form of *Morte villana* betrays its Guittonian pedigree, and indeed the Guittonianism of *Morte villana* is more emphatic than that of the other two *sonetti rinterzati* that we have discussed (*Se Lippo amico, O voi che per la via*).

Commenting on *Morte villana* "as an example of a particular style, a particular rhetoric, a particular flavor," De Robertis lists the stylistic points that reveal the Guittonian style: "We note, in these opening lines – along with the typical figures of *am-*

plificatio, of apostrophe (which basically conditions the entire composition), and of *expolitio* – the solemnity of the images (ll.1–2, and cf. l.7); the accumulation, highlighted by the artificial inversions (the main clause down at l.6), of definitions (ll.1–3, all the way to the etymological pun in l.9); and, at least in the quatrains, the series of rhymed couplets" (*VN*, 58–9). Glossing the flagrant etymological pun that Dante employs in line 9 ("lo tuo fallar d'onni torto tortoso [your fault in every wrongful act of wrong]," De Robertis notes that this trope is "frequent in Guittone" and that it is here "complicated by Dante" in such a way that we end up having a "Dante more Guittonian than Guittone!" (*VN*, 60).

It is also noteworthy, as Gorni points out, that a taste for this trope will return in the *Commedia*, where we find it in uses such as "selva selvaggia" (*Inf.* 1.5) and "più volte vòlto" (*Inf.* 1.36). This style, outdated when we encounter it in the *Vita Nuova*, is one that Dante will eventually renew and reuse.

10 (B VII; FB 12; *VN* VIII.8–11 [3.8–11])

Morte villana, di pietà nemica,	Savage death, compassion's enemy,
di dolor madre antica,	ancient mother of grief,
giudicio incontastabile gravoso,	sentence unappealable, severe,
poi che hai data matera al cor doglioso	since you have given to a grieving heart
ond'io vado pensoso,	a cause for being sad,
6 di te blasmar la lingua s'affatica.	my tongue exhausts itself condemning you.
E s'io di grazia ti voi far mendica,	And if I want to strip you of all worth,
convenesi ch'eo dica	I need to specify
lo tuo fallar d'onni torto tortoso,	the wrongfulness of every wrong of yours,
non però ch'a la gente sia nascoso,	though not because this is unknown to most,
ma per farne cruccioso	but rather to incense
12 chi d'amor per innanzi si notrica.	whoever takes his nourishment from love.
Dal secolo hai partita cortesia	You have deprived this world of courtesy
e ciò ch'è in donna da pregiar vertute:	and what in woman is revered as worth:
in gaia gioventute	in cheerful youthfulness
16 distrutta hai l'amorosa leggiadria.	you have destroyed the grace that love creates.
Più non voi discovrir qual donna sia	I won't disclose here who this lady is
che per le propietà sue canosciute.	except to note her well known qualities.
Chi non merta salute	Those undeserving of salvation
20 non speri mai d'aver sua compagnia.	should never hope to join her company.

METRE: *sonetto rinterzato* of twenty lines with rhyme scheme AaBBbA AaBBbA CDdC CDdC, with a base fourteen-hendecasyllable scheme of ABBA ABBA CDC CDC; cf. *Se Lippo amico* and *O voi che per la via.*

11 La dispietata mente che pur mira

If we take the canzone *Donne ch'avete* as gauge of Dante's full *stil novo*, both from a stylistic point of view (exclusion of all obvious virtuosity, in order to achieve a paradoxical rhetoric of hyperbole that is not showily hyperbolic, of hyperbole that is somehow purified and plain) and from a thematic point of view (nothing is required of the lady, who is simply praised), the canzone *La dispietata mente* can easily be placed in a period that precedes the *stil novo*. *La dispietata mente* not only addresses the lady, asking her for her greeting, but it does so with a certain urgency: "sappiate che l'attender io non posso, / ch'i' sono al fine della mia possanza [please understand I can no longer wait, / for I have reached the limit of my strength]" (29–30). Contini judges it as an early work, "interwoven with 'feudal' and unoriginal motifs" (p. 26). While sharing his judgment of the relative youthfulness of this canzone, I do not agree that it lacks originality or interest.

As in the single-stanza canzone *Lo meo servente core,* the theme is the optimistic experience of the absence of the beloved. The woman in *La dispietata mente* is legible, and the signs are hope-inducing: "ché ciascun che vi mira, in veritate / di fuor conosce che dentro è pietate [for everyone who looks at you, in truth, / will outwardly perceive that pity lies inside]" (51–2). As in *Lo meo servente core,* here too we find a Dante bent on using Sicilian motifs and styles, identifiable above all with Giacomo da Lentini, and on mastering a fluid and limpid style that is the antithesis of the Guittonian mode (as in the sonnets exchanged with Dante da Maiano).

Dante here sends his canzone to *madonna,* from whom he requests a reward. Giacomo da Lentini, who is hardly shy with regard to the reward ("guiderdone") that is expected for his love-service, starts one of his canzoni like this: "Guiderdone aspetto avere / da voi, donna, cui servire / no m'enoia [I hope to earn reward / from you, my fair, in serving whom / I'm not displeased]." In *La dispietata mente* Dante asks for the solace of "vostra salute [your salutation]," as we read at the end of the first stanza: "piacciavi a lui mandar vostra salute / che sia conforto della sua vertute [would you please send along your salutation, / so it may serve to strengthen my resolve]" (12–13). The reward will be invoked even more explicitly at the beginning of the fourth stanza, where the word "dono [gift]" is used outright: "E voi pur siete quella ch'io più amo / e che far mi potete maggior dono [And yet you are the one I love the most, / the one who offers me the greatest gift]" (40–1).

The unfolding of *La dispietata mente* is not so much rigorously logical as it is a series of variations on the theme of absence and of the resultant need for the *saluto/ salute* that only *madonna* can provide. The expression of this need, which acts as a seal on the first stanza, is then elaborated in the following stanza. In the second stanza the obligation of *madonna* to satisfy the need of her lover is compared to the obligation of a "buon signor [honest lord]" who doesn't hold back from helping his servant who calls on him, because in defending the servant he also defends his own honour: "ché buon signor già non ristringe freno / per soccorrer lo servo quando 'l chiama, / ché non pur lui, ma 'l suo onor difende [an honest lord will never hesitate / to aid his servant when he calls for help, / since he defends his honour, not just him]" (17–19). The master/servant trope, here probably used by Dante for the first time, is one that he will turn to not infrequently, in the treatises *De vulgari eloquentia* and *Convivio* and in the *Commedia*: from "ma vergogna mi fé le sue minacce, / che innanzi a buon segnor fa servo forte [but his threats made me feel shame, which before a good lord makes a servant strong]" (*Inf.* 17.89–90) to "Come 'l segnor ch'ascolta quel che i piace, / da indi abbraccia il servo, gratulando / per la novella, tosto ch'el si tace [Like the lord who listens to what pleases him, and then embraces his servant, celebrating the news with him, as soon as he is silent]" (*Par.* 24.148–50). It is a trope that opens a window onto contemporary society. While in *La dispietata mente* the comparison denotes a purely social context, in the moral context of the mature canzone *Doglia mi reca nello core ardire* the metaphor *servo/signore* broadens to become one of the structural metaphors of the canzone's ethical discourse, anticipating the final occurrence of *servo* in the *Commedia*: "Tu m'hai di servo tratto a libertate [You have brought me from servitude to freedom]" (*Par.* 31.85).

The third stanza reveals the urgent desire of the lover, who by now has reached the point of addressing *madonna* directly to ask for the ultimate hope, "l'ultima speme," that is, her greeting: "E ciò conoscer voi dovete, quando / l'ultima speme a cercar mi son mosso [And this you ought to know, since I've begun / my final quest to gain my hope's reward]" (31–2). The fourth stanza forcefully states that only she is capable of helping him. The fifth stanza explains in minute detail how the "salute" of the woman, once having come to comfort the lover's heart – "Dunque vostra salute omai si mova / e vegna dentro al cor, che lei aspetta [So let your greeting now be on its way / and come into my heart, which waits for it]" (53–4) – could not enter without being accompanied by the "messi d'Amor [Love's messengers]" (60).

It has been much discussed whether the woman to whom *La dispietata mente* is addressed is the first screen-woman in the *Vita Nuova* or Beatrice herself. I don't intend to enter here into a discussion that has no empirical basis, but only to indicate the parameters – poetic and hermeneutic, not biographical – within which it is legitimate to formulate the question. The poet of *La dispietata mente* is experimenting. If on the one hand the woman of *La dispietata mente* is treated in the old manner, according to the Sicilian practice of service and reward, on the other hand what Dante asks of her is "vostra **salute**": a new kind of reward that definitely puts us on the road toward the *Vita Nuova*. Precisely as in the *Vita Nuova*, here it is the Guinizzellian motif of the lady's greeting – Guinizzelli's lady "abassa orgoglio a cui dona **salute** [curtails the pride of those she greets]" (*Io voglio del ver la mia donna laudare*, 10) – that signals the potential transition to the new poetic.

Another example of this canzone's originality with respect to traditional motifs is provided by Dante's remarkable variation on the Sicilian topos of the lady painted in the lover's heart. In *La dispietata mente* Dante compares the obligation of the lady towards the lover, who carries her image painted in his heart, to the obligation of God towards human beings created in His image.

The topos of the lady painted in the heart is already used with philosophical rigour by Giacomo da Lentini in *Meravigliosamente*, where it enables an intricate discourse on the relationship between the *vero* (truth) – in this case the real lady – and the veri-similar, the represented reality akin to the truth – in this case the painted image that represents the lady. In other words, the image of the lady painted by Love in the lover's heart – "In cor par ch'eo vi porti, / **pinta** come parete [I seem to bear you in my heart / painted as you appear]" (*Meravigliosamente*, 10–11) – is already, starting with Giacomo, a metadiscourse on representation itself. This metadiscourse will be important to Dante throughout his poetic itinerary, from his lyrics (see the late canzone *Amor, da che convien pur ch'io mi doglia*) to the *Commedia*: for instance, the term "exemplo," used by Giacomo in *Meravigliosamente* ("Com'om che pone mente / in altro exemplo pinge / la simile pintura [As one who contemplates / a model with great care / can paint its replica]" [4–6]), will appear in *Paradiso*.

In one of the extraordinary *translationes* that characterize Dante's *Paradiso*, the image of the lady painted in the lover's heart becomes the human image painted in the "heart" of the Trinity, that is, our image painted in Christ. The second of the three circumferences seen by the pilgrim at the end of *Paradiso*, the one that represents Christ, "parve **pinta** de la nostra effige [seems painted with our image]" (*Par.* 33.131): "pinta" goes all the way back to Giacomo da Lentini. The word "effige," which derives from *effingere* ("to paint"), here replaces the word more typical of the lyric tradition – "figura" ("'nfra lo core meo / porto la tua figura [for in my heart I bear / the portrait of your form]" [*Meravigliosamente*, 8–9]) – and reinforces the importance of "pinta." To emphasize the linearity of the path that brings the old lyrical topos to *Paradiso*, we note that the only other use of "effige" in the *Commedia* refers to the "effige" of Beatrice in *Par.* 31.77: that is, to the ultimate incarnation of the lyric lady.

Instead of "effige" or "figura," the word that Dante employs in *La dispietata mente* is "imagine." By connecting the Sicilian topos of the painted image of the lady to the theological concept of man made in the image of God, Dante already in his youthful canzone projects the Sicilian topos in a new and unexpected theological direction. We might better call it a "theologized" direction, because it has less to do with correct theology than with the young poet's wish to impart a theological flavour.

In *La dispietata mente* the poet states that the suffering of his heart increases when he thinks about how the image of his lady is painted there. The lady ought to care for the heart on which her image is imprinted, exactly in the way that God cares for us human beings because He sees in us the image of Himself. In the verses in which Dante expresses this analogy, note the words "pinta" and "imagine," words that go back to Giacomo on the one hand and that lead to *Paradiso* on the other:

E certo la sua doglia più m'incende
quand'io mi penso ben, donna, che voi
per man d'Amor là entro **pinta** sète:
così e voi dovete
vie maggiormente aver cura di lui,
ché Que' da cui convien che 'l ben s'appari
per l'**imagine** sua ne tien più cari.
(La dispietata mente, 20–6)

[And more intensely is its pain inflamed
when I reflect, my lady, that it's you
inside who's painted by the hand of Love.
And so indeed you must
devote to its well-being much greater care.
For He from Whom we learn about the good
holds us more dear because we bear His image.]

This passage, in which the theology of the incarnation is grafted onto the Sicilian topos of the image of the beloved painted in the heart, is a distant prefiguration of the conclusion of *Paradiso* and bears clear testimony to the precocious originality of *La dispietata mente*.

We have already spoken about the elements in this canzone that anticipate the *Vita Nuova*. The courtly accents of the canzone go beyond the *libello* to the *Commedia*, to two cantos much informed by the courtly world: *Inferno* 2 and *Inferno* 5. The two lines that refer to the "cor che tanto v'**ama**, / poi sol da voi lo **soccorso** attende [my heart which loves you in its plight, / since it expects no help except from you]" (15–16) will be compressed into a single famous verse in *Inferno* 2: "ché non **soccorri** quei che t'**amò** tanto [why do you not help the one who loved you so much]" (*Inf.* 2.104). The idea that the lady ought to care for the heart in which her image is painted – "così e voi dovete / vie maggiormente aver **cura** di lui [And so indeed you must / devote to its well-being much greater care]" (23–4) – anticipates the "tre donne benedette [three blessed ladies]" who "**curan** di te ne la corte del cielo [who care for you in the court of heaven]" (*Inf.* 2.124–5). The use of the technical term "preso" in "saetta / ch'Amor lanciò lo giorno ch'io fui **preso** [the arrow shot by Love / the day that I was made his prisoner]" (57–8) will be recalled in *Inferno* 5. Continuing the courtly motifs, the fifth stanza elaborates a concept that overturns the central metaphor of the *Roman de la rose* (and so also of the *Fiore*), giving to the masculine figure the role that belonged to the lady in those texts: here it is the lover (not the beloved) who has the locked heart, which only she can penetrate.

Characteristic of a much more mature Dante is the vigour of the enjambments accompanied by strong caesuras that we find in the fourth stanza, in the lines "e quelle cose ch'a voi onor sono / dimando e voglio, ogn'altra m'è noiosa [and only things that bring you great renown / I want and need – all else I can't abide" (44–5) and "ché 'l sì e 'l no di me in vostra mano / ha posto Amore, ond'io grande mi tegno [for Love's placed in your hands the power to rule / my destiny – which makes me very proud]" (47–8).

One cannot conclude a discussion of *La dispietata mente* without focusing on the opening and its discourse of memory and desire. The "dispietata mente" of the incipit is the poet's memory, pitiless ("dispietata") in that it makes him suffer by "gazing back / on days that are forever lost in time." Next to the pitiless memory that looks back, to the past, there is the erotic desire that "pulls" him forward, toward the future:

> La dispietata mente che pur mira
> di rieto al tempo che se n'è andato
> da l'un de' lati mi combatte il core,
> e 'l disio amoroso che mi tira
> verso 'l dolce paese c'ho lasciato
> da l'altra part'è con forza d'amore.
> (La dispietata mente, 1–6)

> [Pitiless memory, still gazing back
> on days that are forever lost in time,
> assails my heart upon one side of me,
> and love's desire, which draws me ever toward
> the lovely land that I have left behind,
> has joined with Love upon the other side.]

Dante sketches here a temporal dialectic in which memory (the past) and desire (the future) battle over the lover's heart. But on closer inspection, the future and the past are not so divergent. Desire draws him forward, but where to? Precisely toward a future that is somehow also his past: "verso 'l dolce paese *c'ho lasciato* [toward / the lovely land that I have left behind]" (5). Here we find the idea of time in the form of a spiral – in the form of *terza rima* – in which beginning and end, past and future, are conjoined. These lines seem adapted to the Aristotelian definition of time that will inform the metaphysics and poetics of the *Commedia*, according to which time is "a kind of middle-point, uniting as it does in itself both a beginning and an end, a beginning of future time and an end of past time."[31]

---

31 Aristotle actually refers to the moment, which he considers indistiguishable from time: "Now since time cannot exist and is unthinkable apart from the moment, and the moment is a kind of middle-point, uniting as it does in itself both a beginning and an end, a beginning of future time and an end of past time, it follows that there must always be time" (*Physics* 8.1.251b.18–26; trans. R.P. Hardie and R.K. Gaye, *The Basic Works of Aristotle*, ed. Richard McKeon [New York: Random House, 1941]). For time in the form of a spiral and of *terza rima* and for the temporality of narrative in Dante, see Barolini, *The Undivine Comedy*, chap. 2, "Infernal Incipits: The Poetics of the New," esp. pp. 21–6.

In this canzone one senses how Dante is already exploring human life from an existential perspective: life is the memory of time that is behind us, the hope that pulls us forward, and the present in which the two intersect. This existential meditation is emblematically distilled at the end of the canzone, in the congedo: "Canzone, il tuo cammin vuol esser corto, / ché tu sai ben che poco tempo omai / puote aver luogo quel per che tu vai [My song, your journey must be brief, / for you know well that little time is left / to carry out what makes you now depart]" (68). As will be the case in the *Commedia*, the poet of this canzone feels the yoke of time and articulates the link between time and narrative: the journey of the canzone must "be brief" since "little time is left" (66–7).

The existential journey so suggestively framed at the opening of *La dispietata mente* recalls the poet of the "cammin di nostra vita [journey of our life]" in the first verse of the *Commedia*. The congedo of the canzone returns to the existential note of the "nuovo e mai non fatto cammino di questa vita [new and never travelled road of this life]" (*Convivio* 4.12.15): the journey of life laden with memories and desire, the journey of time that on the one hand stretches behind us to the past and on the other pulls us forward to the future.

11 (B L; C 7; FB 13; DR 12)

La dispietata mente che pur mira	Pitiless memory, still gazing back
di rieto al tempo che se n'è andato	on days that are forever lost in time,
3 da l'un de' lati mi combatte il core,	assails my heart upon one side of me,
e 'l disio amoroso che mi tira	and love's desire, which draws me ever toward
verso 'l dolce paese c'ho lasciato	the lovely land that I have left behind,
6 da l'altra part'è con forza d'amore;	has joined with Love upon the other side.
né dentro sento tanto di valore	I feel that I retain so little strength
che possa lungamente far difesa,	that I am far from mounting a defence,
9 gentil madonna, se da voi non vene:	my lady fair, unless it comes from you.
però, s'a voi convene	So if you find it apt
ad iscampo di lui mai fare impresa,	to undertake the rescue of my heart,
piacciavi a lui mandar vostra salute	would you please send along your salutation,
13 che sia conforto della sua vertute.	so it may serve to strengthen my resolve.
Piacciavi, donna mia, non venir meno	My lady, may it please you not to fail
a questo punto al cor che tanto v'ama,	my heart which loves you in its plight,
16 poi sol da voi lo soccorso attende;	since it expects no help except from you;
ché buon signor già non ristringe freno	an honest lord will never hesitate
per soccorrer lo servo quando 'l chiama,	to aid his servant when he calls for help,
19 ché non pur lui, ma 'l suo onor difende.	since he defends his honour, not just him.
E certo la sua doglia più m'incende	And more intensely is its pain inflamed
quand'io mi penso ben, donna, che voi	when I reflect, my lady, that it's you

per man d'Amor là entro pinta sète:
così e voi dovete
vie maggiormente aver cura di lui,
ché Que' da cui convien che 'l ben s'appari
per l'imagine sua ne tien più cari.

    Se dir voleste, dolce mia speranza,
di dare indugio a quel ch'io vi domando,
sappiate che l'attender io non posso,
ch'i' sono al fine della mia possanza.
E ciò conoscer voi dovete, quando
l'ultima speme a cercar mi son mosso;
ché tutti i carchi sostenere a dosso
de' l'uomo infino al peso ch'è mortale
prima che 'l suo maggiore amico provi,
poi non sa qual lo trovi;
e s'egli avien che gli risponda male,
cosa non è che tanto costi cara,
che morte n'ha più tosto, e più amara.

    E voi pur siete quella ch'io più amo
e che far mi potete maggior dono
e 'n cui la mia speranza più riposa,
che sol per voi servir la vita bramo,
e quelle cose ch'a voi onor sono
dimando e voglio, ogn'altra m'è noiosa.
Darmi potete ciò ch'altri non osa,
ché 'l sì e 'l no di me in vostra mano
ha posto Amore, ond'io grande mi tegno;
la fede ch'eo v'assegno
move dal portamento vostro umano,
ché ciascun che vi mira, in veritate
di fuor conosce che dentro è pietate.

    Dunque vostra salute omai si mova
e vegna dentro al cor, che lei aspetta,
gentil madonna, come avete inteso;
ma sappia che l'entrar di lui si trova
serrato forte da quella saetta
ch'Amor lanciò lo giorno ch'io fui preso;
per che l'entrare a tutt'altri è conteso
fuor ch'a' messi d'Amor, ch'aprir lo sanno
per volontà de la vertù che 'l serra:
onde ne la mia guerra
la sua venuta mi sarebbe danno
sed ella fosse sanza compagnia

---

inside who's painted by the hand of Love.
And so indeed you must
devote to its well-being much greater care.
For He from Whom we learn about the good,
holds us more dear because we bear His image.

    If you were now, sweet hope, to seek delay
in granting me the substance of my wish,
please understand I can no longer wait,
for I have reached the limit of my strength.
And this you ought to know, since I've begun
my final quest to gain my hope's reward:
a man must bear all burdens on his back,
unless the weight should pose the risk of death,
before he places trust in his best friend,
not knowing what he'll find.
For if his friend should turn his plea aside,
there's nothing that could come at greater cost,
since death comes quicker and has greater gall.

    And yet you are the one I love the most,
the one who offers me the greatest gift,
the one in whom my hope most finds repose.
My love of life depends on serving you,
and only things that bring you great renown
I want and need – all else I can't abide.
You're able to provide what no one can,
for Love's placed in your hands the power to rule
my destiny – which makes me very proud.
The trust I place in you
comes from the kindness that your bearing shows,
for everyone who looks at you, in truth,
will outwardly perceive that pity lies inside.

    So let your greeting now be on its way
and come into my heart, which waits for it,
my noble lady, as you've heard me say;
but know the entry leading in is locked
securely by the arrow shot by Love
the day that I was made his prisoner.
And so the entry now is blocked to all
except Love's messengers, who know the way
to open it, from having locked it once before.
So in this strife of mine
its coming would result in injury,
unless escorted by the messengers

65   de' messi del signor che m'ha in balia.   of him who holds me firmly in his power.
    Canzone, il tuo cammin vuol esser corto,   My song, your journey must be brief,
    ché tu sai ben che poco tempo omai   for you know well that little time is left
68   puote aver luogo quel per che tu vai.   to carry out what makes you now depart.

METRE: canzone of five stanzas, each composed of thirteen verses (twelve hendecasyllables and a single *settenario*), with rhyme scheme ABC ABC CDEeDFF and *congedo* of three verses, YZZ. The *fronte* is six verses (3 + 3) and the *sirma* is seven verses. The Y rhyme of the *congedo* has no match elsewhere in the poem. The same rhyme scheme and the same number of stanzas will occur again, but with a different *congedo*, in *Io son venuto al punto de la rota* (the only instance of such repetition in Dante's œuvre).

12 Madonna, quel signor che voi portate

This is a canzone stanza like *Lo meo servente core*, with which *Madonna, quel signor* shares much more than the "archaic" metre already indicated as a point of convergence by Contini (p. 40) (the rhyme scheme is archaic in having only two rhymes in the *fronte*, in the repetition of rhymes of the *fronte* in the *sirma*, and in dividing the *sirma* into two *volte*). Contini follows Barbi in placing it between the two floral ballads *Per una ghirlandetta* and *Deh, Vïoletta*, both Cavalcantian in tone and style. He does so on the basis of the syntagma "soave fiore [delightful flower]" at line 15.

Barbi was influenced by the lively discussions on the identity of the various women in Dante's poetry that occupied critics at the end of the nineteenth century and the first decades of the twentieth (and that he ridicules but nevertheless feels obligated to duly report in his note to *Deh, Vïoletta*). Barbi places this canzone with the two ballads even though he then sums up the situation with this distancing note:

> Zonta thought that this poem signals the passage from love for Fioretta (the first screen-lady of the *Vita Nuova*, according to him) to that for Violetta (the second screen-lady), and would like to attach deep significance to the *nuovo colore*: as though it stood for the passage from one flower to the other. But it is all an arbitrary reconstruction, because nothing entitles us to connect the three poems; and besides, *Fioretta* is too generic to indicate a colour different from *Violetta*. The truth is that we don't know a thing, and we ought to content ourselves with saying that this poem gives the impression of youthfulness (so much so that Zingarelli judged it crude and hardly worthy of Dante). (Barbi-Maggini, p. 209)

In breaking with the Barbian tradition and choosing to give a new placement to *Madonna, quel signor*, I reiterate what I stated in the Introduction to this volume, namely that any editorial ordering of Dante's lyrics is approximate. In the case of this canzone, and in a critical climate in which the "detective story" surrounding Dante's various women is pretty much forgotten, the *senhal* (coded lady's name) based on a flower seems less important as a criterion of order than the many thematic, lexical, and stylistic links that *Madonna, quel signor* shares with *Lo meo servente core* and with *La dispietata mente*.

The three canzoni belong to a Sicilian and Provençal-influenced matrix and sing a love that is fundamentally optimistic. For this reason, all three canzoni feature words such as "conforto [comfort]" and "speranza [hope]": the Love of these poems is not cruel and deadly but, as the poet says in *Madonna, quel signor*, it "draws all good / unto himself, as principle of might": "tragge tutta bontate / a ssé, come principio c'ha possanza" (7–8). In other words, the overwhelming power of Love, "tal che vince ogni possanza [with strength to conquer all opposing might]" (2), is here a benevolent force; in fact, Love "mi dona sicuranza / che voi sarete amica di Pietate [gives me his word / that you will take Compassion for your friend]" (3–4). The woman of *La dispietata mente* was also characterized by "pietate" ("ciascun che vi mira, in veritate / di fuor conosce che dentro è pietate [everyone who looks at you, in truth, / will outwardly perceive that pity lies inside]" [51–2]).

The function of this benevolent Love is to sustain and nourish the lover's hope, as is stated at line 9: "Ond'io **conforto** sempre mia **speranza** [and so I find my hope now reinforced]." This line is connected to "mi tien già **confortato** / di ritornar la mia dolce **speranza** [a pleasant hope / of soon returning here consoles my mind]" of *Lo meo servente core* (7–8) as well as to "che sia **conforto** della sua vertute [so it may serve to strengthen my resolve]" (13) and "'n cui la mia **speranza** più riposa [the one in whom my hope most finds repose]" (42) of *La dispietata mente*. It is specified that Love is on the side of the lover and protects his hope, "la qual è stata tanto combattuta, / che sarebbe perduta, / se non fosse ch'Amore / contr'ogne aversità le dà valore [which, having been so utterly besieged, / would have succumbed / if not for Love / who bolsters it against adversity]" (10–13).

Love uses memory to battle against the possible fading of hope, the possible "desperation" of the lover: "con la sua vista e con la **rimembranza** / del **dolce loco** e del soave fiore [with his appearance and the memory / of that dear place and that delightful flower]" (14–15). If the word "rimembranza" and the theme of memory brings us into the ambience of *Lo meo servente core* (where we find "di me vi rechi alcuna **rimembranza** [bring to you some memory of me]" [4]), the "dolce loco" is an indicator of the link with *La dispietata mente,* where desire "tira [pulls]" the lover "verso 'l **dolce paese** c'ho lasciato [toward / the lovely land that I have left behind]" (5).

In *Madonna, quel signor* the poet recalls not only the "dear place" ("dolce loco") but also the "delightful flower": "la rimembranza / del dolce loco e del soave fiore / che di novo colore / cercò la mente mia, / mercé di vostra grande cortesia [the memory / of that dear place and that delightful flower / which wreathed my mind / with new-found hues, / thanks to the splendour of your courtesy]" (15–18). In these concluding verses the canzone achieves its most innovative poetic formulations, depicting the joy of love with the metaphor of the "new-found hues" that "wreath" the mind. We think, looking forward, of the great canzone *Donne ch'avete intelletto d'amore*, where the lady will be a "cosa nova" and possess "Color di perle" (46–7; see the introductory essay to *Donne ch'avete*). *Madonna, quel signor* concludes, as if becalmed in joy, with the convention of the "cortesia" of *madonna*. In an ending that recalls the final line of *Lo meo servente core* ("gentil mia donna, a voi mi raccomando [my noble lady / it is to you that I commend myself]"), here we find "mercé di vostra grande cortesia [thanks to the splendour of your courtesy]" (18).

12 (B LVII; C 11; FB 22; DR 30)

Madonna, quel signor che voi portate	The lord you bear, dear Lady, in your eyes,
ne li occhi, tal che vince ogni possanza,	whose strength can conquer all opposing might,
mi dona sicuranza	gives me his word
4 che voi sarete amica di Pietate;	that you will take Compassion as your friend,
però che là dov' ei fa dimoranza	for in the place he makes his residence
ed ha in compagnia molta biltate	and has great beauty for his company,
tragge tutta bontate	he draws all good
8 a·ssé, come principio c'ha possanza.	unto himself, as principle of might;
Ond'io conforto sempre mia speranza,	and so I find my hope now reinforced,
la qual è stata tanto combattuta,	which, having been so utterly besieged,
che sarebbe perduta,	would have succumbed
se non fosse ch'Amore	if not for Love
13 contr'ogne aversità le dà valore	who bolsters it against adversity
con la sua vista e con la rimembranza	with his appearance and the memory
del dolce loco e del soave fiore	of that dear place and that delightful flower
che di novo colore	which wreathed my mind
cercò la mente mia,	with new-found hues,
18 mercé di vostra grande cortesia.	thanks to the splendour of your courtesy.

METRE: isolated canzone stanza of eighteen verses (twelve hendecasyllables and six *settenari*), with rhyme scheme ABbA BAaB BCcdD BDdeE. The *fronte* is eight verses (4 + 4) and the *sirma* is ten verses, divided into two *volte* (5 + 5).

13 Deh ragioniamo insieme un poco, Amore

Dante, while travelling, invites Love to converse with him: "ragioniamo insieme" (1). Convivial conversation will distract him from the "ira" (a Provençalism for "suffering," "sorrow") that makes him "feel anguish" ("pensare"): "Deh ragioniamo insieme un poco, Amore, / e tra'mi d'ira, che·mmi fa pensare [Come, Love, let's set aside some time to talk, / to rescue me from thinking of my pain]" (1–2). In the company of Love the lover will exchange pain for pleasure, and the two will delight each other, talking together of the lady they share in common, "our lady" ("nostra donna"): "e se vuol l'un de l'altro dilettare, / trattiam di nostra donna omai, signore [if one of us can bring the other cheer, / let's speak awhile about our lady, lord]" (3–4).[32] Discussing the virtues of *madonna* the journey will be shorter and the return joyous: "Certo il vïaggio ne parrà minore / prendendo un così dolze tranquillare, / e già mi par gioioso il ritornare / audendo dire e dir di suo valore [Indeed our journey will seem half as long, / abiding in such sweet consoling thoughts, / and going back already seems a joy / in hearing and in telling of her worth]" (5–8).

As in *Madonna, quel signor*, so *Deh ragioniamo* depicts a Love entirely well disposed and benign toward his servant. We have seen that in *Madonna, quel signor* it is Love who aids the lover when he is desperate, who restores his hope when it fades, and who "contr'ogne aversità le dà valore [bolsters it against adversity]" (13). Similarly, in *Deh ragioniamo* Love is a benevolent force whose words can relieve the anguish of the lover and soothe him.

Moreover, in this sonnet Dante emphasizes the reciprocity of the relationship between Love and lover, in the expressions "ragioniamo insieme [let's talk]" (1), "l'un de l'altro dilettare [one of us can bring the other cheer]" (3), "nostra donna [our lady]" (4), and "audendo dire e dir [in hearing and in telling]" (8). This last expression is glossed by De Robertis as "speaking continually," but there are some who prefer to gloss it as "hearing talk and talking." Di Benedetto corrected the line in this way and reads "audendo dire e 'n dir" – a reading that reinforces the reciprocity in the behaviour of the two protagonists.

---

32 For a similar situation, in which "la donna nostra" is shared by the god and the lover, see Petrarch, *Apollo, s'anchor vive il bel desio*: "sì vedrem poi per meraviglia inseme / sedere la donna nostra sopra l'erba [so we will then see, to the wonder of us both, / our lady sitting upon the grass]" (*Rvf* 34.12–13). The sonnet of Petrarch's that is commonly linked to *Deh ragioniamo*, because of the shared motif of journeying, is the one that precedes *Apollo, s'anchor vive*, namely *Solo e pensoso* (*Rvf* 35). Maybe Petrarch had *Deh ragioniamo* in mind when he arranged sonnets 34 and 35 contiguously in the *Rerum vulgarium fragmenta*.

While the sestet moves in a less reciprocal direction – here the lover requests that Love should "condescend to keep me company" ("ti dichini a farmi compagnia") (11) – the octave of *Deh ragioniamo* represents a relationship similar to one between close friends.

In fact, the emphasis on confidential reciprocity, on the solidarity of friends, connects *Deh ragioniamo* to the great sonnet of friendship, *Guido, i' vorrei che tu e Lapo ed io*, where too *ragionare* is paramount. With the friends of *Guido, i' vorrei*, the poet desires to "always talk of love": "ragionar sempre d'amore" (12). The difference is that in *Deh ragioniamo* the subject is a fictitious friendship in which the poet dialogues not with others but with a projection of himself (Love), while in *Guido, i' vorrei* the poet talks not *with* Love but *about* love and *with* actual friends – that is, with beings ontologically distinct from him but with whom he desires a relationship of total transparency and reciprocity.

The *ragionare insieme* of poet and Love in *Deh ragioniamo* is repeated in the incipit of the great canzone *Amor che nella mente mi ragiona*, a canzone that Dante invokes again precisely in the context of an idyllic encounter among friends on the shores of Mount Purgatory.[33] It is the friend Casella, he too an artist, a musician, who, singing the canzone, creates a moment of joyous enchantment – "*Amor che ne la mente mi ragiona* / cominciò elli allor sì dolcemente, / che la dolcezza ancor dentro mi suona [*Amor che ne la mente mi ragiona* he started then so sweetly that the sweetness still sounds within me]" (*Purg.* 2.112–14) – similar in sweetness and consolation to the sentiment that the sonnet *Deh ragioniamo* calls "un così dolze tranquillare [such sweet consoling thoughts]" (6). The tranquillity of soul afforded by the sweet singing of a friend in purgatory, a song that used to quiet – "quetar" – all Dante's desires ("mi solea quetar tutte mie voglie" [*Purg.* 2.108]), recalls the "dolze tranquillare" of the early sonnet *Deh ragioniamo*.

The expression "così dolze tranquillare" captures the quality of complete relaxation – born of security and transparency – that Dante associates with friendship, above all the friendship with other artists and poets. The most charming moments of friendship in Dante's repertoire (although also the saddest) occur in an artistic and poetic context, and are patterned on the "così dolze tranquillare" of *Deh ragioniamo*. The key of friendship that one hears in the encounter with Casella in *Purgatorio* 2, and is already plainly present in the sonnet *Guido, i' vorrei*, will be heard again in the purgatorial encounter of Vergil and Statius, perhaps the most splendid of Dante's fictitious friendships. While the palpable friendship of *Guido, i' vorrei* is based on true, historical, and biographical acquaintances, the similarly palpable friendship between Vergil and Statius is the product of Dante's extraordinary capacity to use his imagination to vault the boundaries of time, inspired in this case by the great tribute

---

33 For the episode centred on the autocitation of *Amor che nella mente*, see my *Dante's Poets*, chap. 1, "Autocitation and Autobiography."

to the *Aeneid* with which Statius (the real Statius, the historical Statius) concludes his *Thebaid*.[34]

In the invented scene in purgatory, Vergil invites Statius to engage in the activity that is essential to Dante's understanding of friendship, namely *ragionare*: "Ma dimmi, e come amico mi perdona / se troppa sicurtà m'allarga il freno, / e come amico omai meco **ragiona** [But tell me, and pardon me like a friend if too much confidence loosens the reins, and like a friend now talk with me]" (*Purg.* 22.19–21). To indicate *amicitia* in *Purgatorio* Dante uses the verb that signals friendship for him as early as *Deh ragioniamo* and *Guido, i' vorrei*, but in the *Purgatorio* he adds the knowing repetition of the phrase that makes *amicitia* explicit, "e come amico": "Ma dimmi, **e come amico** mi perdona" (*Purg.* 22.19), "**e come amico** omai meco ragiona" (*Purg.* 22.21).

Dante developed over time what I call a "semantics of friendship," which goes back to the early lyrics; the transfigured use of pronouns as carriers of ontology is apparent in the incipit, "Guido, **i'** vorrei che **tu** e Lapo ed **io**." In the verses of *Purgatorio* 22 cited above Dante recoups his old semantics of friendship, which relies heavily on pronouns (here "dimmi," "mi," "mi," "meco"), as he does again in the beautiful verse from the Forese episode, essentially made of pronouns and verbs: "qual fosti meco, e qual io teco fui [what you were with me, and what I was with you]" (*Purg.* 23.116). The word "amico" itself, which in the earliest lyrics is a coded signifier connected to male rivalry and honour, as in the exchanges with Dante da Maiano, is redeemed as a token of love and intimacy in the *Commedia*, via Dante's by then long familiarity with Cicero's *De Amicitia* and Aristotle's *Nicomachean Ethics*. The beautiful verse "e come amico omai meco ragiona" in *Purgatorio* 22 has its distant origins, both lexical and sentimental, in early sonnets such as *Deh ragioniamo*.

13 (B LX; C 14; FB 18; DR 61)

Deh ragioniamo insieme un poco, Amore,	Come, Love, let's set aside some time to talk,
e tra'mi d'ira, che·mmi fa pensare,	to rescue me from thinking of my pain;
e se vuol l'un de l'altro dilettare,	if one of us can bring the other cheer,
4 trattiam di nostra donna omai, signore.	let's speak awhile about our lady, lord.
Certo il vïaggio ne parrà minore	Indeed our journey will seem half as long,

---

34 In the extraordinary conclusion to the *Thebaid* Statius warns his text not to follow too closely in the footsteps of the illustrious precursor that will always eclipse it: "Vive, precor; nec tu divinam Aeneida tempta, / sed longe sequere et vestigia semper adora [Live, I pray, nor rival the divine *Aeneid*, but follow at a distance and always revere its footsteps]" (*Thebaid* 12.816–17). For discussion of this passage, see my *Dante's Poets*, p. 261; for my reasons for spelling "Vergil" with an "e," see *Dante's Poets*, p. 207, n. 25.

prendendo un così dolze tranquillare,
e già mi par gioioso il ritornare
8   audendo dire e dir di suo valore.

    Or incomincia, Amor, che si convene
e mòviti a far ciò ch'è la cagione
11   che ti dichini a farmi compagnia,
o vuol mercé o vuol tua cortesia;
ché la mia mente il mi' pensier dipone,
14   cotal disio dell'ascoltar mi vène.

METRE: sonnet ABBA ABBA CDE EDC.

abiding in such sweet consoling thoughts,
and going back already seems a joy
in hearing and in telling of her worth.

    Bestir yourself now, Love, the time is ripe,
make haste to justify the reason why
you condescend to keep me company,
through my own merit or your courtesy;
for now my mind dismisses my distress,
so strong is my desire to hear of her.

14 Sonetto, se Meuccio t'è mostrato

Like *Se Lippo amico sè tu che mi leggi*, this sonnet is sent to a friend (perhaps Meuccio Tolomei of Siena). The sonnet to Lippo accompanies the canzone stanza *Lo meo servente core* ("ti guido esta pulcella nuda [I bestow on you this unclothed girl]" [*Se Lippo amico*, 13]); similarly, *Sonetto, se Meuccio* has the task of bringing other poems as gifts. The sonnets are both personified, but while the one to Lippo speaks in the first person ("io che m'apello umil[e] sonetto [a humble sonnet I am called]" [10]), here it is the poet who speaks and gives instructions to his composition, so that the manner of *Sonetto, se Meuccio* is similar to that of an envoy to a canzone (*congedo* in Italian), in which the poet addresses his creation, telling it to whom to go and how to behave. In the *Vita Nuova* Dante defines the *congedo* as "una stanza quasi come ancella de l'altre, ne la quale io dico quello che di questa mia canzone desidero [a stanza that is like a handmaid to the others, one in which I state my wishes for my canzone]" (*VN* XIX.21 [10.32]).

Taking account of Dante's *congedi* in general, one sees that the opening move of this poem – the address to the composition, in this case "Sonetto" – is typical of many *congedi*. In *La dispietata mente*, for example, the *congedo* begins: "Canzone, il tuo cammin vuol esser corto [My song, your journey must be brief]" (66). And in the *congedo* of *Doglia mi reca nello core ardire* there are detailed instructions about the identity of the addressee and the comportment of the canzone when it reaches the addressee: the poet sends the canzone to "una donna / ch'è del nostro paese ... Bianca, Giovanna, Contessa [a woman who is from our land ... Bianca, Giovanna, Contessa]" (148–9, 153), and orders that "A costei te ne va chiusa ed onesta [You go to this woman reserved and dignified]" (154).

The first line of *Sonetto, se Meuccio t'è mostrato* gives us the key to interpretation. Dante is instructing his poem as to how it ought to behave when Meuccio is pointed out to it ("t'è mostrato"): it should greet him immediately, run toward him, and throw itself at his feet, in such a way as to seem "bene acostumato [knowing the proper protocol]" (a Provençalism for "beneducato," polite [4]). It should then take him to one side and deliver its "ambasciata" or message (7), explaining the reason for its visit: "Meuccio, que' che·tt'am'assai / de le sue gioie più care ti manda / per acontarsi al tu' coraggio bono [Meuccio, he who loves you well / sends some of his most precious gems to you, / so as to gain the friendship of your heart]" (9–11). From this reference to "gioie più care," "jewels" or precious poems that the poet will send to gain access to the noble heart of his friend ("acontarsi" and "coraggio" are Gallicisms), Dante moves to the closing exhortation. There is a "primo dono [first gift]" that will arrive at once, for *Sonetto, se Meuccio* has "frati" – sonnet-siblings – that he has brought with him: "Ma fa' che prenda per lo primo dono / questi tuo' frati [But then make sure he takes as his first gift / your sibling sonnets]" (12–13).

Dante will make future use of familial terminology to indicate the relationship that exists between his various compositions. In the *congedo* of the canzone of mourning for the death of Beatrice, *Li occhi dolenti*, the poet refers to "le tue sorelle [your sisters]" (73): other lyrics that, in contrast to *Li occhi dolenti*, "erano usate di portar letizia [used to bring happiness]" (74). Similarly, in the sonnet *Parole mie che per lo mondo siete* there is a reference to "vostre antiche suore [your elder sisters]" (11), and in the sonnet *O dolci rime che parlando andate* we find the phrase "Questi è nostro frate [This one is our brother]" (4), used for the sonnet *Parole mie*. The genetic network among his lyrics that Dante constructs in this manner is an indicator of the high level of self-awareness that informs his poetic activities and that we see in the incipits of these texts: these openings – *Sonetto, se Meuccio*, *Parole mie*, *O dolci rime* – speak to us about poetic creation. In these addresses to his "sonetto," to his "parole," to his "rime," we are witnessing – as also in the congedi of certain canzoni – the dialogue of a creator with his creation, of a "fattore [maker]" with his "fattura [thing he has made]" (*Purg.* 17.102).[35]

These micro-meditations on his own "making" (and we recall that Dante will use the word "fabbro [smith, maker]" for both God and poets) will lead to the poetics of the *Commedia*, to the representation of the divine representation, the violation of the border between truth and truth-like, between is and as, between *res* and *signum*, between signifier and signified.[36] Even if the poetic self-awareness of the *Commedia* is much more complex than that which we find in the lyrics (complicated, above all, by the relationship with the Prime Maker, God), its source is found in early compositions such as *Sonetto, se Meuccio*.

Following this line of interpretation, it is no accident that there is direct speech in *Sonetto, se Meuccio*, dramatically set off by the break between octave and sestet: "e di': 'Meuccio, que' che·tt'am'assai / de le sue gioie più care ti manda' [and say: 'Meuccio, he who loves you well / sends some of his most precious gems to you']" (9–10). Direct speech has a specific and signature valence in Dante's work. It operates as an index of Dante's great enterprise of creating a virtual reality: we think not only of the "visible speech" of the sculpted reliefs on purgatory's terrace of pride, but

---

35 Dante makes explicit the analogy between literary creation and biological generation in *Convivio* 3.9.4: "Per similitudine dico 'sorella'; ché sì come sorella è detta quella femmina che da uno medesimo generante è generata, così puote l'uomo dire 'sorella' de l'opera che da uno medesimo operante è operata; ché la nostra operazione in alcuno modo è generazione [I use the word 'sister' as a metaphor: for just as we call sister a woman who is born of the same parent, so may one call sister a work that is made by the same maker, for our work is, in a sense, begotten]."

36 On the prideful "Arachnean" art that informs the bas-reliefs that seem alive in *Purgatorio* 10–12, an art whose mimesis is so perfect as to compete with divine art – life itself – see Barolini, *The Undivine Comedy*, chap. 6, "Re-presenting What God Presented: The Arachnean Art of the Terrace of Pride."

also of the gate to hell that speaks in the first person. Particularly intense moments of this enterprise are marked by the presence of direct speech: a humble rhetorical technique that is highly effective for crossing the border between *res* and *signum*, "sì che dal fatto il dir non sia diverso [so that the telling does not differ from the deed]" (*Inf.* 32.12). The autoreferentiality becomes vertiginous: if the representation – in this case the sonnet – speaks in direct speech, how does one distinguish the representation from the one who creates the representation, the artifice from the artificer, the sonnet from the poet for whom (literally) it is speaking?

14 (B LXIII; C 17; FB 19; DR 46)

Sonetto, se Meuccio t'è mostrato,
così tosto ·l saluta come ·l vedi,
e va' correndo e gittaliti a' piedi
4 sì·cche tu paie bene acostumato.
E quando sè con lui un poco stato
anche ·l risalutrai, non ti ricredi;
e posci' a l'ambasciata tua procedi,
8 ma fa' che ·l tragghe prima da un lato,
e di': "Meuccio, que' che·tt'am'assai
de le sue gioie più care ti manda
11 per acontarsi al tu' coraggio bono."
Ma fa' che prenda per lo primo dono
questi tuo' frati, e a·llor sì comanda
14 che stean co·llui e qua non tornin mai.

Dear sonnet, when Meuccio's pointed out,
go welcome him as soon as he shows up,
run up and throw yourself before his feet
to show you know the proper protocol.
And after having spent some time with him,
renew your salutation, don't be shy;
and after that proceed to make your point,
though first be sure to usher him aside
and say: "Meuccio, he who loves you well
sends some of his most precious gems to you,
so as to gain the friendship of your heart."
But then make sure he takes as his first gift
your sibling sonnets, and insist on this,
that they remain with him and don't come back.

METRE: sonnet ABBA ABBA CDE EDC.

15 Com più vi fere Amor co' suo' vincastri

The more Love hits you with his rods, his "vincastri" (*vincastri* are the staffs used by shepherds, as in *Inf.* 24.14–15, where the shepherd "prende suo vincastro / e fuor le pecorelle a pascer caccia [takes his staff and drives the sheep out to pasture]"), the more he makes you ready and willing to obey him ("più li vi fate in ubidirlo presto" [2]). In other words, the more pain Love inflicts, the more we are obedient and compliant. This forceful and sexually suggestive opening is the advice ("consiglio" [3]) that Dante offers to an unknown interlocutor (in line 11 mention is made of "vostro buon trovare [your good poetry-writing]," that is, the excellent poetry of the unknown correspondent). Other counsel, declares the poet, cannot be given to you: "non vi si può già dar" (4). Therefore, let whoever is interested fix this counsel well in his mind: "chi vuol l'incastri [whoever wants should learn this well]" (4).

Love, however, is not necessarily cruel in this sonnet. On the contrary: when the right moment comes, Love with his "pleasant remedies" (the "dolci 'mpiastri" of line 5; *impiastro* in this sense is found, as here rhyming with *vincastro*, in *Inf.* 24.18: "e così tosto al mal giunse lo 'mpiastro [and so quickly the plaster reached the hurt]") will dispel all torment, and the pleasure will be well worth waiting for, because Love's suffering does not weigh a sixth of Love's sweetness: "ché 'l mal d'Amor non è pesante il sesto / ver' ch'è dolce lo ben [for torment caused by Love weighs but a sixth / the sweetness of his joy]" (7–8). This optimistic vein continues in the sestet, where the poet suggests his interlocutor follow the supreme power of Love ("lo suo sommo poder [his matchless power]" [10]) and not go astray, because only Love can "bring complete delight" ("tutt'allegrezza dare" [13]) and reward his servants at the right time: "e suo' serventi meritare apunto [and recompense his servants properly]" (14).

What distinguishes *Com più vi fere Amor* is its suggestive physicality at either end of the spectrum of Love's potential treatment of his subjects: both the violence that it ascribes to Love, the menacing sexuality of Love using his *vincastri* to administer physical punishment, and the sonnet's frank appeal to the "allegrezza" of requited passion. Otherwise, its themes are conventional, as can be seen from the above summary. Its form, however, is quite remarkable: *Com più vi fere Amor* boasts harsh and difficult rhymes ("vincastri," "incastri," "'mpiastri," "lastri"), risky metaphors, and bracing caesuras and enjambments. Its stylistic experimentalism is noted by all commentators, who are unanimous in seeing in *Com più vi fere Amor* a precedent for the technical bravura of the *rime petrose* and for the "rime aspre e chiocce [harsh and grating rhymes]" (*Inf.* 32.1) of certain sections of the *Commedia*. I would add that its overt sexuality and reference to sexual violence recur in the *petrose*, especially in the canzone *Così nel mio parlar vogli'esser aspro*.

Contini maintains that in this sonnet, as in the *rime petrose*, Dante is drawing directly on Occitan models and especially on Arnaut Daniel: "Up to now he knew the Provençal poets by ear, through their imitators; but now he goes back to the sources of the *trobar clus*, arriving undoubtedly at Arnaut Daniel, whose sestina he will imitate in the *rime petrose*" (p. 51). I do not share Contini's belief that Dante imitates Arnaut Daniel in *Com più ve fere Amor*; rather, the encounter with Occitan poetry seems to me still mediated by Italians. Many Italian poets well known to Dante, including Guittone and Guinizzelli, had written verse characterized by this same harsh style.

Almost as if to indicate its stylistic pedigree, *Com più vi fere Amor* echoes a noted passage of the great canzone by Guittone, *Ora parrà s'eo saverò cantare*, where we find the same identity rhyme *punto/punto* and the same use of *trovare* in the sense of *poetare* ("to write poetry"). Guittone writes that whoever is not pierced ("punto") by Love does not know how to compose poetry ("trovare"), nor is he worth anything at all ("punto"): "trovare – non sa né valer punto / omo d'Amor non punto [he doesn't know how to write poetry, nor is he worth anything, / a man who is not pierced by Love]" (*Ora parrà*, 6–7). Similarly, in the tercets of *Com più vi fere Amor* we find "punto [wounded]" rhyming with "punto [not even by a bit]" and, alongside the Guittonian rhyme *punto/punto* from *Ora parrà*, we find also the use of "trovare" for writing poetry: "se v'ha sì punto / come dimostra il vostro buon trovare; / e non vi disvïate da lui punto" [if he has wounded you / as deeply as your poetry makes out. / Don't stray from him, not even by a bit]" (10–12).

Very forceful is the strong enjambment between the last line of the octave and the first line of the sestet, made even more emphatic by the use of the unusual verb *lastrare* (*lastricare*, to pave), left suspended at the end of the octave:

Dunque ormai **lastri**
vostro cor lo camin per seguitare
lo suo sommo poder ...   (*Com più vi fere Amor*, 8–10)

[So let your heart / prepare the path that will accommodate / his matchless power, if he has wounded you ...]

This boldly metaphoric use of the imperative "lastri" does not end up, however, expressing a bold sentiment: the poet merely charges his interlocutor to prepare in his heart a path for following the supreme power of Love. While the harsh language of the poem's incipit works well to suggest Love's dominance, there is little correspondence in this latter section of the sonnet between the content – the charge to follow Love – and the form. In the *rime petrose*, by contrast, the stylistic innovations do not exist apart from the powerful grip of ideology; they are the logical consequence of an ideological position regarding Love's complete dominance. Such complete synchronicity between form and content is not yet present in *Com più vi fere Amor.*

15 (B LXII; C 16; FB 7; DR 43)

Com più vi fere Amor co' suo' vincastri
più li vi fate in ubidirlo presto,
ch'altro consiglio, be·llo vi protesto,
4   non vi si può già dar: chi vuol l'incastri.
Poi, quando fie stagion, coi dolci 'mpiastri
farà stornarvi ogni tormento agresto,
ché 'l mal d'Amor non è pesante il sesto
8   ver' ch'è dolce lo ben. Dunque ormai lastri
vostro cor lo camin per seguitare
lo suo sommo poder, se v'ha sì punto
11   come dimostra il vostro buon trovare;
e non vi disvïate da lui punto,
ch'elli sol può tutt'allegrezza dare
14   e suo' serventi meritare apunto.

The more Love strikes you with a shepherd's stick
the quicker you must do as you are told,
for – mark my words – no better counsel can
be had: whoever wants should learn this well.
Then when the time is ripe, he'll medicate
your aches and pains with pleasant remedies,
for torment caused by Love weighs but a sixth
the sweetness of his joy. So let your heart
prepare the path that will accommodate
his matchless power, if he has wounded you
as deeply as your poetry makes out.
Don't stray from him, not even by a bit,
for he alone can bring complete delight
and recompense his servants properly.

METRE: sonnet ABBA ABBA CDC DCD.

16 No me poriano zamai far emenda [Non mi poriano già mai fare ammenda]

Two Redactions

This sonnet with a playful, anecdotal tone, called "la Garisenda" from the name of the famous tower in Bologna that it mentions, was transcribed, in Bolognese and without attribution, by the Bolognese notary Enrichetto delle Querce in his city record of 1287 (Memoriale Bolognese 69 [1287], c. 203v). It was then preserved under the name of Dante in various codices, of which the oldest is Chigiano L VIII 305 (a Tuscan codex produced between 1350 and 1375).[37] The attribution of *No me poriano* to Dante is accepted by Barbi, whose reasons, based on the authority of the Chigiano codex, are available in the Barbi-Maggini commentary (pp. 186–92) and now also in De Robertis.

While accepting the authority of Chigiano L VIII 305 and attributing *No me poriano* to Dante, De Robertis, following in the footsteps of H. Wayne Storey, confers a new and legitimate dignity on the Memoriale Bolognese, which he calls "the first unqualified witness of a composition by Dante" (ed. comm., p. 308). De Robertis in his edition therefore transcribes the text of *No me poriano* in its "Emilian form" (ed. crit., *Testi*, p. 330). For ease of reading, I have followed the Emilian version of the text edited by De Robertis with the Tuscan version edited by Contini.[38]

Among the elements in this poem that make one think of Dante, the most obvious is the description of the same tower in the *Inferno*: "Qual pare a riguardar la Carisenda / sotto 'l chinato, quando un nuvol vada / sovr'essa sì, ched ella incontro penda [As when one looks at the Garisenda / under its leaning side, when a cloud passes /

---

37 Bolognese notaries transcribed poems in their city records in order to fill up the empty space. These poems, by statute always transcribed without attribution, are often the work of noted poets like Guinizzelli. See the discussion in H. Wayne Storey, *Transcription and Visual Poetics in the Early Italian Lyric* (New York: Garland, 1993), pp. 133–5. Storey considers the Bolognese manuscript to be as authoritative as Chigiano L VIII 305, if not more authoritative; he maintains that our deference for the culture that produced the Chigiano codex – a Tuscan and Dante-phile culture – has distracted us from the importance of the older codex and has forced us to accept the Dantean paternity of the sonnet (pp. 143–56). While granting that the Tuscan manuscript has a precise social and cultural orientation that must be considered, this orientation does not in itself constitute, in my opinion, a basis for withdrawing the sonnet from Dante's corpus.

38 De Robertis advances the hypothesis that Dante wrote the sonnet in Bolognese: "the last hypothesis is that this was the original form of the sonnet, with a perfect, functional adaptation to the setting; I advance this hypothesis not in order to take the sonnet from Dante, but to assign it to him also as testament to his incessant linguistic drive, apparent from his earliest years, and as a homage rendered by him to a language [Bolognese] that in *De vulgari eloquentia* 1.15.6 he will recognize as the primary vernacular of all the tongues in Italy" (ed. crit., *Testi*, p. 330).

over it such that the tower leans the more]" (*Inf.* 31.136–8). Necessarily composed before 1287, *No me poriano* attests stylistically to the deftness of the young poet, little more than twenty-one; from the biographical point of view, it indicates at least one visit to Bologna, if not that period of study in the Emilian city conjured by a previous generation of commentators.

The poet scolds his eyes: they will never be able to make amends, other than by going blind, for their "gran fallo" (great offence) (2). What is the "fallo" in question? Looking at the Garisenda tower, they didn't notice "the one (they'll pay for this!) / who ranks supreme among those talked about" ("quella, ma· lor prenda!, / ch'è la maçor dela qual se favelli" // "quella (mal lor prenda) / ch'è la maggior de la qual si favelli") (5–6). The problem here is how to interpret "quella ... ch'è la maçor" // "quella ... ch'è la maggior": are the poet's eyes guilty of having neglected another Bolognese tower, the higher Asinelli one, or for not having recognized a lady celebrated for her beauty?

Carducci accurately noted "the ease of versification; the building up of the verses, one upon the other; the placing of the caesura, especially in line 11; and the bold and forthright movement of the argument from the first to the second tercet" (Barbi-Maggini, p. 188). Striking also is the enjambment between lines 3 and 4, which strongly highlights the name of "la Garisenda / torre," and creates the bold rhyme *emenda/Garisenda/prenda/intenda*.

This set of rhymes provides the key to my discussion of *No me poriano*. It is important to say explicitly what this lyric is *not*, and where we would *not* expect to find it: it is not stilnovist, and we would not expect to find it in the *Vita Nuova*. It is not stilnovist because of its specificity, its historicity – in other words because of words like the proper name "Garisenda." Dante's *stil novo* is achieved by means of a process of elimination, of purification: the lexicon used by Dante in *stil novo* poems is more restricted than his earlier lexicon, although the poet is more mature. Even the *Vita Nuova*'s prose, more detailed and historicized than the poetry, doesn't ever name, for example, the city of Florence that functions as the background of the action.

It is in this stylistic context that we can better appreciate the profound significance of the anecdote about "la Garisenda / torre" that is recounted in this sonnet: the anecdote plunges us into the world of history and lived experience (it does not matter that the particular moment of history is not verified or verifiable), and transports us into the life of the city in all its specific and irreducible detail – the life that was going on in the towers of the magnate families of Bologna. The poet who employs the anecdote about the Garisenda is using a lens for observing the real, not dissimilar to the lens he will one day use to make visible that world full of details, proper names, anecdotes, history, and local life that is the *Commedia*.

In *Inferno* 31 the word "Carisenda" rhymes with "prenda," present in our sonnet, and with "penda," not in the sonnet. The three words that rhyme with "Garisenda" in *No me poriano* (*emenda* or *ammenda/prenda/intenda*) are encountered, again rhyming with each other, in *Inferno* 27, in the passage in which Guido da Montefeltro curses Boniface VIII with the phrase "a cui mal prenda! [to whom may ill befall!]" (*Inf.* 27.70):

> Io fui uom d'arme, e poi fui cordigliero,
> credendomi, sì cinto, fare **ammenda**;
> e certo il creder mio venìa intero,
> se non fosse il gran prete, a cui mal **prenda**!,
> che mi rimise ne le prime colpe;
> e come e *quare*, voglio che m'**intenda**.   (*Inf.* 27.67—72)

[I was a warrior, and then a friar, thinking, corded so, to make amends. And surely my belief would have been fulfilled but for the great priest – to whom may ill befall! – who drew me back to my old ways. And I would like to tell you how and why.]

Guido's imprecation copies the phrase that is found in *No me poriano*, where the offence of his eyes leads the poet to curse: "ma· lor prenda!" // "mal lor prenda" (5). The word "emenda," in the Tuscan form "ammenda," will have a notable history in the *Commedia*: occurring five times, it appears a full four times in rhyme, first in the canto of Guido da Montefelto cited above and then three times in *Purgatorio* 20, where it is one of the very few words (along with "Cristo" and "vidi") that is used in rhyme with itself (see the scathing sarcasm of the thrice repeated "per ammenda [for amends]" in *Purg.* 20.65–9). The lexicon of *No me poriano* assumes therefore a certain weight in Dante's memory.

In addition it is important to note in *No me poriano* the traces of Dante's combinatorial art, an art of continual and irrepressible experimentation. In this instance he mixes highly divergent stylistic elements. Specifically, if in the octave we find the historicist and not at all stilnovist elements that we just talked about, the tercets bring us back to the *stil novo*, thanks to the locution "li mei spirti" // "li miei spirti [my spirits]" (12), and conclude the reprimand of the eyes with the Cavalcantian "scanosenti" // "scanoscenti [lacking in *canoscenza*, knowledge]" (14). Such *contaminatio* is typical of Dante: there are poets who use the forms of the *stil novo* and poets who write in a reality-based and anecdotal vein, but there are few poets indeed who combine these registers in the same text.

16 (B LI; C 8; FB 14; DR 42)
Two Redactions

Redaction 1: Emilian (De Robertis)

No me poriano zamai far emenda	No, never could they hope to make amends
de lor gran fallo gl'ocli mei, set elli	for their mistake, these eyes of mine, except
non s'acecaser, poi la Garisenda	by going blind, for they beheld the tower
4 torre miraro cum li sguardi belli,	of Garisenda with its lovely view
e non conover quella, ma· lor prenda!,	and failed to see the one (they'll pay for this!)

ch'è la maçor dela qual se favelli:
per zo zascun de lor voi che m'intenda
8   che zamai pace no i farò, sonelli
      poi tanto furo, che zo che sentire
    dovean a raxon senza veduta,
11   non conover vedendo, unde dolenti
    sun li mei spirti per lo lor falire;
    e dico ben, se 'l voler no me muta,
14   ch'eo stesso gl'ocidrò quî scanosenti.

who ranks supreme among those talked about:
so both of them have got to understand
that I will never grant them amnesty.

    Such was their fault that what they should have seen
without a look they failed to recognize
while seeing it; and so their oversight
has left my spirits in state of grief,
and I do swear, unless I change my mind,
I'll kill them both myself, these imbeciles.

Redaction 2: Tuscan (Contini)

    Non mi poriano già mai fare ammenda
del lor gran fallo gli occhi miei, sed elli
non s'accecasser, poi la Garisenda
4   torre miraro co' risguardi belli,
    e non conobber quella (mal lor prenda)
    ch'è la maggior de la qual si favelli:
    però ciascun di lor voi' che m'intenda
8   che già mai pace non farò con elli;
      poi tanto furo, che ciò che sentire
    doveano a ragion senza veduta,
11   non conobber vedendo; onde dolenti
    son li miei spirti per lo lor fallire,
    e dico ben, se 'l voler non mi muta,
14   ch'eo stesso li uccidrò, que' scanoscenti.

METRE: sonnet ABAB ABAB CDE CDE.

17 Sonar bracchetti e cacciatori aizzare

To understand *Sonar bracchetti e cacciatori aizzare* it is necessary to consider two other texts. I begin with the sonnet *E di febbraio vi dono bella caccia* from the sonnet cycle on the courtly pastimes enjoyed during each of the months of the year, written by Folgore da San Gimignano, Dante's contemporary (ca. 1270–ca. 1332). In *E di febbraio*, his sonnet on February, Folgore writes about the chivalrous pleasures of the hunt:

> E di febbraio vi dono bella caccia
> di cerbi, cavriuoli e di cinghiari,
> corte gonnelle con grossi calzari,
> e compagnia che vi diletti e piaccia;
> can da guinzagli e segugi da traccia.
> (E di febbraio, 1–5)

> [In February I provide you with fine hunting
> of deer, wild goats, and boars,
> short trousers with boots thigh high,
> and companionship that thrills and pleases you;
> both greyhounds and bloodhounds.]

In the same way that Folgore's first quatrain culminates with the line "and companionship that thrills and pleases" (4), so too, for Dante, the importance of the lively scene that he describes in the first quatrain of *Sonar bracchetti* is in the delight that it produces: "assai credo che deggia dilettare [must surely be a source of great delight]" (5). On the other hand, in Dante's poem there is not the emphasis on the "compagnia" (*E di febbraio*, 4), what Folgore will elsewhere call the "brigata" or group of male comrades.[39] While Folgore's sonnet focuses only and always on the life of the *brigata* (even after the shift, noted by Picone in his commentary, from the outdoor

---

39 The text of *E di febbraio* is edited, with commentary, by Michelangelo Picone in "Le due corone: sonetti della *Semana* e dei *Mesi* con il commento di Michelangelo Picone," in *Il giuoco della vita bella, Folgore da San Gimignano: Studi e testi*, ed. Picone (San Gimignano: Nencini Poggibonsi, 1988), pp. 79–125. On the *brigata* in Folgore and others, see Barolini, "Sociology of the *Brigata*: Gendered Groups in Dante, Forese, Folgore, Boccaccio – From *Guido, i' vorrei* to Griselda," *Italian Studies* 67.1 (2012): 4–22.

hunting scene to the indoor evening parties), Dante's sonnet accomplishes a further shift, from the external life of the hunt to the interior life of the self.

The inner life of the poet brings us to love, and so to the second textual reference. Notable in *Sonar bracchetti* is the opening stylistic move: the accumulation, one after another, of infinitive phrases that function as subjects, as in the octave of *Biltà di donna e di saccente core* by Cavalcanti. This octave lends its first four rhyme-words to *Sonar bracchetti* (*core, genti, amore, correnti*):

> Biltà di donna e di saccente core
> e cavalieri armati che sien genti;
> cantar d'augelli e ragionar d'amore;
> adorni legni 'n mar forte correnti;
> aria serena quand'apar l'albore
> e bianca neve scender senza venti;
> rivera d'acqua e prato d'ogni fiore;
> oro, argento, azzuro 'n ornamenti.
>   (*Biltà di donna e di saccente core*, 1–8)

> [A woman's beauty and her knowing heart
> and knights in armor who are courteous;
> singing of birds and talk of love;
> and ships equipped to sail rough seas;
> gentle breezes at the hour of dawn
> and white snow falling with no wind;
> riverbank and meadow full of every flower;
> silver, gold, and sapphire set in ornaments.]

In this sonnet Cavalcanti lists that which is notably beautiful and "pleasurable" (the form derives from the Provençal genre *plazer*, from the verb "to please") to arrive at the declaration that the beauty and "valore [worth]" of his lady surpass every possible term of comparison.

Therefore, with the sonnet *Sonar bracchetti* Dante enters unequivocally into the field of Cavalcanti's influence. What is more, in the opening of *Sonar bracchetti* Dante combines a poetic register of heightened but recognizable reality – a description of a hunt – with the very different poetic register of the amorous idyll of Cavalcanti. The result is a new and original hybrid: Cavalcantian love-*plazer* + Folgorian delight of the hunt = Dantean hybrid, in which conventions are mixed that usually, in the hands of these poets, do not coexist. The expression of the self via the lover's thought that speaks in direct discourse, for example, is a *stil novo* technique that typically does not coexist with hunting scenes. The rhetorical hybridity of *Sonar bracchetti* is deeply functional: as we shall see, it serves to reinforce the dichotomy between male and female that is the ideological fulcrum of this poem and that constitutes its most remarkable characteristic.

Sonar bracchetti offers a crystal-clear vision of a world that is polarized and dichotomized by gender: indeed, female and male serve here as poles around which two totally different ideologies crystallize. The sonnet takes off with a vigorous verbal explosion of enormous vitality, presenting the male world of action through a series of seven infinitives that evoke the hunt as a flurry of activity: "Sonar bracchetti e cacciatori aizzare, / lepri levare ed isgridar le genti, / e di guinzagli uscir veltri correnti, / per belle piagge volger e 'mboccare [The beagles' belling and the hunters' cries, / the hares flushed out, the cheering of the crowd, / the greyhounds loosed from leashes, dashing by, / careening through the fields in search of prey]" (1–4). All that, says the poet, ought to delight a heart that is free from thoughts of love: "assai credo che deggia dilettare / libero core e van d'intendimenti [must surely be a source of great delight / to any heart not bound by love's demands]" (5–6).

The logic of *Sonar bracchetti* establishes a precise dichotomy: love and its lexicon ("core," "intendimenti") represent the opposite of the hunt, and the hunt and the world it represents can delight only someone free from love. In this way the poet contrasts love with the male world of action that he depicts in the opening lines: love is what might transform someone who is free of love's demands ("van d'intendimenti" [6]) into an individual who is not free and who is burdened with love – into someone therefore incapable of enjoying the baying hounds, leaping hares, and so forth. Love is on one side, with the lady; freedom, the world out of doors, the hunt, the active verbs, and maleness are on the other.[40] Boccaccio, perhaps influenced by Dante's sonnet, used this same formula to conjure maleness in the Proem to the *Decameron*, where a string of infinitives that features many outdoor activities (including *cacciare* and variants thereon) indicate the freedom of being a man, someone who can "andare a torno, udire e veder molte cose, uccellare, cacciare, pescare, cavalcare, giucare o mercatare [go about, see and hear many things, go fowling, hunting, fishing, riding and gambling, or attend to their business affairs]."[41]

Our male poet, however, is unable to enjoy his birthright. Using the sonnet's formal dichotomy as a template for presenting ideological dichotomy, the poem swerves toward the end of the octave (verse 7) to engage a different reality. His inner life enters the scene in the form of a thought that derides him: "Ed io, fra gli amorosi

---

40 Hunting dogs of various types remain in Dante's repertory. A passage in the *Convivio* that establishes a rigid dichotomy of male and female (based on facial hair) constructs an analogy via recourse to hunting dogs: "E qui è da sapere che ogni bontade propria in alcuna cosa, è amabile in quella: sì come ne la maschiezza essere ben barbuto, e nella femminezza essere ben pulita di barba in tutta la faccia; sì come nel bracco bene odorare, e sì come nel veltro ben correre. [Here it should be observed that every goodness proper to a thing is deserving of love in that thing, as in masculinity to have a full beard and in femininity to have the entire face free of hair, just as in the foxhound to have a keen scent, and in the greyhound to have great speed.]" (1.12.8).

41 For the significance of these verbs see my essay "'Le parole son donne e i fatti son maschi': Toward a Sexual Poetics of the *Decameron* (*Dec.* 2.9, 2.10, 5.10)," 1993, rpt. in *Dante and the Origins of Italian Literary Culture*, pp. 281–303.

pensamenti, / d'uno sono schernito in tale affare, / e dicemi esto motto per usanza [But in my thoughts of love I find myself / put down and mocked by one of them; / and as it's done before, it jokes and says]" (7–9). And what exactly does his mocking thought say? It reprimands him severely for abandoning the courtly world of women and love for the "selvaggia dilettanza" of the hunt ("selvaggia dilettanza" is literally "rustic pleasure"; in "selvaggia" we catch overtones of both sylvan and savage). As a result of love, he is now fearful, ashamed, and emotionally and spiritually weighed down, quite the opposite of "libero." Utilizing a keyword from the code of courtly love – *leggiadria* (elegance and gracefulness both inner and outer: the courtly virtue to which Dante will dedicate the canzone *Poscia ch'Amor del tutto m'ha lasciato*) – the thought sarcastically points out that *leggiadria* is a virtue that Dante does not possess, given that he can think of abandoning the ladies for such a pastime: "Or ecco leggiadria di gentil core / per una sì selvaggia dilettanza / lasciar le donne e lor gaia sembianza! [Now here's refinement in a gentleman, / deserting ladies and their gaiety / for such a rough-and-tumble sport as this]" (10–12).

The world of ladies and love is therefore represented as opposing the world of men and male pastimes, by means of a programmatically dichotomized rhetoric. The second part of *Sonar bracchetti* – we could say its "female" part – is as full of static nouns and adjectives as the first – "male" – part is crowded with dynamic verbs. The transition from the male to the female domains of the poem is typified by the transition from "dilettare" (verb) to "selvaggia dilettanza" (abstract noun). While the lexicon of the first part is realistic, specific, and concrete, that of the second part is generic, abstract, codified, and courtly: the nouns, for example, pass from *bracchetti, cacciatori, lepri, genti, guinzagli, veltri, piagge* (beagles, hunters, hares, people, leashes, greyhounds, hillsides) to *core, intendimenti, pensamenti, affare, motto, usanza, leggiadria, dilettanza, donne, sembianza, Amore, vergogna, pesanza* (heart, amorous understandings, thoughts, event, expression, habit, gracefulness, delight, ladies, appearance, Love, shame, heaviness). While the male world is constructed of tumultuous and dynamic verbs (*sonare, aizzare, levare, isgridare, uscire, volgere, imboccare*) and of concrete nouns drawn from daily life and the world as we know it (even if we don't all go hunting, we all know about dogs, rabbits, and yelling onlookers), the female world is instead constructed with a generic and highly stylized lexicon associated with the system of values we label "courtly love."

In *Sonar bracchetti* these two worlds stand opposed: what works in one does not work in the other. The poet therefore stands accused (actually self-accused, by the part of himself associated with love) for his lack of courtly values, for an ideological deficit – for not having enough of the necessary "leggiadria di gentil core." The sign of his deficiency is that he might accept abandoning the world of women for the male world of the hunt, and the sonnet asks him the following pointed question in this regard: how can he, even for a moment, even only in his thoughts, associate with those who "per una sì selvaggia dilettanza" could "lasciar le donne e lor gaia sembianza"?

From the ideological point of view, *Sonar bracchetti* functions both as an ideological correction and as a clue that the "I" of this sonnet experiences his commitment to courtly values with an ambivalence strong enough to require that correction. The sonnet indicates that the poet-lover feels the need to record his internal conflict by means of the two worlds depicted here, and that he feels the need to correct himself in a somewhat aggressive manner through the self-rebuke administered by his thought. It is worth noting that *Sonar bracchetti* is not the only sonnet in which Dante dramatizes such ambivalence. *Volgete gli occhi a veder chi mi tira* opens with an existential drama in which the poet must choose between his friends and love: on the one side are the male friends with whom the poet had intended to go and to whom he addresses himself directly in the incipit, excusing his negligence toward them with the exhortation to look and to see who it is that drags him off in the other direction; on the other side is Love who imperiously "pulls" him. And there is a probing voice that asks him the question with which *Volgete gli occhi* closes: "Dunque, vuo' tu per neente / agli occhi tuoi sì bella donna tôrre? [Would you, for nothing in return, / remove so fair a lady from your eyes?]" (13–14). The question confirms that the only valid choice for the poet-lover is to adore *madonna*; every other activity is annulled, defined as literally "nothing" ("neente").

The reader doesn't know who are the friends of *Volgete gli occhi*, nor with whom the poet went hunting. We can easily imagine a group of friends, all men, like the group of friends who are listed with such precision in the incipit of *Guido, i' vorrei che tu a Lapo ed io* (to whom, however, the sestet will add a group of women, thus creating a company that is sexually mixed, like the one that inhabits the frame-tale of the *Decameron*), and, by doing so, we can glimpse in *Volgete gli occhi* the same tension between the male world and the female world that we have examined in *Sonar bracchetti*. The male social life of the *brigata* of friends – and we recall from the *Decameron* not only the mixed gender *brigata* of the frame-tale, but the hyper-male *brigata* that besieges the poet Guido Cavalcanti in *Decameron* 6.9 – is opposed to the feminized life of the lover under the yoke of Love. From this perspective both *Sonar bracchetti* and *Volgete gli occhi* suggest a less transgressive and less fantastical reality than the one imagined in *Guido, i' vorrei* or in the frame-tale of the *Decameron*; in actual Florentine society of that era the sexes did not casually mix.[42]

While there is a tradition that appropriates the real hunt of the aristocracy for courtly ideology, and for the metaphorical "hunt" of the lover, in the sonnet *Sonar bracchetti* the hunt is constructed in opposition to love: as a literal hunt, one of the favoured activities of the aristocracy and its imitators in mercantile Tuscany, and not as a romantic pursuit.[43] In *Sonar bracchetti* Love intervenes to turn the man away from his world of male activity, from the male hunt, in a sense "feminizing" him. In

---

42 For both normative and non-normative social groups as recorded in literary texts, see my "Sociology of the *Brigata*."

43 Dante himself will reference the hunt in the amatory and not the realistic sense in the sonnet to Cino *I' ho veduto già senza radice.* Here he advises his friend against chasing the lady, using the noun *caccia*: "parmi che ·lla tua **caccia** [non] seguer de' [I don't think you should keep on hunting]" (14).

this either/or universe the lover receives a take-it-or-leave-it proposition: he must decide whether to "lasciar le donne," leave the ladies, for the hunt. The rigid dichotomy between the male and female worlds established by *Sonar bracchetti* is an indicator of the anxiety the young poet felt about the norms imposed by his society.

Dante's ability to violate such norms is on display early in his poetic career: one thinks for instance of the violent reaction of Dante da Maiano to the "favoleggiar" of the sonnet *A ciascun'alma*, and too of Dante's sonnets *Voi che portate la sembianza umile* and *Se' tu colui c' hai trattato sovente*, which show a young poet who wants to take part in the mourning rituals reserved for women in his society. In these texts Dante is already probing the limits with regard to social behaviour dictated by gender. Using *Sonar bracchetti* as a point of departure with respect to the male/female binary, we will be able to trace the itinerary in Dante's thought from the rigid dichotomy on display here to a more complex and nuanced view: in *Paradiso* the lines "E come surge e va ed entra in ballo / vergine lieta, sol per fare onore / a la novizia, non per alcun fallo [And as a happy virgin rises and goes and enters the dance, simply to honour the new bride, not because of any fault]" (*Par.* 25.103–5) refer to Saint John.[44]

17 (B LXI; C 15; FB 16; DR 44)

Sonar bracchetti e cacciatori aizzare,	The beagles' belling and the hunters' cries,
lepri levare ed isgridar le genti,	the hares flushed out, the cheering of the crowd,
e di guinzagli uscir veltri correnti,	the greyhounds loosed from leashes, dashing by,
4 per belle piagge volger e 'mboccare,	careening through the fields in search of prey,
assai credo che deggia dilettare	must surely be a source of great delight
libero core e van d'intendimenti.	to any heart not bound by love's demands.
Ed io, fra gli amorosi pensamenti,	But in my thoughts of love I find myself
8 d'uno sono schernito in tale affare,	put down and mocked by one of them;
e dicemi esto motto per usanza:	and as it's done before, it jokes and says:
"Or ecco leggiadria di gentil core	"Now here's refinement in a gentleman,
11 per una sì selvaggia dilettanza	deserting ladies and their gaiety
lasciar le donne e lor gaia sembianza!"	for such a rough-and-tumble sport as this."
Allor, temendo non che 'l senta Amore,	And fearing then that Love will overhear,
14 prendo vergogna, onde mi ven pesanza.	I feel ashamed and have a heavy heart.

METRE: sonnet ABBA ABBA CDC CDC.

---

44 For the development of Dante's thought on gender, see my essays "*Sotto benda*: Gender in the Lyrics of Dante and Guittone d'Arezzo (with an Excursus on Cecco d'Ascoli)" and "Notes toward a Gendered History of Italian Literature, with a Discussion of Dante's *Beatrix Loquax*," in *Dante and the Origins of Italian Literary Culture*, pp. 333–59, 360–78.

18 Volgete gli occhi a veder chi mi tira

Volgete gli occhi opens with an existential drama: the poet must choose between his friends and Love. This sonnet is thematically connected with *Sonar bracchetti*, where the poet feels obliged to be with the ladies instead of participating in the hunt with his friends. As in *Sonar bracchetti*, *Volgete gli occhi* takes its cue from the internal conflict of the poet, who is here literally tugged in two opposing directions: his friends are on one side beckoning to him to come with them and Love is on the other, pulling him. He had intended to be with his friends; hence now he tells them to turn their eyes and look at the force that prevents him from joining them: "Volgete gli occhi a veder chi mi tira, / per ch'io non posso più venir con voi [Turn round and see the one who tugs at me / so I no more can share your company]" (1–2).

We do not know with whom the poet was expected "to come" nor what he intended to do with them, but the very fact that he uses the plural form of the verb "Volgete" suggests a group – a male *brigata* – with common interests. The use of the verb *venire* gives a feeling of immediacy to the opening: we can imagine the friends saying "Come on!" to Dante. A group of male friends is moreover listed with precision in the opening of *Guido, i' vorrei che tu e Lapo ed io*. Given the primary position of Guido Cavalcanti in that sonnet, it is interesting to note that Guido too uses the verb *venire* in a famous sonnet of reproof directed at Dante that begins with *venire a* (rather than *venire con*): *I' vegno 'l giorno a·tte 'nfinite volte* [I come to you a thousand times a day].

In the opening of *Volgete gli occhi* the poet directly addresses his friends, apologizing for his neglect of them, urging them to consider who is dragging him away, so that they may fully appreciate why he can't come with them. It is not just any force that pulls him from his friends: it is Love, who must be honoured, who makes men suffer on account of women ("e onoratel, che questi è colui / che per le gentil donne altru' martira [and honour him, for he's the one who plies / our noble ladies to wreak others' woe]" [3–4]), and who has the power to kill ("La sua virtute, ch'ancide sanz'ira [this power of his, / which slays sans violence]" [5]).

Stylistically and ideologically, *Volgete gli occhi* hovers between Sicilian conventions and a new, more Cavalcantian style. The image of Love painting the lady in the mind of her lover is Sicilian; it is an image that we have seen in the canzone *La dispietata mente*, where we find as well the syntagma "mi tira" ("'l disio amoroso che mi tira [love's desire, which draws me]" [4]). In this case the lady's nobility painted in his mind is such that all the poet's strength hurries to kneel before her feet: "e pingevi una donna sì gentile / che tutto mio valore a' piè le corre [depicting there a lady of such worth / that all my strength kneels down before her feet]" (10–11).

In terms of ideology, the love of *Volgete gli occhi* is tyrannical, powerful, and "fero" (fierce, acting with force or violence): "ch'elli m'è giunto fero nella mente [for he has forced his way inside my mind]" (9). While this position can easily be conventional, Dante's Sicilian-style poems tend to sing a benevolent and optimistic love: it is possible therefore that this cruel and "fero" love already reflects the influence of Cavalcanti. Dante's use in *Volgete gli occhi* of the Sicilian topos of the lady painted in the heart lends itself to a Cavalcantian interpretation. We saw that the "valore" of the lover kneels at *madonna*'s feet. The image of the lady painted within the lover leads thus to the lover's self-abasement rather than to his elevation, precisely as in Cavalcanti's poems, where the figure of the lady frequently has the effect of reducing or negating the existential worth of the lover (and the word "valore," used in precisely this sense, is very Cavalcantian; see note 47 in the essay on *Guido, i' vorrei*).

The concluding move of *Volgete gli occhi* is explicitly stilnovistic: a refined and gentle voice speaks within the poet, and its words take the form of direct speech (the fragmentation of the "I" into various speaking entities is also a Cavalcantian speciality). Here the soft voice that speaks has the same tone of reprimand, though not as sharp, that we witnessed in the words of the speaking thought of *Sonar bracchetti*. There, the thought sarcastically asserts what it does not think is true, that the lover's behaviour is a sign of courtesy: "Or ecco leggiadria di gentil core [Now here's refinement in a gentleman]" (*Sonar bracchetti,* 10). Here, the soft voice puts a rhetorical question to the protagonist that reconnects to the existential drama at the start of the sonnet: "Dunque, vuo' tu per neente / agli occhi tuoi sì bella donna tôrre? [Would you, for nothing in return, / remove so fair a lady from your eyes?]" (13–14).

This question asserts again that the only valid choice on the poet-lover's part is to adore *madonna* (hence not to turn his eyes away from her), given that every other activity – such as, for example, passing time with friends – is classified as literally "neente" (nothing). To the rather aggressive question with which the sonnet closes, "vuo' tu per neente / agli occhi tuoi sì bella donna tôrre?" the only acceptable response clearly is "No, there is no sufficient motive for depriving my eyes of the sight of such a beautiful lady." But the response remains implicit, and the dominant note of *Volgete gli occhi* is therefore tension: the tension of the imperative with which the sonnet opens and the tension of the question, left hanging, with which it ends.

From this tension we can deduce that the young Dante is not without ambivalence in his adherence to the values of courtly love, values that (as too in *Sonar bracchetti*) separate him from the world of friends, from the world of men.

18 (B LIX; C 13; FB 17; DR 45)

Volgete gli occhi a veder chi mi tira,	Turn round and see the one who tugs at me
per ch'io non posso più venir con voi,	so I no more can share your company,
ed onoratel, che questi è colui	and honour him, for he's the one who plies

4   che per le gentil donne altru' martira.
     La sua virtute, ch'ancide sanz'ira,
     pregatel che mi laghi venir poi,
     e io vi dico, de li modi suoi
8   cotanto intende quanto l'uom sospira;
      ch'elli m'è giunto fero nella mente
     e pingevi una donna sì gentile
11   che tutto mio valore a' piè le corre;
     e fammi udire una boce sottile
     che dice: "Dunque, vuo' tu per neente
14   agli occhi tuoi sì bella donna tôrre?"

our noble ladies to wreak others' woe.
Beseech him to allow this power of his,
which slays sans violence, to enter me;
I tell you this: one understands his ways
according as one suffers from his might;
    for he has forced his way inside my mind,
depicting there a lady of such worth
that all my strength kneels down before her feet:
he makes me listen to a gentle voice
that says: "Would you, for nothing in return,
remove so fair a lady from your eyes?"

METRE: sonnet ABBA ABBA CDE DCE.

19 Guido, i' vorrei che tu e Lapo ed io

In this sonnet Dante writes about friendship, a subset of love.[45] Friendship is one of
Dante's great themes, with roots in his earliest lyrics, as discussed in the introductory
essays to *Deh ragioniamo*, *Sonar bracchetti*, and *Volgete gli occhi*. The social life of a
group of male friends is common to *Guido, i' vorrei*, *Sonar bracchetti*, and *Volgete gli
occhi*; only in *Guido, i' vorrei*, however, do we find Dante linking friendship to poetry.
The friends named in *Guido, i' vorrei* include at least one poet, Guido Cavalcanti, and
more than one poet if we take "Lapo" to refer, as is traditional, to Lapo Gianni. (I do
not follow De Robertis in substituting the traditional "Lapo" by "Lippo," because the
reasons he gives for his choice do not convince me.)[46] The first friend to be named, the
one to whom the sonnet is addressed, and who responds, in the sonnet *S'io fosse quelli
che d'Amor fu degno*,[47] is the poet whom Dante calls "primo de li miei amici [the first

---

45 Aristotle dedicates books 8 and 9 of the *Nicomachean Ethics* to friendship. In the treatise *De Amicitia* Cicero explains the etymological link between *amor* and *amicitia*: "Amor enim, ex quo amicitia
nominata est [For it is 'amor' (love) from which the word 'amicitia' (friendship) is derived]" (8.26).

46 "Lapo" is the reading of almost all the manuscripts traditionally accepted by editors of the *Rime*,
who think of Lapo Gianni de' Ricevuti, Florentine poet and notary. De Robertis opts for "Lippo"
instead of "Lapo" in the wake of Guglielmo Gorni, who suggested Lippo Pasci de' Bardi (to whom
Dante wrote the sonnet *Se Lippo amico*) rather than Lapo Gianni as the third protagonist of this sonnet; see *Il nodo della lingua e il verbo d'amore* (Florence: Olschki, 1981), pp. 99–124. The reasons
given by De Robertis are extratextual and therefore not compelling: "The stemma ... definitely puts
Lippo in the minority with respect to *Lapo*, popularly *Lapo Gianni*, who until now was seen as present in the invitation and so a member of the society of *stilnovisti* ... The fact is that after Gorni's
suggestion ... various documents turn out to be marked by an equivalence of *Lippo-Lapo,* more than
once *Lippus seu Lapus* (*Lippo* or *Lapo*) ... To write *Lapo* is to write *Lippo*: and the variant *Lippo,*
totally neutral, here firmly adopted, simply means *not* Lapo Gianni" (crit. ed., *Testi*, p. 306). In his
2005 commentary edition, De Robertis writes, more simply, "Lippo or Lapo" (comm. ed., p. 288).
In a case where the choice of variant is, in De Robertis' words, "totally neutral," and the change is
made for reasons that are explicitly nontextual but interpretative, I prefer not to change the text. See
Lino Leonardi, "Nota sull'edizione critica delle *Rime* di Dante a cura di Domenico De Robertis,"
Medioevo Romanzo 28 (2004): 63–113, who points out on p. 104 that the change in this incipit creates a contradiction with Cavalcanti's *Se vedi Amore*, where a "Lapo" is a member of the group of
friends: "Se vedi Amore, assai ti priego, Dante, / in parte là 've Lapo sia presente [I pray you, Dante,
if you should see Love / in any place where Lapo's present too]"). And see Giunta, pp. 166–7, for his
reasons for retaining "Lapo" in his edition.

47 Guido's response to *Guido, i' vorrei* is typical of what we call the Cavalcantian mode: it evinces a
pessimistic view of love based on the abject nature of the lover-poet, his lack of worth. Thus, Guido
courteously refuses to participate in Dante's vision of happiness in the *vasello* because of his own
lack of "valore" (the last word of *S'io fosse quelli*): "S'io fosse quelli che d'Amor fu degno, / del

of my friends]" in the prose of the *Vita Nuova* (III.14 [2.1]), where he explains that Guido's response to *A ciascun'alma* "was more or less the beginning of the friendship between him and me" ("fue quasi lo principio de l'amistà tra lui e me") (*VN* III.14 [2.1]). In this passage of the *Vita Nuova* Dante makes explicit the link between making poetry and making friends.[48] *Guido, i' vorrei* thus offers a privileged early vantage on the tight bond that Dante forges between poetry and friendship and on Guido's "primacy" ("primo de li miei amici") in both domains.

We find a fascinating confirmation of the link between making poetry and being friends in Cavalcanti's *I' vegno 'l giorno a·tte 'nfinite volte*, the famous sonnet in which Guido reprimands Dante for the condition to which he has sunk after Beatrice's death: he now has an "anima invilita [degraded soul]" (14). Here Guido indicates that his friendship with Dante had a textual dimension, resulting in Guido's collection of Dante's lyrics: "di me parlavi sì coralemente / che·ttutte le tue rime avìe ricolte [of me you used to speak so cordially / that I would welcome every poem you sent]" (*I' vegno 'l giorno*, 7–8). Similarly, Guido's disappointment in Dante also has a textual dimension, for now he feels obliged to reject his friend's poetry, his "dir": "Or non ardisco, per la vil tua vita, / far mostramento che·ttu dir mi piaccia [I now dare not, since you've demeaned yourself, / acknowledge that I like your poetry]" (*I' vegno 'l giorno*, 9–10). I would classify *I' vegno 'l giorno* as an "anti-consolatory" poem, a poem that applies to the ailing friend an electric jolt rather than a warm hug. The friend who wrote instead the canonic *consolatoria* to Dante on Beatrice's death (*consolatoria* is the term used to denote a canzone of consolation), Cino da Pistoia, will take Guido's place as canonic friend-poet in Dante's subsequent writings.[49]

· After the *Vita Nuova*, in which the figure of Guido Cavalcanti is first among friends, we pass to the treatise *De vulgari eloquentia*, where the catalogues of vernacular poets contain traces of Dante's friendships. The Italian poets are listed in the *De vulgari eloquentia*'s catalogue of Book 2, chapter 6 in this manner: Guido Guinizzelli, Guido Cavalcanti, Cino da Pistoia, and "his [Cino's] friend" (*DVE* 2.6.6). The last poet,

---

qual non trovo sol che rimembranza, / e la donna tenesse altra sembianza, / assai mi piaceria siffatto legno [If I were one who still was worthy of Love, / of which I only have a memory, / and if my lady had a different air, / a boat like this would please me very much]" (1–4). Thus, Guido does not accept – not even in fantasy – Dante's more positive view of love.

48 The word *amico* is rather rare in the lyrics: it appears in the sonnets exchanged with Dante da Maiano, in the incipit of *Se Lippo amico*, and then more generically in *La dispietata mente*, *Tre donne*, and *Doglia mi reca*. It does not appear in this great poem dedicated to friendship. It is not, however, rare in the prose of the *Vita Nuova*. As can be seen in the two passages of the *Vita Nuova* just cited – "primo de li miei amici" and "lo principio de l'amistà tra lui e me" – one of the tasks of the prose is to thematize friendship. In chapter XXXII (21) Dante situates Beatrice's brother within his hierarchy of friendship: "uno, lo quale, secondo li gradi de l'amistade, è amico a me immediatamente dopo lo primo [one who, in degree of friendship, is the friend of mine right after the first]" (*VN* XXXII.1 [21.1]).

49 The *consolatoria* by Cino is the canzone *Avegna ched el m'aggia più per tempo*. See the introductory essay to *Li occhi dolenti* for further discussion of *I' vegno 'l giorno a·tte* as an "anti-*consolatoria*."

referred to by the periphrasis "amicus eius," is Dante himself. The perfect expression of the symbiosis between poetry and friendship is the phrase "amicus eius," used repeatedly in the *De vulgari eloquentia*: instead of using the name "Dante" to place himself in the lists of vernacular poets, Dante calls himself "amicus eius." By calling himself the friend of the poet who precedes him in the catalogues, Cino da Pistoia,[50] Dante performs the idea that the friend is as Cicero says, another self.

Dante reinforces the link between poetry and friendship in the *Commedia*, pairing every citation of his own canzoni to an encounter with a friend, and putting onstage many friendly encounters among poets in the otherworld.[51] Among these let us recall the moments when Dante imagines himself welcomed by the great poets of antiquity as "sesto tra cotanto senno [sixth among so much wisdom]" (*Inf.* 4.102) and when Statius realizes he is in the presence of his adored Vergil (*Purg.* 21; for this moment see the introductory essay to *Deh ragioniamo*). In fact, if there are tight-knit male *brigate* in the *Commedia*, they are composed of poets, able to become fast friends and always to find something to chat about (but not to share with outsiders to the group): Dante walks with the poets in Limbo "talking about things of which it is best to remain silent" ("parlando cose che 'l tacere è bello" [*Inf.* 4.104]), and as he follows Vergil and Statius he "listened to their words that gave me understanding of poetry" until the novelty of the upside-down tree interrupted "the sweet conversing" ("le dolci ragioni" [*Purg.* 22.128–30]). As discussed in the essay on *Deh ragioniamo*, "ragionar" (talking) is the social activity preferred by Dante's poets. Similarly, in *Guido, i' vorrei* the line "e quivi ragionar sempre d'amore [and here to talk always about love]" (12) is an indicator of being in the company of poets.

In this sonnet, friendship is experienced as an enchanted state that permits complete transparency untrammelled by our existence as differentiated ontological beings – in effect, a transparency and unity uncontaminated by difference. This fantasy of oneness causes exquisite pleasure but also sadness: the total reciprocity and transparency that is longed for cannot be grasped in human life and the enchantment is therefore veiled by melancholy. *Guido, i' vorrei* expresses a desire: the desire for a magic space of impossible and perfect non-difference.[52] The afflatus with which the name "Guido" is pronounced at the poem's opening is the breath of friendship itself.

---

50 The poem that represents Cino in the catalogue of *DVE* 2.6.6 is precisely the *consolatoria* on the death of Beatrice. Lapo Gianni too is mentioned in *DVE*, as one who – with Dante, Guido Cavalcanti, and Cino da Pistoia – had made use of an excellent vernacular ("vulgaris excellentiam cognovisse" [*DVE* 1.13.3]). Gorni maintains that in this case as well the common reading *Lapum* is to be put aside as *facilior* and that Dante's text actually refers to Lippo Pasci de' Bardi.

51 See the first chapter of my *Dante's Poets* for Dante's autocitations – the first paired with Casella, the second with Forese, and the third with Carlo Martello – and chapters 2 and 3 for the encounters with poets.

52 As in my book *The Undivine Comedy*, I use "difference" in the way that Dante uses it ("In the abstract it means the 'divergence' between two or more elements"; Fernando Salsano, s.v. "differenza," *Enciclopedia dantesca*, gen. ed. Umberto Bosco, 6 vols. [Rome: Istituto dell'Enciclopedia Italiana, 1970–78]), and essentially in the way that Thomas Aquinas uses *distinctio*: "any type of non-identity

The expression of this desire controls and governs the sonnet from the beginning, even syntactically: we encounter right off, after the vocative "Guido," the verb of desire, "i' vorrei [I wish]," on which the syntax of the entire sonnet depends. (The conditional "vorrei" is followed by imperfect subjunctives, as befits a classic conditional contrary-to-fact construction.) The transition from the incipit to the following line indicates the parameters of the fantasy. From the recitation of names and pronouns that mark the fully individuated and hence plural state of the three friends – Guido, Lapo, and Dante himself are three subjects who are ontologically and grammatically separate and different – we move to the unitary state of the plural verb at the beginning of the second line: "Guido, i' vorrei che tu e Lapo ed io / *fossimo* presi ... [Guido, I wish that Lapo, you, and I / were carried off ...]" (1–2). The *three* plural identities, which preserve their individuality underscored by the pronouns "I" and "you," would be, in this fantasy, part of *one* magic circle. Here we find a distant preview of the many attempts in *Paradiso* to give poetic life to the idea that Three can become One while always remaining Three. Or, switching cultural contexts, we think of Cicero's *De Amicitia*, where a friend is "another self" – "alter idem" (21.80) – and friendship results in such a mixing of souls as to "almost make one of two" ("ut efficiat paene unum ex duobus!") (21.81), and the power of friendship is such as to make one soul where there was a plurality of souls: "Nam cum amicitiae vis sit in eo ut unus quasi animus fiat ex pluribus [the effect of friendship is to make, as it were, one soul out of many]" (25.92).

In Dante's imagination the magical protected space of friendship takes the form of a boat in which he wishes the three friends could together navigate the sea of life, the sea that in *Paradiso* will have become the metaphysical "gran mar de l'essere [the great sea of being]" (*Par.* 1.113). Or we could think of the sea of love, of which one day Dante will write "tratto m'hanno del mar de l'amor torto, / e del diritto m'han posto a la riva [they took me from the sea of erroneous love and placed me on the shore of right love]" (*Par.* 26.62–3). In this vessel of his imagination,[53] the friends would be immune from the wearying and perilous passions of life/love: the wind that typically afflicts the poet-lover of the love lyric,[54] instead of opposing them, here

---

between objects and things. Often called diversity or difference" (T. Gilby, *Glossary*, in Thomas Aquinas, *Summa theologiae*, Blackfriars ed. [New York: McGraw-Hill/London: Eyre and Spottiswoode, 1964–81], 8:164). In other words, as is clear in the discussion on time and difference in *The Undivine Comedy*, my use is essentially Aristotelian.

53 Contini connects the *vasel* with Merlin's vessel in the Arthurian romances, recalled also in *Mare amoroso,* lines 212–16 ("E se potesse avere una barchetta, / tal com' fu quella che donò Merlino / a la valente donna d'Avalona, / ch'andassi sanza remi e sanza vela / altressì ben per terra com' per aqua [And if he could have a little boat like the one that Merlin gave to the excellent lady of Avalon, which went without oars and without a sail as well on earth as through water]") and 226–9.

54 See Giacomo da Lentini: "Lo vostr'amor che m'ave / in mare tempestoso, / è sì como la nave / c'a la fortuna getta ogni pesanti [My love for you, which places me / upon a stormy sea, / is like a ship in peril / that must cast overboard its heavy bulk]" (*Madonna, dir vo voglio,* 49–52).

concurs with their every desire: "in un vasel ch'ad ogni vento / per mare andasse al voler vostro e mio; / sì che fortuna od altro tempo rio / non ci potesse dare impedimento [and set upon a ship to sail the sea / where every wind would favour our command, / so neither thunderstorms nor cloudy skies / might ever have the power to hold us back]" (3–6).

Throughout the octave the friends' unity is emphasized. To the multiplicity ("ogni vento [every wind]") and difficulty of life ("fortuna od altro tempo rio [thunderstorms or cloudy skies]") is contrasted the unitary force of their friendship (*"un vasel"* [one boat], "voler *vostro e mio*" [your will and mine]), with which the poet wishes they could face any "impedimento." He also wishes they could be united in a single desire, a single wish (*"un* talento"), such that their "disio [desire]" to be together would grow: "anzi, vivendo sempre in un talento, / di star insieme crescesse il disio [but rather, cleaving to this single wish, / that our desire to live as one would grow]" (7–8). The resolution of the many into the one makes unity grow, and from love more love is born, precisely as will be theorized in *Purgatorio*: "E quanta gente più là sù s'intende, / più v'è da bene amare, e più vi s'ama [And the more people up there are in love, the more there are to love truly, and the more they love each other]" (*Purg.* 15.73–4).[55]

In the octave Dante imagines a state of complete and timeless harmony, in which the friends are protected from the flux of time and multiplicity. Dante's dream includes immortality, living *"sempre* [forever] in un talento." In this atemporal state of absolute nondifferentiation (time is that which condemns us to difference, being "number of motion in respect of 'before' and 'after'"),[56] the desire for further harmony – of being together, "star *insieme*" – could not but grow: this is a virtuous circularity, in which always living together with one sole desire will increase the desire to continue living together. And who wouldn't choose to be together in conditions so different from those of real life? The sonnet imagines individuals who, while remaining individuals – while continuing to be Dante, Guido, and Lapo – are able to suspend all individual desires and thus all "impediments," or conflicts. In real life individual desires are the origin of the conflicts that lessen the desire to be together; if we shared a single desire, conflicts would necessarily diminish, indeed would disappear.

Dante proposes to eliminate the differing wishes of the three protagonists, without however doing away with their irreducible and separate individual selves, indicated

---

55 On the question of the tension between the one and the many in Dante's *Paradiso*, see Barolini, *The Undivine Comedy*, esp. chap. 8, "Problems in Paradise: The Mimesis of Time and the Paradox of *più e meno.*"

56 The citation is from *Physics* 4.11.219b1. Dante writes: "Lo tempo, secondo che dice Aristotile nel quarto de la Fisica, è 'numero di movimento, secondo prima e poi'; e 'numero di movimento celestiale,' lo quale dispone le cose di qua giù diversamente a ricevere alcuna informazione [Time, as Aristotle says in the fourth book of the *Physics*, is 'number of motion, with respect to before and after,' and 'number of celestial movement' is that which disposes things here below to receive the informing powers diversely]" (*Conv.* 4.2.6).

by means of the brilliant series of names and pronouns that opens the poem. This use of pronouns is part of a long-term "semantics of friendship" developed early by Dante (see the introductory essay to *Deh ragioniamo*). Pronouns are markers of intimate bonds of male friendship in the *Commedia*, for instance in the devastatingly beautiful verse that memorializes Dante's friendship with Forese Donati: "qual fosti meco, e qual io teco fui [what you were with me, and what I was with you]" (*Purg.* 23.116). We think too of the verses that celebrate the friendship of Statius and Vergil: "Ma dimmi, e come amico mi perdona" (*Purg.* 22.19) and "e come amico omai meco ragiona" (*Purg.* 22.21). The most intense use of pronouns to suggest complete interchangeability of being between one person and another occurs not, in the *Commedia*, in an exchange between a man and a woman but in that between Dante and another old friend, Carlo Martello, which features the coinage of intense verbs of mutual penetration made of pronouns: "s'io m'intuassi, come tu t'inmii [if I were to in-you myself as you in-me yourself]" (*Par.* 9.81).

In *Guido, i' vorrei* the pronouns and names indicate separate identities that set up an aporia – how can the one and the many coexist? – that Dante will eventually treat in *Paradiso* in philosophical terms but that now he approaches by using a profane and magical setting. In life as we know it separate identities (identities indicated by the names "Guido," "Lapo," and by the pronouns "tu," "io," and – the last word of our sonnet – "noi")[57] necessarily carry divergent wills. Absent a supernatural or theological context, perfect unity is not possible without violating individual identity; the various attempts in human history to enforce unity of will in political terms have led to forms of totalitarianism. *Guido, i' vorrei* does not go in that direction; it belongs rather to an enchanted state that is knowingly unreal.

If it is true that the intensity of this longed-for unity diminishes in the transition from the octave to the sestet, where we encounter the poets' ladies ("monna Vanna" and "monna Lagia" are the ladies loved, respectively, by Guido and Lapo),[58] it is also true that the very presence of the ladies is important: the impulse to reconcile difference is so strong in *Guido, i' vorrei* that women are present in the boat. As we can surmise from the segregation of men and women notable in the *Vita Nuova*, the presence of ladies in this boat testifies to an idealized situation, one that is outside the quotidian societal norm. Their altogether unusual presence helps us to understand the risk that Boccaccio took in creating his mixed company of men and women in the frame-tale of the *Decameron*. Dante does not need to defend the probity of the ladies in his boat, as Boccaccio continually defends the virtue of the female members of

---

57 Proper names are signifiers of irreducible historicity in epic poetry (we recall the catalogue of ships in the second book of the *Iliad*, which comes to Dante via the seventh book of the *Aeneid*). Dante's own equivalent of the *Iliad*'s catalogue of ships is the catalogue of Florentine names in *Paradiso* 16; see Barolini, *The Undivine Comedy*, pp. 139–40.

58 The name "Vanna" appears again – this time together with "monna Bice" – in the sonnet *Io mi senti' svegliar*. A "monna Lagia" (the diminutive of Alagia) is referenced also in the incipit of *Amore e monna Lagia e Guido ed io* and in Cavalcanti's sonnet *Dante, un sospiro messagger del core*.

his *brigata*, because the conditions in which they are placed are explicitly unreal and magical: the ladies are placed in the boat by a magician ("con noi ponesse il buono incantatore [borne to us ... / by our good enchanter's wizardry]" [11]). It is important to note that Dante, imagining perfection, should include women. As we will see also in the essays on the sonnets *Voi che portate la sembianza umile* and *Se' tu colui c' hai trattato sovente*, Dante's imagination is not boxed in by his society's norms of appropriate comportment.

On the other hand, there is a clear lowering of intensity in the sestet. The poets' ladies are added to the dream of friendship in a second installment, formally separate in the sestet. And to the desire that those in the boat may always talk about love (12) – let us imagine that the ladies are taking part in the conversation, as in the *Decameron* – is added the hope, shadowed by the implicit possibility of failure, that "ciascuna di lor fosse contenta [each of them would find herself content]" (13).

Even if the sestet offers another occurrence of the adverb "sempre" ("ragionar *sempre* d'amore" [always talking about love]) (12), the dream of perfect unity is no longer intact: the tear in the fabric (the crack in the golden bowl) shows in the stubborn presence of singularity among the ladies, in the fact that the poet refers to "*ciascuna* di lor" – "*each* of them" – when in the case of the men the plural pronoun "noi" – "we" – is sufficient. And it is worth noting, without entering into discussion as to whether "quella ch'è sul numer de le trenta [(she) who's number thirty]" (10) is the first screen-lady of the *Vita Nuova* or not (Barbi maintains she is), that the use of a number for referring to one's lady (in *Vita Nuova* VI.2 [2.11] Dante mentions a lost *serventese* in which he names the sixty most beautiful women in Florence) can only increase the sense of a multiplicity that is hardly amenable to unity.

There is, therefore, tension in *Guido, i' vorrei*: tension reflected in the structural division between octave (the friends) and sestet (their ladies). However, if this structural dichotomy recalls *Sonar bracchetti*, the comparison between the two sonnets only highlights how in *Guido, i' vorrei* the poet's will is directed towards eliminating dichotomy and difference while creating instead the privileged space of unity. *Guido, i' vorrei* is a dream of floating, light as the foam of the sea, far from any division: distant not only from the divisions that can separate a man from a woman, but distant as well – perhaps above all, given the strong male identities of the incipit – from the divisions that can separate a man from another man. The authentic privileged space of the sonnet is the male space of the octave, before the addition of the ladies to the sestet. Is there a latent homoeroticism in this sonnet? We note that the past participle associated throughout the courtly tradition with erotic love, *preso*, is used for the men who are "*presi* per incantamento [carried off by some enchanter's spell]" (2).

In the case of the two men separated by the space of the first verse – "Guido" on the one side, "I" on the other – their friendship was not able to withstand division, and so it is difficult to avoid attributing the melancholy of this sonnet in part to an obscure foreboding of the poetic and ideological falling-out that will eventually rupture the harmony between Dante and his "first" friend, differentiating them in a way that can no longer be overcome. We have already mentioned the sonnet written

by Guido after Beatrice's death, *I' vegno 'l giorno a·tte 'nfinite volte*. At that stage a
rupture had not yet occurred, given that Guido still "comes" every day, insistently,
to find his friend. But, however it came about, the rupture did ultimately occur: in
the end, this boat landed, if you will, on the shore of the River Styx. By this I do not
want to suggest that I subscribe to the view according to which Dante condemns
Guido with his father Cavalcante de' Cavalcanti in the tenth canto of the *Inferno*
(even less that he is already thinking about such a condemnation when he wrote
Guido, i' vorrei); I have always maintained that Dante is deliberately ambiguous with
regard to the destiny of the friend who, in the fiction of the *Commedia*, is explicitly
"co' vivi ancor congiunto [still among the living]" (*Inf.* 10.111).[59] And in any case
Dante does not condemn sons for the sins of their fathers: one need only recall the
examples – which Dante is at pains to provide us – of Manfredi and Bonconte. But
on the other hand there is no doubt that the move of *Inferno* 10 contaminated the
historical reception of Guido Cavalcanti – as the story about Guido Cavalcanti in
the *Decameron* (6.9) demonstrates – and that Dante in this sense cast a shadow on
Guido's reputation, linking the name of his friend in perpetuity to hell and damnation
in the cultural imaginary.[60]

But it is not necessary to think of the future to access the melancholy of *Guido, i'
vorrei*. The melancholy is inherent in the very subject of the sonnet: in the fact that
this dream of escaping difference remains, even in the consciousness of the poet
who dreams it, only a dream. The many similarities with passages in *Paradiso* are
instructive. In *Paradiso* these dreams are recounted in the present or future tense, not
in the conditional. For example, to stay within the context of multiple wills pacified
by a single will, Dante does not write in *Paradiso* 3 "*vorrei* che nella sua volontade
fosse nostra pace" – "I wish that in his will were our peace" – but "' n sua volontade
è nostra pace [in his will is our peace]" (*Par.* 3.85). In other words, *Paradiso* offers
not dreams, but imagined realities, while in *Guido, i' vorrei* the poet's imagination
remains in the state of desire, without reaching the state of lived imaginary reality.

The syntax of *Guido, i' vorrei*, the fact that all the conjugated verbs up to the last
line are subjunctives that depend on the initial "vorrei," keeps the discourse afloat but
on a sea that is explicitly unreal, not even dreamed as real, but as part of an "enchantment" brought about by a "good enchanter" (11). Nor does the final verse change the
perspective. In fact, it serves to encapsulate the problem and reproduce it with utter
clarity in the restricted confines of a single verse, replacing the verb of the incipit
with a new verb: "credo" (I believe). The problem of a "noi" that is longed for but
reached only conditionally is not resolved; if anything it is reinforced and encapsulated by the last verse: "sì come *credo* che *sarémo* noi [just as I think that we should

---

59 See Barolini, *Dante's Poets*, p. 148.

60 On the relationship between Dante and Guido see Barolini, *Dante's Poets*, esp. chap. 2, and my essay
    "Dante and Cavalcanti (On Making Distinctions in Matters of Love)," 1998, rpt. in *Dante and the
    Origins of Italian Literary Culture*, pp. 70–101.

likewise be]" (14). The true enchantment of this sonnet resides in its dream of a perfect friendship but even more in its awareness: this dream of evasion knows that it cannot evade its own evanescence.

19 (B LII; C 9; FB 15; DR 35)
Dante to Guido Cavalcanti

Guido, i' vorrei che tu e Lapo ed io
fossimo presi per incantamento
e messi in un vasel ch'ad ogni vento
4   per mare andasse al voler vostro e mio;
sì che fortuna od altro tempo rio
non ci potesse dare impedimento,
anzi, vivendo sempre in un talento,
8   di star insieme crescesse il disio.
E monna Vanna e monna Lagia poi
con quella ch'è sul numer de le trenta
11   con noi ponesse il buono incantatore:
e quivi ragionar sempre d'amore,
e ciascuna di lor fosse contenta
14   sì come credo che sarémo noi.

Guido, I wish that Lapo, you, and I
were carried off by some enchanter's spell
and set upon a ship to sail the sea
where every wind would favour our command,
so neither thunderstorms nor cloudy skies
might ever have the power to hold us back,
but rather, cleaving to this single wish,
that our desire to live as one would grow.
And Lady Vanna were with Lady Lagia
borne to us with her who's number thirty
by our good enchanter's wizardry:
to talk of love would be our sole pursuit,
and each of them would find herself content,
just as I think that we should likewise be.

METRE: sonnet ABBA ABBA CDE EDC.

20 Amore e monna Lagia e Guido ed io

My decision to include this sonnet despite the not complete certainty of its textual tradition is based on various considerations. *Amore e monna Lagia* is, among the lyrics of uncertain attribution, the one traditionally held to be most certain: Barbi places it first in a list that moves from more to less certainty of Dantean paternity; and Contini, while following Barbi in placing it among the "Rime dubbie," writes that "the attribution to Dante can be considered secure" (p. 229). Two codices give the sonnet to Cavalcanti, only one (less authoritative) to Dante, but, "if the problem is to choose between Dante and Guido Cavalcanti, there cannot be any doubt of Dante's paternity – Guido being excluded because referred to in the text of the sonnet in the third person" (Barbi-Pernicone, p. 663).

And in fact the attribution to Dante is based on non-codicological criteria, such as the presence in the sonnet of "Guido" noted by Barbi-Pernicone. Similarly, Contini refers to the characters named in the poem, not to material evidence. The presence of lady Lagia calls for Lapo Gianni: "Dante and Lapo must therefore be on the one hand the author and on the other the unnamed protagonist of the sonnet; and since the tradition has never assigned this poem to Lapo, one can safely attribute it to Dante" (p. 229).

De Robertis, however, takes *Amore e monna Lagia* out of the *rime dubbie* and places it among the lyrics certainly written by Dante, but his procedure lacks the methodological transparency that would induce unreserved confidence in his readers.

De Robertis cuts the number of the doubtful lyrics from Barbi/Contini's twenty-six to sixteen, adding eight compositions to the regular canon and completely excluding two (*Deh, piangi meco tu, dogliosa petra* and *Nulla mi parve più crudel cosa*). The eight doubtful lyrics readmitted into the canon are *Aï faus ris, Quando 'l consiglio degli ucce' si tenne, Amore e monna Lagia e Guido ed io, Se 'l viso mio a la terra si china, Questa donna ch'andar mi fa pensoso, Non v'accorgete voi d'un che·ssi more, Io sento pianger l'anima nel core*, and *Degli occhi di quella gentil mia dama*.

The problem, as I noted previously, is lack of transparency in the classification. Consulting De Robertis, one finds that he classifies differentially the eight lyrics that he readmits to the canon, without offering an explanation of his different classificatory rubrics. Two carry the rubric "restored to Dante" ("restituita/o a Dante"), four the rubric "probably Dante's" ("probabilmente di Dante"), and two have no rubric at all:

18 [restored to Dante]	*Aï faus ris, pour quoi traï aves*
34 [restored to Dante]	*Quando 'l consiglio degli ucce' si tenne*[61]
41	*Amore e monna Lagia e Guido ed io*
51 [probably Dante's]	*Se 'l viso mio a la terra si china*
53 [probably Dante's]	*Questa donna ch'andar mi fa pensoso*
54 [probably Dante's]	*Non v'accorgete voi d'un che·ssi more*
55 [probably Dante's]	*Io sento pianger l'anima nel core*
59	*Degli occhi di quella gentil mia dama*

Given the lack of explanation, it is difficult to interpret these rubrics. Do they indicate a hierarchy according to which the lyrics with no rubric are presumed the most certain, those "restored to Dante" a little less certain, and those that are "probably Dante's" still less certain? Perhaps.[62] But in this case, *Amore e monna Lagia* shares the advantage of silence with *Degli occhi di quella gentil mia dama*, a sonnet whose Dantean paternity is much less convincing. In his review of De Robertis' edition, Leonardi writes regarding *Degli occhi di quella gentil mia dama* that "the consensus of what is moreover a scant tradition fails to justify the authenticity of this 'awkward' sonnet" ("goffo" or "awkward" is Contini's word for *Degli occhi di quella gentil mia dama*), and concludes, "in sum, I would have left it among the poems of doubtful attribution" (p. 88).

If *Amore e monna Lagia* is printed here beside *Guido, i' vorrei*, it is because of the many considerations expressed over many years by Barbi, Contini, De Robertis, and others, and not because of the reattribution recently carried out by De Robertis. The transfer of eight lyrics from the doubtful to the canonical list will have to be studied and De Robertis' reasons will have to be scrutinized, text by text. When philologists have reached a widely shared consensus, on the basis of considerations that one hopes will be made transparent to all (it is unfortunately not rare for "philological" decisions to be based on considerations that are not strictly philological, but stylistic or ideological),[63] then we will be able to decide how to proceed.

---

61 For my reasons against accepting De Robertis' stylistic arguments for Dantean paternity of this *sonetto rinterzato*, see the introductory essay to *Se Lippo amico*.

62 So interprets Lino Leonardi, in "Nota sull'edizione critica delle *Rime* di Dante," pp. 63–113: "four sonnets are recovered from that Appendix and placed in the canon, but with the cautionary label 'probably Dante's'; three more sonnets and the trilingual canzone 18 *Aï faus ris* are more decisively 'restored to Dante,' as the label states however only for 18 and 34" (p. 86).

63 Other examples of ideological or interpretive rather than philological reasoning are De Robertis' choice of "Lippo" over "Lapo" in *Guido, i' vorrei* and his choice of "Licenza" over "Lisetta" in *Per quella via*; see the introductory essays to the poems in question. See too my discussion of De Robertis' stylistic reasons for accepting Dantean paternity of *Quando 'l consiglio* in the introductory essay to *Se Lippo amico*. More on this topic may be found in my "Editing Dante's *Rime* and Italian Cultural History," 2004, rpt. in *Dante and the Origins of Italian Literary Culture*, pp. 245–78.

* * *

Contini called *Amore e monna Lagia* "this obscure (but smiling) sonnet" (p. 229), and the sonnet is in fact difficult to interpret, above all because of its allusiveness. Like the sonnets exchanged between Dante and Forese Donati, *Amore e monna Lagia* gives the impression of being immersed in the ordinary quotidian flux of social life, in this case of a group of friends, and "presupposes that it is sufficient for the state of things to be known to those involved" (DR, ed. comm., p. 304). The result is that there are many questions to which it is not possible to respond. According to Contini, the presence of Lapo Gianni "is absolutely demanded by that of his friend, lady Lagia ... Dante and Lapo must therefore be on the one hand the author and on the other the unnamed protagonist of the sonnet" (p. 229). The unnamed protagonist is the "ser costui [certain sir]" (2) – who is thanked ironically for having caused the break-up ("che·nn'ha partiti [for parting us]" [3]) of the group that served Love, and whose name must remain "in oblio [out of mind]" (4):

> Amore e monna Lagia e Guido ed io
> possiamo ringraziar un ser costui
> che·nn'ha partiti sapete da cui
> (no·l vo' contar per averlo in oblio).
> > (*Amore e monna Lagia,* 1–4)

> [Guido, lady Lagia, Love and I
> must show a certain sir our gratitude
> for parting us from him, and you know who,
> though I won't say, to keep him out of mind.]

Lapo is thus responsible for "a general change of the situation and for the dissolution of a pact of fidelity and 'service' that bound the members of the group together in the name of Love" (DR, ed. comm., p. 304).

From *Amore e monna Lagia* emanates a trace "scent" of the life of the *brigata* – of the authentic social life of Duecento Florence – as also from *Sonar bracchetti*, *Volgete gli occhi*, and *Guido, i' vorrei*. It is interesting to note that the social group of this sonnet, like that of *Guido, i' vorrei* (and that of the frame-tale of the *Decameron*) is mixed-gender, composed of women and men, while the *brigata* of hunters in *Sonar bracchetti* is exclusively male.

The little bit of information offered regarding the members of the company piques our belated curiosity. The group that is dissolving because of "ser costui" consists of three members, "monna Lagia e Guido ed io [Guido, lady Lagia and I]" (1), who manifest three different behaviours. The woman takes back her heart from her "servant" ("ch'eran serventi di tal guisa a lui [who used to serve him with such loyalty]" [6]), and so is no longer to be numbered among the *fedeli d'amore*: "la donna saggia / che[d] in quel punto li ritolse il core [that lady then who prudently / reclaimed her heart]" (10–11). (Note the presence of a "saggia donna" also in *Amore 'l cor gentil sono una cosa*: "Bieltate appare in saggia donna pui [Then beauty in a worthy lady's seen]" [9].) Guido proves immune, in Contini's words, "from infatuation for the alleged god of love" (p. 230): "e Guido ancor, che·nn'è del tutto fore [and Guido next, who keeps his distance now]" (12). Only the author, "alone, would like to yield or still yields to the power of the one from whom the other characters named in the first verse are liberated" (Contini, p. 230): "ed io ancor che 'n sua vertute caggia [and I, although I fall beneath his spell]" (13). The yielding – literally "falling" ("caggia" from *cadere*) – to the power of Love is an old topos of Dante's.

The verse dedicated to Guido stands out above all: "e Guido ancor, che·nn'è del tutto fore [and Guido next, who keeps his distance now]" (12). It is one of those verses that has a strange hold on the reader of today, because it seems to capture in highly concentrated form the whole myth of Guido Cavalcanti, a myth still in the making at the time of the writing of *Amore e monna Lagia.* Standing alone in splendid isolation, "completely outside" ("del tutto fore"), marginalized, not part of the group, somewhat haughty with respect to communal endeavours:[64] all this, later brought to life in the story about Guido Cavalcanti in *Decameron* 6.9, a story featuring Guido's rejection of the *brigata* of Betto Brunelleschi, is already distilled and gathered into the early verse, written when the two poets were still "hanging out" – "e Guido ancor, che·nn'è del tutto fore."

The adverb "fore" – "outside" – distils the very essence of Cavalcanti: the poet whose most benign vision materializes in the form of alien, foreign creatures, literally "outsiders" or "foresette" (for Cavalcanti's *foresette*, see his poems *Era in penser d'amor* and *Gli occhi di quella gentil foresetta*, and the discussion of the role of the *foresette* in the introductory essay to *Cavalcando l'altr'ier*). Cavalcanti is the poet sent out of Tuscany, into the physical exile invoked in the famous *ballata Perch'i' no spero di tornar giammai*, a physical exile that corresponds to his existential exile and to the interior alienation of his poetry. He is the poet who exhorts Dante to flee "la noiosa gente" ("Solevanti spiacer persone molte, / tuttor fuggivi la noiosa gente [You once would treat crowds with contempt / and always fled from those who are

---

64 Frank O'Hara wonderfully captures the Cavalcantian persona in "A Poem in Envy of Cavalcanti" (*The Collected Poems of Frank O'Hara*, ed. Donald Allen [Berkeley: University of California Press, 1995]):

Oh! my heart, although it sounds better
in French, I must say in my native tongue
that I am sick with desire. To be, Guido,
a simple and elegant province all by myself
like you, would mean that a toss of my head,
a wink, a lurch against the nearest brick
had captured painful felicity and all its opaque
nourishment in a near and cosmic stanza, ah!
But I only wither to the earth, my personal
mess, and am unable to utter a good word.

mundane]" [*I' vegno 'l giorno a·tte*, 5–6]). He is the poet whom Dante himself "will hunt from the nest" ("caccerà del nido") (*Purg.* 11.99): will expel from the domestic circle of poet-friends that emerges from these sonnets.

Perhaps the psychological distance that separates the non-infatuated Guido of *Amore e monna Lagia e Guido ed io*, the Guido "che·nn'è del tutto fore," from the disillusioned Guido of canto 10 of the *Inferno*, is after all, from Dante's perspective, not so great. The haughty isolationist quality of being "del tutto fore" seems to have darkened over time in Dante's imagination, crystallizing ultimately into its infernal variant, "disdegno": "forse cui Guido vostro ebbe a disdegno [whom perhaps your Guido held in disdain]" (*Inf.* 10.63).[65]

20 (B D. I; C 59; DR 41)

Amore e monna Lagia e Guido ed io	Guido, lady Lagia, Love and I
possiamo ringraziar un ser costui	must show a certain sir our gratitude
che·nn'ha partiti sapete da cui	for parting us from him, and you know who,
4 (no·l vo' contar per averlo in oblio).	though I won't say, to keep him out of mind.
Poi questi tre più non v'hanno disio,	For these three wish to cling to him no more,
ch'eran serventi di tal guisa a lui,	who used to serve him with such loyalty
che veramente più di lor non fui	that even I was not more dutiful
8 imaginando ch'elli fosse iddio,	in thinking that he was indeed a god.
sia ringraziato Amor che se n'accorse	So let's give thanks to Love, who first perceived
primeramente; e poi la donna saggia	the truth, that lady then who prudently
11 che[d] in quel punto li ritolse il core;	reclaimed her heart from him just afterward,
e Guido ancor, che·nn'è del tutto fore;	and Guido next, who keeps his distance now;
ed io ancor che 'n sua vertute caggia:	and I, although I fall beneath his spell,
14 se poi mi piacque, no·l si crede forse.	how much I loved him no one will believe.

METRE: sonnet ABBA ABBA CDE EDC.

---

65 On Guido's *disdegno*, see Barolini, *Dante's Poets*, pp. 145–6.

21 Per una ghirlandetta

The commentators, De Robertis included, usually place this poem, a *ballata*, in a small cluster that also contains *Madonna, quel signor che voi portate* and *Deh, Vïoletta, che 'n ombra d'Amore*. The canzone-stanza *Madonna, quel signor* is traditionally included in this group on the strength of the "soave fiore [delightful flower]" of line 15, but its decidedly Sicilian and Occitan-inspired manner has convinced me to move it forward. *Per una ghirlandetta* and *Deh, Vïoletta* remain together in my order, and in a position in which they can bear witness to the increasing importance of Guido Cavalcanti's poetry in the production of the young Dante.

Cavalcanti has been present in all the introductory essays from *No me poriano* on. If in *No me poriano* Cavalcanti is glimpsed only briefly (in the term "scanoscenti"), *Sonar bracchetti* renders homage to him quite explicitly: the syntactic form of the octave of *Sonar bracchetti* is indebted to Cavalcanti's *Biltà di donna*. *Volgete gli occhi* contains some Cavalcantian moves, and as for *Guido i' vorrei* we need only cite the first word that announces to the whole world the bond between Dante and the man who in the *Vita Nuova* is called "primo de li miei amici [the first of my friends]" (*VN* III.14 [2.1]).

Per una ghirlandetta and *Deh, Vïoletta* are both *ballate*. The very form of the *ballata* can be considered an homage from Dante to Guido: while the latter cultivated the *ballata* (Guido wrote, in a collection of fifty-two poems, a full eleven of them) and avoided the canzone, for Dante the opposite is true. The *ballata* is a rather marginal form for Dante; in a collection of at least eighty-eight texts, there are only six.

Per una ghirlandetta takes up from Cavalcanti's *ballate* both their motif of the lady associated with the world of flowers and spring and their delicate musicality. In particular, we hear echoes of *Fresca rosa novella*, a *ballata* that is usually attributed to the young Cavalcanti, and which, according to one of the primary witnesses, Chigiano L VIII 305, was dedicated to Dante. In the first lines of this poem, which identify the lady with newness and rebirth – "Fresca rosa novella, / piacente primavera [Fresh new rose, / delightful spring]" (1–2) – it seems that Dante may have seen a *senhal* for Cavalcanti's lady, as suggested by the *Vita Nuova*: "E lo nome di questa donna era Giovanna, salvo che per la sua bieltade, secondo che altri crede, imposto l'era nome Primavera [And this woman's name was Giovanna, except that she was given the name Primavera, or Spring – because of her beauty, as others believe]" (*Vita Nuova* XXIV.3 [15.3]).

The lady whom Dante sings about in *Per una ghirlandetta* is called Fioretta: "S'ïo sarò là dove sia / Fioretta mia bella a sentire [If I should find myself / where my fair

Fioret may hear]" (11–12). The fact that she is not anonymous has given rise to much conjecture, including whether Fioretta and Violetta are the same person, if she is the first or second screen-lady, and so on. While we are not able to recover a historical reality for these ladies, we can observe that Dante's imagination in this period of his life is crowded with female presences and that two of their various *senhal*s – Fioretta and Violetta – have clear Cavalcantian connotations, echoing as they do the floral delicacy of "Fresca rosa novella / piacente primavera."

The feminine presences in Dante's lyrics are existentially individuated through the use of proper names or words that function as names: Fioretta, Violetta, Beatrice, Lisetta, the *donna gentile*, the *pargoletta*, the *pietra*. These are names that bear poetic testimony: they trace a meandering path that includes the more Cavalcantian-inspired *senhal*s like Fioretta and Violetta and the more original Dantean choice of Beatrice. Like Fioretta and Violetta, Beatrice is a very early name in Dante's canon, appearing in the youthful canzone *Lo doloroso amor* (see the introductory essay to *Lo doloroso amor* for discussion of the name "Beatrice").

The diminutives of *Per una ghirlandetta* – "ghirlandetta" is repeated two times, then "angiolel," "Fioretta," "parolette," "novelle" – constitute another Cavalcantian stylistic feature (less present in *Deh Vïoletta*, where the only diminutive is the addressee's name). Dante is echoing the relatively optimistic, lightly sensual Cavalcanti of *Fresca rosa novella* and *In un boschetto trova' pasturella*; the importance of the latter *ballata* for the *Commedia*, especially for the earthly paradise and for the figure of Matelda, who appears "scegliendo fior da fiore [choosing flower from flower]" (*Purg.* 28.41), is well established.[66] We think also of Lia, who makes a garland for herself in the dream of *Purgatorio* 27: "movendo intorno / le belle mani a farmi una ghirlanda [moving around my lovely hands to make myself a garland]" (*Purg.* 27.101–2).

Matelda and Lia are imagined by Dante as lyric ladies transposed by a number of registers, and their floral activities are part of constructing them on the lyric template. In the *Commedia* the noun *ghirlanda* – a fundamental motif of the lady in love poetry, as we saw in Dante da Maiano's *Provedi, saggio* – appears as an attribute of Lia and then again to describe the wise men in the heaven of the sun, who are fascinatingly feminized and lyricized by being likened to a *ghirlanda* shortly after being compared to ladies who pause while dancing.[67]

Typical of Dante's *stil novo* are both the adjective *umile*, in the sense of *dolce/soave* (sweet/mild), which refers to the angel who flies above the garland of flowers worn by the lady (garlands were a typical ornament of Florentine women, above all in May Day celebrations) – "e sovr'a·llei vidi volare / un angiolel d'amore umìle

---

66 See the discussion of *In un boschetto* and the earthly paradise in Barolini, *Dante's Poets*, chap. 2, pp. 148–53.

67 Of the *Commedia*'s four uses of *ghirlanda* (three in the singular and one plural), two apply to the wise men in the heaven of the sun (*Par.* 10.92 and *Par.* 12.20).

[and over it / I saw an angel full of gentle love]" (6–7) – and the verb *laudare*, present in the angel's song: "e 'l suo cantar sottile / dicea: 'Chi·mmi vedrà / lauderà 'l mio signore' [and singing gracefully / he said: 'Whoever looks on me / will praise my noble lord']" (8–10). The concept of praise will be of primary importance for the *Vita Nuova* and for Dante's *stil novo*, which sets itself to praise *madonna* rather than asking for the *guiderdone* (reward) of the courtly tradition. In *Per una ghirlandetta* the "angiolel d'amore" (little angel of love), whose very existence is a declaration of divine goodness, inspires the onlooker to the praise of God. In the later *stil novo* poems we will see transferred from *angiolel* to lady both the quality of humility and the sacramental function – worthy of praise – of being the visible sign of invisibile grace.

The image of the *ghirlandetta* suggests to the reader of this *ballata* the idea of circularity, later to be exploited by Dante when he refers to the circles of wise men in the heaven of the sun as "due ghirlande" (*Par.* 12.20). A circular form is encountered immediately in the *ripresa* – "Per una ghirlandetta / ch'i' vidi, mi farà / sospirare ogni fiore [For a little garland / that I saw / all flowers make me sigh]" (1–3) – and again at the start of the first strophe: "I' vidi a voi, donna, portare / ghirlandetta di fior' gentile [I saw you, Lady, wearing / a garland made of lovely flowers]" (4–5). The angel who flies above the circlet of flowers worn by *madonna*, and who sings with a gentle voice, is a distant prefiguration of the "circulata melodia" of *Paradiso* 23, where the archangel Gabriel sings and circles the Virgin: "'Io sono amore angelico, che giro / l'alta letizia' ... Così la circulata melodia / si sigillava ['I am angelic love, who circles the high joy' ... In this way the circling melody sealed itself]" (*Par.* 23.103–4, 109–10).

Of the lady in *Per una ghirlandetta* it is said that, "per crescer disire [to increase desire]" (a locution that recalls "crescesse il disio [our desire ... would grow]" in *Guido, i' vorrei*), she "will come / crowned by Love": "verrà / coronata d'Amore" (16–17). In the sonnet *Tanto gentile* the lady will be, in a similar rhetorical locution, "d'umiltà vestuta [dressed in humility]" (6).

If Fioretta seems in some sense to incarnate the flowers that adorn her, almost as if she were Botticelli's Primavera, the same can be said about the *ballata* that pays her honour, it too made of flowers: "Le parolette mie novelle / che di fior[i] fatt'han ballata [These freshly minted words of mine, / which knit a ballad out of flowers]" (18–19). The word "ballata" recalls the technical term "sonetto" in *Se Lippo amico* and in *Sonetto, se Meuccio*; the "vesta" of line 21 recalls the musical dress of *Se Lippo amico*. For Dante the implicit meditation on his own poetic activity is never out of place, not even in the wispiest, most delicate lyric. And in fact the confusion generated by the "parolette mie novelle / che di fior[i] fatt'han ballata" is intriguing: De Robertis' questions, "Are they a *ballata* on the theme of flowers? Are they flowers in the form of a *ballata*?" (ed. comm., p. 269), suggest that once again our *fabbro* was playing with border-crossing, in this case the border between the flowers of the *ghirlandetta* and the *ballata* that sings them.

21 (B LVI; FB 21; C 10; DR 28)

Per una ghirlandetta	For a little garland
ch'i' vidi, mi farà	that I saw
3 sospirare ogni fiore.	all flowers make me sigh.
I' vidi a voi, donna, portare	I saw you, Lady, wearing
ghirlandetta di fior' gentile,	a garland made of lovely flowers,
e sovr'a·llei vidi volare	and over it
7 un angiolel d'amore umìle;	I saw an angel full of gentle love;
e 'l suo cantar sottile	and singing gracefully
dicea: "Chi·mmi vedrà	he said: "Whoever looks on me
10 lauderà 'l mio signore."	will praise my noble lord."
S'ïo sarò là dove sia	If I should find myself
Fioretta mia bella a sentire,	where my fair Fioret may hear,
allor dirò la donna mia	I'll say my lady wears
14 che port'in testa i mie' sospire.	my sighs around her head.
Ma per crescer disire	But to increase desire
[la] mia donna verrà	my lady will come
17 coronata d'Amore.	crowned by Love.
Le parolette mie novelle	These freshly minted words of mine,
che di fior[i] fatt'han ballata,	which knit a ballad out of flowers,
per leggiadria ci hanno tolt'elle	have taken as an ornament
21 una vesta ch'altrui fu data:	a dress another was to wear:
però siate pregata,	and so I now request,
qual uom la canterà,	whoever sings its tune,
24 che·lli facciate onore.	please greet him graciously.

METRE: *ballata* with *ripresa* xyz and three stanzas of seven verses, with rhyme scheme ab ab byz. The *fronte* is four *novenari* (2 + 2), and the *volta* is three *settenari*.

22 Deh, Vïoletta, che 'n ombra d'Amore

This *ballata* is less delicately ornamental and more passionate than *Per una ghirlandetta*. With the exception of the lady's name, Violetta, which is mentioned two times, the floral motif is absent and now the lover, instead of "sospirare ogni fiore" (sighing at all flowers) (*Per una ghirlandetta,* 3), more conventionally asks the lady to have "pietà del cor che tu feristi, / che spera in te e disïando more [pity on the heart that you did wound, / which trusts in you and dies now of desire]" (*Deh, Vïoletta,* 3–4).

The dominant motif in *Deh, Vïoletta* is the fire of love. With her beauty, "tuo piacer" in verse 7 (Francesca too uses "piacer" in the sense of "beauty" in *Inf.* 5.104), Violetta has ignited a fire in the lover: with an "atto di spirito cocente [flaming spirit's forceful act]" she has aroused hope in him: "foco mettesti dentro in la mia mente / col tuo piacer ch'io vidi; / poi con atto di spirito cocente / creasti spene [you've set my mind ablaze through beauty / that I saw in you; / and through a flaming spirit's forceful act, / you brought forth hope]" (6–9). Violetta's "atto di spirito cocente" evokes *Donne ch'avete intelletto d'amore*, where from Beatrice's eyes "escono spirti d'amore inflammati [issue spirits aflame with love]" (52). Maintaining the same metaphorical system, the poet exhorts his lady: "ma drizza gli occhi al gran disio che m'arde [look at the great desire that burns in me]" (12).

Perhaps the most interesting aspect of this poem is in the characterization of Violetta as possessing "more than human form": "Vïoletta, in forma più che umana [Violetta, surpassing human form]" (5). More than a generic "*stil novo*-style transhumanizing" (Contini, p. 43), we have here a reference to the Cavalcantian *ballata* that I singled out as a point of reference for both *Per una ghirlandetta* and *Deh, Vïoletta*. At the end of the second strophe of *Fresca rosa novella* Cavalcanti places his lady in a superhuman setting with the following rhetorical question: "tanto adorna parete / ch'eo non saccio contare: / e chi poria pensare – oltra natura? [you appear so lovely / that I cannot convey it: / and who could think – beyond nature?]" (29–31). Then, using the Provençal technique of *coblas capfinidas*, in which the first words of the new stanza take up the last words of the previous one, Cavalcanti starts off the third stanza by repeating "oltra natura" and adding "umana," underscoring in this way the idea of the supernatural lady: "Oltra natura umana / vostra fina piagenza [Beyond human nature / your graceful loveliness]" (32–3).

If it is true that these early *ballate* of Dante's are variants of Cavalcanti's *Fresca rosa novella*, it is also instructive to note the points of divergence. Domenico De Robertis, in his commentary on Cavalcanti, notes that *Fresca rosa novella* "with the three following sonnets represents a phase – call it auroral – in which the discovery of love does not involve ascertaining its passionate nature: the only 'difficulty' is the inconceivability of the lady's worth" (p. 3). In other words, in these early poems the tragic and negative vision of Cavalcantian love does not yet appear. The only block to his love at this stage is that the cognitive capacity of the poet is not up to comprehending the lady's existential value, precisely because one's thought cannot go beyond human nature, to a supernatural domain: "e chi poria pensare – oltra natura?"

But this difficulty in fact already contains *in nuce* the whole Cavalcantian problematic, which is epistemological, rotating around the word (non-)*canoscenza*. The Cavalcantian lady, even when she is not "fera" (fierce), remains in any case inaccessible. The basic problem for Cavalcanti is always one of an insurmountable epistemological distance. His lady does indeed have value and worth and power, in fact she has "troppo valore [too much worth/power]" (cf. *Io non pensava che lo cor giammai:* "Tu non camperai, / ché troppo è lo valor di costei forte [You won't survive / because this woman's power is much too great]" [7–8]). Precisely because it is "troppo," excessive with respect to the human capacity of the poet, her power is unattainable and incomprehensible, unusable by him. From the poet's point of view, the lady's power serves only to emphasize his epistemological failure.

In Dante's poetry a completely different situation obtains. Armed with peerless epistemological vigour, Dante does not hesitate to imagine that his lady is "in forma più che umana" and also that – undeterred by her superhuman status – he can have access to her. Moreover, he can reach her not only when she is alive but also when she is dead: *Oltra la spera che più larga gira*, the last sonnet of the *Vita Nuova*, imagines that a "sospiro ch'esce del mio core [sigh that issues from my heart]" (2) passes beyond the crystalline sphere to reach his lady. The opening of *Oltra la spera* seems like a response to Cavalcanti's question. One asks: "e chi poria pensare – oltra natura?" The other responds, repeating the keyword "oltra": "Oltra la spera che più larga gira / passa 'l sospiro ch'esce del mio core [Beyond the sphere that makes the widest sweep / proceeds the sigh that issues from my heart]" (1–2).

There is no trace in *Deh, Vïoletta* of the negative implications of the superhuman nature of Cavalcanti's lady. The cognitive deficiencies of the poet with respect to the power of his lady, to which *Fresca rosa novella* clearly alludes, are not present in *Deh, Vïoletta*, where the fact that the lady possesses "forma più che umana" seems not to pose any obstacle to her lover. In fact, the fire created by her creates hope in him.

22 (B LVIII; C 12; FB 23; DR 29)

Deh, Vïoletta, che 'n ombra d'Amore	Ah, Violetta, you who in Love's form
nelli occhi miei sì sùbito apparisti,	appeared before my eyes so suddenly,
aggi pietà del cor che tu feristi,	take pity on the heart that you did wound,
4 che spera in te e disïando more.	which trusts in you and dies now of desire.
Tu, Vïoletta, in forma più che umana	You, Violetta, surpassing human form,

foco mettesti dentro in la mia mente	have set a fire ablaze within my mind
col tuo piacer ch'io vidi;	through beauty that I saw;
poi con atto di spirito cocente	and through a flaming spirit's forceful act,
creasti spene che 'n parte mi sana	you brought forth hope that heals me partially
10 là dove tu mi ridi.	when you just smile at me.
Deh non guardare perch'a·llei mi fidi,	Ah, disregard the fact I trust in hope,
ma drizza gli occhi al gran disio che m'arde,	look at the great desire that burns in me,
ché mille donne già, per esser tarde,	for many ladies, being slow to act,
14 sentit'han pena de l'altrui dolore.	have known the pain of others' suffering.

METRE: *ballata*, with *ripresa* XYYX and a single stanza of ten verses (eight hendecasyllables and two *settenari*), with rhyme scheme ABc BAc CDDX. The *fronte* is six verses (3 + 3) and the *volta* is four verses.

23 Cavalcando l'altr'ier per un cammino

This sonnet, placed by Dante in *Vita Nuova* IX (4), describes a journey and an encounter between the lover and Love. Perhaps because of the journey motif, its pace is more narrative than lyrical. The lover is unhappy because he finds the journey that he is taking unpleasant; he is "pensoso de l'andar che mi sgradia [taking little pleasure as (he goes)]" (2). The sonnet does not explain why the journey is disagreeable, but one presumes that the cause of suffering is the distance from the lady about whom Love speaks: "e disse: 'Io vegno di lontana parte, / ov'era lo tuo cor per mio volere; / e recolo a servir novo piacere' [and (he) said: "I've travelled from a distant land / where your heart dwelled by my command; / I bring it back to serve another love]" (10–12). After the two initial verses that describe the situation and the lover's state of mind, almost the whole rest of the sonnet is dedicated to the description of Love, who is unusually represented "in abito leggier di peregrino [attired in simple clothes that pilgrims wear]" (4), and to the words that Love spoke.

Dante adds to the theme of absence another very important theme, that of the potential transition to a new object of desire, to what Beatrice will later call a "novità," when she chastises Dante for having desired "o pargoletta / o altra novità con sì breve uso [either a girl or some other novelty with such a short-lived use]" (*Purg.* 31.59–60). The issue of "the new" – *il novo* – is fundamental to Dante's thinking:[68] a subset of the theme of desire, it focuses on the volatility of the will, on the changeableness of desire that transfers itself from one object to another, new object, here indicated by the words "novo piacere" (new pleasure) (12). This is the problem that Dante considers important enough to discuss with his friend Cino da Pistoia in *Epistle* 3 (dated 1303–6), in which he responds in the affirmative to the question "utrum de passione in passionem possit anima transformari [whether the soul can move from one passion to another]" (*Ep.* 3.2). The question of how the soul ought to behave in the face of a "novo piacere" will occupy a fundamental place in Dante's ethical system, first in his lyrics and finally in the *Commedia*. The "novo piacere" in verse 12 of *Cavalcando l'altr'ier per un cammino* anticipates the "altra novità con sì breve uso" of *Purgatorio* 31.60.

Cavalcando l'altr'ier is the sonnet with which Dante inaugurates the manifestly Cavalcantian section of the *Vita Nuova*, after having traversed Sicilian-Guittonian territory and before arriving at the Guinizzellian new world with the discovery of the

---

68 For the new in Dante, see Barolini, *The Undivine Comedy*, chap. 2, "Infernal Incipits: The Poetics of the New," esp. pp. 21–6.

new style. The most explicit textual presence of Cavalcanti in the *Vita Nuova* is in chapters XIV (7) through XVI (9), and is concentrated in the three sonnets belonging to the "gabbo [mocking]" episode, sonnets strewn with anxious "spiriti," trembling souls, and inner breakdowns. The story of Cavalcanti in the *Vita Nuova* starts earlier, however, back at *Cavalcando l'altr'ier* and at the poem that follows it, *Ballata, i' voi che tu ritrovi Amore* (*Vita Nuova* XII [5]), texts whose first words – "Cavalcando," "Ballata" – immediately testify to the presence of Cavalcanti.[69]

The presence of Cavalcanti is felt in the unusual presentation of the figure of Love, who is "attired in simple clothes that pilgrims wear"[70] and has a miserable appearance, like a lord deposed from his lordship: "Ne la sembianza mi parea meschino, / come avesse perduto segnoria; / e sospirando pensoso venia, / per non veder la gente, a capo chino [By his appearance he seemed destitute, / as if he'd lost his due authority; / and sighing in distress he came along, / his head bowed down so others couldn't see]" (5–8). The figure of dejection that we find here corresponds to the Cavalcantian imaginary. Fascinatingly, however, Dante has constructed the figure of Love, not on the basis of Cavalcantian Amore, a despotic and fearsome figure, but on that of the Cavalcantian *lover*, who is precisely dejected, miserable, and dismayed (*sbigottito*: the adjective that describes Love in the prose of the *Vita Nuova* IX [4]), prey to an interior fragmentation that destines him to be forever in search of himself – forever a "pilgrim" in an existential "misadventure" (the signature Cavalcantian word is "disaventura").

To comprehend the stand taken in the *Vita Nuova* with regard to Cavalcanti's ideology, it is necessary to understand that his radical negativity, displayed in theoretical dress in the canzone *Donna me prega*, manifests in his poetry also through an insistent recourse to mediation: the lady, whom Cavalcanti in *Donna me prega* proclaims unknowable for epistemological reasons, in the sonnets and *ballate* is simply rendered unknowable by the presence of various other creatures, like the "giovane donna di Tolosa [the young lady of Tolouse]" and the "foresette nove [young country girls]," who put her out of the picture.[71] Even though these presences are benign in themselves, they have the effect of making the possibility of "knowledge" ("canoscenza" is another signature Cavalcantian term) still more remote, by pushing the source of knowledge and epistemological vigour (the lady) still further away. For example, in the *ballata Era in penser d'amor quand'i' trovai* "due foresette nove" screen "la Mandetta," who in her turn screens the original lady (according to the son-

---

69 "In my opinion, the first words of each composition – 'Cavalcando' and 'Ballata' – are intended to refer to Cavalcanti, one directly to his name ("Cavalcando" is a *hapax* in the *Vita Nuova* and Dante's lyric production in general, and is especially striking in its initial capitalized position), and the other to his favorite genre, the *ballata*" (Barolini, *Dante's Poets,* p. 137).

70 On Love's clothing see the long note in Barbi-Maggini, pp. 45–50.

71 See the introductory essay to *Amore e monna Lagia* for the deep significance of "foresette" – etymologically connected to "fore," outside – within the economy of a Cavalcantian poetics of outsideness.

net *Una giovane donna di Tolosa*), thus placing the poet at two removes from the first catalyst of his desire.

We find an analogous situation in *Cavalcando l'alt'ier*, where Love suggests to the poet that he turn to the "novo piacere" in a manner that is very similar to what happens in Cavalcanti's *ballata* with the "foresette nove." The result – according to the account of the *Vita Nuova* prose – is extremely negative: the loss of Beatrice's greeting.

The prose of *Vita Nuova* IX (4) narrates how Dante, going away from Beatrice, encounters Love, who tells him that it will be necessary to transfer his heart from the first to the second screen-lady. The "novo piacere" of the sonnet in this way becomes the *Vita Nuova*'s second screen-lady. The change of perspective from the sonnet to the *libello* requires a recontextualization of the underlying ethical issue. Instead of the variability of desire, the *Vita Nuova* instructs us that the topic of the sonnet is the simulation of desire: "simulato amore [simulated love]" (*VN* IX.6 [4.6]). The screen-ladies, whose function is to screen or protect from others' eyes the love that Dante has for Beatrice, are creatures imported from the sociology and ideology of the court; they come from the courtly world of *lauzengiers*, the spies and eavesdroppers who create the need to simulate one's passion. The narrative of the first part of the *Vita Nuova* is full of such courtly imports, because Dante has set himself the task of reproducing and unmasking one by one the various empty and artificial games of courtly love. As part of this overall strategy "simulato amore" is first performed and then promptly unmasked, insofar as the simulation leads to an undesirable outcome: the result of all these games will be not to help Dante but to drive Beatrice to deny him her greeting.

Of all this material added to the sonnet by the prose of the *Vita Nuova* – of screen-ladies, simulated love, Beatrice – there is not a trace in *Cavalcando l'altr'ier*. Or better, there is only an indirect trace, through Cavalcanti: Cavalcanti and his ideology are present in the sonnet, and Cavalcanti had drawn on the Occitan and courtly world, above all from the *pastorella* genre, in his making of the "foresette nove," precursors of Dante's "novo piacere."

Dante found in *Cavalcando l'altr'ier* a vehicle through which he could introduce Cavalcanti into the *Vita Nuova*'s program to deconstruct traditional courtly values. The Cavalcantian move of populating his poems with creatures benign in themselves, but whose mediating presence contributes to the tragic unknowableness of the original desired object, thus comes to be part of the wrong way indicated here: the way of "simulato amore," which the lover in this section of the *Vita Nuova* pursues, is made of *novi piaceri* similar to Cavalcanti's *foresette*. Dante gives a name to this path – "lo cammino de li sospiri [the way of sighs]" (*VN* X.1 [5.1]) – which is tantamount to saying "the way of Cavalcantian poetics."

I began by observing that this sonnet's character is more narrative than lyrical, and conclude by noting the narratological features that prefigure the *Commedia*: not only certain words and phrases ("per un cammino" [down a road], "peregrino" [pilgrim], "in mezzo de la via" [in the middle of the road]) but modalities of narration such as the use of the gerund ("Cavalcando" [While riding]). Most important in prefiguring the *Commedia* is the construction of the narrative background with the imperfect tense ("sgradia" [was feeling bad], "parea" [seemed], "venia" [was coming]), against which the key events of the sonnet are etched in the past absolute ("trovai Amore" [I found Love], "Quando mi vide" [When he saw me], "mi chiamò per nome" [he called me by name]). From the "novo piacere" of *Cavalcando l'altr'ier per un cammino* we move to the "nuovo e mai non fatto cammino di questa vita [new and never travelled road of this life]" (*Conv.* 4.12.15) to arrive at the "poetics of the new" of the *Commedia.*

23 (B VIII; FB 20; *VN* IX.9–12 [4.9–12])

Cavalcando l'altr'ier per un cammino,
pensoso de l'andar che mi sgradia,
trovai Amore in mezzo de la via
4   in abito leggier di peregrino.
Ne la sembianza mi parea meschino,
come avesse perduto segnoria;
e sospirando pensoso venia,
8   per non veder la gente, a capo chino.
    Quando mi vide, mi chiamò per nome,
e disse: "Io vegno di lontana parte,
11   ov'era lo tuo cor per mio volere;
e recolo a servir novo piacere."
Allora presi di lui sì gran parte,
14   ch'elli disparve, e non m'accorsi come.

While riding down a road the other day
and taking little pleasure as I went
I came on Love before me in the road
attired in simple clothes that pilgrims wear.
By his appearance he seemed destitute,
as if he'd lost his due authority;
and sighing in distress he came along,
his head bowed down so others couldn't see.
    When he saw me, he called me by my name
and said: "I've travelled from a distant land
where your heart dwelled by my command;
I bring it back to serve another love."
And then I took from Love so much of him
he disappeared, without my knowing how.

METRE: sonnet ABBA ABBA CDE EDC.

24 Ballata, i' voi che tu ritrovi Amore

The longest of Dante's six *ballate*, *Ballata, i' voi* is the only *ballata* included in the *Vita Nuova*, where Dante places it in chapter XII (5). With the sonnet *Cavalcando l'altr'ier* that precedes it and the four sonnets that follow, it is part of an arc of texts that together constitute the most manifestly Cavalcantian section of the *Vita Nuova*. In the case of this composition, the Cavalcantian turn is further marked by the presence of a genre much favoured by Guido, as is underscored by the first word, which is both technical and metapoetic: "Ballata."

However, differently from the sonnets that follow, *Ballata, i' voi* is not an especially Cavalcantian poem; it is rather a generic courtly lyric. As discussed in the essay on *Cavalcando l'altr'ier*, Dante in the first part of the *Vita Nuova* constructs a plot that dramatizes the failure of courtly values: so long as the protagonist of the *Vita Nuova* behaves according to such values, participating for example in a "simulated love" for the screen-ladies, he will be blocked, incapable of setting out on the new path that he finds first after being challenged about his love by certain unnamed Florentine ladies, loses during the encounter with the *donna gentile*, and finds again at the end of the *libello*.

The various Occitan genres that are utilized by Dante in the first part of the *Vita Nuova* are inserted into the prose frame as emblems of an outworn ideology. We have already seen that the sonnet *Piangete, amanti* belongs to the Occitan genre of lamentation or *planh*. *Ballata, i' voi* openly declares its provenance from the Occitan *escondig*: the *ballata* presents itself with Love before *madonna* "sì che la scusa mia, la qual tu cante, / ragioni poi con lei lo mio segnore [so that my Lord can then explain to her / the crux of my defence, which you will sing]" (3–4). Saying that the *ballata* sings "my defence," "la scusa mia" (and "scusa" occurs again at line 20), Dante is informing us that this poem belongs to the courtly genre in which the lover defends himself from slanderous gossip.

To *Ballata, i' voi* is entrusted the task of calming the indignation of *madonna* ("di me adirata [annoyed with me]" [12]), and explaining to her that, even if Love had forced the poet to look at other women ("li fece altra guardare [made him look at someone else]" [23]), his love for her remains unchanged. Here we see the theme of the will's fickleness and variability already discussed in connection with *Cavalcando l'altr'ier*. The poet, however, declares he never had a change of heart: "non mutò 'l core" (24). His heart has preserved a fidelity so staunch – "sì fermata fede" (26) – that his every thought has prodded him to serve her: "che 'n voi servir l'ha 'mpronto onne pensero [that all his thoughts compel (his) serving you]" (27).

The lexicon of *Ballata, i' voi*, with its insistence on *servire*, to serve ("servire" [27], "servidore" [34], "servo" [40]), reflects its courtly provenance: the *ballata* goes to *madonna* "sì cortesemente [so courteously]" (5). Testifying to Occitan influence is also the conspicuous Provençalism and *hapax* "sdonnei," in line 36. *Sdonneare* is the opposite of *donneare*, which derives from Provençal *domnejar*, that is, "to court, to be with ladies in a courtly manner." The verb *donneare* is present again in the canzone dedicated to courtly morality, *Poscia ch'Amor*; Dante will use it finally twice in *Paradiso*, where we find "La mente innamorata, che donnea / con la mia donna sempre [The mind in love that ever amorously courts my lady]" (*Par.* 27.88–9) and "La Grazia, che donnea / con la tua mente [Grace, which amorously courts your mind]" (*Par.* 24.118–19). The use of courtly *donneare* in *Paradiso*, by now fully theologized, has its distant origin in line 36 of *Ballata, i' voi*. For the courtly lexicon of *Paradiso*, see also the discussion of *leggiadria* in *O voi che per la via d'Amor passate*.

If we consider this *ballata* in isolation, we find a poem whose courtly formulas harbour the theme of the heart's volatility, which in this case touches on the theme of simulation. As we noted in the discussion of *Cavalcanto l'altr'ier*, these themes, both fundamentally ethical, will have a long history in Dante's poetry. If instead we consider *Ballata, i' voi* as a way station in the Cavalcantian section of the *Vita Nuova*, we come back to the problem of mediation, as discussed with respect to *Cavalcando l'altr'ier*: Cavalcanti adopts the presence of mediating figures as obstacles to "immediate" (unmediated) contact with the lady, which is to say, as obstacles to immediate/unmediated contact with *canoscenza*. In this part of the *Vita Nuova* Dante dramatizes the crisis of mediation, presented in such a way as to implicate not only courtly culture in general but Cavalcanti in particular.

Before arriving at *Ballata, i' voi* the *Vita Nuova* prose is carefully stocked with phrases and words dear to Guido. For example, to describe the effect of Beatrice's greeting Dante speaks of the "spirito d'amore," which, "distruggendo tutti li altri spiriti sensitivi, pingea fuori li deboletti spiriti del viso [destroying all the other spirits of the sensitive soul, would drive out the weak spirits of sight]" (*VN* XI.2 [5.5]). De Robertis notes that this experience is described "according to the Cavalcantian model and by way of the typical mechanics of the 'spirits' in the sonnet *Con l'altre donne*," and that "the expression *li deboletti spiriti* [the weak spirits] harkens back to Guido's sonnet *Voi che per li occhi*" (*VN*, p. 70). Immediately after, the theme of mediation is broached: Love, we are told, is not "tal mezzo" – such a mediator – that he can temper "la intollerabile beatitudine [the unbearably powerful bliss]" of Beatrice's greeting (*VN* XI.3 [5.6]). Gorni notes with respect to "intollerabile" that it is "a synthetic definition of a state that Cavalcanti describes in *Veggio negli occhi*" (*VN*, p. 53). The "soverchio di dolcezza [excess sweetness]" (*VN* XI.3 [5.6]) provoked by the greeting features another "Cavalcantian word" (De Robertis, *VN*, p. 71): in *Io non pensava* Cavalcanti uses the phrase "soverchio de lo su' valore [excess of her worth/ power]" (49) to indicate the excessive – hence intolerable and inaccessible – worth of *madonna*.

This concept is fundamental for Cavalcanti: in the same canzone Love declares, "Tu non camperai / ché troppo è lo valor di costei forte [You won't survive / because this woman's worth/power is much too great]" (*Io non pensava,* 7–8). Far from helping its devotee, the excessive and supernatural *valore* of the Cavalcantian lady constitutes the obstacle that blocks the lover's search: her *troppo valore* functions in relation to him as an obstacle that is harmful and indeed (as testified by "Tu non camperai") deadly.

The Cavalcantian lady possesses *troppo valore* and so needs to be mediated, as in the *Vita Nuova* Love serves as a "mezzo" – mediator, medium – between Dante and Beatrice. But Dante's path will bring him to an entirely different destination, to a system radically opposed to that of Cavalcanti. In Dante's system the lady is a *beatrice*, one who blesses: that is, not only is she unmediated and thus im-mediate but she herself functions as mediator, giving access to and knowledge of a reality even more vast and significant than she. The Love who commands Dante to use *Ballata, i' voi* as a "mezzo," an intermediary – "Queste parole fa che siano quasi un **mezzo** [Make it so that your words are a kind of intermediary]" – because Beatrice might become indignant if he addressed her "immediatamente" – "sì che tu non parli a lei **immediatamente** [so that you do not speak to her directly]" (*VN* XII.8 [5.15]) – is a Cavalcantian Love who gives Cavalcantian advice. The advice given by this Love is wrong. It is discredited in the *Vita Nuova*, and of course in the *Commedia*: as we know, in the *Commedia* Dante speaks to Beatrice "immediatamente."

I will add that, when Dante goes beyond the courtly norm that it is discourteous to address the lady directly, not only does he give freedom to speak to himself but he also gives it to her: the Beatrice of the *Commedia* is anomalous also inasmuch as she is an erstwhile lyric lady who speaks. There is a first hint of this *Beatrix loquax* in the *Vita Nuova* not long after this *ballata*, where certain speaking ladies (an oxymoron in the courtly tradition, where young shepherd girls speak, but never ladies) liberate Dante from courtly ideology. As Beatrice will do in the *Commedia* – where she declares, "amor mi mosse, che mi fa *parlare* [love moves me, making me *speak*]" (*Inf.* 2.72)[72] – the Florentine ladies in *Vita Nuova* XVIII (10) speak in order to offer greater access to knowledge, to spur Dante on to a higher level of understanding.

But we are getting too far ahead of ourselves. Returning to *Ballata, i' voi*, it is important to note that this is the first poem in the *libello* that, according to the account of the *Vita Nuova*, had been written specifically for Beatrice. Let me conclude by affirming in lapidary fashion what Barbi, writing at a different critical moment, had to

---

72 On the importance of this *parlare* see my "Notes Toward a Gendered History of Italian Literature, with a Discussion of Dante's *Beatrix Loquax*," in *Dante and the Origins of Italian Literary Culture*, pp. 371–3: "In this declaration that love moved her and makes her speak, Dante both conjures Beatrice's past and scripts for her a radically new future. This future, which will unfold in the *Commedia*, is contained in the verb *parlare*, a verb betokening an activity utterly alien from the agenda of the lyric lady" (p. 371).

use six pages to explain (Barbi-Maggini, pp. 54–60): there is no reason to think that *Ballata, i' voi* was actually written for the *gentilissima*. As we have discussed, the *ballata*, if taken on its own, outside the context of the prose, is not even a particularly *stil novo* composition. It lends itself very well, however, being an *escondig*, to the task assigned it within the economy of the *Vita Nuova*, which is to create another occasion to try (and to fail) to build a relationship with *madonna* according to the outdated schemas of the old courtly ideology.

24 (B IX; FB 24; *VN* XII.10–15 [5.17–22])

Ballata, i' voi che tu ritrovi Amore,	My ballad, I request you seek out Love
e con lui vade a madonna davante,	and with him join my lady's company,
sì che la scusa mia, la qual tu cante,	so that my Lord can then explain to her
4 ragioni poi con lei lo mio segnore.	the crux of my defence, which you will sing.
Tu vai, ballata, sì cortesemente,	Your conduct, ballad, is so courteous
che sanza compagnia	that even on your own
dovresti avere in tutte parti ardire;	you should feel gallant going anywhere;
ma se tu vuoli andar sicuramente,	but if you wish to have security,
retrova l'Amor pria,	then first you must find Love,
10 ché forse non è bon sanza lui gire;	for without him perhaps you'd best not go,
però che quella che ti dee audire,	since she who must give you an audience,
sì com'io credo, è ver di me adirata:	I rather think, is quite annoyed with me.
se tu di lui non fossi accompagnata,	If you were not accompanied by him,
14 leggeramente ti faria disnore.	she'd likely greet you with discourtesy.
Con dolze sono, quando se' con lui,	With soothing melodies, take up these words,
comincia este parole,	when you are next with him,
appresso che averai chesta pietate:	as soon as you have asked for sympathy:
"Madonna, quelli che mi manda a vui,	"My lady, he who sends me forth to you,
quando vi piaccia, vole,	desires, with your consent,
20 sed elli ha scusa, che la m'intendiate.	that his defence be made to you by me.
Amore è qui, che per vostra bieltate	For Love is here, who through your loveliness
lo face, come vol, vista cangiare:	can make him change his outward look at will:
dunque perché li fece altra guardare	so why Love made him look at someone else
24 pensatel voi, da che non mutò 'l core."	judge for yourself, he's had no change of heart."
Dille: "Madonna, lo suo core è stato	Tell her: "My lady, ever has his heart
con sì fermata fede,	remained so truly firm
che 'n voi servir l'ha 'mpronto onne pensero:	that all his thoughts compel its serving you:
tosto fu vostro, e mai non s'è smagato."	it was all yours at once, and it's not strayed."
Sed ella non ti crede,	If she should then demur,
30 dì che domandi Amor, che sa lo vero:	tell her to question Love, who knows the truth:
ed a la fine falle umil preghero,	and at the end please ask her humbly,

lo perdonare se le fosse a noia,
che mi comandi per messo ch'eo moia,
34   e vedrassi ubidir ben servidore.
    E dì a colui ch'è d'ogni pietà chiave,
avante che sdonnei,
che le saprà contar mia ragion bona:
"Per grazia de la mia nota soave
reman tu qui con lei,
40   e del tuo servo ciò che vuoi ragiona;
e s'ella per tuo prego li perdona,
fa che li annunzi un bel sembiante pace."
Gentil ballata mia, quando ti piace,
44   movi in quel punto che tu n'aggie onore.

if she should find forgiveness difficult,
that she decree my death by messenger,
and faithfully her servant will obey.
    And say to Love, who's keeper of all mercy,
(before you take your leave),
who will know how to make my case to her:
"In virtue of my pleasant melody
stay here awhile with her,
and speak about your servant as you will;
and if she pardons him because you spoke,
let her kind face announce to him his peace."
Now go, my gentle ballad, when you please,
at such time you'll be met with courtesy.

METRE: *ballata*, with *ripresa* XYYX and four stanzas of ten verses (eight hendecasyllables and two *settenari*), with rhyme scheme AbC AbC CDDX. The *fronte* is six verses (3 + 3) and the *volta* is four verses.

25 Tutti li miei penser parlan d'Amore

The incipit of *Tutti li miei penser* announces the theme, dear to the troubadours, of conflicting thoughts: among the examples of similar Occitan verses proposed by Barbi-Maggini (p. 60), critical attention has settled on the incipit by Peire Vidal, *Tuiz mei cossir son d'amor et de chan*. The poet's thoughts are united in all talking of Love – "*Tutti* li miei penser parlan d'Amore [*All* my thoughts now speak to me of Love]" – but they show great variety of perspective: "e hanno in lor sì gran varietate [and yet they share such great diversity]" (2).

The various points of view of the divergent thoughts are then listed one by one, and seem to recapitulate the Italian lyrical tradition prior to Dante. The first thought, which represents the generically courtly point of view and which one might identify, in the Italian context, with the Sicilian tradition, "mi fa voler potestate [compels me to desire its power]" (3). In other words, the first thought compels the poet to accept the power of Love. The second thought brings to mind Guittone, who in the canzone *Ora parrà* declares "ché 'n tutte parte ove distringe Amore / regge follore – in loco di savere [because wherever Love takes hold, / folly rules in place of knowledge]" (10–11). This thought maintains that Love's rule is "folle," irrational: "altro folle ragiona il suo valore [another claims its rule is foolishness]" (4). The third thought, optimistic in a way that recalls Guinizzelli, gives the lover hope and therefore sweet happiness – "altro sperando m'apporta dolzore [another brings delight by means of hope]" (5) – while the fourth, tragic à la Cavalcanti, has the opposite effect, since "pianger mi fa spesse fiate [another oftentimes will make me weep]" (6). All these thoughts agree only in requesting pity for the lover: "e sol s'accordano in chere pietate, / tremando di paura che è nel core [they find their sole accord in seeking pity, / by trembling for the fear within my heart]" (7–8).

Moving from cause in the octave to effect in the sestet (a common division of labour in the early sonnet), Dante goes on to elaborate the result of the condition he has just described: he finds himself in such a state of uncertainty – of "amorosa erranza [confused by love]" (11) – that he ends up saying, "Ond'io non so da qual matera prenda [So I know not from which to take my theme]" (9). Not knowing what line of thought to choose, he is blocked poetically: "e vorrei dire, e non so ch'io mi dica [I'd like to speak, but don't know what to say]" (10). In other words, he has reached an impasse.

Note the semantic play of this tercet, a play centred on the metaphor of a poetic path that can be lost or blocked, like the "cammin riciso [cut-off path]" across which the sacred poem must leap in *Paradiso* 23: "e così, figurando il paradiso / convien saltar lo sacrato poema / come chi trova suo cammin riciso [and so, in figuring paradise, the sacred poem has to leap across, as does a man who finds his path cut off]" (*Par.* 23.61–3). In the "amorosa erranza" – literally "amorous wandering" – of this early sonnet one can glimpse the long history of the double valence of the metaphor of the path for Dante: a metaphor that Dante applies not only to the experience of living, to the "cammin di nostra vita [journey of our life]," but also to the experience of writing, as in the "cammin riciso" of *Paradiso* 23.63.[73]

The prose of *Vita Nuova* XIII (6), where Dante puts *Tutti li miei penser parlan d'Amore*, seeks to emphasize the metaphor implicit in the word "erranza" (from the verb *errare*, to wander) and to reinforce the sense of the poetic journey – in this case blocked – that is implicit in the first tercet of the sonnet: "Ond'io non so da qual matera prenda; / e vorrei dire, e non so ch'io mi dica: / così mi trovo in amorosa erranza! [So I know not from which to take my theme; / I'd like to speak, but don't know what to say: / that's why I find myself confused by love]" (9–11). In an excellent example of how the *Vita Nuova*'s prose, by emphasizing and unpacking, can shed light on apparently secondary, easily neglected aspects of the poetry, the metaphor that is implicit in the sonnet is made plain and explicit in the prose: "E ciascuno mi combattea tanto, che mi facea stare quasi come colui che non sa per qual via pigli lo suo cammino, e che vuole andare e non sa onde se ne vada; e se io pensava di volere cercare una comune via di costoro, cioè là ove tutti s'accordassero, questa era via molto inimica verso me [And each of these thoughts battled within me so much, they made me like someone who doesn't know which way to take for his journey – who wants to go but doesn't know where he is headed. And when I considered the way they all had in common – the one they agreed on, in other words – it was a highly hostile one from my point of view]" (*VN* XIII.6 [6.6]).

Dante intervenes here with notable energy, loading the metaphor of "erranza" with one of the very few similes of the *Vita Nuova*. The result is a paradigmatic passage in the repertory of Dante's metaphoric journeys: "come colui che non sa per qual via pigli lo suo cammino, e che vuole andare e non sa onde se ne vada [like someone who doesn't know which way to take for his journey – who wants to go but doesn't know where he is headed]" (*VN* XIII.6 [6.6]).

Another aim of the prose that glosses *Tutti li miei penser* is to "Cavalcanti-ize" it, to render the poem more Cavalcantian. As has been noted, the poems of this section of the *Vita Nuova* are part of a Cavalcantian arc that stretches from *Cavalcando l'altr'ier* in chapter IX (4) to *Spesse fiate vegnonmi a la mente* in chapter XVI (9), passing through the episode of the *gabbo* (mocking). In the case of *Ballata, i'voi che tu ritrovi Amore*, a poem not in itself particularly Cavalcantian, we saw that the work of the prose is to create a Cavalcantian atmosphere; in the case of *Tutti li miei penser parlan d'Amore*, which has certain Cavalcantian aspects, the aim of the prose is to reinforce them.

---

73 For the poetic "cammino" see Barolini, *The Undivine Comedy*, chap. 2 and passim; for the *cammin riciso* of *Par.* 23, see esp. chap. 10, "The Sacred Poem Is Forced to Jump: Closure and the Poetics of Enjambment."

Among the potentially Cavalcantian aspects of *Tutti li miei penser parlan d'Amore* is the characterization (noted by Foster-Boyde) of the poet's conflicted thoughts as projections of his own interiority. However, the typically Cavalcantian anxiety of such internal fragmentation is a creation of the *Vita Nuova*'s prose, which introduces the metaphor of combat and battle, absent from the sonnet. In the prose that precedes *Tutti li miei penser*, Dante writes "mi cominciaro molti e diversi pensamenti a *combattere* [several contending thoughts started to *fight* in me]" (XIII.1 [6.1]); in the prose that follows *Tutti li miei penser* we even find the very Cavalcantian metaphor of the "*battaglia* de li diversi pensieri [the *battle* of various contending thoughts]" (XIV.1 [7.1]). With respect to Cavalcantian language in the sonnet, however, the only notable feature is the verse "tremando di paura che è nel core [by trembling for the fear within my heart]" (8). I thus fully endorse the view of De Robertis, the only one among the *Vita Nuova*'s commentators who consistently emphasizes the divergence between prose and poetry, that "any allusion by the sonnet to the Cavalcantian poetic experience (only l. 8 suggests it) is the work of the prose" (*VN*, p. 86).

25 (B X; FB 26; *VN* XIII.8–9 [6.8–9])

Tutti li miei penser parlan d'Amore;	All my thoughts now speak to me of Love,
e hanno in lor sì gran varietate,	and yet they share such great diversity
ch'altro mi fa voler sua potestate,	that one compels me to desire its power,
4 altro folle ragiona il suo valore,	another claims its rule is foolishness,
altro sperando m'apporta dolzore,	another brings delight by means of hope,
altro pianger mi fa spesse fiate;	another oftentimes will make me weep;
e sol s'accordano in cherer pietate,	they find their sole accord in seeking pity,
8 tremando di paura che è nel core.	by trembling for the fear within my heart.
Ond'io non so da qual matera prenda;	So I know not from which to take my theme;
e vorrei dire, e non so ch'io mi dica:	I'd like to speak, but don't know what to say:
11 così mi trovo in amorosa erranza!	that's why I find myself confused by love.
E se con tutti voi fare accordanza,	If I should wish to harmonize them all,
convenemi chiamar la mia nemica,	I'd need to call upon my enemy,
14 madonna la Pietà, che mi difenda.	the Lady Pity, to defend my cause.

METRE: sonnet ABBA ABBA CDE EDC.

26 Con l'altre donne mia vista gabbate
First Redaction

In this sonnet, based on the motif, conventional in the Occitan lyric, of the "gabbo" (the act of making fun of, teasing), the poet addresses *madonna* directly. That lack of screens or mediators is notable; not only does the poet talk to *madonna* without intermediaries but he does it in a particularly sharp way, expressing himself in the present as if the action he is complaining about were contemporary to the act of writing: "Con l'altre donne mia vista gabbate / e non guardate, donna, onde si mova [With other ladies you deride my looks, / not thinking, lady, how it comes about]" (1–2). The lady who is teasing him with her companions isn't worried about the fact that she herself is the cause of the change in his face ("mia vista"). A pattern of circular behaviour emerges: the beauty of the woman whom the poet is addressing – "la vostra beltate" (your beauty) (4) – provokes the change in his appearance; his appearance in turn provokes the negative reaction in her and her companions ("altre donne"): "che vi risembro sì figura nova / quando risguardo la vostra beltate [that you should see in me so strange a look / when I regard the beauty you possess]" (3–4).

If *madonna* knew the effect that she has on him, Pity would not remain hostile: "Se·llo saveste, non poria Pietate / più ver di me tener l'usata prova [Were you to know this, Pity would not have / the power to treat me as it's wont to do]" (5–6; in *Tutti li miei penser parlan d'Amore* too, there is a personification of "la mia nemica, / madonna la Pietà [my enemy, / the Lady Pity]" [13–14]). The transition from the descriptive to the analytical, indicated by the hypothetical sentence ("Se·llo saveste, non poria Pietate ..."), gives new retrospective force to the opening of this sonnet, where the exceptional use of the present tense amounts to an attack on *madonna*.

The first part of *Con l'altre donne mia vista gabbate* is unusual in its expressive vigour and for a form of direct address to *madonna* that is not at all the deferential address of Dante to Beatrice in the *Commedia*. At the end of the octave the sonnet goes in a different direction: Love appears ("ch'Amor, quando sì presso a voi mi trova, / prende baldezza e tanta sicurtate [for Love, in finding me so close to you, / becomes so brazen and so confident]" [7–8]), and after his arrival the sonnet takes a notable stylistic turn, becoming a catalogue of Cavalcantian motifs and features. In a very Cavalcantian manner, the lover's vital "spirits" enter the scene, spirits that Love, already frightened, wounds, kills, and drives away: "che fiere tra i miei spiriti paurosi / e qual ancide e qual pinge di fore [he takes my frightened spirits by assault, / and some he slays, and others he drives out]" (9–10). The lover, literally "transfigured" (he was already a "figura nova" in line 3) because of the slaughter of his spirits brought about by Love, has changed so much in his appearance that he is no longer himself: "ond'io mi cangio in figura d'altrui [thus I take on the look of someone else]" (12). However, his mutation does not keep him from hearing the lamentations of his exiled, tormented spirits: "ma non sì ch'io non senta bene allore / li guai de li scacciati tormentosi [but not so much that I don't hear full well / the torment of those spirits he drove out]" (13–14). With the manifestly Cavalcantian line "li guai de li scacciati tormentosi" the sonnet ends.

In the case of *Con l'altre donne mia vista gabbate*, an authentically Cavalcantian sonnet, there is not the discrepancy between prose and poem that we saw in the cases of the two preceding poems. (I follow De Robertis, as always, in printing the redaction prior to that of the *Vita Nuova* when such a redaction exists.) The prose frame of *Vita Nuova* XIV (7) elaborates the Cavalcantian themes of the sonnet. Free of the burden of having to create a Cavalcantian ambience absent from the poem, the prose glosses and adds density to those aspects of the sonnet that are especially important from the point of view of the *libello*.

An element of the sonnet that is emphasized and elaborated in the prose is the expression "figura nova," particularly meaningful in a text entitled *Vita Nuova*, which is glossed with the spiritually and metaphysically significant words "trasfigurazione" and "trasfiguramento": "accorgendosi de la mia *trasfigurazione* [noticing my transfiguration]" (*VN* XIV.7 [7.7]); "la cagione del mio *trasfiguramento* [the cause of my transfiguration]" (*VN* XIV.10 [7.10]). Meanings that are only adumbrated in the sonnet's "figura nova" (but we should not forget that the word *novo* is always important in Dante's usage) become manifest with the word "trasfigurazione," whose prefix, *tras*, leads directly to the *trasumanar* of *Paradiso*. Similarly, the prose suggests a wider metaphysical context in which to situate the Cavalcantian love-death, in itself a death that is exquisitely lyrical and absolute. By contrast, the prose of the *Vita Nuova* invokes a death that is not absolute, a death that leads to resurrection: "*resurressiti* li morti spiriti miei [my dead spirits now resurrected]" (*VN* XIV.8 [7.8]). This is a death that already foreshadows a possibility not considered in Cavalcanti's system: a death that is transfiguration, metamorphosis, and rebirth of the soul in a "figura nova."

26 (B XI; FB 27; DR 52; *VN* XIV.11–12 [7.11–12])
First Redaction

Con l'altre donne mia vista gabbate	With other ladies you deride my looks,
e non guardate, donna, onde si mova	not thinking, lady, how it comes about
che vi risembro sì figura nova	that you should see in me so strange a look
4 quando risguardo la vostra beltate.	when I regard the beauty you possess.
Se·llo saveste, non poria Pietate	Were you to know this, Pity would not have
più ver di me tener l'usata prova,	the power to treat me as it's wont to do,
ch'Amor, quando sì presso a voi mi trova,	for Love, in finding me so close to you,
8 prende baldezza e tanta sicurtate	becomes so brazen and so confident

148 Con l'altre donne mia vista gabbate

che fiere tra i miei spiriti paurosi
e qual ancide e qual pinge di fore,
11 sì che solo rimane a veder voi:
ond'io mi cangio in figura d'altrui;
ma non sì ch'io non senta bene allore
14 li guai de li scacciati tormentosi.

he takes my frightened spirits by assault,
and some he slays, and others he drives out,
so he alone remains to look at you.
Thus I take on the look of someone else,
but not so much that I don't hear full well
the torment of those spirits he drove out.

VN 2. non pensate – 3. Ch'io vi rasembri – 4. riguardo – 6. Tener più contra me – 8. baldanza – 10. quale a.

METRE: sonnet ABBA ABBA CDE EDC.

27 Ciò che m'incontra, nella mente more
First Redaction

This sonnet, placed by Dante in *Vita Nuova* XV (8) but here printed in the earlier redaction put forward by De Robertis, is at the centre of the Cavalcantian section of the *libello*. The motif of the *gabbo*, dominant in *Con l'altre donne mia vista gabbate*, is here taken up again in a minor key: thus " 'l vostro gabbo" at line 12. The dominant motif is now the erotic death of the courtly lyric: thus, "il vostro gabbo ancide [your mocking slays]." De Robertis comments that the verb "more" (dies) of the incipit, "which is, in any case, a Cavalcantian trademark, inaugurates the main thematic thrust of the whole sonnet" (*VN,* p. 99).

The poet returns here to the effect brought about by the sight of his lady. It is a paradoxical effect, making him desire that which is fatal for him, as summed up in the concluding line of the sonnet: "degli occhi, c'hanno di lor morte voglia [within my eyes that wish themselves to die]" (14). The lines that precede this longed-for death – note the strong antithesis created by the two nouns "death" and "desire" joined in the final position ("morte voglia") – offer a close examination of the modalities of such a death and of the concept that death brought about by desire is desireable and desired.

In this essay I will draw attention to the provenance of these modalities, which has received little critical attention. I will show that much of the description of the "death" experienced by the lover of *Ciò che m'incontra* comes from the mystical tradition and that therefore we see here in this very youthful composition – a sonnet that exists in a pre–*Vita Nuova* redaction – a very early engagement with mysticism on Dante's part.

When the lover is about to see his lady, the occurrences of his life vanish from his memory: "Ciò che m'incontra, nella mente more / quando vegno a veder voi, bella gioia [What comes to pass dies in my memory / when I am in your company, my joy]" (1–2). As in mystical experiences, so in this experience the protagonist exits the flux of normal space-time events: "ciò che m'incontra" – literally, "that which meets me" – is a phrase that encompasses all events and happenings in the course of quotidian living, all the things that "encounter" us as we go along the path of life. The outer world disappears, what happens to the lover "dies" in his memory, giving him the freedom to exist fully in the interior space created by Love. We see here too the simultaneous presence of erotic and mystical modalities: on the one hand the opening of *Ciò che m'incontra* plunges us into the midst of mystical experience, while on the other hand the two opening lines conclude with the courtly *senhal* used by Guittone d'Arezzo for his lady, "bella gioia" (lovely jewel or joy).

The sense found in this sonnet of the inwardness of mystical experience, of its estrangement from the things of the world, of alienation from that which happens to us, will later be articulated in *Purgatorio*, in the context of the ecstatic visions in cantos

15 and 17. This purgatorial *narratio* of "visione / estatica" (*Purg.* 15.85–6) provides us with a key to Dante's phenomenology of mystical experience.[74] Here Dante explains that after the vision "l'anima mia tornò di fori / a le cose che son fuor di lei vere [my soul came back to the things that are real outside it]" (*Purg.* 15.115–16), clearly indicating the existence of various dimensions of reality: the dimension of things that are true within the soul and the dimension of things that are true outside it, "fuor di lei vere."

While in the fifteenth canto of *Purgatorio* Dante portrays the moment in which the soul returns to the things that exist outside of it, re-entering the flux of everyday life, in the sonnet *Ciò che m'incontra* he portrays the opposite moment, marked by the fading out of external things, which "die" to the lover upon experiencing the "vision" of *madonna* ("quando vegno a veder voi, bella gioia"). The encounter with *madonna* cancels what the lover encounters outside himself and provokes the beginning of a "mystical" experience, in the sense of an experience during which the soul leaves the quotidian flux and enters a different dimension of reality.

In *Ciò che m'incontra*, when the lover is near his lady ("e quando vi son presso [when I stand near you]" [3]), he hears Love advising him, using – significantly – direct address: "sento Amore / che dice: 'Fuggi, se 'l morir t'è noia' [I hear Love say: / 'Flee now, if you disdain the thought of death']" (3–4). The use of direct address is typical of Cavalcanti's interior dialogic dramas; later it will mark the ecstatic visions in *Purgatorio*, and, in general, Dante's mystical style, where direct address confers immediacy and intensity on visionary experience. Direct address, employed by Dante as a means for crossing boundary lines between various dimensions of the real, is a rhetorical constant of his mystical-visionary style; in his early work we encounter it again in the prophetic and visionary account of the death of *madonna* in *Vita Nuova* XXIII (14). The origins of this staple harken back to *Ciò che m'incontra*.

I should add that the Cavalcantian contribution to Dante's mystical style is yet to be explored. For the *contaminatio* in Dante's writing between lyrical/erotic/Cavalcantian modes and mystical/theological modes, one need think only of *piovere* in Cavalcanti's use – "E' **piove** / gioco d'amore in noi [Amorous delight / rains down on us]" (*Era in penser d'amor*, 3–4) – and in Dante's: "Poi **piovve** dentro all'alta fantasia / un crucifisso [Then rained down within the high fantasy one crucified]" (*Purg.* 17.25–6). In the case of *Ciò che m'incontra*, the words expressed in direct address by Love – "Fuggi, se 'l morir t'è noia" – pursue the theme of lyrical death in a Cavalcantian key.[75]

The sonnet accurately delineates the phenomenology of a mystical transport, from

---

74 For mystical experience as defined by this passage of *Purgatorio*, which contains the word "estatica," a *hapax* in all Dante's production, see Barolini, *The Undivine Comedy*, chap. 7, "Nonfalse Errors and the True Dreams of the Evangelist."

75 The final redaction of *Ciò che m'incontra* offers instead "se 'l perir t'è noia," in a change typical of the transition from first redaction to the redaction used in the *Vita Nuova*: while the sense does not change, the substitution of "perir" (perish) for "morir" (die) in a context where there are already many forms of *morire* and *morte* adds variety and linguistic range.

the pallid face to the listless body that starts to faint and leans wherever: "Lo viso mostra lo color del core / che tramortendo ovunque pò s'appoia [My face reveals the colour of my heart, / which, swooning, seeks whatever help it can]" (5–6). The image of a staggering man is then reinforced by what follows. His heart's tremours have inebriated the poet, to the point that he thinks he hears the stones of the wall on which he is leaning start to assail him, saying "Moia moia" (note the direct address): "e per l'ebrïetà del gran tremore / le pietre par che dican: 'Moia, moia!' [and as I tremble in this drunken state / the stones appear to shout out: 'Die! Die!']" (7–8). Inebriation as a sign of mystical *raptus* is found in Jacopone da Todi, who describes Christ with the words "Come ebrio per lo mondo spesso andavi [You often went through the world as though drunk]" (*Amor de caritate*, 203). After the experience of the first group of ecstatic visions in *Purgatorio*, Dante says that he walks "a guisa di cui vino o sonno piega [as one whom wine or sleep bends over]" (*Purg.* 15.123).

Among the notable textual links that connect this sonnet to the mystical section of the end of *Purgatorio* 15, I would include the vision of Saint Stephen during his martyrdom: "Poi vidi genti accese in foco d'ira / con pietre un giovinetto ancider, forte / gridando a sé pur 'Martira, martira!' [Then I saw people stirred up in fiery rage killing a young man with stones, shouting loudly to each other repeatedly 'Kill, kill!']" (*Purg.* 15.106–8). This terzina describes a young man who is killed "with stones" by people "shouting" – in direct address – "Martira, martira!": the line in *Purgatorio* "gridando a sé pur: 'Martira, martira!'" recalls the rocks that shout "Moia, moia" in the redaction of *Ciò che m'incontra* that we read in the *Vita Nuova*. The *Vita Nuova* redaction of the sonnet includes the brilliant substitution of *gridare*, to shout ("le pietre par che **gridin**: 'Moia, moia'") for *dire*, to say ("le pietre par che **dican**: 'Moia, moia!'"), and thus anticipates even more directly the lines in *Purgatorio* that describe the vision of Saint Stephen's martyrdom.[76]

The mystical modalities of the *Commedia* are already largely anticipated in the *Vita Nuova*. I will give another example, taken again from the conclusion of *Purgatorio* 15. The condition of one who "guarda pur con l'occhio che non vede, / quando disanimato il corpo giace [looks fixedly with the eye that does not see, when the body lies without its soul]" (*Purg.* 15.134–5) – lines that evoke Saint Augustine's description of ecstasy, where the soul is "alienated from the senses of the body" ("a sensibus corporis alienata") (*De genesi ad litteram* 12.5.14)[77] – is already present in the prose of *Vita Nuova* XI (5): "lo mio corpo ... molte volte si movea come cosa grave inanimata [my body ... often moved like a heavy, inanimate object]" (*VN* XI.3 [5.6]). The "trembling" of the soul provides, moreover, an example of how Dante navigates the transition from lyric subjectivity to objective other-world reality. The "tremare" of these sonnets, which is situated within the narrating self, will later be projected onto

---

76 I note that *gridare,* never used by the more toned-down Cavalcanti, appears rather frequently in Dante's lyrics: in two canzoni of violent eros (*E' m'incresce di me, Così nel mio parlar*), in two theologized canzoni (*Donne ch'avete, Donna pietosa*), and in this sonnet.

77 See chapter 7 of Barolini, *The Undivine Comedy* for discussion of Augustine's *De genesi ad litteram* in the context of *raptus*.

the landscape of hell, where it provokes the same effect of mystical transport: we recall the earthquake at the end of *Inferno* 3, because of which "la buia campagna / tremò sì forte [the dark countryside shook so powerfully]" (*Inf.* 3.130–1), causing the pilgrim to fall "come l'uom cui sonno piglia [like the man taken by sleep]" (*Inf.* 3.136) and wake up again literally "transported" to the other shore of the river Acheron. The shaking of self and shaking of earth are already associated in Dante's imagination in these early sonnets. Thus, *Spesse fiate vegnonmi a la mente* (the sonnet that follows in the *Vita Nuova*) refers to the "tremoto" (13) or "earthquake" of his heart: "nel cor mi si comincia uno tremoto, / che fa de' polsi l'anima partire [a tremour in my heart begins to rise / that drives my soul completely from my blood]" (*Spesse fiate*, 13–14).

In the sestet of *Ciò che m'incontra*, the poem becomes a more conventional sonnet in the manner of Cavalcanti. The first tercet focuses on the compassion that the frightened state of the lover ought to provoke in whoever sees him: "Peccato face chi allor mi vede / se l'alma sbigottita non conforta / sol dimostrando che di me li doglia [Whoever sees me, then, commits a sin / if he does not console my troubled soul, / at least by showing that he shares my grief]" (9–11). But the pity that is aroused by the sight of his appearance – by his "vista morta [look of death]" – is killed by *madonna* ("'l vostro gabbo ancide [your mocking slays]" [12]), the very lady whom the eyes of the poet desire to see even though she causes their death.

27 (B XII; FB 28; DR 57; *VN* XV.4–6 [8.4–6])
First Redaction

Ciò che m'incontra, nella mente more	What comes to pass dies in my memory
quando vegno a veder voi, bella gioia;	when I am in your company, my joy;
e quando vi son presso, sento Amore	and when I stand near you, I hear Love say:
4 che dice: "Fuggi, se 'l morir t'è noia."	"Flee now, if you disdain the thought of death."
Lo viso mostra lo color del core	My face reveals the colour of my heart,
che tramortendo ovunque pò s'appoia,	which, swooning, seeks whatever help it can;
e per l'ebrïetà del gran tremore	and as I tremble in this drunken state
8 le pietre par che dican: "Moia, moia!"	the stones appear to shout out: "Die! Die!"
Peccato face chi allor mi vede	Whoever sees me, then, commits a sin
se l'alma sbigottita non conforta	if he does not console my troubled soul,
11 sol dimostrando che di me li doglia,	at least by showing that he shares my grief,
per la pietà che 'l vostro gabbo ancide,	by means of pity, which your mocking slays,
la qual si cria nella vista morta	the pity that is nurtured by the look of death
14 degli occhi, c'hanno di lor morte voglia.	within my eyes that wish themselves to die.

VN 2. Quand'i' v. – 3. quand'io vi – io sento – 4. 'l perir – 8. che gridin – 9. allora

METRE: sonnet ABAB ABAB CDE CDE.

28 Spesse fiate vegnonmi a la mente

Spesse fiate vegnonmi a la mente is the last poem of the Cavalcantian section of the
Vita Nuova, which stretches from *Cavalcando l'altr'ier* to the discovery of the new
style in *Donne ch'avete*. Like *Ciò che m'incontra*, it places the narrating self at the
centre of the discourse. Placed by Dante in *Vita Nuova* XVI (9), this sonnet leaves
behind the theme of the *gabbo* to focus on the "dark" state of the lover – the "oscure
qualità" inflicted on him by Love – and on the consequent pity that he feels for himself. The motif of self-pity, very Cavalcantian (the standard reference is Cavalcanti's
incipit *A me stesso di me pietate vène*), is presented at the start of the sonnet: reflecting on his suffering, the lover finds that self-pity arises in him ("e venmene pietà"
[3]), with the result that he wonders rhetorically (in a refined move that reveals the
narcissism of the narrator) if there can be any others who experience similar suffering or if he is the only one so afflicted. The words that the self speaks are recorded as
direct speech, in the Cavalcantian manner: "io dico: 'Lasso!, avviene elli a persona?'
[I often ask: 'Alas, do others ever feel this way?']" (4).

There follows a description of the assault by Love, who takes his life, leaving
alive only the spirit that talks about *madonna*: "ch'Amor m'assale subitanamente, /
sì che la vita quasi m'abbandona: / campami un spirto vivo solamente, / e que' riman
perché di voi ragiona [For Love assails me unexpectedly, / so that my life all but
abandons me: / a single spirit only holds on fast, / and it survives because it speaks of
you]" (5–8). It would seem – between deadly Love, fragile life, and spirits destroyed
but for one that barely survives – that the sonnet could not become any more Cavalcantian, but the sestet manages, if possible, to outdo the tragic tone of the octave. The
lover, dead in appearance and, Cavalcanti-like, lacking in all force and existential
worth ("e così smorto, d'onne valor voto [and pale as death, and drained of all my
might]" [10]), tries to see his lady, believing (why, is anyone's guess!) that the sight
of her will heal him ("vegno a vedervi, credendo guerire [I come to see you hoping
to be healed]" [11]), while instead she makes him plummet back into the trembling
already so dramatically described in *Ciò che m'incontra* (recall the "gran tremore"
of line 7 in that sonnet). *Spesse fiate* ends with the death of the lover, whose soul
departs because of the internal "earthquake" that he feels when he raises his eyes to
gaze on *madonna*: "e se io levo li occhi per guardare, / nel cor mi si comincia uno
tremoto,[78] / che fa de' polsi l'anima partire [but if I lift my eyes to look at you, / a
tremour in my heart begins to rise / that drives my soul completely from my blood]"

---

78 Gorni changes Barbi's reading into the nonsyncopated and more familiar form *un terremoto*.

(12–14). The essay on *Ciò che m'incontra* treats the link between the lover's interior "earthquakes" in these early sonnets and the later external earthquakes that will be analogously "transporting" (as at the end of *Inferno* 3).

In the economy of the *Vita Nuova*, Dante structurally joins together the three sonnets that are usually referred to as the *gabbo* poems – *Con l'altre donne mia vista gabbate, Ciò che m'incontra, nella mente more*, and *Spesse fiate vegnonmi a la mente* – binding them in the real and material sequence of the *libello*. He also joins them together thematically, not as much by means of the *gabbo* motif as by the fact that in these sonnets he does something he does not do elsewhere in the *Vita Nuova*: he directly addresses *madonna* (in the sonnets we do not know who this might be, in the *Vita Nuova* she is Beatrice) to talk to her about himself. Dante underscores this point in the prose that follows *Spesse fiate*, where he writes of "questi tre sonetti, ne li quali parlai a questa donna che fuoro narratori di tutto quasi lo mio stato [these three sonnets in which I addressed this lady directly, since they told almost everything about my state]," then deciding, in the same sentence, to be silent and say no more about himself: "tacere e non dire più però che mi parea di me assai avere manifestato [to be silent and write no more since I felt I had explained enough about myself]." He concludes that "a me convenne ripigliare matera nuova e più nobile che la passata [I needed to take up new and nobler subject matter than that of the past]" (*VN* XVII.1 [10.1]).

In their lyrical dress these sonnets are part of a courtly world (*Con l'altre donne*) made ever more tragic and Cavalcantian (*Ciò che m'incontra* and *Spesse fiate*). In their more than lyrical dress, in the narrative and ideological dress created by the invention of the unitary and unifying prose of the *Vita Nuova*, these same three sonnets become emblems of that part of the world inherited by Dante that is destined to fail and that he will have to discard and surpass. Inserting these sonnets in the *Vita Nuova* in the order in which we find them, an order that moves inexorably towards the death of the poet, and commenting on them within the prose setting, Dante uses them as signs of the self-mutilating narcissism of the lyrical culture that precedes him – a culture that, as he proclaims, he will replace with a "matera nuova e più nobile che la passata."

28 (B XIII; FB 29; *VN* XVI.7–10 [9.7–10])

Spesse fiate vegnonmi a la mente	I often call to mind the spells of grief
le oscure qualità ch'Amor mi dona,	that Love inflicts on me, and then I feel
e venmene pietà, sì che sovente	such pity for myself I often ask:
4 io dico: "Lasso!, avviene elli a persona?";	"Alas, do others ever feel this way?"
ch'Amor m'assale subitanamente,	For Love assails me unexpectedly,
sì che la vita quasi m'abbandona:	so that my life all but abandons me:
campami un spirto vivo solamente,	a single spirit only holds on fast,

8   e que' riman perché di voi ragiona.
     Poscia mi sforzo, ché mi voglio atare;
   e così smorto, d'onne valor voto,
11 vegno a vedervi, credendo guerire:
   e se io levo li occhi per guardare,
   nel cor mi si comincia uno tremoto,
14 che fa de' polsi l'anima partire.

and it survives because it speaks of you.
   I try to summon strength to help myself,
and pale as death, and drained of all my might,
I come to see you hoping to be healed.
But if I lift my eyes to look at you,
a tremour in my heart begins to rise
that drives my soul completely from my blood.

METRE: sonnet ABAB ABAB CDE CDE.

29 Degli occhi della mia donna si move

We have reached the point in Dante's trajectory in which Cavalcantian influence begins not so much to lose its grip as to mingle with Guinizzellian motifs. Contini defines *Degli occhi della mia donna* as "a typical and one might say average *stil novo* sonnet," because "to the general Guinizzellian motif of the salutary lady, of the extraordinary effects of her gaze," with which the sonnet opens "is added the Cavalcantian motif of 'paura' [fear]" (p. 55), a theme that we have seen in *Ciò che m'incontra* and *Spesse fiate*. This formula of uniting Guinizzellian and Cavalcantian motifs will be elaborated, as we shall see, in the great early canzoni *Lo doloroso amor* and *E' m'incresce di me*.

The light that moves from the eyes of *madonna* is such "that where it is manifest / things are revealed that cannot be described / because they are uncommon and sublime": "che dove appare / si veggion cose ch'uom non può ritrare / per lor altezze e per lor esser nove" (2–4). Here we find the Dantean theme of representation, seen from the perspective of that which "cannot be described" ("uom non può ritrare"), in other words, from the perspective of our incapacity to represent things in the face of a reality that surpasses our ability for representation. The meta-theme of "ritrare" functions as a mirror: as the poet is incapable at his craft of making representations, so the lover is an abject being, defeated and "vinto [subdued]" (9). He experiences "paura [fear]" (6; also see "gli occhi paurosi [my frightened eyes]" [10]), rejection ("Qui non voglio mai tornare [I'll never go back there again]" [7]), loss of self ("ma poscia perdo tutte le mie prove [but after all my efforts come up short]" [8]), failure ("e tornomi colà dov'io son vinto [I go back to the place where I'm subdued]" [9]), and annihilation – not only of his eyes ("ed e' son chiusi [they're closed up tight]" [12]) but also of his desire itself: "lo disio che li mena qui è 'stinto [the desire that brought them here is spent]" (13). *Degli occhi della mia donna* is a catalogue of the inadequacies of the lover, one that brings him inexorably to a conclusion in which, no longer able to attend to himself, he puts himself in the hands of Love: "però proveggi a lo mio stato Amore [so then let Love provide for my well-being]" (14).

The most notable aspect of this sonnet is the poet's declaration that he can see, illuminated by the eyes of his lady, things that cannot be portrayed "because they are uncommon and sublime": "per lor altezze e per lor esser nove" (4). The theme of the new that we find in "per lor esser nove" is of primary importance in Dante: it will eventually result in the "poetics of the new" of the *Commedia*, but harkens back to the earliest lyrics. We must remember that Dante himself glosses the word *nuovo* in the phrase "nuovo e mai non fatto cammino di questa vita [new and never travelled road of this life]" (*Convivio* 4.12.15). The primary meaning of the word in Dante's usage always preserves a temporal dimension (*nuovo* = "mai non fatto," literally "never before done"), and so also a figural one. As creator, God is an artist who "presents" rather than "re-presenting": God is "Colui che mai non vide cosa nova [He who never saw a new thing]" (*Purg.* 10.94) because His is a condition of omniscience that precedes history, that precedes the new things that we encounter on the path of life, that is always *prius* ("semper enim quod naturalius est prius est [that which is more natural is always first]," says Saint Thomas, *ST* I-II, q. 49, a. 2). Dante instead, as re-presenter, delivered over to the flux of history and of the new, is in search of the newest new thing, the most special created being, the one that will give him an advantage over other re-presenters. The figure of his lady serves him to this end: "Poi la reguarda, e fra se stesso giura / che Dio ne 'ntenda di far cosa nova [He looks at her and to himself he swears / that God intends to make a thing that's new]" (*Donne ch'avete intelletto d'amore*, 45–6). His lady is a "cosa nova," who gives him access to a *stil novo*.

29 (B LXV; C 18; FB 30; DR 58)

Degli occhi della mia donna si move
un lume sì gentil, che dove appare
si veggion cose ch'uom non può ritrare
4   per lor altezze e per lor esser nove;
e li suo' razzi sovra 'l mio cor piove
tanta paura, che mi fa tremare,
e dicer: "Qui non voglio mai tornare";
8   ma poscia perdo tutte le mie prove,
    e tornomi colà dov'io son vinto
riconfortando gli occhi paurosi
11   che sentier prima questo gran valore.
    Quando son giunti, lasso!, ed e' son chiusi;
lo disio che li mena qui è 'stinto:
14   però proveggi a lo mio stato Amore.

A light emerges from my lady's eyes
so noble that where it is manifest
things are revealed that cannot be described
because they are uncommon and sublime.
And in her radiance my heart is bathed
with fear so much I tremble and am forced
to say: "I'll never go back there again."
But after all my efforts come up short
    I go back to the place where I'm subdued,
providing comfort to my frightened eyes,
which were the first to feel that powerful glance.
When they arrive, alas, they're closed up tight,
and the desire that brought them here is spent:
so then let Love provide for my well-being.

METRE: sonnet ABBA ABBA CDE DCE.

30 Ne le man vostre, gentil donna mia

The sonnet has an explicitly biblical opening, for the first words of the poet-lover, "Ne le man vostre, gentil donna mia, / raccomando lo spirito che more [My gentle noble lady, in your hands / I now entrust my spirit as it dies]," echo the words of Christ on the cross: "In manus tuas commendo spiritum meum [Into your hands I commend my spirit]" (Luke 23:46). The lover, as he "dies," addresses his lady with the words that Christ – as he died – spoke to God. In the analogy established by these lines, the lover is compared to Christ and the lady to God. The analogy is excessive and does not easily gain the reader's assent.

Characterized by the mix of Cavalcantian elements and biblical elements, *Ne le man vostre* is part of an experimental phase that carries Dante to the verge of the *Vita Nuova*, a text that too makes use of biblical elements and mixes them with courtly elements. The hybrid result of the *Vita Nuova* is, however, very different from that of this sonnet – so different, in fact, that the exclusion of *Ne le man vostre* from the *libello* comes as no surprise. I disagree with the observation of Contini, according to whom in the "spirito" of the second line there is a "fusion of the biblical spirit with the *stil novo* spirit," a fusion that makes it "less easy than for other lyrics ... to come up with a plausible hypothesis as to why this sonnet was not put into the *Vita Nuova*" (p. 58). Much more to the point is De Robertis, who notes that the words of the dying Christ, "Into your hands I commend my spirit," are "here integrated with the phrase 'che more' ('as it dies'), which is a Cavalcantian addition" (ed. comm., p. 339).

In other words, the textual fusion carried out in *Ne le man vostre* is not of biblical elements with generically *stil novo* elements, as in the sonnet *O voi che per la via d'Amor passate* – a sonnet that Dante *did* place in the *Vita Nuova*. Rather, in *Ne le man vostre* biblical elements are mixed with Cavalcantian elements. The result of this formula, Bible + Cavalcanti, is a text akin to a great canzone from this same poetic period, also excluded from the *Vita Nuova*, whose Cavalcantian pedigree is clearly stated in its opening words: *E' m'incresce di me sì duramente*.

There are two biblical allusions in *Ne le man vostre*, the first at the sonnet's opening and a second at lines 7–8, where the dying spirit invokes Love with more words from the Passion of Christ: "Segnore, / qualunque vuoi di me, quel vo' che sia [My Lord, / what you should wish of me, I wish as well]" (echoing Mark 14:36: "non quod ego volo, sed quod tu [yet not what I will, but what thou wilt]"). These biblical citations set up analogies that might, if not analysed, seem like those that underlie the *Vita Nuova*, but in fact they are profoundly divergent. The analogies of *Ne le man vostre* do not function correctly from the point of view of the spiritual economy of the *libello*.

In the *Vita Nuova* Dante theologizes the courtly lady, the same "gentil donna mia" who is invoked in the opening and again in line 12 of *Ne le man vostre* ("Gentil mia donna"), positing an analogy between Beatrice and Christ: both are bringers of beatitude, salutary, worthy of all praise and able to redeem the lover even after death. In contrast, in *Ne le man vostre* it is the lover and not the beloved who is compared to Christ: the lover suffers and dies in the way that Christ suffers and dies.

Barbi is therefore incorrect when he states that "far from any sense of desecration, the religious tone [of this sonnet] is the same as in many passages of the *Vita Nuova*" (Barbi-Maggini, p. 231). In the *Vita Nuova* the Christological language of the Passion is never used for the suffering lover. For instance, when Dante echoes the catastrophes that precede the Passion (the dishevelled women, the sun going dark, the birds falling down dead, the earthquakes; cf. *VN* XXIII.5 [14.5]), he does so not with respect to the lover but to the imagined death of *madonna*.[79]

Also of note is the use of the adjective *consolato* in the line "per tal ch'i' mora consolato in pace [so I at least might die a peaceful death]" (13). This word, meaning "one who has received consolation," is drawn from a religious matrix (see the examples of *consolazione* in *TLIO*).[80] Its presence contributes to the unstable religiosity of *Ne le man vostre*, to its tone of profanation, owing to the idea that *consolatio* can be offered by a living woman to her dying lover. In sharp contrast, in a canzone such as *Li occhi dolenti*, on the death of Beatrice, *consolatio* is offered by the dead lady to her living lover. In *Li occhi dolenti*, the analogy is aligned "correctly": Beatrice, dead, gives renewed hope to her lover crying over her death, in this way reaffirming the connection between her and Christ.

We can learn from *Ne le man vostre* what Dante himself must have learned: it is one thing to theologize the courtly system in a Guinizzellian direction, always expanding upon the salutary effects of the *donna gentile*, but it is quite another to theologize on a Cavalcantian base, concentrating on the sufferings of the poet-lover. One road leads to a poetics of sublimation, of exaltation, to a poetics that strives – like the "sospiro ch'esce del mio core [the sigh that issues from my heart]" in the last sonnet of the *Vita Nuova* – to go "Oltra la spera [Beyond the (crystalline) sphere]." We might define this as a successfully spiritualized poetics (despite the attempts of Cecco Angiolieri and of the heroic minority that attempted from the beginning to strip away its spiritual authority), successful precisely because the terms of the analogy are acceptable to the reader. The other road leads to the inevitable collapse of the spiritualizing and theologizing thrust, a collapse that occurs when the terms of the analogy are not acceptable to the reader, when they appear "excessive": Cavalcanti's imaginary world is not capable of sustaining the comparison between the death of the

---

79 "This and the other 'signs' of the death of Beatrice are a part of the biblical repertoire of the signs of the death of Christ, and still more of the wrath of God and the end of the world" (De Robertis, *VN*, p. 153).

80 *Tesoro della lingua italiana delle origini,* http://tlio.ovi.cnr.it/TLIO.

courtly lover and the Passion of Christ. *Ne le man vostre* is an experiment that Dante rejected because it did not provide a workable model for the theologized program of the *Vita Nuova*.

30 (B LXVI; C 19; FB 31; DR 50)

Ne le man vostre, gentil donna mia,	My gentle noble lady, in your hands
raccomando lo spirito che more:	I now entrust my spirit as it dies:
e' se ne va sì dolente, che Amore	such pain does its departure bring that Love,
4 lo mira con pietà, che ·l manda via.	who bids it leave, looks on with sympathy.
Voi lo legaste a la sua segnoria,	You bound it fast to Love's authority
sì che non ebbe poi alcun valore	so that it then no longer had the strength
di poter lui chiamar se non: "Segnore,	to utter any words except: "My Lord,
8 qualunque vuoi di me, quel vo' che sia."	what you should wish of me, I wish as well."
Io so ch'a voi ogni torto dispiace;	I know that you dislike what is unjust,
però la morte, ch'i' non ho servita,	and that is why this death, so undeserved,
11 molto più m'entra ne lo core amara.	besets my heart with greater bitterness.
Gentil mia donna, mentr'i' ho de la vita,	My noble lady, while I'm still alive,
per tal ch'i' mora consolato in pace,	so I at least might die a peaceful death,
14 vi piaccia a li occhi miei non esser cara.	do not deny my eyes the sight of you.

METRE: sonnet ABBA ABBA CDE DCE.

31 Lo doloroso amor che mi conduce

As clearly indicated by its first words, the canzone *Lo doloroso amor* is about "painful love." Barbi places *Lo doloroso amor* immediately after the other great early canzone of tormented and sorrowful love, *E' m'incresce di me sì duramente*. Contini follows Barbi with respect to placement, here as elsewhere, noting, however, that "in an ideal chronology of the *rime dolorose* for Beatrice, this canzone is certainly the oldest" (p. 67). Features that support an early date of composition are the two unrhymed lines in every stanza and in the *congedo*, the *congedo* that does not correspond to the *sirma*, and the use of an imperfect rhyme at line 26. Foster and Boyde pick up on the implicit suggestion in Contini's comment, putting *Lo doloroso amor* first among Dante's *rime dolorose*, including those from the *Vita Nuova*. In this way, Foster and Boyde place *Lo doloroso amor* literally in the "posto più antico" of this thematic group and take advantage of the programmatic quality of the incipit. And yet, for reasons that I will explain, De Robertis places it last among the canzoni.

As discussed in the Introduction to this volume, every editorial attempt to order Dante's lyrics – whether it be an order that seeks an approximate chronology like that of Barbi, Contini, Foster-Boyde, and myself or an order that follows in the footsteps of the editorial tradition like that of De Robertis – is necessarily an invention: editorial, not authorial. All editors of Dante's *rime* are working in the absence of an authorial ordering, with the exception of the authorial orderings that we find in Dante's hybrid texts of prose mixed with poetry: the *Vita Nuova* and *Convivio*.

In the absence of a Dantean ordering of the *rime*, various editorial solutions have been proposed in the course of the centuries-long commentary tradition. The poems were traditionally divided by genre, the canzoni isolated from the sonnets and *ballate*; more recently, in the last century, the ordering by genre gave way to the attempt to put the poems in a chronological order. In 2002, De Robertis returned to the traditional ordering by genre, placing the canzoni first, as is traditional in ancient anthologies; with respect to the order of the canzoni he follows Boccaccio, who transcribed fifteen of Dante's canzoni. These are the so-called *canzoni distese*, an expression that derives from the phrase with which Boccaccio concludes his transcription in codex Chigiano L.V.176 ("finiscono le canzoni distese di Dante").

Boccaccio (or someone before him, according to a recent proposal)[81] thus chose

---

81 Giuliano Tanturli has advanced the idea that the anthology of fifteen canzoni existed before Boccaccio; see Tanturli, "L'edizione critica delle *Rime* e il libro delle canzoni di Dante," *Studi Danteschi* 68 (2003): 250–66, and the discussion in the Introduction to this volume.

the ordering of the canzoni that we find in De Robertis' edition. But Boccaccio omitted the canzone *Lo doloroso amor* from his transcription of *canzoni distese*. Given the non-inclusion of *Lo doloroso amor* among Boccaccio's fifteen *canzoni distese*, the canzone is placed by De Robertis in the sixteenth position in his edition, after the fifteen canzoni transcribed by Boccaccio. This position is given to *Lo doloroso amor* despite the fact that it is, according to the unanimous consensus of Dante's editors (including De Robertis), an early canzone.

I cannot endorse De Robertis' editorial solution, which puts *Lo doloroso amor* in a marginal position, suspended between the post-exilic canzone *Amor, da che convien* and the nonexistent canzone (cited in *De vulgari eloquentia*) *Trag[g]emi de la mente Amor la stiva*. Nor do I follow Foster-Boyde, who separate *Lo doloroso amor* from *E'm'incresce di me*, in order to place it first among the *rime dolorose*. Rather, I take this opportunity to place *Lo doloroso amor* immediately before its sister canzone, *E' m'incresce di me*, in order to produce a reading of maximum ideological cohesion.

Foster and Boyde consider *Lo doloroso amor* an archaic canzone, stylistically linked to *La dispietata mente*, a canzone with Sicilian features but "not specifically Cavalcantian" (p. 72). I, on the other hand, consider *Lo doloroso amor* profoundly Cavalcantian. Moreover, it is a canzone to whose Cavalcantian matrix theologized elements are added, exactly as seen in the sonnet that precedes it in my order, *Ne le man vostre*, and as will be seen again in the canzone that follows it, *E' m'incresce di me*, where we encounter not just generically theologized elements but elements pertaining to the *Vita Nuova*. In fact, the canzoni *Lo doloroso amor* and *E'm'incresce di me* are hermeneutically linked and lend themselves to a unitary interpretation, as Barbi suggested by placing them next to one another (but in inverted order, with *E' m'incresce di me* coming first). Given the elements typical of the *Vita Nuova* that can be found in *E m'incresce di me*, these canzoni suggest a reading based on an ideological/poetic path that was first experimented with and then discarded. Specifically, a commentary that connects *Lo doloroso amor* and *E' m'incresce di me* allows us to see that Dante experimented with what seems retrospectively like an ideological oxymoron: a Cavalcantian *Vita Nuova*.

The great interest of the canzoni *Lo doloroso amor* and *E' m'incresce di me* lies precisely in their relationship with the *Vita Nuova*: the text from which they were excluded and that their very existence helps us to better comprehend. These canzoni clearly demonstrate that Dante imagined a course antithetical to the one he later followed in the *libello*. On the basis of these canzoni, we can infer that Dante conceived of an experience that could be defined in the oxymoronic terms of a Cavalcantian *Vita Nuova*. Cavalcanti's hold on Dante's imagination is still very strong – and we should not forget that his hold extends beyond the *Vita Nuova*: Dante wrote mature lyrics that are Cavalcantian.[82]

---

82 On this theme and for an examination of Cavalcantianism in Dante's lyrics and beyond, see my essay "Dante and Guido Cavalcanti (On Making Distinctions in Matters of Love)," 1998, rpt. in *Dante and the Origins of Italian Literary Culture*, pp. 70–101.

The canzoni *Lo doloroso amor* and *E' m'incresce di me* offer interpretive clues fundamental for the reconstruction of Dante's itinerary up to the threshold of the *Vita Nuova*. They provide tools with which to understand the creation of the figure of Beatrice: they show us that the making of Beatrice as she is presented in the *Vita Nuova* was a gradual process, a *gradatio* that we can to some degree reconstruct. In these canzoni we witness an "unholy matrimony": on the one hand there are the traces of an event that is already conceived of as miraculous, hyperbolic, and theologized, but on the other hand these innovations are presented against a background whose ideology is still courtly and/or Cavalcantian.

Above all, the beloved lady in *Lo doloroso amor* is explicitly called Beatrice, but the Beatrice in question retains the features of Cavalcanti's "homicidal" ("micidiale") lady. From this it can also be deduced that Dante found the name "Beatrice" before arriving at a final decision on how to take advantage of the meaning of that name. Even more, the canzone indicates that Dante was originally quite capable of treating the *Vita Nuova*'s principle "nomina sunt consequentia rerum" ironically, and of linking the *nomen* Beatrice to an explicitly non-beatifying *res*. She is, in fact, not a giver of life but of death: the verse in which Dante names her – the name "Beatrice" is present only here in the lyrics excluded from the *Vita Nuova*[83] – is "Per quella moro c'ha nome Beatrice [I die for her whose name is Beatrice]" [14]). Here Dante does not name Beatrice casually, as he names Violetta, Fioretta, or Lisetta, other ladies in his lyrics; rather, he records her name as the structural equivalent of his own death. The extraordinary verse in which he does so – "Per quella moro c'ha nome Beatrice" (14) – is the concluding verse of the first stanza.

When, in *Purgatorio* 27.41–2, Dante writes of "il nome / che ne la mente sempre mi rampolla [the name that's always flowering within my mind]," we should think, à propos the "always" in "*sempre* rampolla," of *Lo doloroso amor*: the first recorded flowering of the name "Beatrice" in Dante's mind occurs in this early canzone. But this is a perverse flowering, for in the canzone we learn that though the name of Beatrice may be sweet, yet it makes his heart bitter, and he experiences this bitterness every time that he sees it written (interesting proof of the intense writerliness of our poet, confirmed by the supporting metaphor of the self as glossator in the *Vita Nuova*): "Quel dolce nome che mi fa il cor agro, / tutte fïate ch'i' lo vedrò scritto / mi farà nuovo ogni dolor ch'i' sento [The sweet name that embitters so my heart / each time I see it written down someplace / will make the pain I feel renew itself]" [15–17]). These verses begin the second stanza, and they underline the concluding message of the preceding stanza. In the event that the reader did not sufficiently grasp line 14's affirmation regarding the name that does not function as it ought to, the incipit of the second stanza reinforces the antithesis *Beatrice/moro* with the chiasmus *dolce-nome/cor-agro* that underlines it.

---

83 In the lyrics not in the *Vita Nuova*, the name "Beatrice" appears only in *Lo doloroso amor*; in the lyrics that are in the *Vita Nuova* it occurs two times in the canzone *Li occhi dolenti* and once in the sonnet *Oltra la spera*, while the sonnet *Deh pellegrini* contains the noun "beatrice." The diminutive "Bice" occurs only in the sonnet *Io mi senti' svegliar*, included in the *Vita Nuova*.

This play *in malo* on the name "Beatrice" is placed by Dante in a position of high relief, in the concluding verse of the first stanza. The first stanza provides in this way a model that will serve for the whole canzone, insofar as it is typical of *Lo doloroso amor* to begin the stanzas in a fairly conventional manner and to then conclude them with material that is more hyperbolic than normal, more theologized. Thus the first stanza begins with a sorrowful love, conventionally lethal, that is retroactively radicalized by the introduction of the name "Beatrice" in the final verse. That the poet suffers from a "doloroso amor che mi conduce / a·ffin di morte per piacer di quella / che lo mio cor solea tener gioioso [painful love that leads me to my end / in death – resulting from an act of her / who used to fill my heart with joyfulness]" [1–3]) is not particularly notable; nor is it notable that the effect of the lady on the lover is antithetical to her *senhal* (think of Guittone's *bella gioia*, who brings him so much *noia*). What is notable is the exasperation of these conventional motifs brought about by their fusion with theological motifs, as happens through the introduction of the name "Beatrice."

From this point of view, *Lo doloroso amor* anticipates *Donne ch'avete intelletto d'amore*, where, too, a conventionally erotic discourse is projected onto a theological backdrop and in this way radically transformed. The major difference between *Lo doloroso amor* and *Donne ch'avete* is that in the first canzone the theologized material is used in a systematically deviant manner: in this perverse variant of the *Vita Nuova* (a label that can be applied even more rigorously to *E' m'incresce di me*), "nomina NON sunt consquentia rerum" and Beatrice is not a principle of life but of death. *Lo doloroso amor* and *E' m'incresce di me* give the impression that Dante posed himself the problem of making the sum Guinizzelli + Cavalcanti to see what the result would be: to the Guinizzellian strategy of theologizing the erotic-courtly code is added the theme of lethal love presented in a hyper-Cavalcantian key (and in fact not even Guido addresses a *congedo* to "Morte," as Dante does uniquely in *Lo doloroso amor*).

The second stanza of *Lo doloroso amor* prolongs the initial antithesis ("Quel dolce nome che mi fa il cor agro") with the idea that the name of the lady will give the lover not new life and hope but instead (in a motif that will be dear to Petrarch) renewed pain: "mi farà nuovo ogni dolor ch'i' sento [will make the pain I feel renew itself]" (17). The suffering continues as the dominant motif in a canzone that opens with "painful love that leads me to my end / in death" and that closes when the lover imagines himself having arrived at the death to which love has led him: the circle closes as it opened, and the last word of *Lo doloroso amor* is "dolore."

In the second stanza, where the lover is still going along the journey towards the death of the *congedo*, the poet documents the afflictions that consume him, leaving him so wasted, "sì magro / della persona [my body wasted]" (18–19), that "it will then take but a little breeze / to sweep me off so that I fall down dead": "non trarrà sì poco vento / che non mi meni, sì ch'io cadrò freddo" (21–2). These verses, which include the only occurrence in Dante's lyrics of *magro* (or its variant *macro*), will be remembered in the *Commedia*: in the *Paradiso*, it is the "poema sacro," rather than *doloroso amor*, "che m'ha fatto per molti anni macro [sacred poem ... that made me thin through many years]" [*Par.* 25.1–3]). In the context of paradise, thinness assumes the odour, not of sexual passion, but of holiness: Saint Peter and Saint Paul are "magri e scalzi [thin and barefoot]" [*Par.* 21.128]).

In the canto of *Inferno* dedicated to lust, we find instead a situation similar to that of our canzone. The "bufera infernal [che] mena li spirti" ("infernal whirlwind [that] drives the spirits" [*Inf.* 5.31–2]) echoes the "vento / che non mi meni" of *Lo doloroso amor*, and the concluding verse, "E caddi come corpo morto cade [and I fell as a dead body falls]" [*Inf.* 5.142]), recalls "sì ch'io cadrò freddo" of the canzone. Moreover, the first verses of our canzone, "Lo doloroso **amor** che mi **conduce** / a·ffin di **morte** per **piacer** di quella," are echoed in Francesca's celebrated verses: in "mi prese del costui **piacer** sì forte [seized me with his beauty so strongly]" [*Inf.* 5.104]) and above all in "**Amor condusse** noi ad una **morte** [Love led us to one death]" [*Inf.* 5.106]), which strips away "doloroso" and "a·ffin" to arrive at the essential building blocks of *amore, condurre,* and *morte. Lo doloroso amor* and its companion canzone, *E' m'incresce di me,* where these building blocks are also present, served as incubators for an ideology that Dante will reject, but to which he will also give voice through Francesca, whose culminating "Amor condusse noi ad una morte" is imprinted on the opening of *Lo doloroso amor* syntactically, lexically, and above all ideologically.

It is curious that this same second strophe of *Lo doloroso amor,* which will endure in the memory of the later eschatological masterpiece, concludes by introducing into the canzone its own erotic eschatology. Here Dante follows in the footsteps of Giacomo da Lentini (in this way also recalling the canzone *La dispietata mente,* which dialogues significantly with the Sicilian poet), whose sonnet *Io m'aggio posto in core a Dio servire* avails itself of the *paradiso/viso* rhyme and makes it emblematic of the interior struggle of the poet, who feels "diviso" between God ("Io m'aggio posto in core a Dio servire, / com'io potesse gire in **paradiso** [I've set my heart on serving God, / so as to visit Paradise]" [1–2]) and his lady ("Sanza mi **donna** non vi voria gire, / quella c'à blonda testa e claro viso [I would not go without my love, / whose face is bright and hair light blond]" [5–6]). Using the same *paradiso/viso* rhyme to indicate the same internal division, Dante openly declares that paradise is worth nothing in comparison with the memory of the sweet face of his lady: "ricordando la gioia del dolce **viso** / a che nïente pare il **paradiso** [remembering the joy of her sweet face, / beyond compare of even paradise]" [27–8]).

And that is not all: the third and last strophe delineates the drama of the lover against a backdrop that is more and more exaggeratedly eschatological and theologized. Here the poet takes up again the dilemma of Giacomo and the courtly world and in the strongest and most explicit manner aligns himself not on the side of God but on that of the lady. "Reflecting on what love has made me feel," the poet declares that "my soul desires no other happiness": "Pensando a quel che d'amor ho provato, / l'anima mia non chiede altro diletto" (29–30). Further, the love that he felt in life protects him from fear of the beyond ("né il penar non cura il quale attende [nor will it fear the torment it awaits]" [31]), since when he dies, love will accompany his soul to God. The phrase "l'**amor** che m'ha sì **stretto** [the love that's bound me so to it]"

(33), which in the canzone is rhymed with "l'anima mia non chiede altro **diletto**" (30), constitutes another echo of *Lo doloroso amor* destined for the fifth canto of *Inferno*, where we find the proximity of "diletto" not with the past participle of *stringere* ("stretto") but with the *passato remoto* "strinse": "Noi leggiavamo un giorno per diletto / di Lancialotto come **amor** lo **strinse** [We were reading one day, for pleasure, of Lancelot and how Love bound him]" (*Inf.* 5.127–8).

In the third strophe, Dante creates a perverse variant of the famous *congedo* of Guido Guinizzelli's *Al cor gentil rimpaira sempre amore*, where the Bolognese poet imagines having to justify his love for his lady before a divine tribunal, declaring: "Tenne d'angel sembianza / che fosse del Tuo regno; / non me fu fallo, s'in lei posi amanza [She had an angelic look, / as if from Your kingdom; / it was no fault in me, if I placed my love in her]" (*Al cor gentil*, 58–60). Here the theologizing of the amorous discourse serves to elevate the earthly (the "vano amor" of which God accuses the poet) towards the divine and thus to exculpate the poet: it is not a "fault" to love the lady precisely because she belongs to the divine kingdom; indeed, if fault there is, it is God's, who created women so similar to the angels of his kingdom. But even if Guinizzelli indulges in the daring game of throwing back at the Creator the accusation that was levelled at himself, we still remain in a context in which God – not the lady – is the point of reference.

In *Lo doloroso amor*, Dante inverts the terms, making the lady the point of reference instead. The poet details the situation of his soul, which has – as in Guinizzelli's *congedo* – arrived before the divine tribunal: if God does not pardon the soul its sins, it will depart with the punishments it deserves ("e se del suo peccar pace no i rende, / partirassi col tormentar ch'è degna [and should He grant its sin no amnesty, / it will depart with torments that are just]" [35–6]), but in such a way as to not be afraid ("sì·cche non ne paventa [but which it does not dread]" [37]). How can it be that the soul of the poet will not be afraid of the punishments of hell? Because, in another reprise of Giacomo, here the Sicilian topos of the image of the lady painted in the heart of the lover, the poet explains that his soul will be so intent on imagining his lady that it will not feel any pain: "e starà tanto attenta / d'immaginar colei per cui s'è mossa, / che nulla pena averà che ella senta [it will be so intent / on contemplating her who made it leave / that there will be no pain that it might feel]" (38–40).

In an overturning of the normative hierarchy between Creator and creature, here the poet makes the lady the absolute point of reference of his universe. She is, in fact, "she for whom my soul set off on its course": the journey of his life, the journey towards the death described by the canzone, the spiritual movement of his soul – all of it is a function of her, defined literally as "colei per cui [l'anima sua] s'è mossa" (39). Intent and concentrated on imagining his lady, the poet will be immunized to the punishments of hell, pains that in fact he will not even feel. The old topos of the *guiderdone* finds in these verses a new and eschatological vitality: here finally is the true recompense lavished by Love on the faithful! If Love was sparing with him in this life, "'n questo mo[n]do" (41), it will instead be generous in the next: "sì·cche se 'n questo mo[n]do i' l'ho perduto, / Amor nell'altro me ·n darà tributo [and thus if I have lost it in this world, / Love in the other will repay me well]" (41–2).

The importance of *Lo doloroso amor* derives in great part from the strong eschatological bent of this last strophe, by the underlined contrast between "questo mondo" and "l'altro." Dante is here experimenting with the same theologized elements, of Guinizzellian heritage, that will make the style of *Donne ch'avete intelletto d'amore* "new." But, given the sorrowful theme of *Lo doloroso amor*, these elements here take on a perverse and non-normative colouring.

The eschatological elements in *Lo doloroso amor* have a history in Dante's repertory, one that extends beyond *Inferno* 5 all the way to the seventh canto of *Paradiso*, where we find the same combination of the name of Beatrice, first divided "into *Be* and *ice*" ("pur per *Be* e per *ice*" [*Par.* 7.14]), and then written whole in verse 16, with the hyperbole of the lover who does not feel the punishments of hell:

Ma quella reverenza che s'indonna
di tutto me, pur per *Be* e per *ice*,
mi richinava come l'uom ch'assonna.
Poco sofferse me cotal Beatrice
e cominciò, raggiandomi d'un riso
tal, che nel foco faria l'uom felice.   (*Par.* 7.13–18)

[But that reverence that lords over all of me, even just with *Be* and with *ice*, made me
bow like a man falling asleep. Beatrice didn't leave me in this state for long, and she
began to speak, shining on me with the rays of such a smile as would make a man happy
in the fire.]

Here are the vestiges of *Lo doloroso amor*: the courtly world invoked in the neologism "s'indonna," a verb denoting "to lord over someone as feudal mistress or *donna*" (*Par.* 7.13); the name made sign by the division into syllables, *Be* and *ice*, as though "written," as stipulated in the words of *Lo doloroso amor*, "The sweet name that embitters so my heart / each time I see it *written down*" (15–16); and above all the description of the lady's laughter, capable of immunizing her lover from the pains of hell: "un riso / tal, che nel foco faria l'uom felice" (*Par.* 7.17–18).

Lo doloroso amor is important in reconstructing Dante's ideological path because its key verse, "Per quella moro c'ha nome Beatrice" (14), is antithetical to the values of the poet Dante became, whose epigraph could well be "Per quella vivo c'ha nome Beatrice": I live for/because of her whose name is Beatrice. *Lo doloroso amor* thus executes an ideological oxymoron: it anticipates on the one hand the Beatrician and theologized *Vita Nuova* and on the other the fatal love of the *rime petrose*. It is as though the lethal lady of the *rime petrose* were called not "petra" (stone) but "she who makes happy, she who gives *beatitudine*." The extremism of *Lo doloroso amor* lies in its commingling of elements that will be antithetical in the Dantean universe as ultimately scripted.

In conclusion, I offer a note on the transmission of *Lo doloroso amor*. In this most existential of contexts, *Lo doloroso amor* holds a very particular position: a position of precarious marginality with respect to Dante's other canzoni. *Lo doloroso amor* is, as De Robertis notes, "estravagante tra le estravaganti [an outsider among the outsiders]" [*Introduzione*, vol. 2, p. 756]),[84] and in fact the history of its transmission is the history of its absence. This canzone was not a part of the fortunate group of fifteen canzoni copied by Boccaccio, a group destined to be transmitted as a corpus in their Boccaccian order. Excluded from Boccaccio's collection, *Lo doloroso amor* was then excluded from the first printed edition of Dante's lyrics, the Giuntina of 1527. Given its exclusion from what De Robertis calls "la grande tradizione" of Dante's lyric poems, *Lo doloroso amor* has had a less privileged transmission than Dante's other canzoni: "The codices, for this canzone, are not counted in the hundreds as for the others, or in tens, if we make a single witness out of the extremely copied Boccaccian tradition (but a single witness with enormous influence for almost two centuries); rather they are counted on the fingers of one hand" (De Robertis, *Introduzione*, vol. 2, p. 1152). The absence of *Lo doloroso amor* from Boccaccio's *canzoni distese* has thus contributed to its marginal position, a marginality reified by De Robertis in his recent edition. It is as though *Lo doloroso amor* were less canonical, less Dante's canzone than the others.

It is difficult to repress the suspicion that it is precisely the verse "Per quella moro c'ha nome Beatrice" that created strong doubts in the copyists, Boccaccio included, and in this way damaged the transmission of the canzone that contains it. If that were the case, one could say that in a certain sense the copyists showed themselves to be shrewd readers. They understood – and attempted to eliminate – the challenge posed by *Lo doloroso amor* to the dominant myth of himself that Dante so ably constructed and passed on to posterity.

31 (B LXVIII; C 21; FB 25; DR 16)

Lo doloroso amor che mi conduce	The painful love that leads me to my end
a·ffin di morte per piacer di quella	in death – resulting from an act of her
3 che lo mio cor solea tener gioioso	who used to fill my heart with joyfulness –
m'ha tolto e toglie ciascun dì la luce	has robbed and robs me still each day of light
ch'avean li occhi miei di tale stella,	my eyes were used to claiming from her star
6 che non credea di lei mai star doglioso;	such that I thought she'd never make me sad:
e 'l colpo suo, c'ho portato nascoso,	this wound, which I have kept concealed from view,
omai si scuopre per soperchia pena,	can now be seen because of my deep pain,
la qual nasce del foco	engendered by the fire
che m'ha tratto di gioco,	that robbed me of my joy,

---

84 In *filologia dantesca* (Dantean philology) the word "estravagante" is used to refer to Dante's poems not included in the *Vita Nuova* and in the *Convivio,* the poems kept "out," and thus forced to remain "wandering outsiders"; on the cultural freight of *estravaganti* see my essay "Editing Dante's *Rime* and Italian Cultural History," 2004, rpt. in *Dante and the Origins of Italian Literary Culture*, pp. 245–78.

11 sì·cch'altro mai che male io non aspetto;
    e 'l viver mio – omai de' esser poco –
    fin a la morte mia sospira e dice:
14 "Per quella moro c'ha nome Beatrice."
        Quel dolce nome che mi fa il cor agro,
    tutte fïate ch'i' lo vedrò scritto
17 mi farà nuovo ogni dolor ch'i' sento;
    e della doglia diverrò sì magro
    della persona, e 'l viso tanto afflitto
20 che qual mi vederà n'avrà pavento.
    E allor non trarrà sì poco vento
    che non mi meni, sì ch'io cadrò freddo;
    e per tal verrò morto,
    e 'l dolor sarà scorto
25 co·ll'anima che se ·n girà sì trista,
    e sempre mai co·llei starà ricolto
    ricordando la gioia del dolce viso
28 a che nïente pare il paradiso.
        Pensando a quel che d'amor ho provato,
    l'anima mia non chiede altro diletto,
31 né il penar non cura il quale attende;
    ché poi che 'l corpo sarà consumato
    se n'anderà l'amor che m'ha sì stretto
34 co·llei a Quel ch'ogni ragione intende;
    e se del suo peccar pace no i rende,
    partirassi col tormentar ch'è degna,
    sì·cche non ne paventa,
    e starà tanto attenta
39 d'inmaginar colei per cui s'è mossa,
    che nulla pena averà che ella senta:
    sì·cche se 'n questo mo[n]do i' l'ho perduto,
42 Amor nell'altro me ·n darà tributo.
        Morte, che·ffai piacere a questa donna,
    per pietà, innanzi che·ttu mi discigli,
    va' da·llei, fatti dire
    perché m'avien che la luce di quegli
47 che mi fan tristo mi sia così tolta.
    Se per altrui ella fosse ricolta,
    fa' ·lmi sentire, e trarra'mi d'errore,
50 e assai finirò con men dolore.

so that I now expect just pain alone.
My life (what little now remains of it)
will sigh to me right to my death and say:
"I die for her whose name is Beatrice."
    The sweet name that embitters so my heart
each time I see it written down someplace
will make the pain I feel renew itself;
I think I will become so changed by grief,
my body wasted and my face distraught,
that those who see me will recoil in fear.
And it will then take but a little breeze
to sweep me off so that I fall down dead;
and that is how I'll die,
my anguish to escort
my sullen soul that must now fade away;
and it will always keep her company,
remembering the joy of her sweet face,
beyond compare of even paradise.
    Reflecting on what love has made me feel,
my soul desires no other happiness,
nor will it fear the torment it awaits;
for once my body has been turned to dust,
the love that's bound me so to it will rise
aloft to Him who comprehends all things;
and should He grant its sin no amnesty,
it will depart with torments that are just,
but which it does not dread;
it will be so intent
on contemplating her who made it leave
that there will be no pain that it might feel:
and thus if I have lost it in this world,
Love in the other will repay me well.
    Death, you who implement this lady's will,
for pity's sake, before you ruin me,
go up to her and ask
why is it that the light of those fair eyes
that sadden me has been withdrawn this way.
If someone else instead receives this light,
end my illusion now by telling me,
so I can suffer death less painfully.

METRE: canzone of three stanzas, each composed of fourteen verses (twelve hendecasyllables and two *settenari*), with rhyme scheme ABC ABC CXddYDEE and *congedo* of eight verses, XAyABBCC. The *fronte* is six verses (3 + 3) and the *sirma* is eight verses. X and Y indicate verses that do not rhyme: verses 8 and 11 of each stanza, as well as two verses in the *congedo*.

32 E' m'incresce di me sì duramente

Whether or not as a result of its scandalous thematic content, *Lo doloroso amor* experienced an anomalous reception: it was not included by Boccaccio in his group of fifteen heavily anthologized canzoni. In the case of *E' m'incresce di me*, such marginalization did not occur, but this canzone – also sorrowful, also theologized; if anything, even more theologized, with features that approach the *Vita Nuova* – joins its fellow in its ability to provoke scholarly anxiety. Such anxiety was expressed in the futile *querelle* on the identity of the murderous lady of *E' m'incresce di me*, and in the prolonged refusal, documented by Barbi (pp. 244–56), to concede the obvious: that this lady too is Beatrice. All because *E' m'incresce di me* does not contain a verse, like "Per quella moro c'ha nome Beatrice [I die for her whose name is Beatrice]" [*Lo doloroso amor*, 14]), which renders the identity of the lethal lady undeniable.

Exegetes have nonetheless concurred with Barbi's formulation according to which, like *Lo doloroso amor*, *E' m'incresce di me* "should be placed in the period of strong love, of painful love, a love represented in the *Vita Nuova* only by the four sonnets of chapters XIII–XVI" (Barbi-Maggini, p. 256).

E' m'incresce di me begins in a strongly Cavalcantian key, delineating the self-pity that the lover feels for himself because of the death inflicted on him by his lady's eyes, eyes that will be protagonists throughout the canzone. In this primordial moment of the drama, they are "belli occhi [alluring eyes]" (7) that seem "piani, / soavi e dolci [gentle, kind and tender]" (10–11), but later they will be "occhi micidiali [murderous eyes]" (49), and in the last stanza her dominion will be sealed by a gaze bestowed by those same eyes: "che sarà donna sopra tutte noi / tosto che fia piacer degli occhi suoi [who will reign as mistress of us all, / as soon as it is pleasing to her eyes]" (83–4). If in the first stanza her eyes "undertook / to bring about my death" ("incominciaro / la morte mia" [12–13]), in the second they leave him for dead on the battlefield that is love. From the moment that the lady's eyes take in their victory "di loro intelletto [by their own reasoning]" (18) – thus demonstrating an "intelletto d'amore" of a very different order from that possessed by the ladies of *Donne ch'avete intelletto d'amore*! – they depart with the banners of Love, with the result that "my soul now grieves / when it expected comfort": "è rimasa trista / l'anima mia che n'attendea conforto" (24–5).

The abandoned soul is the protagonist of the third stanza, where it is depicted as dejected, crying, and disconsolate, in a typically Cavalcantian register: "Innamorata se ne va piangendo / for di questa vita / la sconsolata, che la caccia Amore [Still full of love my soul, disconsolate, / departs this life of ours / with tears of sorrow, driven out by Love]" (29–31). The Cavalcantian tone, melancholic and elegiac, is prolonged for the whole third strophe:

Ristretta s'è entro 'l mezzo del core
con quella vita che rimane spenta
solo in quel punto ch'ella se· n va via,
ed ivi si lamenta
d'Amor che for d'esto mondo la caccia,
e spessamente abraccia
li spiriti che piangon tuttavia,
però che perdon la lor compagnia.
        (*E' m'incresce di me*, 35–42)

[The soul retreats inside the inner heart
to join what little life remains to fade
the very instant that it takes its leave.
And there it censures Love,
who forces it to leave this world behind,
embracing more than once
the spirits that lament unceasingly
the painful loss of its sweet company.]

In the third stanza we note the recurrence of the verb *cacciare*, used twice to denote existential exile. Love is portrayed as the hunter, and the soul is literally hunted "out of this life" and "out of this world": "fora di questa vita / la sconsolata, che la **caccia** Amore [departs this life of ours / with tears of sorrow, driven out by Love]" (30–1); "ed ivi si lamenta / d'Amor che for d'esto mondo la **caccia** [and there it censures Love, / who forces it to leave this world behind]" (38–9). If the exilic locutions "fora di questa vita" and "for d'esto mondo" are Cavalcantian, the verb *cacciare* is not; to the contrary, it imports into the Cavalcantian melancholy a vitality and robustness that are instead very Dantean, and anticipates the idiosyncratically and innovatively Dantean tone of the fourth and fifth stanzas.

The double presence of the verb *cacciare* in the third stanza of *E' m'incresce di me* may have a bearing on the complex drama between Dante and his "primo amico," Guido Cavalcanti. Maybe when Dante wrote in *Purgatorio* of the poet who will hunt Guido Guinizzelli and Guido Cavalcanti from the nest – "Così ha tolto l'uno a l'altro Guido / la gloria de la lingua; e forse è nato / chi l'uno e l'altro **caccerà** del nido [Thus has one Guido taken from the other the glory of our language, and perhaps he is born who will hunt one and the other from the nest]" (*Purg.* 11.97–9) – he recalled what is plausibly his first use of the verb *cacciare*, in the youthful Cavalcantian canzone *E' m'incresce di me*.[85] Certainly a Love that "hunts" breaks with Cavalcanti,

---

85 Other than a use of *scacciare* similar to what we find in *E' m'incresce di me* in the sonnet *Onde venite voi così pensose?* ("sì·mm'ha in tutto Amor da·ssé **scacciato** [so completely has Love driven me away from him]" [10]), the other uses both of the verb *cacciare* and of the noun *caccia* in Dante's lyrics come from his more mature poems. In the canzone *Amor che movi tua vertù dal cielo*,

who never uses the verb *cacciare* in his love poems. Guido uses *cacciare* only in two correspondence sonnets, one to Guido Orlandi and the other to Dante. In the sonnet *I' vegno 'l giorno a·tte*, Guido harshly reproves his friend for "la vil tua vita" and concludes in this way: "Se 'l presente sonetto spesso leggi, / lo spirito noioso che·tti **caccia** / si partirà dall'anima invilita [If you reread this sonnet several times, / the loathsome spirit persecuting you (literally, that hunts you) / will be dispelled from your degraded soul]" (12–14). Perhaps this rather aggressive use of "caccia" on the part of his friend is what Dante remembered as he penned his own aggressive verses in *Purgatorio* 11.

E' m'incresce di me divides into two halves of three strophes each, as the narrative emphasis shifts from the lover to the lady, or, in Contini's words, "from a subjective, internal point of view" to "an objective, historical point of view" (p. 61). The fourth stanza opens with the imposing figure of the victorious lady who installs herself in the mind of the lover (the word "mente" will be used four times in *E' m'incresce di me*, more than in any other of Dante's poems; here it anticipates the "libro della mente" of the next stanza): "L'imagine di questa donne siede / sù nella mente ancora [The image of this lady still holds sway / within my intellect]" (43–4). Onto the scene erupts a lady-assassin who "raises up her murderous eyes [alza gli occhi micidiali]" (49) and celebrates her absolute dominion with a shout, whose sadistic content is registered through the immediacy of direct discourse: "e **grida** / sovra colei che piange il suo partire: / 'Vanne, misera, fuor, vattene omai' [she castigates my soul that weeps for death: / 'Get out of here, you wretch, now go away']" (49–51).[86] The verb *gridare*, "to scream or shout out," which Dante uses again in the following verse – "Questo **grida** il disire [Such words desire speaks]" (52) – could not be less Cavalcantian: literally, given that Cavalcanti never uses it. The same could be said of the adjective *micidiale* used by Dante for the "occhi micidiali" of the lady, another word that does not appear in the more restricted diction – calmer, more resigned – of Cavalcanti.

The fourth stanza of *E' m'incresce di me* marks the birth of a new poetics of passion. Moving away from the calm, rational desperation of Cavalcanti, Dante here is inventing the diction and the register of erotic aggression that he will exploit with so much success in the *rime petrose* and, beyond the *rime petrose*, in the prose treatises

---

the poet describes the actions of Love, as in *E' m'incresce di me*, but portrays a Love who acts not cruelly but virtuously: "tu **cacci** la viltà altrui del core [you banish baseness from all hearts]" (7). In the sonnet to Cino *I' ho veduto già senza radice*, Dante advises his friend not to pursue the "giovane donna": "parmi che·lla tua **caccia** [non] seguer de' [I don't think you should keep on hunting]" (14). And in the canzone of exile, *Tre donne*, the political *congedo* features the verb *cacciare*: "canzone, **caccia** con li neri veltri [canzone, hunt with the black greyhounds]" (102).

86 It is altogether unusual for the courtly lady to speak, never mind shout, even if it is true that these words could be put in the mouth of Love and are not at all indicative of her subjectivity or inner state. The use of *gridare* in Dante's lyrics will be discussed again in the introductory essay to *Donne ch'avete*.

and ultimately in the *Commedia*: passion and aggression are essential to Dante's poetics. Dante is as hot and impassioned, even (especially) when dealing with the intellect, as Cavalcanti is detached and cool, even (especially) when dealing with passion. The verb *gridare* and the adjective *micidiale* appear together in *E' m'incresce di me* and again in the most aggressive of the *petrose*, *Così nel mio parlar*, in which the lover struggles with a lady who is "micidiale e latra [murderous and thieving]" (58).

At this point, it might seem that Dante had already accomplished enough in this canzone, but in fact it is the fifth stanza that moves the poet most significantly along his poetic itinerary. The fifth stanza of *E' m'incresce di me* is essentially a trial run for the *Vita Nuova*, in the sense that the lady – this same aggressive, cruel, and lethal lady – will be presented as a being who is special and miraculous in absolute terms, not only within the subjectivity of the lover but objectively and historically. Situating his narration on a stage that now encompasses the whole world, the poet takes an enormous step backward in history in order to return to the day of the birth of his lady and to the effects of this birth on his youthful body. He says that he is able to read these effects "in the book of memory" ("nel libro della mente"):

> Lo giorno che costei nel mondo venne,
> secondo che si truova
> nel libro della mente che vien meno,
> la mia persona pargola sostenne
> una passïon nova,
> tal ch'io rimasi di paura pieno.
>   (*E' m'incresce di me*, 57–62)

> [The day on which she came into this world,
> according to the book
> of memory that falters more and more,
> my youthful body was subjected to
> a feeling so unknown
> I sank into a state of fearfulness.]

Here we see elements of the miraculous and theologized history of the *Vita Nuova*, still linked syntactically to the Cavalcantian love that provokes fear and death. For instance, in verse 59, the image of the "libro della mente," which before long will ornament the prose opening of the *Vita Nuova*, is destabilized by the Cavalcantian faltering of "vien meno" (to fail); similarly, the "passïon nova" that the lover feels is not such as to cause ecstasy, but such that "I sank into a state of fearfulness" ("tal che rimasi di paura pieno") (61–2). If on the one hand the poem affirms – as does the *Vita Nuova* – an experience that is absolutely new and different, that can miraculously make itself felt by the childish body of the poet in the moment of her birth, on the other hand it is still about a passion that causes fear and trembling and that carries the soul towards death:

e se 'l libro non erra,
lo spirito maggior tremò sì forte
che parve ben che morte
per lui in questo mondo giunta fosse;
ma or ne 'ncresce a quei che questo mosse.
(*E' m'incresce di me*, 66–70)

[and if this book is right,
the greater spirit trembled with such force
that it became quite clear
that death was just about to claim its life.
But He who did ordain this now repents.]

In the last verse of the fifth stanza, the death of the self awakens pity in the ordainer of these events, God, already invoked in verse 34, where "its Maker hears its plea with sympathy": "ascolta con pietate il suo Fattore" (34). *E' m'incresce di me* thus moves from self-pity in its first verse to God's pity: Dante's field has broadened. But she who is born with such cosmic effects in *E' m'incresce di me* is not yet endowed with the beneficent qualities of the lady of *Donne ch'avete intelletto d'amore*; to the contrary, in this canzone the intellective faculty of the lover realizes that "its affliction had been born": "che 'l suo male era nato" (76). We are still dealing with the Beatrice of *Lo doloroso amor*, of whom the poet wrote "Per quella moro c'ha nome Beatrice."

The canzoni *Lo doloroso amor* and *E' m'incresce di me* are evidence of an interior drama: they show that the road Dante travelled to arrive at the Beatrice of the *Vita Nuova* was far from overdetermined. Dante experimented with various formulas, and *E' m'incresce di me* was one of these experimentations, a canzone in which the poet combines Cavalcanti's lethal love with a new erotic aggression all Dante's own, and then sets the whole drama in a cosmic and supernatural frame. The result is a fascinating ideological aporia: a lady who is miraculous but also Cavalcantian.

32 (B LXVII; C 20; FB 32; DR 10)

E' m'incresce di me sì duramente,
ch'altrettanto di doglia
3 mi reca la pietà quanto 'l martiro,
lasso, però che dolorosamente
sento contra mia voglia
6 raccoglier l'aire del sezzaio sospiro
entro 'n quel cor che' belli occhi feriro
quando li aperse Amor co· le sue mani
per conducermi al tempo che mi sface.

I feel such deep compassion for myself
that pity makes me bear
in equal measure sorrow and great pain,
and so excruciatingly, alas,
I feel unwillingly
the final sigh swell up within my heart
that those alluring eyes of hers struck hard
when Love with his own hands first opened them
to lead me to the hour of my demise.

10 Oïmè, quanto piani,
      soavi e dolci ver' me si levaro
      quand'elli incominciaro
      la morte mia, che tanto mi dispiace,
14 dicendo: "Nostro lume porta pace."
          "Noi darem pace al core, a voi diletto"
      diceano agli occhi miei
17 quei della bella donna alcuna volta;
      ma poi che sepper di loro intelletto
      che per forza di lei
20 m'era la mente già ben tutta tolta,
      co· le 'nsegne d'Amor dieder la volta;
      sì che la lor vittorïosa vista
      poi non si vide pur una fïata:
24 ond'è rimasa trista
      l'anima mia che n'attendea conforto;
      ed ora quasi morto
      vede lo core a cui era sposata,
28 e partir la conviene innamorata.
          Innamorata se ne va piangendo
      fora di questa vita
31 la sconsolata, che la caccia Amore.
      Ella si move quinci sì dolendo,
      ch'anzi la sua partita
34 l'ascolta con pietate il suo Fattore.
      Ristretta s'è entro 'l mezzo del core
      con quella vita che rimane spenta
      solo in quel punto ch'ella se ·n va via,
38 ed ivi si lamenta
      d'Amor che for d'esto mondo la caccia,
      e spessamente abraccia
      li spiriti che piangon tuttavia,
42 però che perdon la lor compagnia.
          L'imagine di questa donna siede
      sù nella mente ancora,
45 là ove la puose quei che fu sua guida;
      e non le pesa del mal ch'ella vede,
      anzi vie più bella ora
48 che mai e vie più lieta par che rida,
      ed alza gli occhi micidiali, e grida
      sovra colei che piange il suo partire:
      "Vanne, misera, fuor, vattene omai!"
52 Questo grida il disire
      che mi combatte così come suole,

How gentle and how kind,
how tender was the look that they displayed
the day they undertook
to bring about my death, so painfully,
and said to me: "Our light will bring you peace."
    "We'll bring peace to your heart, and joy to you,"
her eyes said to my eyes,
the ones my lady used to show at times;
but once they knew, by their own reasoning,
that through her power my mind
had been completely torn away from me,
they turned and fled beneath Love's gonfalon,
so that the look they had in victory
was never to be seen again, not once:
and so my soul now grieves
when it expected comfort from their light,
and must now look upon
my heart near death, to which it once was wed,
and has to take its leave still full of love.
    Still full of love my soul, disconsolate,
departs this life of ours
with tears of sorrow, driven out by Love.
In going forth it suffers so much pain
that, just before it leaves,
its Maker hears its plea with sympathy.
The soul retreats inside the inner heart
to join what little life remains to fade
the very instant that it takes its leave.
And there it censures Love,
who forces it to leave this world behind,
embracing more than once
the spirits that lament unceasingly
the painful loss of its sweet company.
    The image of this lady still holds sway
within my intellect,
where it was placed by him who was her guide.
But it's not troubled by the harm it sees,
indeed she's lovelier
than in the past and smiles with greater joy;
and as she raises up her murderous eyes,
she castigates my soul that weeps for death:
"Get out of here, you wretch, now go away!"
Such words desire speaks,
assailing me as it has always done,

avegna che men duole,
però che 'l mio sentire è meno assai
56 ed è più presso al terminar de' guai.
      Lo giorno che costei nel mondo venne,
secondo che si truova
59 nel libro della mente che vien meno,
la mia persona pargola sostenne
una passïon nova,
62 tal ch'io rimasi di paura pieno;
ch'a tutte mie virtù fu posto un freno
subitamente, sì ch'io caddi in terra
per una luce che nel cuor percosse;
66 e se 'l libro non erra,
lo spirito maggior tremò sì forte
che parve ben che morte
per lui in questo mondo giunta fosse;
70 ma or ne 'ncresce a quei che questo mosse.
      Quando m'aparve poi la gran biltate
che sì mi fa dolere,
73 donne gentili a cui i' ho parlato,
quella virtù c'ha più nobilitate,
mirando nel piacere,
76 s'accorse ben che 'l suo male era nato;
e conobbe il disio ch'era creato
per lo mirare intento ch'ella fece,
sì che piangendo disse a l'altre poi:
80 "Qui giugnerà, in vece
d'una ch'i' vidi, la bella figura
che già mi fa paura,
che sarà donna sopra tutte noi
84 tosto che fia piacer degli occhi suoi."
      I' ho parlato a voi, giovani donne
ch'avete gli occhi di bellezze ornati
e la mente d'amor vinta e pensosa,
88 perché raccomandati
vi sian li detti miei ovunque sono;
e 'nnanzi a voi perdono
la morte mia a quella bella cosa
92 che me n'ha colpa e mai non fu pietosa.

though now the pain is less
because my power to feel is less intense
and is far closer to the end of woe.
      The day on which she came into this world,
according to the book
of memory that falters more and more,
my youthful body was subjected to
a feeling so unknown
I sank into a state of fearfulness;
and it arrested all my faculties
so suddenly I fell right to the ground,
because a light had pierced me in the heart:
and if this book is right,
the greater spirit trembled with such force
that it became quite clear
that death was just about to claim its life.
But He who did ordain this now repents.
      When I first saw her wondrous loveliness
that brings such pain to me,
dear noble ladies who've now heard me speak,
the faculty that stands above the rest,
while gazing on her face,
perceived that its affliction had been born
and recognized the yearning brought to life
by having gazed on her so steadfastly;
and so it told the other faculties, in tears:
"In place of her I saw
will come the lovely image of that one,
which I already fear
and who will reign as mistress of us all,
as soon as it is pleasing to her eyes."
      Young ladies, I have spoken now to you,
whose eyes hold beauty as an ornament
and who are ruled by painful thoughts of love,
in order that my poem
commend itself to you where it is heard:
before you, I forgive
that lovely one for having caused my death,
who bears all blame and never showed me pity.

METRE: canzone of six stanzas, each composed of fourteen verses (ten hendecasyllables and four *settenari*), with rhyme scheme AbC AbC CDEdFfEE and *congedo* with rhyme scheme identical to that of the *sirma*. The *fronte* is six verses (3 + 3) and the *sirma* is eight verses.

33 Donne ch'avete intelletto d'amore

Among his own canzoni, *Donne ch'avete* was Dante's personal favourite. In two key moments of his writer's life – in the *Vita Nuova* and then in the *Commedia* – Dante cites it and explicitly states that for him it holds a privileged place, and that he assigns it a central role in constructing his identity as poet, in his poetic autobiography. In the linguistic treatise *De vulgari eloquentia*, where Dante cites several of his own canzoni, *Donne ch'avete* again holds a prominent position, cited where the canzone genre is defined (2.8) and again as an example of a canzone whose stanzas are composed entirely of hendecasyllables (2.12). In *Vita Nuova* XIX (10), *Donne ch'avete* is a canzone-manifesto, which assumes a programmatic function in the *libello* (a role that is then cemented by the explicit echoes of *Donne ch'avete* in the canzone on the death of Beatrice, *Li occhi dolenti*): it has the role of breaking with the past, of ushering in the new, and of alerting readers to all that is new and different in the *stil novo* with respect to earlier poetics. Composed of five stanzas of fourteen lines each (the fifth functions as a *congedo*), *Donne ch'avete* is the first canzone in the *Vita Nuova* and represents a new beginning, in writing as well as in life, a new beginning that Dante underscores in the prose, emphasizing the canzone's birth, its "cominciamento": "Queste parole io ripuosi ne la mente con grande letizia, pensando di prenderle per mio cominciamento; onde poi, ritornato a la sopradetta cittade, pensando alquanti die, cominciai una canzone con questo cominciamento [Then, returning to the above-named city, after thinking about it for several days, I started to compose a canzone with this opening]" (*VN* XIX.3 [10.14]).

The programmatic, foundational role of *Donne ch'avete* will be confirmed many years later, when it is precisely this poem that inspires Bonagiunta da Lucca to conjure the label *dolce stil novo*, sweet new style, in the celebrated encounter of *Purgatorio* 24. We might say that in the *Vita Nuova*, where Dante's *stil novo* is *in fieri*, *Donne ch'avete* "acts," that is, it actualizes the new style: the canzone actively shows us what is new about the *stil novo*. In *Purgatorio*, on the other hand, *Donne ch'avete*, which in its time had broken with the past, has become the past: it is emblematic of the poetic history that Dante is now writing and codifying, a history that – long since institutionalized in Italian historiography with the purgatorial label – was for Dante distilled in the early canzone.

Dante, a poet in an age when lyrics usually remained uncollected, discovered a foolproof method for conferring upon a single lyric a special value in the economy of his overall work: he understood that he could exercise choice as author-cum-editor-publisher, and that through the act of choosing and reusing he could give a lyric, which was already living a "first life" as an autonomous poem, a "second life" within a macrotext. Thirty-one poems were in this way chosen and assigned to the macro-text of the *Vita Nuova*, three canzoni to the macrotext of the unfinished *Convivio*, and the opening lines of three canzoni to the macrotext of the *Commedia*. The three autocitations allocated to the *Commedia* all come from other macrotexts, so that the *Commedia* confers upon them a "third life": *Amor che nella mente mi ragiona*, previously the second of the three canzoni of the *Convivio*, is cited in *Purgatorio* 2; *Donne ch'avete intelletto d'amore*, from the *Vita Nuova*, in *Purgatorio* 24; and *Voi che 'ntendendo il terzo ciel movete*, the first of the canzoni of the *Convivio*, in *Paradiso* 8. The central poem of this intertextual and autobiographical discourse inscribed in the *Commedia*, the only one that is not subjected to the slightest criticism or retroactive revision, is the favoured canzone *Donne ch'avete*.[87]

When we consider this canzone in the context of Dante's lyrics, it is important to read it for itself, and not through the lens of Dante's self-mythologizing, which in this case is a lens of endorsement and a potential magnifying glass. On the other hand, the rhetorical and ideological achievements of this canzone, seen from the perspective of what Dante previously wrote – canzoni such as *La dispietata mente*, *Lo doloroso amor*, and *E' m'incresce di me* – are real and indisputable: if Dante was searching for a way that would lead him to the *Commedia*, *Donne ch'avete* constitutes a fundamental step in getting there. And we can say this without resorting to the *Vita Nuova*'s prose, but on the basis of the canzone taken in itself.

Donne ch'avete, in fact, is extraordinary without an assist from the prose: the substance of the canzone is entirely radical on its own, entirely innovative, entirely theologized. (I prefer to speak of the canzone as "theologized" rather than "theological," because Dante is endowing his courtly discourse with a theologized patina, not engaging in a careful use of theology.) While there are slight love lyrics in the *Vita Nuova* that are puffed up by the prose with a metaphysical and theologized meaning that is not intrinsic to them (for example the sonnet *Io mi senti' svegliar dentro a lo core* in *Vita Nuova* XXIV [15]), *Donne ch'avete* does not belong to this category: its metaphysical claims have no need of the prose because they are intrinsic to the canzone as such. For this very reason there is no rewriting of the canzone's thematic kernel in the prose frame that introduces *Donne ch'avete*, as happens in the prose frames to *Io mi senti' svegliar* and other poems. In the case of *Donne ch'avete* the introductory prose aims not to decipher it but to shed light on the circumstances of its creation and above all to announce its absolute newness as a love lyric dictated not by the desire to possess but by the desire to praise: "E però propuosi di prendere per matera de lo mio parlare sempre mai quello che fosse loda di questa gentilissima [So I decided that the subject matter for my poetry from then on would be praise for this most gracious of women]" (*VN* XVIII.9 [10.11]).

---

87 For a reading of the three autocitations within the *Commedia*, and for the retroactive revisions to which *Amor che nella mente* and *Voi che 'ntendendo* are subjected, see Barolini, *Dante's Poets*, chap. 1, "Autocitation and Autobiography."

The newness of *Donne ch'avete intelletto d'amore* is already in the incipit, which hails a partnership between reason and love that is fully characteristic of Dante, and which rejects and overturns the Cavalcantian vision according to which love is non-rational: "non razionale, – ma che sente [not rational, – but that feels]" (*Donna me prega*, 31).[88] In the incipit of *Donne ch'avete* Dante establishes a link between *intelletto* and *amore* – antithetical values in Cavalcanti's system. It is interesting from this point of view to recall the formal similarity between *Donne ch'avete*, which opens with a break with Cavalcantian dogma, and *Donna me prega*, Guido's canzone-manifesto: both are canzoni made up entirely of hendecasyllables, cited together as examples of that category in *De vulgari eloquentia* 2.12. Dante does not comment, in the Latin treatise, on another similarity that he would have noticed, and that is that *Donna me prega* and *Donne ch'avete* also share the same stanza length of fourteen lines, the length of a sonnet. (The fourteen-line stanza is typical of the canzoni in the *Vita Nuova*: the length is shared by *Donne ch'avete*, *Donna pietosa*, *Li occhi dolenti*, and *Sì lungiamente*; only *Quantunque volte* diverges from this pattern.) These formal similarities highlight the ideological abyss that separates *Donne ch'avete* from *Donna me prega* and the fundamental divergence in their visions of the role of desire in human life, a divergence that extends beyond ideology to embrace existential attitude: Cavalcanti parses passion as "not rational" with a cold and rigorous logic, in rationalistic terminology, while Dante sings of the "intellect of love" with a warm, impassioned exuberance that at times verges on illogicality.

The first stanza of *Donne ch'avete*, which in the prose Dante calls "proemio de le sequenti parole [the proem for the words that follow]" (XIX.5 [10.26]), provides the interpretative key: this canzone dramatizes the word itself, not just any word, but the word that praises the poet's lady. The prose account explains that beatitude resides "In quelle parole che lodano la donna mia [In those words that praise my lady]" (*VN* XVIII.6 [10.8]). Thus *Donne ch'avete*, rather than explaining, acts: the canzone is the acting out of "those words that praise my lady." In an understated, plain style, the poet declares his intention "de la mia donna dire, / non perch'io creda sua laude finire, / ma ragionar per isfogar la mente [to speak to you about my lady, / not that I think I can exhaust her praise, / but rather to alleviate my mind]" (2–4). The following verses continue to focus on the speech act, indicating for example – in what may be a sign of the metaphysical bent that the canzone will assume – a restriction on the group of possible interlocutors: only the "donne e donzelle amorose [ladies, maidens, who know love]" (13) can be his audience, "ché non è cosa da parlarne altrui [for this is something others should not hear]" (14). The less restricted group that the poet ad-

---

88 There will nonetheless be "relapses" into Cavalcantianism as late as Dante's last canzone, *Amor, da che convien*. For the twists and turns of Dante's path and for his clear ideological divergence from Cavalcanti already in the moral canzone *Doglia mi reca*, see my essay "Dante and Cavalcanti (On Making Distinctions in Matters of Love)," in *Dante and the Origins of Italian Literary Culture*, pp. 70–101.

dressed in *A ciascun'alma presa e gentil core* is no longer relevant. The first stanza is laced with a lexicon that insists on the act of speaking: "Io dico" (5), "farei parlando" (8), "E io non vo' parlar" (9), "ma tratterò del suo stato gentile" (11), "che non è cosa da parlarne altrui" (14). Although the poet's voice is for now the only one to make itself heard, the first stanza begins to create the sense of a choral world that rotates around *madonna*.

At the start of the second stanza, this world changes vertiginously. From the "donne e donzelle amorose" (13), the poet shifts without warning to a celestial scene, and in place of the plain, modest *trattare* of the poet we hear the resounding angelic *clamare*: "Angelo clama in divino intelletto / e dice [An angel clamours in the mind of God, / and says]" (15–16). The world stage on which the lady of *Donne ch'avete* is projected is vast, and the chorus that rises "with respect to her" ("a respetto a lei" [12]) is truly cosmic. The leap from the first stanza to the second is immense.

The canzone performs this immense leap in such a way, however, as to maximize thematic coherence: *Donne ch'avete* remains a poetic text dedicated to the act of speech and specifically to the act of praising *madonna*. Although the angel communicates "in divino intelletto," that is, directly in the divine mind without the medium of words (*De vulgari eloquentia* teaches that human beings require language because we cannot enter into others' minds as angels can: "Nec per spiritualem speculationem, ut angelum, alterum alterum introire contingit [Nor is it given to us to enter into each other's minds by means of spiritual reflection, as the angels do]" [*DVE* 1.3.1]), what the angel has to "say" is recorded by the poet in human words in the form of direct address. Still more impressive is the fact that God speaks – "che parla Dio" (23) – and that his words too are reported by the poet, also given as direct address. The chorality of *Donne ch'avete* expands and rises to the point that it encompasses the divine word.

It is not the first time an angel is heard speaking in Dante's lyrics: in *Per una ghirlandetta* the poet invents "an angel full of gentle love" (7) who sings "Whoever looks on me / will praise my noble lord" (9–10). This delicate ("sottile") voice of the diminutive angel ("angiolel") of *Per una ghirlandetta*, who speaks with lexical and syntactic simplicity, contrasts with the majestic presence of the non-diminutive angel who "clamours" in *Donne ch'avete* and whose form of linguistic expression is much more complex: "Sire, nel mondo si vede / maraviglia ne l'atto che procede / d'un'anima che 'nfin qua su risplende [My Lord, on earth a miracle / in act is seen proceeding from a soul / whose shining light extends as far as here]" (16–18). In De Robertis' gloss, *madonna* is defined by the angel as a "miracle (in the etymological sense of a marvelous thing or effect) in act, incarnate" (*VN*, p. 120).

The notion that *madonna* is a miracle is presented against a background that is impressively vertical: the splendour of her soul down in the world "extends as far as here" ("'nfin qua su risplende" [18]). The cosmic background anticipates the "corte del cielo [court of heaven]" of *Inferno* 2; the canzone features not three beatified women talking among each other but the discourse of angels, saints, and God himself. The conceits that originate with this strange mixture of courtly love and Christianity are mostly, in Foster-Boyde's words, "theologically absurd" (p. 100), as in fact it is theologically absurd that "Heaven, whose only imperfection is / the lack of her, implores its Lord to ask / for her, and all saints favour this request": "Lo cielo, che non have altro difetto / che d'aver lei, al suo segnor la chiede, / e ciascun santo ne grida merzede" (19–21).[89] We witness here not theological accuracy but rather a manifest wish on the part of the young poet to theologize courtly discourse: a wish already evident, though expressed differently, in the canzoni *Lo doloroso amor* and *E' m'incresce di me*.

A cosmic chorus of voices rises with the express purpose of praising *madonna*, and among the verbs of speech is *gridare*, used for the saints in paradise who "cry out" for the grace of having *madonna* among them, in the verse just quoted: "e ciascun santo ne grida merzede" (21). De Robertis notes that "*Grida* responds to *clama* in line 15" (*VN*, p. 120). These "clamorous" verbs are part of the chorality of this canzone, of the mise-en-scène of the voices – from God's voice to Love's voice, from the angel's voice to the poet's voice – that arise to proclaim the absolute newness of *madonna*, a courtly lady of whom it can be said that "My lady is desired in highest heaven": "Madonna è disiata in sommo cielo" (29). It is also interesting to note how the theologizing context legitimizes the use of a verb, *gridare*, that in a purely courtly context functions in an entirely different manner: we saw how the unusual use of *gridare* in the canzone *E' m'incresce di me* belongs to a new lexicon of erotic aggression that will later lead to the *rime petrose*. The sort of shout that occurs in *Donne ch'avete* is, rather, the salvific clamour that we will see again in *Donna pietosa*, where all the angels "gridavan tutti: *Osanna* [were crying out *Hosanna*]" (61).

In *Donne ch'avete* even God speaks, in a move inherited from Guinizzelli (whose God speaks in the congedo of *Al cor gentil*) that the mature Dante will reject. God does not speak in the *Commedia*, suggesting that Dante upon reflection grasped that this is a narrative move from which there is little to gain and much to lose (compare Tasso, who has God speak in his epic *Gerusalemme liberata*). But he does speak in *Donne ch'avete*, where Dante assigns him direct discourse *within* his direct discourse. God, speaking in direct discourse, makes reference to what will be *said* about the lady in hell, which he cites verbatim, also in direct discourse:

che **parla** Dio, che di madonna intende:
"Diletti miei, or sofferite in pace
che vostra spene sia quanto me piace
là 'v'è alcun che perder lei s'attende,

---

89 An excellent example of how courtly love has stayed alive in poetry – as it does still in popular songs – is the lyric "Annabel Lee" by Edgar Allan Poe, which expresses a concept similar to *Donne ch'avete*, 19–21: "I was a child and she was a child, / In this kingdom by the sea; / But we loved with a love that was more than love – / I and my Annabel Lee; / With a love that the winged seraphs of heaven / Coveted her and me ... The angels, not half so happy in heaven, / Went envying her and me ..."

> e che **dirà** ne lo inferno: O mal nati,
> io vidi la speranza de' beati."
>
> (*Donne ch'avete*, 24–8)

[so God, referring to my lady, says:
"Beloveds, accept with patience that the one
you wish for must, as long as I desire,
remain below with someone who foresees
her loss and who will say in Hell: 'Lost souls,
I have beheld the hope of all the blessed.'"]

The "words that praise my lady" of which we learned in *VN* XVIII.6 (10.8) thus encompass the words expressed by one hypothetical damned soul to other damned ("I have beheld the hope of the blessed"), words cited by God "who speaks" to his saints: a vertical line of praise for *madonna* stretches from hell ("lo inferno") (27) to the highest heaven ("sommo cielo") (29), from one end of the universe to the other.

These themes will culminate in *Paradiso*: when Dante writes of Beatrice, "Se quanto infino a qui di lei si dice / fosse conchiuso tutto in una loda [If all said of her up to here were encapsulated in one hymn of praise]" (*Par.* 30.16–17), he is evoking a lexical journey that stretches back in time to the first praise-poems; and when he writes that Beatrice's beauty is such "che solo il suo fattor tutta la goda [that only her maker may enjoy it all]" (*Par.* 30.21), he is returning to the mise-en-scène of *Donne ch'avete*.

The reference to the damned soul "ne lo inferno" in line 27 should not be taken literally. This is a hyperbole that provides another way to gauge the internal contradictions and the exuberant theological immaturity of this canzone (a lover of *madonna* could not find himself in hell if, in fact, "one who's spoken with her can't be damned" [42]). A similar hyperbolic flourish may be found in the third stanza of *Lo doloroso amor*, where the lover imagines himself damned but free from suffering because he is protected by the image of Beatrice (there the lady is explicitly named "Beatrice," a name that is not present in *Donne ch'avete*, which is why I limit myself to referring generically to *madonna*).[90] In *Lo doloroso amor* the eschatological hyperbole functions as a violent declaration of extreme passion; in *Donne ch'avete* it functions as an extreme eulogy.

The literally "culminating" point to which all the eulogies of the second stanza of *Donne ch'avete* lead is the first line of stanza three: "Madonna è disiata in sommo

---

90 The only canzone in the *Vita Nuova* that has the name "Beatrice" in it is *Li occhi dolenti*, where it is used twice. The name also appears once in the sonnet *Oltra la spera*, while the sonnet *Deh pellegrini* contains the noun "beatrice." The diminutive "Bice" occurs only in the sonnet *Io mi senti' svegliar*, included in the *Vita Nuova*. In the lyrics not in the *Vita Nuova*, the name "Beatrice" appears only in *Lo doloroso amor.*

cielo [My lady is desired in highest heaven]" (29). From this "sommo cielo" or highest peak the canzone descends to earth. In the words of the sonnet *Tanto gentile e tanto onesta pare*, it descends "da cielo in terra a miracol mostrare [from heaven to earth to show a miracle]" (8), as confirmed by the *Vita Nuova* prose: "Poscia quando dico: *Angelo clama*, comincio a trattare di questa donna. E dividesi questa parte in due: ne la prima dico che di lei si comprende in cielo; ne la seconda dico che di lei si comprende in terra, quivi: *Madonna è disiata* [Then when I say: *An angel speaking*, I begin to talk directly about my lady. This section has two parts: in the first I describe how she is perceived in heaven; in the second I describe how she is perceived on earth, beginning with, *My lady is desired*]" (*VN* XIX.17 [10.28]).

And in fact the third stanza of *Donne ch'avete* is less radical than the preceding stanzas, following in the footsteps of the Guinizzellian sonnet *Io voglio del ver la mia donna laudare* in listing the prodigious and virtuous effects of the lady: "or voi di sua virtù farvi savere [now let me tell you of her qualities]" (30). What follows is the most conventionally laudatory part of *Donne ch'avete*, where we find explicit echoes not only of the earlier tradition but also of Dante's own praise-sonnets in which the lady passes "per via" and exercises her salvific influence:

> Dico, qual vuol gentil donna parere
> vada con lei, che quando va per via,
> gitta nei cor villani Amore un gelo,
> per che onne lor pensero agghiaccia e pere;
> e qual soffrisse di starla a vedere
> diverria nobil cosa, o si morria.
>
> (Donne ch'avete, 31–6)

> [To wit, that any lady who would show
> her noble worth should keep her company,
> for when she passes Love benumbs base hearts
> so every thought of theirs will freeze and die;
> and any who endured to look at her
> would gain nobility, or else expire.]

We note the links to Dante's sonnets *Negli occhi porta la mia donna Amore* and above all *Tanto gentile e tanto onesta pare*, whose incipit echoes in the words "qual vuol gentil donna parere" (31). The presence of *madonna* creates a new moral order: "Ancor l'ha Dio per maggior grazia dato / che non pò mal finir chi l'ha parlato [God's given her an even greater grace: / that one who's spoken with her can't be damned]" (41–2).

In the third stanza Dante follows in the footsteps of Guinizzelli, but he surpasses his precursor. Guinizzelli in the canzone *Al cor gentil* justifies his desire for *madonna* on the basis of her "likeness to an angel" (*Al cor gentil*, 58), whereas Dante creates a situation in which there is no need to justify his desire, given that the angels themselves feel it. Similarly, God speaks in *Al cor gentil* to reprimand the lover for praising a mortal woman, a "vano amor [profane love]" (*Al cor gentil*, 54), whereas God speaks in *Donne ch'avete* in order to participate himself in praising her. In *Al cor gentil* the lover explains to God that praising *madonna* cannot constitute a "fault," given that she belongs to "Your kingdom" (*Al cor gentil*, 58–60), whereas Dante places the "fault" of desiring and praising her in the celestial kingdom itself.

In this way Dante makes still more radical the already radical Guinizzellian mise-en-scène. The profundity of Dante's *inventio* is then further on display in the fourth stanza of *Donne ch'avete*, which opens with the provocative question of a new interlocutor, Love: "Dice di lei Amor: 'Cosa mortale / come esser pò sì adorna e sì pura?' [Love says of her: 'How can a mortal thing / be so attractive and as well so pure?']" (43–4). Mortality and purity, usually antithetical values (a mortal being is by definition that which is subject to corruption), are here united. This is the stanza that, according to the prose, treats "la nobilitade del suo corpo [the nobility of her body]" (*VN* XIX.18 [10.29]), and it is important to note the dignity that Dante here confers upon the body, the "cosa mortale." The "cosa mortale" is not eliminated or absorbed or sublimated (as in Guinizzelli's "d'angel sembianza") but rather sacralized: Love teaches us that this *cosa mortale* is "so attractive and so pure" (44), and that "God intends to make a thing that's new" (46). She is, remarkably, both "cosa mortale" and "cosa nova." These two facts – her mortality and her miraculousness – are tightly bound together, even by the *dispositio* of the poem, wherein "cosa mortale" and "cosa nova" mirror one another at the ends of their respective verses:

> Dice di lei Amor: "**Cosa mortale**
> come esser pò sì adorna e sì pura?"
> Poi la reguarda, e fra se stesso giura
> che Dio ne 'ntenda di far **cosa nova.**
> (*Donne ch'avete*, 43–6)

> [Love says of her: "How can a mortal thing
> be so attractive and as well so pure?"
> He looks at her and to himself he swears
> that God intends to make a thing that's new.]

The fourth stanza of *Donne ch'avete* presents a woman who is a miraculous being but who at the same time preserves the features of a mortal woman: "Color di perle ha quasi, in forma quale / convene a donna aver, non for misura: / ella è quanto de ben pò far natura [Her colour is like pearl, of such a hue / as well befits a lady, not too much. / She is the best that nature can create]" (47–9). She is not, like Cavalcanti's lady in *Fresca rosa novella*, "oltra natura [beyond nature]" (31); rather, "she is the best that nature can create" (49). The phrase "Color di perle" indicates the materiality of *madonna*: a materiality, like that of pearls, of utmost delicacy, purity, and preciousness. Dante often uses the word "colore" to reveal physical characteristics, and hence to offer psychological insight: he uses it to show his own prostration in *Ciò che m'incontra* ("Lo viso mostra lo color del core [My face reveals the colour of my heart]" [5]), *Donna pietosa* ("Elli era tale a veder mio colore [So pallid was the colour of my face]" [21]), and *Li occhi dolenti* ("che mi tramuta lo color nel viso [that all the colour in my face is lost]" [48]), and to indicate the pity of the ladies in *Voi che portate* ("'l vostro colore / par divenuto de pietà simile [your colour seems / to have become so similar to pity]" [3–4]). In the most spectacular instance, the opening of *Color d'amore e di pietà sembianti*, a woman's *colore* displays both pity and love. All feeling is instead chastely veiled by "Color de perle ha quasi," a description that incites wonder and admiration without revealing the state of mind of the "cosa nova."

Dante does not deny the mortality of *madonna* in the canzone that confirms her radical extraordinariness, her "newness." Her mortality is essential, as will be seen in the encounter with Beatrice in *Purgatorio* 31, where "cosa mortale" echoes our canzone: "e se 'l sommo piacer sì ti fallio / per la mia morte, qual **cosa mortale** / dovea poi trarre te nel suo disio? [and if the highest pleasure so failed you with my death, what **mortal thing** should then have drawn you to desire it?]" (*Purg.* 31.52–4). Dante's idiosyncratic breakthrough is to construct his lady as a both/and, both a "cosa mortale" and a "cosa nova": simultaneously within and without the natural order.

The canzone's final pairing – the simultaneity of "cosa mortale" and "cosa nova" – is prefigured by its beginning: by the radical copula "intelletto d'amore," whose fusion of intellect and will anticipates *Paradiso*. We need only think – to give two examples among many – of the fusion of the faculties of intellect and will in the verses "Imagini, chi bene intender cupe [Imagine this, you who crave to understand]" (*Par.* 13.1), where "intender" is a verb of intellection and "cupe" is a verb of will, and "Affetto al suo piacer, quel contemplante [Rapt in his pleasure, that contemplative]" (*Par.* 32.1), where the first clause coincides with the will and the second with the intellect. The mystical fusion of the faculties at the end of *Paradiso* is anticipated by the preposition *di* in the *iunctura* "intelletto d'amore": entirely different, much less forceful and suggestive, would be "Donne ch'avete intelletto *ed* amore." The young poet's "intelletto d'amore" will become the "luce intellettüal, piena d'amore [intellectual light, full of love]" of *Paradiso* 30.40.

33 (B XIV; FB 33; *VN* XIX.4–14 [10.15–25])

<table>
<tr><td>

Donne ch'avete intelletto d'amore,
i' vo' con voi de la mia donna dire,
non perch'io creda sua laude finire,
4   ma ragionar per isfogar la mente.
Io dico che pensando il suo valore,

</td><td>

Ladies who have intellect of love,
I wish to speak to you about my lady,
not that I think I can exhaust her praise,
but rather to alleviate my mind.
I know that when I think about her worth

</td></tr>
</table>

Amor sì dolce mi si fa sentire,
che s'io allora non perdessi ardire,
8   farei parlando innamorar la gente.
E io non vo' parlar sì altamente,
ch'io divenisse per temenza vile;
11   ma tratterò del suo stato gentile
a respetto di lei leggeramente,
donne e donzelle amorose, con vui,
14   ché non è cosa da parlarne altrui.
   Angelo clama in divino intelletto
e dice: "Sire, nel mondo si vede
maraviglia ne l'atto che procede
18   d'un'anima che 'nfin qua su risplende."
Lo cielo, che non have altro difetto
che d'aver lei, al suo segnor la chiede,
e ciascun santo ne grida merzede.
22   Sola Pietà nostra parte difende,
che parla Dio, che di madonna intende:
"Diletti miei, or sofferite in pace
25   che vostra spene sia quanto me piace
là 'v'è alcun che perder lei s'attende,
e che dirà ne lo inferno: O mal nati,
28   io vidi la speranza de' beati."
   Madonna è disiata in sommo cielo:
or voi di sua virtù farvi savere.
Dico, qual vuol gentil donna parere
32   vada con lei, che quando va per via,
gitta nei cor villani Amore un gelo,
per che onne lor pensero agghiaccia e pere;
e qual soffrisse di starla a vedere
36   diverria nobil cosa, o si morria.
E quando trova alcun che degno sia
di veder lei, quei prova sua vertute,
39   ché li avvien, ciò che li dona, in salute,
e sì l'umilia, ch'ogni offesa oblia.
Ancor l'ha Dio per maggior grazia dato
42   che non pò mal finir chi l'ha parlato.
   Dice di lei Amor: "Cosa mortale
come esser pò sì adorna e sì pura?"
Poi la reguarda, e fra se stesso giura
46   che Dio ne 'ntenda di far cosa nova.
Color di perle ha quasi, in forma quale
convene a donna aver, non for misura:

I feel Love's sweetness so entirely
that if this did not render me less bold,
by speaking I'd make people fall in love.
But I don't plan to speak too loftily,
for fear that I could never measure up;
instead I'll speak of her nobility
in language less exalted than she is,
with you, dear ladies, maidens, who know love,
for this is something others should not hear.
   An angel clamours in the mind of God
and says: "My Lord, on earth a miracle
in act is seen proceeding from a soul
whose shining light extends as far as here."
Heaven, whose only imperfection is
the lack of her, implores its Lord to ask
for her, and all saints favour this request.
Yet only Pity will defend our cause,
so God, referring to my lady, says:
"Beloveds, accept with patience that the one
you wish for must, as long as I desire,
remain below with someone who foresees
her loss and who will say in Hell: 'Lost souls,
I have beheld the hope of all the blessed.'"
   My lady is desired in highest heaven:
now let me tell you of her qualities.
To wit, that any lady who would show
her noble worth should keep her company,
for when she passes Love benumbs base hearts
so every thought of theirs will freeze and die;
and any who endured to look at her
would gain nobility, or else expire.
And when she finds a person who deserves
to look at her, he feels her worth within,
so that her gift promotes his excellence,
which humbles him so he forgets all slights.
God's given her an even greater grace:
that one who's spoken with her can't be damned.
   Love says of her: "How can a mortal thing
be so attractive and as well so pure?"
He looks at her and to himself he swears
that God intends to make a thing that's new.
Her colour is like pearl, of such a hue
as well befits a lady, not too much.

ella è quanto de ben pò far natura;
50 per essemplo di lei bieltà si prova.
De li occhi suoi, come ch'ella li mova,
escono spirti d'amore inflammati,
53 che feron li occhi a qual che allor la guati,
e passan sì che 'l cor ciascun retrova:
voi le vedete Amor pinto nel viso,
56 là 've non pote alcun mirarla fiso.

    Canzone, io so che tu girai parlando
a donne assai, quand'io t'avrò avanzata.
Or t'ammonisco, perch'io t'ho allevata
60 per figliuola d'Amor giovane e piana,
che là 've giugni tu diche pregando:
"Insegnatemi gir, ch'io son mandata
a quella di cui laude so' adornata."
64 E se non vuoli andar sì come vana,
non restare ove sia gente villana:
ingegnati, se puoi, d'esser palese
67 solo con donne o con omo cortese,
che ti merranno là per via tostana.
Tu troverai Amor con esso lei;
70 raccomandami a lui come tu dei.

She is the best that nature can create;
by her example beauty is appraised.
Her eyes, wherever she should turn her gaze,
send spirits forth, inflamed with love, that pierce
the eyes of anyone who looks at her
and penetrate so each one finds the heart:
you will see Love depicted in her look,
on which no one can concentrate his gaze.

    My song, I know that you will go and speak
to many ladies when I send you forth.
Because I raised you as a child of Love,
obedient and meek, I bid you now
to ask this favour everywhere you go:
"Show me the way to go, since I must reach
the lady with whose praises I'm adorned."
And if you do not wish to go in vain,
avoid the kind of people who are base:
do all you can to introduce yourself
to ladies and to men of worth alone,
who'll guide you to her by the quickest path.
You'll find Love in the company of her;
speak well of me to him, as well you must.

METRE: canzone of five stanzas, each composed of fourteen hendecasyllables, with rhyme scheme ABBC ABBC CDD CEE. The *fronte* is eight verses (4 + 4) and the *sirma* is six verses (3 + 3). The final stanza functions as a *congedo*.

34 Amore e 'l cor gentil sono una cosa

Dante placed the sonnet *Amore e 'l cor gentil sono una cosa* right after *Donne ch'avete*, in *Vita Nuova* XX (11). This placement is significant; in *Purgatorio* 24 the "nove rime" (new lyrics) are said to begin with *Donne ch'avete intelletto d'amore*: "Ma dì s'i' veggio qui colui che fore / trasse le nove rime, cominciando / *Donne ch'avete intelletto d'amore* [But tell me if I see here the one who brought forth the new lyrics, beginning *Donne ch'avete intelletto d'amore*]" (*Purg.* 24.49–51). As noted previously, the *Vita Nuova* is also the history of Dante's poetic journey, the history of precursors who are rejected and of those who are embraced. In the latter category, Guido Guinizzelli is pre-eminent, "il padre / mio e de li altri miei miglior che mai / rime d'amor usar dolci e leggiadre [my father and the father of my betters who ever used love's sweet and elegant rhymes]" (*Purg.* 26.97–9). This sonnet is the homage due to "father" Guinizzelli, here celebrated as "il saggio [the wise man]": "sì come il saggio in suo dittare pone [affirms the wise man in his poetry]" (2). The first verse states that "Love and the noble heart are one sole thing," thus restating the key concept of Guinizzelli's canzone-manifesto, *Al cor gentil rimpaira sempre amore*: "né fe' amor anti che gentil core, / né gentil core anti ch'amor, Natura [and Nature did not make the noble heart / ere love, nor made love ere the noble heart]" (*Al cor gentil*, 3–4).

However, as Foster-Boyde note, Dante moves beyond the Guinizzellian identity of "amor" and "cor gentil" to an investigation of the genesis of love. Love is created simultaneously with the noble heart and then remains *in potentia* in the "dwelling place" of the heart, "sleeping" ("dentro la qual dormendo si riposa / tal volta poca e tal lunga stagione [wherein he lies in dormancy, at times / just briefly and at others quite a while]" [7–8]), until "awakened" – activated, from potency to act (Aristotelian terminology not present in the sonnet but added by Dante in the *Vita Nuova* prose) – by the lady's beauty: "Bieltate appare in saggia donna pui, / che piace a li occhi sì, che dentro al core / nasce un disio de la cosa piacente; / e tanto dura talora in costui, / che fa svegliar lo spirito d'Amore [Then beauty in a worthy lady's seen / that is so pleasing to the eyes that in / the heart desire is born for what is pleasing; / and this desire at times will linger there / until Love's spirit is aroused from sleep]" (9–13). The interest shown here in the genesis of love will be seen later in the encounter with Francesca and Paolo, when Dante asks a question aimed at illuminating the origin of their love: "Ma dimmi: al tempo d'i dolci sospiri, / a che e come concedette amore / che conosceste i dubbiosi disiri? [But tell me: in the time of the sweet sighs, by what and in what way did love grant that you knew hesitant desire?]" (*Inf.* 5.118–20).

Amore e 'l cor gentil demonstrates Dante's new poetic affinities, and not only with the incipit that so blatantly echoes Guinizzelli's *Al cor gentil*. The presence of a simile in lines 3–4, the stylistic move favoured by Guinizzelli, further indicates the pedigree of the sonnet. In addition, the analogy established by the terms of the simile, according to which the relationship between love and the noble heart is analogous to the relationship between the rational soul and reason – "e così esser l'un sanza l'altro osa / com'alma razional sanza ragione [and one can no more lack the other / than intellect can lack intelligence]" (3–4) – serves to separate Dante from Cavalcanti: a poet for whom love and the rational soul do not coexist.

Amore e 'l cor gentil is an anti-Cavalcantian poem, because it insists on the ethical and rational basis of love. For this reason, the beauty that awakens love sleeping in man comes not from just any woman but from a "wise lady" ("saggia donna") (9), and the man who evokes a similar reaction in the heart of the lady is a "man of worth" ("omo valente") (14). Beauty and virtue are balanced in this vision of an ethically ordered passion. Dante will express this view not only in the *Commedia* but also in some lyrics, above all in the mature canzone *Doglia mi reca nello core ardire*, where, however, it is negatively articulated as the precept that women ought not to love men without virtue.[91]

The importance of the last line of *Amore e 'l cor gentil* has not been appreciated sufficiently by the critical tradition; the equality between man and woman expressed here should not be neglected. The line "E simil face in donna omo valente" – literally, "A worthy man causes a similar effect in a lady" – means that Dante does not exclude the lady from the experience theorized in this sonnet: from the world of free agents endowed with will and capable of ethically based desire. In Dante's conception, therefore, the woman is not merely the passive object of the man's love; according to the concluding verse of *Amore e 'l cor gentil*, a woman can actively love. In other words, Dante conceives of women as moral actors: not only love's objects but also its subjects. Even if only sketched in the last line of the sonnet, and not elaborated, the idea put forward by "E simil face in donna omo valente" is important and is the basis of future representations of women in the *Commedia*.

Dante here anticipates his mature position, as expressed in the didactic canzone *Doglia mi reca*: the moral instructions directed at the ladies of *Doglia mi reca*, however paternalistic, indicate that the poet conceives of women as agents and interlocutors capable of acting and therefore in need of teaching.[92] Moreover, Dante dramatizes the concept sketched in *Amore 'l cor gentil* in the sonnet *Color d'amore*, where a lady is decidedly the protagonist of her love affair.

---

91 On *Doglia mi reca* as the site of Dante's mature formulation of balanced reason and desire, see my essay "Guittone's *Ora parrà*, Dante's *Doglia mi reca*, and the *Commedia*'s Anatomy of Desire," in *Dante and the Origins of Italian Literary Culture*, pp. 47–69.

92 This position is elaborated in my essay "*Sotto benda*: Gender in the Lyrics of Dante and Guittone d'Arezzo (with an Excursus on Cecco d'Ascoli)," in *Dante and the Origins of Italian Literary Culture*, pp. 333–59.

Dante himself does not gloss over the idea of gender equality present in the last verse when he divides the sonnet in the prose: "Poscia quando dico: *Bieltate appare*, dico come questa potenzia si riduce in atto; e prima come si riduce in uomo, poi come si riduce in donna, quivi: *E simil face in donna* [Then when I say, *Beauty appears*, I tell how this potentiality is made actual in a man, then how it is made actual in a woman: *The same is true of women*]" (*VN* XX.8 [11.8]). This equality is emphasized lexically as well. Dante chooses to describe the lady precisely with the adjective "saggia" (wise) after using the same word in the masculine for Guinizzelli, "il saggio" of the second line: "sì come il saggio in suo dittare pone." In a sonnet-tribute to Guinizzelli, the transfer of the epithet dedicated to him is significant; there is no more emphatic way of suggesting the intellectual (and therefore ethical) capacities of the lady.

34 (B XVI; FB 34; *VN* XX.3–5 [11.3–5])

Amore e 'l cor gentil sono una cosa,	Love and the noble heart are one sole thing,
sì come il saggio in suo dittare pone,	affirms the wise man in his poetry,
e così esser l'un sanza l'altro osa	and one can no more be without the other
4 com'alma razional sanza ragione.	than intellect can lack intelligence.
Falli natura quand'è amorosa,	Nature makes them when inclined to love,
Amor per sire e 'l cor per sua magione,	Love as the lord, the heart his dwelling place,
dentro la qual dormendo si riposa	wherein he lies in dormancy, at times
8 tal volta poca e tal lunga stagione.	just briefly and at others quite a while.
Bieltate appare in saggia donna pui,	Then beauty in a worthy lady's seen
che piace a li occhi sì, che dentro al core	which is so pleasing to the eyes that in
11 nasce un disio de la cosa piacente;	the heart desire is born for what is pleasing;
e tanto dura talora in costui,	and this desire at times will linger there
che fa svegliar lo spirito d'Amore.	until Love's spirit is aroused from sleep.
14 E simil face in donna omo valente.	The same is true of women as of men.

METRE: sonnet ABAB ABAB CDE CDE.

35 Negli occhi porta la mia donna Amore

First Redaction

In the introductory prose to this sonnet in *Vita Nuova* XXI (12), Dante links *Negli occhi porta la mia donna Amore* to the preceding sonnet, *Amore e 'l cor gentil sono una cosa*. While the "donna saggia" of *Amore e 'l cor gentil* is capable of "awakening" love that "sleeps" in the heart of the noble lover, Beatrice operates so miraculously ("mirabilmente operando") that she can cause love to come about even where it did not exist before: "Poscia che trattai d'Amore ne la soprascritta rima, vennemi volontade di volere dire anche in loda di questa gentilissima parole, per le quali io mostrasse come per lei si sveglia questo Amore, e come non solamente si sveglia là ove dorme, ma là ove non è in potenzia, ella, mirabilmente operando, lo fa venire [After I wrote about Love in the above poem, I was taken with a wish to write something in praise of this most gracious of women, by means of which I would show how love awakens through her, and how it awakens not only where it is dormant but also where it is not even in potential: working miraculously, she brings it forth]" (*VN* XXI.1 [12.1]). But there is no clear trace of this miraculous comportment in a sonnet that declares, certainly, that the appearance of the beloved when she smiles is "a rare and noble miracle" ("è novo miracolo e gentile") (14), but that lists no miraculous details beyond those already seen in other *stil novo* verses. *Negli occhi porta* is an excellent example of how Dante, himself "mirabilmente operando," uses the framework of the *Vita Nuova* to make a sonnet that is a mixture of *stil novo* themes without great thematic novelty the occasion for celebrating a woman with literally divine characteristics.

Noteworthy in *Negli occhi porta* is the word *miracolo* of the concluding verse, a word that Dante will use in the sonnet that for him represents the perfection of his new style, *Tanto gentile e tanto onesta pare*, a sonnet with which *Negli occhi porta* shares both themes and lexical elements. The prose of *Vita Nuova* XXI (12) plays on the etymological link between *miracolo* and *mirabile* – as Dante will do more extensively in the prose that precedes *Tanto gentile* – and underscores the importance of the declaration that this woman is a "novo miracolo e gentile."

In this way, Dante theologizes this slight sonnet. These are the verses of *Negli occhi porta* that can lend themselves to the idea of the lady as a *faber*/maker who, "mirabilmente operando," creates love ex nihilo: "Ogni dolcezza, ogni pensiero umìle / nasce nel core a chi parlar la sente [All sweetness and all humble thoughts are born / within the heart of those who hear her speak]" (9–10). Perhaps the verb "nasce" in line 9 may have suggested to Dante the completely artificial link established in the *Vita Nuova* between this sonnet and its predecessor: in *Amore e 'l cor gentil* love sleeps in the lover's heart; in *Negli occhi porta* love is born there.

Negli occhi porta la mia donna Amore (here printed in a pre–*Vita Nuova* redaction that does not contain notable divergences from the version in the *libello*), presents the typical effects induced by the *stil novo* lady when she walks along the street:

> per che si fa gentil ciò ch'ella mira;
> là dove passa, ogn'om ver' lei si gira
> e cui saluta fa tremar lo core,
> sì che sbassando il viso tutto smore
> e d'ogni suo difetto allor sospira:
> fugge dinanzi a·llei Superbia e Ira.
>
> (*Negli occhi porta*, 2–7)

> [which renders noble all she looks upon;
> all turn to look at her when she walks by,
> and when she greets someone his heart beats fast,
> he bows his head as colour leaves his face,
> and then he sighs remembering his faults:
> before her, pride and wrath are forced to flee.]

We hear echoes of Cavalcanti's *Chi è questa che vèn* ("Chi è questa che vèn, ch'ogn'om la mira, / che fa tremar di chiaritate l'âre [Who's this who comes along, whom all admire, / who sets the air atremble with bright light]") and of Guinizzelli's *Io voglio del ver la mia donna laudare* ("Passa per via adorna, e sì gentile / ch'abassa orgoglio a cui dona salute [She passes by adorned, with so much grace / that she curtails the pride of those she greets]" [9–10]). There are clear similarities with the third stanza of *Donne ch'avete*, where Dante lists the salvific influences of *madonna*, and with the sonnet *Tanto gentile e tanto onesta pare*, with which *Negli occhi porta* shares the rhyme *mira/sospira* and the idea of the lady-*miracolo*.

The unusual imperative "aiutatemi" addressed at the end of the octave to ladies heretofore not present – "Aiutatemi, donne, farle onore [My ladies, help me now to honour her]" (8) – gives a pinch of dramatic tension to the sonnet's framework of stilnovist chorality, in which ladies in the plural often act as a passive background to the single lady about whom the poet is writing. (The imperative "aiutatemi" also anticipates the invocation to the Muses of *Inferno* 2: "O muse, o alto ingegno, or m'aiutate [O muses, o high genius, now help me]" [*Inf.* 2.7].) If the task of a *stil novo* poem, not now in the generic sense but in the sense elaborated by Dante in the *Vita Nuova* and confirmed in *Purgatorio* 24, includes the elimination of the presence of the self (taking as the norm *Tanto gentile e tanto onesta pare*), then the strong presence of the "I" in the imperative "aiutatemi" indicates a fissure in the total adherence of *Negli occhi porta* to the new style.

The concluding tercet – "Quel ch'ella par quand'un poco sorride / non si può dicer né tenere a mente, / tant'è novo miracolo e gentile [What she looks like when she begins to smile / cannot be told or held within the mind, / so rare and noble is this miracle]" (12–14) – makes effective use of the verb *parere*, which Dante will use in the opening of *Tanto gentile e tanto onesta pare*. As in *Tanto gentile*, the verb *parere* means "to manifest oneself." Here what manifests is the miraculous presence of the lady when "un poco sorride" – literally, when "she smiles a little." The smile, which is not a motif of *Tanto gentile*, constitutes the most original feature of this sonnet and closes the thematic circle that opens in the incipit with her eyes.

35 (B XVII; FB 35; DR 63; *VN* XXI.2–4 [12.2–4])
First Redaction

   Negli occhi porta la mia donna Amore,
per che si fa gentil ciò ch'ella mira;
là dove passa, ogn'om ver' lei si gira
4   e cui saluta fa tremar lo core,
sì che sbassando il viso tutto smore
e d'ogni suo difetto allor sospira:
fugge dinanzi a·llei Superbia e Ira.
8   Aiutatemi, donne, farle onore.
   Ogni dolcezza, ogni pensiero umìle
nasce nel core a chi parlar la sente,
11   ond'è laudato chi prima la vide.
   Quel ch'ella par quand'un poco sorride
non si può dicer né tenere a mente,
14   tant'è novo miracolo e gentile.

   My lady carries Love within her eyes,
which renders noble all she looks upon;
all turn to look at her when she walks by,
and when she greets someone his heart beats fast,
he bows his head as colour leaves his face,
and then he sighs remembering his faults:
before her, pride and wrath are forced to flee.
My ladies, help me now to honour her.
   All sweetness and all humble thoughts are born
within the heart of those who hear her speak,
and therefore he who saw her first is blessed.
What she looks like when she begins to smile
cannot be told or held within the mind,
so rare and noble is this miracle.

VN 3. Ov'ella p. – 5. bassando – 14. Sì è

METRE: sonnet ABBA ABBA CDE EDC.

36 Voi che portate la sembianza umile

This sonnet and its companion piece, *Se' tu colui c' hai tratto sovente*, belong to the same narrative moment in the *Vita Nuova*, where they are anthologized together by Dante in chapter XXII (13). They belong to a group of four sonnets, of which two are included in the *Vita Nuova* and two are left out of it, thus offering the critic a rare and important opportunity to reflect on Dante's editorial choices with respect to the *libello*. We will return to the question of inclusion/exclusion in the comments on the excluded sonnets, *Onde venite voi così pensose?* and *Voi donne, che pietoso atto mostrate*.

According to the prose of *Vita Nuova* XXII (13), *Voi che portate la sembianza umile* was occasioned by the death of Beatrice's father and by the suffering caused by this loss; in the context provided by the *Vita Nuova*, then, the ladies in the sonnet are Beatrice's female friends who accompany her in mourning. The sonnets, however, do not offer any such information: no mention is made of the identity of the dead person – no hint as to the person's sex or age – nor of the identity of the lady who is mourning the death. The reader knows only that she, "nostra donna gentile [our worthy lady]" (5), is loved by the poet. The sonnet describes collective suffering, publicly manifested in the act of ritual weeping, and shared not only by the ladies but also by the poet. The poet's desire to participate in mourning is the theme of this group of sonnets, with the result that they are situated on the borderline between the world of public ritual and that of private suffering.

The narrator of the *Vita Nuova* relates the gathering of the mourning ladies around Beatrice: "molte donne s'adunaro colà dove questa Beatrice piangea pietosamente [many women gathered where this Beatrice was weeping pitifully]." Because he is "in a place where most of the women passed who were coming from her" ("in luogo onde se ne giano la maggiore parte di quelle donne che da lei si partiano") (*VN* XXII.4 [13.4]), the poet can hear the women talking among each other. Because he remains "in the same place" ("nel medesimo luogo"), the ladies pass near to him: "dimorando ancora nel medesimo luogo, donne anche passaro presso di me [as I was staying where I was other women passed by near to me]" (*VN* XXII.5 [13.5]). Given their physical proximity to Dante, the women note that he is weeping. (One wonders how Dante's first readers construed this unspecified "luogo," where so much physical proximity between male and female can occur under such circumstances.) The ladies note the unusual participation on the part of the poet, a man, for weeping is typically reserved for women's ritual grieving. They comment very precisely, asking who is this man who weeps as though he had participated in mourning as much as they? They further comment on his distraught appearance: "'Questi ch'è qui piange né più né meno come se l'avesse veduta, come noi avemo.' Altre poi diceano di me: 'Vedi questi non pare esso, tal è divenuto!' ['This man is crying neither more nor less than he would if he had seen her, as we have.' Still others were saying nearby, 'Look at how this man is so changed he doesn't seem himself!']" (*VN* XXII.6 [13.6]).

The narrator of the *Vita Nuova* at this point transitions to a description of the poet's interior life. After hearing the comments of the ladies about himself, Dante imagines that he can speak to them, and in his imagination he invents the queries he would put to them if such a dialogue were acceptable within Florentine social norms. The sonnet *Voi che portate* is portrayed as the fruit of this fantasy, as the questions he would have asked the ladies were it not improper to do so: "Onde io poi, pensando, propuosi di dire parole, acciò che degnamente avea cagione di dire, ne le quali parole io conchiudesse tutto ciò che inteso avea da queste donne; e però che volentieri l'averei domandate se non mi fosse stata riprensione, presi tanta matera di dire come s'io l'avesse domandate ed elle m'avessero risposto [Thinking about it later, I planned to write some verses, since I had a theme worthy of poetry, in which I would put all I had heard these women saying. And since I would have liked to ask them something, if it were not considered improper to do so, I arranged my subject matter as if I had questioned them and they had responded]" (*VN* XXII.7 [13.7]).

Dante immediately establishes the link between the two sonnets of *Vita Nuova* XXII (13), explaining that he had written one in which to pose his imaginary questions and a second in which he imagines the ladies' responses: "E feci due sonetti; che nel primo domando, in quello modo che voglia mi giunse di domandare; ne l'altro dico la loro risponsione, pigliando ciò ch'io udio da loro sì come lo mi avessero detto rispondendo [I wrote two sonnets. In the first I ask in the way the wish to ask came over me; in the other I give their response, taking what I heard them saying as if they had responded to me]" (*VN* XXII.8 [13.8]).

In the *Vita Nuova*, therefore, *Voi che portate* and its companion *Se' tu colui* are explicitly presented as compensatory acts in which the poet can allow himself an experience prohibited by the society in which he lives.

As I have pointed out previously, the prose of the *Vita Nuova*, although intentionally vague and imprecise (substituting, for example, "la sopradetta cittade" for the name "Firenze"), reveals social and quotidian pressures that are not as clearly visible in the poems. Besides explaining that the reason for the collective sorrow is the death of the beloved's father – a fact that cannot be verified in the sonnet – the prose offers a rich background of elements gathered from daily life, including the separation of men and women in the choreography of mourning: "secondo l'usanza de la sopradetta cittade, donne con donne e uomini con uomini s'adunino a cotale tristizia [in keeping with the customs of the city mentioned earlier, women with women and men with men come together on such sad occasions]" (XXII.3 [13.3]).

Although not as rich as the prose, the sonnet too offers a social context that would merit further historical or anthropological investigation. In many premodern societies women as a group act as spokespeople for the suffering of the community, a function that is discharged both by their comportment and by their appearance, as in the first verses of *Voi che portate*: "Voi che portate la sembianza umile, / con li occhi bassi, mostrando dolore [You who bear a mournful countenance, / with downcast eyes, revealing your distress]" (1–2). They engage in rigorously choreographed movements, as described throughout *Voi che portate*, where we move from "onde venite che 'l vostro colore / par divenuto de pietà simile? [where do you come from that your colour seems / to have become so similar to pity?]" (3–4), to "perch'io vi veggio andar sanz'atto vile [for I can see you move with dignity]" (8), and finally to "e veggiovi tornar sì sfigurate [and I see that you return in such distress]" (13). Taken together, these verses allude to precisely scripted ritual movement – a coming, a going, a returning from and towards prescribed places and locales – as described in the pages of Davidsohn:

> In ancient times, it was considered an essential part of the funeral ritual that the women relatives or the women friends of the deceased person tear their hair, rip their clothes, and scratch their faces bloody, but in the Duecento these exaggerated manifestations of mourning were prohibited; in Florence only the widow was permitted to loosen her veil and tear her hair as she wept. Female friends rushed to her or to the daughters of the dead man, and to men in mourning relatives came by, and guild associates; however for the two sexes to be together on such occasions was considered inappropriate.[93]

But *Voi che portate* also alludes to a behaviour that is not part of the prescribed ceremony and of the accepted ritual. The invitation proffered by the poet to the mourning ladies – "piacciavi di restar qui meco alquanto, / e qual che sia di lei, nol mi celate [may it please you to stay with me awhile, / and what you know of her disclose to me]" (10–11) – describes an encounter and a dialogue that could not happen in reality, since, as Davidsohn notes, "for the two sexes to be together on such occasions was considered inappropriate." Were such an encounter and dialogue to occur, they would be cause for "rebuke" ("riprensione" according to the more explicit *Vita Nuova* prose).

In other words, *Voi che portate* gives us a glimpse of a Dante who is not comfortable with the social norms with which he lives, a poet who uses poetry to create occasions for dialogue and encounter that are not permitted by the world around him. His intense desire to participate in the female work of mourning – caught in the imperatives "Ditelmi, donne [tell me, ladies]" (7) and "nol mi celate [don't hide it from me]" (11) – verges on impropriety. His is a desire that threatens to trespass the rigid social barrier placed between male and female and that also risks feminizing him. We will see in the next sonnet how the ladies take action to re-establish the normal divisions between the sexes and between their roles.

Barbi-Maggini's commentary on mourning customs in Florence sends the reader of *Voi che portate* to the *Decameron*: "Era usanza, sì come ancora oggi veggiamo

---

93 Trans. from Robert Davidsohn, *Storia di Firenze*, 7 vols. (Florence: Sansoni, 1965), 7:708–9.

usare, che le donne parenti e vicine nella casa del morto si ragunavano, e quivi con quelle che più gli appartenevano piagnevano; e d'altra parte dinanzi la casa del morto co' suoi prossimi si ragunavano i suoi vicini e altri cittadini assai [It had once been customary, as it is again nowadays, for the women relatives and neighbours of a dead man to assemble in his house in order to mourn in the company of the women who had been closest to him: moreover his kinsfolk would forgather in front of his house along with his neighbours and various other citizens]" (*Decameron*, Introduction to the First Day, 32). *Voi che portate* is clearly informed by the custom described by Boccaccio, and contains two explicit references to ritualized female weeping: "Vedeste voi nostra donna gentile / bagnar nel viso suo di pianto Amore? [Did you now just behold our worthy lady / bathing Love with tears upon her face?]" (5–6) and "Io veggio li occhi vostri c'hanno pianto [I see your eyes, which show that you have wept]" (12).

We are not able to ascertain the occasion by which this sonnet was originally triggered. Placed in the *Vita Nuova*, *Voi che portate* advances the sense of impending mortality that hangs over the work: soon enough the narrator will move from the death of Beatrice's father to the death of the *gentilissima* herself.

36 (B XVIII; FB 36; *VN* XXII.9–10 [13.9–10])

Voi che portate la sembianza umile,	You who bear a mournful countenance,
con li occhi bassi, mostrando dolore,	with downcast eyes, revealing your distress,
onde venite che 'l vostro colore	where do you come from that your colour seems
4 par divenuto de pietà simile?	to have become so similar to pity?
Vedeste voi nostra donna gentile	Did you now just behold our worthy lady
bagnar nel viso suo di pianto Amore?	bathing Love with tears upon her face?
Ditelmi, donne, che 'l mi dice il core,	O tell me, ladies, what my heart tells me,
8 perch'io vi veggio andar sanz'atto vile.	for I can see you move with dignity.
E se venite da tanta pietate,	And if you come from grief that's so intense,
piacciavi di restar qui meco alquanto,	may it please you to stay with me awhile,
11 e qual che sia di lei, nol mi celate.	and what you know of her disclose to me.
Io veggio li occhi vostri c'hanno pianto,	I see your eyes, which show that you have wept,
e veggiovi tornar sì sfigurate,	and see that you return in such distress
14 che 'l cor mi triema di vederne tanto.	that my heart trembles at the sight of it.

METRE: sonnet ABBA ABBA CDC DCD. *Voi che portate* shares the same rhyme scheme as the other mourning sonnets, *Se' tu colui*, *Onde venite*, and *Voi donne*.

37 Se' tu colui c' hai trattato sovente

The narrative premise of the prose framework of *Vita Nuova* XXII (13) is the death of Beatrice's father and the consequent suffering not only of the *gentilissima* but also of her companions. In essence the framework of chapter XXII (13) is that of the "corrotto" (archaic term for funeral lament). Beatrice's companions are the ladies with whom Dante imagines an encounter and dialogue not permitted in the social reality in which he lives. The dialogue not permitted in the prose of *Vita Nuova* XXII (13), but dearly wished for by him, is realized in a series of sonnets. These take the form of a fictive quasi-*tenzone*, imitating the classical *botta e risposta* structure (a tart comment with a quick reply) typical of the genre: *Voi che portate la sembianza umile*, in which Dante addresses imaginary questions to the ladies, is replied to by its companion piece, *Se' tu colui c' hai trattato sovente*, in which Dante imagines their responses.

Se' tu colui begins with the opening query of the ladies: they want to make sure of the identity of their interlocutor, whose appearance ("figura") is disfigured by grief (similarly, the grieving ladies are "sfigurate" in the preceding sonnet: "e veggiovi tornar sì sfigurate" (*Voi che portate* [13]). Barbi-Maggini recall the encounter with Forese Donati in *Purgatorio* 23, in which Dante's friend Forese is rendered physically unrecognizable by his emaciated appearance: "Mai non l'avrei riconosciuto al viso; / ma ne la voce sua mi fu palese / ciò che l'aspetto in sé avea conquiso" ("I never would have recognized him by his face; and yet his voice made plain to me what from his appearance was erased" [*Purg.* 23.43–5]). As in purgatory Forese, so here Dante is recognized by his voice: "Tu risomigli a la voce ben lui, / ma la figura ne par d'altra gente [The tenor of your voice resembles his, / but by your look you're clearly someone else]" (3–4). Identification by "voice" is particularly suited to a poet, and these ladies know and classify Dante as a poet: "Se' tu colui c' hai trattato sovente / di nostra donna, sol parlando a nui? [Are you the one who's often written poems / about our lady, speaking just to us?]" (1–2). De Robertis notes that Dante is here identified specifically "as a poet who has 'spoken to ladies,' alluding to *Donne ch'avete*," and that the ladies' question "anticipates that of Bonagiunta in *Purg.* 24.49–51, a typical identification of the poet by his work" (*VN*, p. 150).

Recognition by means of voice is a topos that connects to Florentinity, in our sonnet and with Forese in *Purgatorio*; and indeed, one has to know someone first hand to recognize his voice. (A variant is provided by Farinata, a Florentine from the previous generation who recognizes not Dante's voice but his inflection: "La tua loquela ti fa manifesto / di quella nobil patrïa natio [Your speech shows that you are a native of that noble homeland]" [*Inf.* 10.25–6].) The sounds of life in Florence are present in these sonnets. In *Se' tu colui* we hear the mourning of the Florentine community, a practice that is recorded lexically in the sonnet's five uses of *piangere* and *pianto*: "E perché piangi tu sì coralmente [Why do you weep so inconsolably]" (5); "Vedestù pianger lei [Is it because you saw her weep]" (7); "Lascia piangere noi [Leave weeping to us]" (9); "che nel suo pianto l'udimmo parlare [for we're the ones who heard her speak with tears]" (11); "sarebbe innanzi lei piangendo morta [she would have died before her shedding tears]" (14).

In this sonnet and in its predecessor, Dante imagines being able to cross over the social boundary that separates women from men in the rigid context of the *corrotto*: he wants to participate in the women's work of weeping. The very existence of this imaginary dialogue is proof of Dante's wish to trespass an established boundary – or rather, of his wish to test a boundary that he then ends up reaffirming. This reaffirmation comes by means of the imagined response of the women, who do not show themselves as even slightly open to the role-change implicitly suggested by the poet. Rather, they strongly reconfirm the division of tasks established by the social structure: "E perché piangi tu sì coralmente, / che fai di te pietà venire altrui? / Vedestù pianger lei, che tu non pui / punto celar la dolorosa mente? [Why do you weep so inconsolably / that you make others want to pity you? / Is it because you saw her weep that you / cannot conceal the sorrow that you feel?]" (5–8).

There is a thinly disguised reprimand in the ladies' rhetorical question, "Vedestù pianger lei," literally "Did you see her weep?": they know that Dante did not have the experience, permitted only to the company of women, of direct participation in *madonna*'s mourning. He did not see her weep: how then can he insist that he suffers as they do, when they have seen her and have had full rights to such participation? His public suffering is excessive, not socially legitimate or acceptable, given that he does not belong to the family circle and is not part of the group – a female group – to which is designated the task of mourning. It would be better if he could refrain from the too-public manifestation of a grief that is experienced "sì coralmente" (literally, in such a heartfelt fashion). Given that he has not seen *madonna*, and given that he does not have the right to see her – given, in other words, that he is a man – he ought to be able to conceal his sorrow. The public display of grief belongs to women, while men have the duty of behaving discreetly and of knowing how to hide their suffering ("celar la dolorosa mente").

When the women say, "Lascia piangere noi e triste andare [Leave weeping and unhappiness to us]" (9), they are reaffirming the division of social duties on the basis of sex. The duties of women described in verse 9 of *Se' tu colui* are those of weeping – "piangere" – and of proceeding sadly: "triste andare." The allusion to the ladies' ceremonial procession in the phrase "triste andare," which echoes their "andar sanz'atto vile" in the preceding sonnet, reflects the practice whereby, in the Duecento, Florentine women participated in the funeral procession:

The corpse was carried to the parish chuch or to one chosen beforehand by the dead person on the shoulders of friends and guild associates; it was followed by relatives, acquaintances, neighbours, and friends, by invitation of the guild itself. The women followed, and the female relatives nearest to the dead person were accompanied and supported on either side by friends or relatives.[94]

The ladies of the sonnet *Se' tu colui* re-establish the duties and roles accepted by the norms of their society, and use pronouns to delineate the various areas of competence: there are duties that are prescribed for us ("noi" in line 9) and not for you ("tu" in line 7). The tercet "Lascia piangere noi e triste andare / (e fa peccato chi mai ne conforta), / che nel suo pianto l'udimmo parlare [Leave weeping and unhappiness to us / (to try to comfort us would be a sin), / for we're the ones who heard her speak with tears]" (9–11) returns to the fact that only the ladies had direct contact with the mourner. The obligation of giving comfort is strictly delegated to them by the community – "Lascia piangere a noi" – and not to self-selected others.

Se' tu colui ends up respecting and reaffirming the norms of communal life in Dante's Florence; indeed it is sinful to interfere (10). Although this sonnet-exchange permits a fantasy dialogue with women, a dialogue not allowed in real life, the women of Dante's fantasy reassert the status quo of the society in which Dante lives. But there is no doubt that Dante here shows himself to be an adventurer in social and psychic space, willing to cross over pre-established boundaries in matters involving gender differentiation, sex roles, and normative male behaviour.

37 (B XIX; FB 37; *VN* XXII.13–16 [13.12–15])

Se' tu colui c' hai trattato sovente	Are you the one who's often written poems
di nostra donna, sol parlando a nui?	about our lady, speaking just to us?
Tu risomigli a la voce ben lui,	The tenor of your voice resembles his,
4 ma la figura ne par d'altra gente.	but by your look you're clearly someone else.
E perché piangi tu sì coralmente,	Why do you weep so inconsolably
che fai di te pietà venire altrui?	that you make others want to pity you?
Vedestù pianger lei, che tu non pui	Is it because you saw her weep that you
8 punto celar là dolorosa mente?	cannot conceal the sorrow that you feel?
Lascia piangere noi e triste andare	Leave weeping and unhappiness to us
(e fa peccato chi mai ne conforta),	(to try to comfort us would be a sin),
11 che nel suo pianto l'udimmo parlare.	for we're the ones who heard her speak with tears.
Ell'ha nel viso la pietà sì scorta,	So clearly does her face reveal her pain
che qual l'avesse voluta mirare	that had some lady wished to look at her,
14 sarebbe innanzi lei piangendo morta.	she would have died before her shedding tears.

METRE: sonnet ABBA ABBA CDC DCD. See metrical notation to *Voi che portate*.

---

94 Trans. from Davidsohn, *Storia di Firenze*, 7:710. For the procession, see Sharon Strocchia, *Death and Ritual in Renaissance Florence* (Baltimore: Johns Hopkins University Press, 1992), pp. 8–11, who also explains that in the Trecento women began to be excluded from the funeral procession.

38 Onde venite voi così pensose?

In this sonnet, as in *Voi che portate la sembianza umile*, the poet sees some ladies pass by "pensose [distraught]," and he questions them to find out whence they come: "Onde venite voi così pensose? [Where have you been that makes you so distraught?]" Is a visit to *madonna* the cause of their grief?: "Ditemel, s'a voi piace, in cortesia, / ch'i' ho dottanza che·lla donna mia / non vi faccia tornar così dogliose [Please tell me, in the name of courtesy, / because I fear my lady is the reason / your return is burdened with such pain]" (2–4). *Onde venite* is commonly held to be an earlier and less successful version of *Voi che portate*: less successful because less concentrated on *madonna*'s grief, to which the love-sufferings of the poet are now "inappropriately" (the word is Contini's) added. If it is true, as Contini suggests in a plausible hypothesis, that *Onde venite* "is a trial run, a first draft" (p. 74), then this poetic episode offers us three distinct archeological layers of textuality.

According to this hypothesis, the earliest layer, the first poetic attempt to imagine a dialogue between the poet and ladies on the question of a sorrowful beloved (Barbi and Contini refer to Beatrice, but *madonna* is not identified in the poems, nor is it specified why she is grieving), is constituted by *Onde venite* and *Voi donne, che pietoso atto mostrate*. The next layer, constituted by *Voi che portate* and *Se' tu colui*, is a second and more successful attempt, also in sonnet form, to imagine the same dialogue involving the same theme of grieving; again, the reader does not know who *madonna* is or for whom she weeps. Only in the last layer, the one added by the prose of the *Vita Nuova*, does Dante declare that the beloved of these sonnets is Beatrice, and that her grief has been elicited by her father's death.

In *Onde venite*, as in *Voi che portate*, the poet wants to dialogue with the grieving ladies. The Florentinity quotient of these mourning sonnets, discussed vis-à-vis *Se' tu colui*, is here further enhanced, since here he sees the ladies in the very street where he is ("in questa via") and begs them to pause a while ("ristare alquanto"): "Deh gentil donne, non siate sdegnose / né di ristare alquanto in questa via / e dire al doloroso che disia / udir della suo donna alquante cose [Ah, noble ladies, don't disdain my plea / to pause a while along the path you take / to have a word with one who's suffering / and longs to have some news about his lady]" (5–8). De Robertis notes that the reference to "questa via" in line 6 "adds that minimum of 'local' color that chapter 13 (XXII) of the *Vita Nova* will develop" (ed. comm., p. 356). The verb "venite" in the opening and the line "ristare alquanto in questa via" allude to the same choreography of mourning treated in the essays on the two preceding sonnets. In the sestet of *Onde venite*, however, attention shifts away to the love-sufferings of the poet: "avvegna che gravoso m'è l'udire: / sì·mm'ha in tutto Amor da·ssé scacciato / ch'ogni suo atto mi trae a·fferire [though hearing it may well be hard to bear, /

since Love's rejected me so utterly / that all his deeds are meant to bring me harm]"
(9–11). The concluding tercet moves toward a Cavalcantian style tinged by an aggressive narcissism that leads the poet to urge the ladies to pay attention to him and
to comfort him for his lovesickness: "Guardate bene s'i' son consumato, / ch'ogni
mie spirto / comincia a·ffuggire / se da voi, donne, non son confortato [Just see how
wholly worn away I am, / and know my spirits will begin to flee, / if you, dear ladies,
do not comfort me]" (12–14).

Onde venite is split between the theme of mourning and that of the suffering
lover. The lesser usefulness to Dante of *Onde venite* compared to *Voi che portate* –
the reason that one is included in the *Vita Nuova* and the other is not – derives from
this thematic inconsistency. As Contini notes, the motif of mourning is "inappropriately" combined with "the subjective anguish of the poet" (p. 74). Or, in the amusing
words of Barbi: "Was that really the moment to put himself forward in that way, he
along with his unfortunate love?" (Barbi-Maggini, p. 269). When we recall that the
fundamental project of the *Vita Nuova* is that of extracting personal subjectivity and
personal suffering from the act of loving, in order to escape the traps of ego and narcissism, we understand why *Onde venite*, whose octave is devoted to the grieving of
madonna and whose sestet is devoted to the suffering of the self, was not chosen for
the *libello*.

38 (B LXX; C 23; FB 38; DR 56)

Onde venite voi così pensose?	Where have you been that makes you so distraught?
Ditemel, s'a voi piace, in cortesia,	Please tell me, in the name of courtesy,
ch'i' ho dottanza che·lla donna mia	because I fear my lady is the reason
4 non vi faccia tornar così dogliose.	your return is burdened with such pain.
Deh gentil donne, non siate sdegnose	Ah, noble ladies, don't disdain my plea
né di ristare alquanto in questa via	to pause a while along the path you take
e dire al doloroso che disia	to have a word with one who's suffering
8 udir della suo donna alquante cose,	and longs to have some news about his lady,
avegna che gravoso m'è l'udire:	though hearing it may well be hard to bear,
sì·mm'ha in tutto Amor da·ssé scacciato	since Love's rejected me so utterly
11 ch'ogni suo atto mi trae a·fferire.	that all his deeds are meant to bring me harm.
Guardate bene s'i' son consumato,	Just see how wholly worn away I am,
ch'ogni mie spirto comincia a·ffuggire	and know my spirits will begin to flee,
14 se da voi, donne, non son confortato.	if you, dear ladies, do not comfort me.

METRE: sonnet ABBA ABBA CDC DCD. See metrical notation to *Voi che portate*.

39 Voi donne, che pietoso atto mostrate

Voi donne, che pietoso atto mostrate concentrates within itself the imaginary *tenzone* enacted by the two sonnets set in *Vita Nuova* XXII (13), *Voi che portate* and *Se' tu colui*. The octave of *Voi donne* contains the questions that the poet addresses to the ladies (elaborated in *Voi che portate*), and the sestet contains their response (elaborated in *Se' tu colui*), leading Contini to the conclusion that "*Voi donne* is certainly prior to the final arrangement" (p. 76). Even if generally considered superior to the preceding sonnet, given the excessive self-pity of *Onde venite*, *Voi donne* still demonstrates clear traces of inadequacy with respect to the theme that dominates *Vita Nuova* XXII (13): the theme of public mourning, which will be taken up again at the end of the *libello* in *Deh pellegrini che pensosi andate*. Again, as with *Onde venite*, the problem is one of focus. The poet begins by referring to *madonna*'s grief – "chi è 'sta donna che giace sì vinta? [Who is this lady lying fallen here?]" (2) – but then changes direction to focus on the relationship that ties the beloved to him, falling back on the old Sicilian topos of the lady painted in the heart of her lover: "Sarebbe quella ch'è nel mio cor pinta? [Is she the one who's painted in my heart?]" (3).

There are other interesting features that suggest *Voi donne* was written before Dante had fully conceptualized the situation of *Voi che portate* and *Se' tu colui*, two sonnets that breathe life into the topic of mourning as a public event and into the dynamic (seen in a quasi-anthropological light) between those who can participate in the *corrotto* and those who – like the poet himself – cannot. Above all, *Voi donne* conjures an implausible situation, for in *Voi donne* the lover is physically present in the space where the beloved is. In other words, the grieving lady is not physically distant from the man who observes her, and the questions put by the lover to the lady's companions aim at verifying what he indeed already knows:

> Deh, s'ell'è dessa, più non me ·l celate.
> Ben ha le sue sembianze sì cambiate
> e la figura sua mi par sì spenta,
> ch'al mio parere ella non rapresenta
> quella che fa parer l'altre beate.
>
> > (*Voi donne*, 4–8)

> [Ah, if it's she, do not hide her from me.
> Her features are so utterly transformed,
> her look so changed, that she no longer seems
> to me to bear the likeness of the one
> who makes all others shine with blessedness.]

A situational analysis offers further confirmation of Contini's suggestion that this poem was written before the two on the same topic that were placed in the *Vita Nuova*. If the poet can imagine himself in the presence of his grieving lady it means that he has not yet devised the basic situation of *Voi che portate* and *Se' tu colui*, which is founded on actual social convention: the strict separation of men and women that was imposed by contemporary social customs. In *Voi che portate* and *Se' tu colui* Dante dramatizes the rigid boundaries that he opposes – at least in his imagination. If he is in the same room with *madonna*, all this vanishes: there is no boundary to transgress.

And in fact there is no reprimand in *Voi donne*, as there is in *Se' tu colui*. "Non pianger più, tu sè già tutto sfatto [but weep no more, for you are quite destroyed]" (14), addressed by the ladies to the poet in *Voi donne*, is a comforting gesture, not a rebuke, as in the parallel verse of *Se' tu colui*: "Lascia piangere noi [Leave weeping to us]" (9). In *Voi donne* the "do not weep" motif belongs to the ladies' attempt to comfort the lover, who is "quite destroyed," and is a development of the situation of *Onde venite*, where the poet voices his wish to be comforted: "ch'ogni mie spirto comincia a·ffuggire / se da voi, donne, non son confortato [and know my spirits will begin to flee, / if you, dear ladies, do not comfort me]" (*Onde venite*, 13–14). In *Se' tu colui*, by contrast, the "do not weep" motif functions not to comfort but to reprimand: you, man, do not belong to the group designated to do the weeping, so go back within your borders and "leave the weeping to us."

The sonnets *Voi che portate* and *Se' tu colui* are more realistic than *Voi donne*, in the sense that they reflect the real segregation of the sexes in Florentine society, while *Voi donne* takes place in an imaginary world in which the poet is free to go wherever he wants, even into *madonna*'s room. By inserting elements of daily life and of its governing social norms, Dante creates in *Voi che portate* and *Se' tu colui* the dramatic tension that is lacking in *Voi donne*.

The true theme of *Voi donne*, in contrast to the theme of mourning that will be developed in *Voi che portate* and *Se' tu colui*, is that of the relation between our self-representation and our self: if the outer features of *madonna* are "so transformed" ("sì cambiate") that "she no longer seems / to me to bear the likeness of the one / who makes all others shine with blessedness" (7–8), is it possible that she is no longer she? In Italian these verses feature the verb *rappresentare*[95] ("e la figura sua mi par sì spenta, / ch'al mio parere ella non **rapresenta** / quella che fa parer l'altre beate"), which helps us to see that the question here posed is: What is the relationship between our self-representation in the world and our essence? The ladies reassure the lover on the identity between *figura* and essence, telling him that they too could not recognize *madonna* when they first saw her ("Se nostra donna conoscer non pòi, / ch'è sì conquisa, non mi par gran fatto, / però che quel medesmo avenne a noi [It's

---

95 The verb *rappresentare* appears in the lyrics only here and in the canzone *Amor che nella mente mi ragiona*; for its story in the *Commedia*, see Barolini, *The Undivine Comedy*, p. 128.

not at all surprising that you fail / to recognize our lady in this state, / because this happened just as well to us]" [9–11]), but add that if he looks carefully at her eyes, seeking her interiority, he will recognize her: "Ma se tu mirerai el gentil atto / degli occhi suoi, cognosceraila poi [But if you gaze upon the noble glance / of her sweet eyes, then you will know it's she]" (12–13). The link between *res* and *signum*, between the physical manifestation of *madonna* and her essence, is intact: this is the actual comfort offered by *Voi donne*.

39 (B LXXI; C 24; FB 39; DR 65)

"Voi donne, che pietoso atto mostrate,
chi è 'sta donna che giace sì vinta?
Sarebbe quella ch'è nel mio cor pinta?
4 Deh, s'ell'è dessa, più non me ·l celate.
Ben ha le sue sembianze sì cambiate
e la figura sua mi par sì spenta,
ch'al mio parere ella non rapresenta
8 quella che fa parer l'altre beate."
"Se nostra donna conoscer non pòi,
ch'è sì conquisa, non mi par gran fatto,
11 però che quel medesmo avenne a noi.
Ma se tu mirerai el gentil atto
degli occhi suoi, cognosceraila poi.
14 Non pianger più, tu sè già tutto sfatto."

"You ladies who show pity in your eyes,
who is this lady lying fallen here?
Is she the one who's painted in my heart?
Ah, if it's she, do not hide her from me.
Her features are so utterly transformed,
her look so changed, that she no longer seems
to me to bear the likeness of the one
who makes all others shine with blessedness."
"It's not at all surprising that you fail
to recognize our lady in this state,
because this happened just as well to us.
But if you gaze upon the noble glance
of her sweet eyes, then you will know it's she:
but weep no more, for you are quite destroyed."

METRE: sonnet ABBA ABBA CDC DCD. The B rhyme, where *i* rhymes with *e*, is Guittonian. See metrical notation to *Voi che portate*.

40 Donna pietosa e di novella etate

Of *Donna pietosa*, Foster-Boyde write that it has been "since the nineteenth century the most admired of Dante's early canzoni" (p. 114). This popularity says much about the challenge represented by *Donne ch'avete* and its radical work of theologizing the courtly tradition, and by contrast indicates the more accessible nature of *Donna pietosa*, a canzone of pronounced narrativity and remarkable dramatic flourish. Although *Donna pietosa* is also highly theologized, its visionary fabric renders its "theology" less severe (more "Gothic," in the nineteenth-century sense) and more responsive to our tastes than the sermonizing divinity of *Donne ch'avete*. Moreover, Dante's dream of his dead lady, not only dead but dead and beautiful ("Morta è la donna tua, ch'era sì bella [Your lady's dead, who was so beautiful]" [56]), confers a pathos, a tenderness, and a painterly quality on this canzone that again render it more appetizing to modern tastes (to say nothing of the early modern taste of Petrarch, the poet of "cosa bella mortal passa, et non dura [this beautiful mortal creature passes, and does not endure]" [*Rvf* 248.8]). The English painter and writer Dante Gabriel Rossetti, translator of both *Donne ch'avete* and *Donna pietosa*, did not paint the scene described in *Donne ch'avete* but painted several times a scene taken from *Donna pietosa*, which he entitled *Dante's Dream at the Time of the Death of Beatrice*.

Placed by Dante in *Vita Nuova* XXIII (14), the second and longest canzone of the *libello* (*Donna pietosa* has six stanzas of fourteen lines each, while *Donne ch'avete* has five stanzas of the same length) is a lyric that in its story-telling narrativity verges on the cadences of prose, while at the same time maintaining an exquisite lyrical delicacy (created metrically by the presence of two *settenari* per stanza). For this reason also *Donna pietosa* merits its literally central position in a book that, being a *prosimetrum*, is a continuous meditation on the dialectic between prose and poetry, between the "distesa lingua" (*Par.* 11.23) of prose, "open" and unregulated, and poetry, defined as "quel parlare che 'n numeri e tempo regolato in rimate consonanze cade [speech whose cadences are regulated by rhythm and metre to produce rhymed consonances]" (*Convivio* 4.2.12).

The overlap between *Donna pietosa* and the prose that precedes it in *Vita Nuova* XXIII (14), "an unusually precise paraphrase" in the words of De Robertis (*VN*, p. 152), has caused critics to suspect that *Donna pietosa* was written specially for the *Vita Nuova*, at the same time as the prose: "the essential likeness of the two narratives [that of the prose and that of the canzone], both in terms of content and form (apart from the different listener), and ultimately the lack of any real gain in the prose ... with respect to the canzone (a canzone that, moreover, has unusual narrative characteristics) – all this leads one to believe in a contemporaneity of inspiration of the two texts, as if both were composed for the *Vita Nuova* (which is not to say: in the order of the *Vita Nuova*)" (De Robertis, *VN*, p. 158).

The "contemporaneity of inspiration of the two texts" is a plausible thesis, although it cannot be verified and I will argue against it on a variety of grounds. There are a number of ways in which the prose adds to the poem, counter to De Robertis' claim that there is a "lack of any real gain in the prose," and one such divergence is critical: in the canzone *Donna pietosa* the name Beatrice is missing. Continually invoked in the prose that precedes it, the name of Beatrice is never present in the canzone. And we know that Dante is capable of naming Beatrice in early lyrics from this time period, because *Lo doloroso amor* pointedly includes her name: "'Per quella moro c'ha nome Beatrice.' / Quel dolce nome che mi fa il cor agro ['I die for her whose name is Beatrice.' / The sweet name that embitters so my heart]" (14–15). *Li occhi dolenti*, the *Vita Nuova*'s canzone-lament for Beatrice's death, records the *gentilissima*'s name twice.

The lack of her name in the canzone *Donna pietosa* and its hyper-presence in the prose generate extremely divergent results. For instance, in the canzone *Donna pietosa*, a meditation on his own mortality leads the poet to think of the inexorable death of the beloved, "la mia donna": "per che l'anima mia fu sì smarrita, / che sospirando dicea nel pensero: / 'Ben converrà che la mia donna mora' [This made my soul so utterly distraught / I spoke these words, while sighing, in my thought. / 'My lady someday surely has to die']" (32–34). In the prose the same meditation and the same thought inexorably lead to Beatrice's name: "Onde, sospirando forte, dicea fra me medesimo: 'Di necessitade convene che la gentilissima Beatrice alcuna volta si muoia' [Then, letting out a great sigh, I told myself: 'There is no escaping the fact that the most gracious Beatrice will have to die some day']" (*VN* XXIII.3 [14.3]).

The prose of *Vita Nuova* XXIII (14) begins wtih the "dolorosa infermitade [painful illness]" that strikes the poet and because of which he suffers "per nove dì amarissima pena [bitter pain for nine days in a row]"; on the ninth day the thought of his lady comes over him and with it awareness of the mortality of every living thing, including himself: "E quando ei pensato alquanto di lei, ed io ritornai pensando a la mia debilitata vita; e veggendo come leggiero era lo suo **durare**, ancora che sana fosse, sì cominciai a piangere fra me stesso di tanta miseria [And after having thought about her for a while, I went back to thinking about my incapacitated life; and seeing how fleeting it was, even when it was healthy, I started to weep over such misery]" (*VN* XXIII.3 [14.3]). The thought of Beatrice makes the poet aware of universal entropy, signalled by the verb *durare*, present in the prose and in the canzone: "Mentr'io pensava a la mia frale vita, / e vedea 'l suo **durar** com'è leggiero [While I was thinking of my frail life, / and saw how my survival was unsure]" (29–30).

From the fleetingness of all life, the poet arrives at a realization of Beatrice's death, expressed in the form of direct discourse: "dicea fra me medesimo: 'Di necessitade convene che la gentilissima Beatrice alcuna volta si muoia' [I told myself: 'There is no escaping the fact that the most gracious Beatrice will have to die some day']" (*VN* XXIII.3 [14.3]). The use of direct discourse is important; as I noted in the essay on the sonnet *Ciò che m'incontra*, direct discourse is a rhetorical marker of Dante's mystical-visionary mode. Here it prepares for the transition from everyday reality to the alternative reality of Dante's delirious visions: "E però mi giunse uno sì forte smarrimento, che chiusi li occhi e cominciai a travagliare sì come farnetica persona ed a imaginare in questo modo [As a result, such powerful turmoil came over me that I closed my eyes and started to suffer like a delirious person, imagining things]" (*VN* XXIII.4 [14.4]).

The adjective *farnetico* (delirious) and the verb *farneticare* (to be in a state of delirium) are present in Dante's oeuvre only in the prose of this chapter of the *Vita Nuova*: "sì come farnetica persona [like a delirious person]" (XXIII.4 [14.4]), "poi che io lasciai questo farneticare [after I left off being in this state of delirium]" (XXIII.30 [14.30]). It is worth recalling that it is precisely this sort of behaviour, the *farneticare* recorded in another visionary text, *A ciascun'alma*, that arouses the contemptuous reaction of Dante da Maiano in his response to Alighieri's sonnet: "sol c'hai farneticato, sappie, intendo [I only mean, please know, you were delirious]" (*Di ciò che stato sè dimandatore*, 11; see the introductory essay to *A ciascun'alma*). The careful use of the word *farneticare* in chapter XXIII (14) of the *Vita Nuova*, a text dedicated to the phenomenology of vision, would seem therefore to be a defense on Dante's part of his youthful comportment: Dante da Maiano's offensive use – "sol c'hai farneticato, sappie, intendo" – is here duly dismissed. To behave "sì come farnetica persona" is legitimate, as will be emphasized in the *Commedia* when the pilgrim is subject to ecstatic visions and walks "a guisa di cui vino o sonno piega [as one whom wine or sleep bends over]" (*Purg.* 15.123). To understand that there can be a legitimate *farneticare* it is, however, necessary to leave behind the intellectual provincialism of Dante da Maiano. It is also necessary to be less afraid of crossing gendered boundaries of comportment than Dante da Maiano appears to have been. As we can see from the discussion of the poems that precede *Donna pietosa* in the *Vita Nuova*, the mourning sonnets *Voi che portate* and *Se' tu colui*, Dante Alighieri was not afraid to cross such boundaries.

At this point in the prose Dante begins the narration "de lo errare che fece la mia fantasia [of the wandering about of my fantasy]" (*VN* XXIII.4 [14.4]), elaborating the visions that are recounted more succinctly in the canzone. He imagines dishevelled women telling him that he will die, then that he is dead; he comes to an unknown place where he sees ladies crying on the street, the sun darkened so that the stars seem to weep, the birds falling dead, earthquakes. He imagines a male friend who tells him Beatrice has died. He begins to weep, not only within the *fantasia* but in real life. He looks up and sees multitudes of angels singing *Osanna in excelsis*. His heart then tells him that Beatrice lies dead. He goes to see her body and his *erronea fantasia* shows him Beatrice dead, and ladies covering her head with a white veil, and he sees her face and its expression. He then calls upon death. When he has completed all the tasks assigned to care for the bodies of the dead he imagines that he returns to his room, and there he looks at heaven and begins to speak to Beatrice.

The prose account allows Dante to insist on visionary modalities, as for example when he specifies that "non solamente piangea ne la imaginazione, ma piangea con li occhi, bagnandoli di vere lagrime [I wasn't crying only in imagination but I was crying with my eyes, wetting them with real tears]" (*VN* XXIII.6 [14.6]); such synchrony between fantasy experience and bodily experience is typical of vision literature. Language that one might call "technical" with respect to the *narratio* of a vision, present but less emphatic in the canzone, is highlighted in the prose: the continual use of direct discourse and of the verbs *vedere* and *parere*, and the insistence on the paradoxical coexistence of truth and falsehood. *Donna pietosa* and the chapter of the *Vita Nuova* to which it belongs are early experiments in the visionary mode of "nonfalse errors," as distilled by verses in *Purgatorio* 15 that express *in nuce* much of Dante's thought on visionary experience: "Quando l'anima mia tornò di fori / a le cose che son fuor di lei vere, / io riconobbi i miei non falsi errori [When my soul returned to the things that are true outside of it, I recognized my nonfalse errors]" (*Purg.* 15.115–17).[96]

In the prose the poet is "awakened" from the visionary state after having assisted in the funeral rites for Beatrice: "E quando io avea veduto compiere tutti li dolorosi mestieri che a le corpora de li morti s'usano di fare, mi parea tornare ne la mia camera [And when I had seen all the mournful rites that are customarily done with the bodies of the dead, it seemed that I returned to my room]" (*VN* XXIII.10 [14.10]). To the gaunt corresponding verse of the canzone, "Poi mi partia, consumato ogne duolo [Once the last rites were done I went away]" (80), the prose adds the information that the "mournful rites" have to do with "the bodies of the dead," thus enriching what we might call the sociology of the *corrotto* (funeral lament), as introduced by the previous chapter, *Vita Nuova* XXII (13). Earlier as well, regarding the veil that covers the dead woman, there is a significant addition in the prose: where the canzone indicates only that the ladies cover *madonna* "d'un velo" – "vedea che donne la covrian d'un velo [I saw those ladies wrap her in a veil]" (68) – the prose specifies the colour of the veil and the part of the body (again the emphasis on "the bodies of the dead") that is covered: "e pareami che donne la covrissero, cioè la sua testa, con uno bianco velo [and it seemed that women were covering her – that is, her head – with a white veil]" (XXIII.8 [14.8]). I cannot therefore agree with De Robertis when he claims that there is not "any real gain in the prose" (*VN*, p. 158); the prose here adds notable information about Florentine social life, as elsewhere in the *Vita Nuova*. This shift suggests that *Donna pietosa*, too, was composed before the prose and not contemporaneously.

In his vision the poet is able to steal into the room where the cadaver of *madonna* is lying and participate fully in mourning. Now he does precisely what he was prevented from doing in the two preceding sonnets of the *Vita Nuova*. He finds himself exactly where he wanted to be in the sonnets *Voi che portate* and *Se' tu colui*: not

---

96 Another lyric that treats the phenomenology of visions is the sonnet *Ciò che m'incontra*. For a more developed examination of the rhetorical features that make up Dante's visionary manner, see chap. 7 of Barolini, *The Undivine Comedy,* "Nonfalse Errors and the True Dreams of the Evangelist."

at the margins of the mourning process, not at the periphery, but at the centre of the funeral activities. Now, however, it is not *madonna* who is mourning, as in the preceding sonnets, but *madonna* who is mourned.

The protagonist of the prose narration awakens with a "doloroso singulto di pianto [an agonized tearful sob]" (*VN* XXIII.11 [14.11]) that shakes up a lady seated beside his bed, "who was joined to me by the closest of blood ties [la quale era meco di propinquissima sanguinitade congiunta]" (*VN* XXIII.12 [14.12]). This precise designation of kinship is not present in the poem and represents another substantial addition of social information by the prose. Once that lady has departed – she has been identified by commentators as a sister of the poet[97] – the other ladies "si trassero verso me per isvegliarmi, credendo che io sognasse, e diceanmi: 'Non dormire più,' e 'Non ti sconfortare' [drew near me to wake me up, believing that I was dreaming, and they said to me: 'Don't sleep anymore,' and, 'Don't despair']" (*VN* XXIII.12 [14.12]). From here the prose winds towards its conclusion, in which the poet comes out of the "powerful fantasy at the very moment when I was about to say, 'O Beatrice, blessed are you'; and I had already said, 'O Beatrice'" ("forte fantasia entro in quello punto ch'io volea dicere: 'O Beatrice, benedetta sie tu'; e già detto avea 'O Beatrice'") (*VN* XXIII.13 [14.13]), and feels ashamed of having named Beatrice publicly. A parallel moment is Dante's waking up in the earthly paradise, where, however, Beatrice's name can be declared without shame: "E tutto in dubbio dissi: 'Ov'è Beatrice?' [And full of doubt I said: 'Where is Beatrice?']" (*Purg.* 32.85). The stress on the name that escapes from him is very strong in the prose – "I was about to say, 'O Beatrice, blessed are you'; and I had already said, 'O Beatrice'" – which makes its absence from the canzone all the more noteworthy.

Reassured that the name he pronounced has not been heard and comprehended by the ladies around his bed, the poet sets himself to recount "quello che veduto avea, tacendo lo nome di questa gentilissima [what I had seen, staying silent about the name of this most gracious of women]" (*VN* XXIII.15 [14.15]). All that then remains is to reconfirm the fundamental fiction of the *Vita Nuova*, which holds that the poems were written for the occasions described in the prose: "Onde poi, sanato di questa infermitade, propuosi di dire parole di questo che m'era addivenuto, però che mi parea che fosse amorosa cosa da udire; e però ne dissi questa canzone [Later, having recovered from this illness, I planned to compose a poem about what happened to me, since it seemed to me to be a love theme worthy of an audience; and so I wrote this canzone]" (*VN* XXIII.16 [14.16]).

The very presence of this routine confirmation of what is elsewhere not true, namely that the poem was composed specifically for the occasion described in the prose, further suggests that in this case, as elsewhere, the canzone was not contempo-

---

97 "In light of what will be said of Beatrice's brother – 'distretto di sanguinitade con questa gloriosa [a close relation of this glorious woman]' in 21.1 [XXXII.1], and who is, to put it clearly, her *frate* [brother] in 22.4 [XXXIII.4] – we are dealing here with a sister of the poet" (Gorni, *VN*, p. 129).

raneous with but actually preceded the prose, and that it was not originally written for the never-named Beatrice. The evidence gathered here suggests that the canzone and prose were not composed contemporaneously: Beatrice is never named in the canzone, as she is obsessively in the prose; the prose includes many details of social and material life not present in the canzone; Dante utilizes the same technique of relating that the poem was composed for the occasion described in the prose that he uses throughout the *Vita Nuova*, a technique that we know to be deliberately misleading.

Analysing the narrative blocks that make up the prose, we can point to three macro-episodes: (1) the poet's illness; (2) the delirious visions; (3) his waking up again surrounded by ladies, among whom is first of all his sister. It is important to note, with respect to Dante's commitment to the phenomenology of visionary experience in the *Vita Nuova*, that in the prose the visionary material precedes the matter-of-fact information that he is in his sickbed surrounded by concerned ladies. The prose reverses the order of the canzone, which begins with the episode that is last in the prose: *Donna pietosa e di novella etate* starts with the person that the prose designates his sister – the "lady youthful and compassionate" of the incipit – and with the moment in which the poet comes to consciousness beside her and then tells the other compassionate ladies all that has happened to him except for the name of the *gentilissima*. This story narrated by the poet to the ladies around his bed, which does not appear as such in the prose, is instead the gist of the canzone, which therefore takes the form of a story within a story: both the opening illness and the vision are narrated in the canzone not in the sequence in which they were experienced but in the form of a flashback told by the poet to his gracious interlocutors.

The poet of *Donna pietosa* is at the centre of the scene: he is sick, in bed, at the centre of attention of a group of women. This literally central position of the protagonist is highlighted by the formal structure of the canzone, where the sick poet's interactions with the women who are his healers and interlocutors frame his telling of his story: first comes the description of the ladies, then his recounting of his story to them, then a closing interaction with the ladies. In this way, the poet's narrative about himself is literally and materially central in the disposition of the canzone.

As the ladies physically surround the bed of the protagonist, so formally his dialogue with them frames his story: the last line of the canzone, "Voi mi chiamaste allor, vostra merzede [Then, by your mercy, you called out to me]" (84), marks the exit from the flashback and the return of the poet to the "reality" of his conversation with the women. If therefore on the one hand the prose is richer than the poem with historical and sociological detail – for example, the particular about the kinship of the "donna pietosa e di novella etate" – on the other hand the canzone is endowed with a much more complex narrative structure, which the prose unpacks and embroiders. Organized in the form of one discourse (the poet's illness, the consequent visions) framed by another (the conversation with the consoling ladies), the complexity of the structure is such that it is useful to visualize *Donna pietosa* in outline form:

First stanza: Begins where the prose ends, with the kind lady (in the prose identified as his sister) sitting by his bed, hearing the words of his delirium and beginning to weep. The other ladies, just as in the prose, become aware of him because of her weeping, send her away, and approach him to hear what he is saying. They speak consoling words to him. He leaves "la nova fantasia [my strange imaginings]" as a result of their intervention.

Second stanza: Still proemial. His voice was so broken by his weeping that he alone understood the name in his heart, "ch'io solo intesi il nome nel mio core" (17). In other words, the ladies were unable to catch the beloved's name: note how the prose unpacks the potential social trespass, while the poem stays within the lyric frame of the amorous/erotic. They ask him what he saw, and he tells them that he will tell them: "io dissi, 'Donne, dicerollo a vui'" (28). Speech within speech begins.

Third stanza: "While I was thinking of my frail life": here begins the flashback to what he was imagining while delirious. Now the poem treats the visionary material where the prose begins. Thinking of the frailty of his own life, he says to himself (in direct discourse of course) that his lady will die: "Ben converrà che la mia donna mora [My lady someday surely has to die]" (34). Just as in the prose, reflections on his own mortality lead to the certainty of her mortality. He experiences such *smarrimento* as a result of this thought that he closes his eyes and his spirits are confused and he begins to imagine ("e poscia imaginando" [39]) the faces of women who say to him (in direct discourse): "Morra'ti, morra'ti [You'll die, you'll die]" (42).

Fourth stanza: The "vano imaginare ov'io entrai [deceptive vision that I had]" (44): the poet is in an unspecified place (as in the prose), where he sees precisely what the prose relates in greater detail, in the same sequence. He sees: "donne andar per via disciolte [ladies walked whose hair was left unbound]" (46); "turbar lo sole e apparir la stella [the sun grow dim and then the stars appear]" (50); "cader li augelli [birds fall from the sky]" (52); "la terra tremare [the earth then quake]" (53). The final vision is a man who appears and announces the lady's death: "ed omo apparve scolorito e fioco, / dicendomi: 'Che fai? Non sai novella? / Morta è la donna tua, ch'era sì bella' [and someone pale and indistinct appears, / who said to me: 'Have you not heard the news? / Your lady's dead who was so beautiful']" (54–6). This "omo scolorito e fioco" is the "alcuno amico" of the prose.

Fifth stanza: Still within the vision. He looks up and sees the angels returning to heaven after which they cry out *Osanna*; if they had said anything more, says the poet, I would tell you (that last curious statement is missing from the prose). Love speaks: "Più non ti celo; / vieni a veder nostra donna che giace [No longer will I hide the truth: / come and behold our lady who lies dead]" (63–4). His "imaginar fallace [false imagining]" (65) leads him to look upon his dead lady; once he has seen her, the ladies cover her with a veil, and she seems to say, "Io sono in pace [I am at peace]" (70).

Sixth stanza: Still within the vision. He addresses death, whom he now finds sweet; he desires death. Then, once all the funeral preparations are taken care of ("consumato ogne duolo"; the prose adds that these preparations are for "le corpora de li morti"), he remains alone and, looking towards heaven, speaks to his dead lady: "Beato, anima bella, chi te vede [Whoever sees you, lovely soul, is blessed]" (83).

These words, which anticipate the end of the *Vita Nuova*, are the penultimate line of the canzone, but they remain technically within the poet's account of his "strange imaginings." Only in the very last verse of the canzone does the poet leave the trance and return from his vision to reality. The canzone concludes with the poet addressing the ladies, recalling the moment when they interrupted his vision by calling to him: "Voi mi chiamaste allor, vostra mercede" (84).

The construction of *Donna pietosa* anticipates that of the second canto of *Inferno*, another text made up of embedded speeches. Just as in *Inferno* 2, where there is a relay of female compassion that motivates the ladies of the court of heaven to help the lost pilgrim, *Donna pietosa* opens with the pity of one lady that elicits the compassion of others: "E altre donne, che si fuoro accorte / di me per quella che meco piangia, / fecer lei partir via, / e appressarsi per farmi sentire [And other ladies, learning of my plight / because of her who wept there by my side, / sent her away / and came to aid in my recovery]" (7–10). Shaken by their concerned comments and questions – "Qual dicea: 'Non dormire,' / e qual dicea: 'Perché sì ti sconforte?' [One said: 'Wake up!' / Another asked: 'Why are you so distraught?']" (11–12) – the poet comes to. The first stanza of *Donna pietosa* ends with him awaking and calling out his lady's (unspecified) name: "Allor lassai la nova fantasia, / chiamando il nome de la donna mia [I then forsook my strange imaginings, / as I was calling out my lady's name]" (13–14).

As already noted, "il nome de la donna mia" is not specified; so too unspecified is the kinship of the "Donna pietosa e di novella etate, / adorna assai di gentilezze umane [A lady youthful and compassionate, / so well adorned with human gentleness]" (1–2). If his sister, then the "gentilezze" of which the "donna pietosa" is "adorna" constitute not only a reference to her nobility of spirit but also a first indication of the great importance that Dante attaches (protestations notwithstanding) to his nobility of blood, that "nobiltà di sangue" that he shares with Cacciaguida and of which he boasts at the beginning of *Paradiso* 16.

The scene of the poet just having woken up and being surrounded by female attention continues in the second stanza, where we learn that, because of his voice "rotta sì da l'angoscia del pianto [broken by the anguish of my tears]" (16), the ladies did not hear the name of his heart: the line "io solo intesi il nome nel mio core" (I alone understood the name in my heart) (17) is an interesting reminder of the "dolce nome che mi fa il cor agro [sweet name that embitters so my heart]" in the canzone that names Beatrice, *Lo doloroso amor* (15). His pallor rouses compassion that leads to the ladies' wish to console – "'Deh, consoliam costui' / pregava l'una l'altra umilemente ['Let's comfort him,' / each one of them implored kindheartedly]" (23–4)[98] – and to their curiosity, which takes the form of the question, already implicitly visionary: "Che vedestù, che tu non hai valore? [What have you

---

98 This feminine consolation brings to mind the *Consolatio Philosophiae* of Boethius and the consolatory and Boethian role of Lady Philosophy in the *Convivio*. *Consolare* will be discussed further in the introductory essay to *Li occhi dolenti* with due distinction between consolation from real and embodied sources and consolation from allegorical constructs.

seen that takes away your strength?]" (26).[99] The second stanza concludes with the poet's offer to narrate what he saw in his delirium to the ladies: the last line of the second stanza – "Donne, dicerollo a vui [I'll tell you, ladies, what I saw]" (28) – is the beginning of the poet's account that will continue uninterrupted until the penultimate line of the canzone, requiring four of the six stanzas of *Donna pietosa* for its unfolding. The emphatic position of the meta-discursive "Donne, dicerollo a vui" underscores the importance of what follows.

The third stanza of *Donna pietosa* begins the flashback with the meditation on his own mortality – "Mentr'io pensava la mia frale vita, / e vedea 'l suo durar com'è leggiero [While I was thinking of my frail life, / and saw how my survival was unsure]" (29–30) – that leads to the recognition of the beloved's mortality, followed by panic and confusion: "Io presi tanto smarrimento allora, / ch'io chiusi li occhi vilmente gravati [I then became so wholly mystified / I closed my eyes, weighed down with cowardice]" (35–6). The stanza ends with the first vision and with the insistent rhythm of death: "visi di donne m'apparver crucciati, / che mi dicean pur: 'Morra'ti, morra'ti' [I saw the looks of ladies suffering / who said repeatedly: 'You'll die, you'll die!']" (41–2).

The situation outlined in *Donna pietosa* broadly anticipates the beginning of the *Commedia*. In the canzone too the protagonist is *smarrito* – "per che l'anima mia fu sì smarrita [this made my soul so utterly distraught]" (32) – and enters a new reality where he sees frightening things: "Poi vidi cose dubitose molte, / nel vano imaginare ov'io entrai [Then I saw many things that frightened me / in the deceptive vision that I had]" (43–4). He witnesses a cosmic scene of lament, "donne andar per via disciolte [ladies walk(ing) whose hair was left unbound]" (46), followed by a series of natural dislocations – "turbar lo sole e apparir la stella ... cader li augelli ... e la terra tremare [The sun grow dim and then the stars appear ... birds ... fall from the sky, / the earth then quake]" (50, 52, 53) – that culminate with the apparition of a tragic messenger: "ed omo apparve scolorito e fioco, / dicendomi: 'Che fai? non sai novella? / Morta è la donna tua, ch'era sì bella' [And someone pale and indistinct appear, / who said to me: 'Have you not heard the news? / Your lady's dead, who was so beautiful']" (54–6).

If the fourth stanza anticipates aspects of *Inferno* and echoes the story in the Gospels about the death of Christ, the fifth anticipates aspects of *Purgatorio* and *Paradiso*, echoing, among other biblical passages, a psalm: the beginning of the fifth stranza, "Levava li occhi miei [I lifted up my eyes]" (57), repeats the beginning of Psalm 120, "Levavi oculos meos in montes," a verse translated in *Paradiso* 25.38.

---

99 Regarding this verse, commentators note the Cavalcantian use of *valore* to indicate strength, vigour, as for example in "ho perduto ogni valore [I have lost all strength]" (*Poi che di doglia*, 4). We recall too the incipit of the sonnet with which Guido responds to the first sonnet of the *Vita Nuova*: *Vedeste, al mio parere, onne valore*. Guido's incipit combines *vedere* and *valore*, just as in verse 26 of *Donna pietosa*: "Che vedestù, che tu non hai valore?"

Raising his gaze, the poet sees "li angeli che tornavan suso in cielo, / e una nuvoletta avean davanti, / dopo la qual gridavan tutti: *Osanna* [the angels, ... / ascending in the sky, returning home, / together with a little cloud in front, / behind which they were crying out '*Hosanna*']" (59–61), in a scene that "is like a combination of Christ's Ascension ... and the Assumption" (Gorni, *VN*, p. 137). As for the angels who shout *Osanna* (the verb *gridare*, to shout, is used in a similarly theologized context in *Donne ch'avete*), De Robertis recalls that *Osanna* "resonates in Scripture only for the entrance of Christ into Jerusalem" (*VN*, p. 164), while Gorni specifies that the verse that follows in the Gospels, "Benedictus qui venit in nomine Domini [Blessed is he who comes in the name of the Lord]" (Matt. 21:9, Mark 11:9–10, John 12:13), "is then significantly recited in *Purgatorio* 30.19, 'Tutti dicean: Benedictus qui venis!' in the moment in which Beatrice reappears" (Gorni, *VN*, p. 137).

In sum, *Donna pietosa* functions as an incubator of fundamental aspects of the *Commedia*, among which the analogy between *madonna* and Christ and the capacity of the poet to perceive a truth invisible to eyes that perceive only quotidian reality.

However, while Beatrice in the *Commedia* is never represented in her earthly form, the canzone *Donna pietosa* concludes its visionary sequence with the representation of "my dead lady": "*madonna morta*." After the ascent of the angels into heaven, Dante writes that Love "mi condusse a veder madonna morta [led me to see my lady's lifeless form]" (66); here begins the vision that inspired the painter Dante Gabriel Rossetti. The stanza that begins with the poet's gaze lifted towards the sky, following the upward flight of the angels – "Levava li occhi miei bagnati in pianti, / e vedea, che parean pioggia di manna, / li angeli che tornavan suso in cielo, / e una nuvoletta avean davanti [I lifted up my eyes, still wet with tears, / and saw the angels, like a mist of manna, / ascending in the sky, returning home, / together with a little cloud in front]" (57–60) – concludes with the vision of the dead lady, covered by a veil. In *Purgatorio* Dante fuses the angels and the veil in the apparition of a resurgent Beatrice covered by a "candido vel [white veil]" (*Purg.* 30.31; this veil recalls the "bianco velo" of *VN* XXIII.8 [14.8]) and triumphant in a cloud of angelic flowers:

> così dentro una nuvola di fiori
> che da le mani angeliche saliva
> e ricadeva in giù dentro e di fori,
> sovra candido vel cinta d'uliva
> donna m'apparve, sotto verde manto
> vestita di color di fiamma viva.
> (Purg. 30.28–33)

[thus inside a cloud of flowers that from the angelic hands rose and fell back down inside and outside, over a white veil crowned with olive a woman appeared to me, under a green mantle dressed in the colour of living flame.]

The last two stanzas of *Donna pietosa* alternate between sky and earth, between the gaze raised upward and the gaze turned downward. The sixth and last stanza continues the scene of "madonna morta" with which the preceding stanza had concluded, passing to the reaction of the poet who sees "in lei tanta umiltà formata [such humility in her / incarnate]" (72) and to his invocation of Death. Then, when he is alone, after having completed the funeral rites (the pronounced narrative flow of the canzone follows every movement of the protagonist), Dante again raises his gaze. This is the first time that Dante follows his lady to heaven with his thoughts, as he will later do in the sonnet *Oltra la spera*: "e quand'io era solo, / dicea, guardando verso l'alto / regno: / 'Beato, anima bella, chi te vede!' [And when I was alone / I said, while looking toward the realm above: / 'Whoever sees you, lovely soul, is blessed!']" (81–3).

In the vision narrated in the canzone, therefore, Dante inserts another virtually visionary act: the desire to see the "anima bella" of his lady in heaven. In line 83 of *Donna pietosa*, "Beato, anima bella, chi te vede!," Dante imagines the act of seeing the beatified lady and the beatifying consequences of such a sight: he imagines the beatitude – the adjective *beato* is a signal that we are, at least etymologically and potentially, in the presence of the *beatrice* – which will be the consequence of seeing his lady in paradise. In this way, Dante anticipates much of his poetic future and renews the oldest motif of the Italian lyric: we recall the sonnet *Io m'aggio posto in core a Dio servire* by Giacomo da Lentini, which concludes with the verse "veggendo la mia donna in ghiora stare [to see my love in glory's realm]." But here, in the highly complex structure of *Donna pietosa*, the gaze of the reader is brought back one last time to earth, and we find ourselves again in a Florentine room with a poet who breaks the enchantment, saying to the ladies around him: "Voi mi chiamaste allor, vostra merzede [Then, by your mercy, you called out to me]" (84).

40 (B XX; FB 40; *VN* XXIII.17–28 [14.17–28])

	Donna pietosa e di novella etate,	A lady youthful and compassionate,
	adorna assai di gentilezze umane,	so well adorned with human gentleness,
3	ch'era là 'v'io chiamava spesso Morte,	who heard me, nearby, often call on Death,
	veggendo li occhi miei pien di pietate,	and seeing my anguished eyes so full of tears
	e ascoltando le parole vane,	and hearing all the ravings of my speech,
6	si mosse con paura a pianger forte.	began to weep most bitterly with fear.
	E altre donne, che si fuoro accorte	And other ladies, learning of my plight
	di me per quella che meco piangia,	because of her who wept there by my side,
	fecer lei partir via,	sent her away
10	e appressarsi per farmi sentire.	and came to aid in my recovery.
	Qual dicea: "Non dormire",	One said: "Wake up!"
	e qual dicea: "Perché sì ti sconforte?".	Another asked: "Why are you so distraught?"

Allor lassai la nova fantasia,
14   chiamando il nome de la donna mia.
     Era la voce mia sì dolorosa
     e rotta sì da l'angoscia del pianto,
17   ch'io solo intesi il nome nel mio core;
     e con tutta la vista vergognosa
     ch'era nel viso mio giunta cotanto,
20   mi fece verso lor volgere Amore.
     Elli era tale a veder mio colore,
     che facea ragionar di morte altrui:
     "Deh, consoliam costui"
24   pregava l'una l'altra umilemente;
     e dicevan sovente:
     "Che vedestù, che tu non hai valore?"
     E quando un poco confortato fui,
28   io dissi: "Donne, dicerollo a vui.
     Mentr'io pensava la mia frale vita,
     e vedea 'l suo durar com'è leggiero,
31   piansemi Amor nel core, ove dimora;
     per che l'anima mia fu sì smarrita,
     che sospirando dicea nel pensero:
34   'Ben converrà che la mia donna mora.'
     Io presi tanto smarrimento allora,
     ch'io chiusi li occhi vilmente gravati,
     e furon sì smagati
38   li spirti miei, che ciascun giva errando;
     e poscia imaginando,
     di caunoscenza e di verità fora,
     visi di donne m'apparver crucciati,
42   che mi dicean pur: 'Morra'ti, morra'ti.'
     Poi vidi cose dubitose molte,
     nel vano imaginare ov'io entrai;
45   ed esser mi parea non so in qual loco,
     e veder donne andar per via disciolte,
     qual lagrimando, e qual traendo guai,
48   che di tristizia saettavan foco.
     Poi mi parve vedere a poco a poco
     turbar lo sole e apparir la stella,
     e pianger elli ed ella;
52   cader li augelli volando per l'are,
     e la terra tremare;
     ed omo apparve scolorito e fioco,
     dicendomi: 'Che fai? non sai novella?

I then forsook my strange imaginings
as I was calling out my lady's name.
   My voice was so afflicted by my pain
and broken by the anguish of my tears
that my heart only heard her spoken name.
And yet in spite of all the shame I felt,
which had appeared so plainly on my face,
Love made me turn to see the ladies there.
So pallid was the colour of my face
that it made them begin to speak of death.
"Let's comfort him,"
each one of them implored kind-heartedly.
They often asked:
"What have you seen that takes away your strength?"
And after being somewhat comforted,
I said: "I'll tell you, ladies, what I saw.
   While I was thinking of my frail life,
and saw how my survival was unsure,
Love wept inside my heart, where it abides;
this made my soul so utterly distraught
I spoke these words, while sighing, in my thought:
'My lady someday surely has to die.'
I then became so wholly mystified
I closed my eyes, weighed down with cowardice;
so shaken were
my spirits that they wandered all about;
and while I dreamed,
deprived of consciousness and knowing truth,
I saw the looks of ladies suffering
who said repeatedly: 'You'll die, you'll die!'
   Then I saw many things that frightened me
in the deceptive vision that I had;
I came into an unfamiliar place
where ladies walked whose hair was left unbound,
some weeping, others voicing their laments,
that shot forth fiery shafts of agony.
And gradually it seemed to me I saw
the sun grow dim and then the stars appear,
all weeping tears,
birds flying through the air fall from the sky,
the earth then quake,
and someone pale and indistinct appear,
who said to me: 'Have you not heard the news?

56 Morta è la donna tua, ch'era sì bella.'	Your lady's dead, who was so beautiful.'
Levava li occhi miei bagnati in pianti,	I lifted up my eyes, still wet with tears,
e vedea, che parean pioggia di manna,	and saw the angels, like a mist of manna,
59 li angeli che tornavan suso in cielo,	ascending in the sky, returning home,
e una nuvoletta avean davanti,	together with a little cloud in front,
dopo la qual gridavan tutti: *Osanna*;	behind which they were crying out *'Hosanna.'*
62 e s'altro avesser detto, a voi dire'lo.	And if they had said more, I'd tell you now.
Allor diceva Amor: 'Più nol ti celo;	Love said: 'No longer will I hide the truth:
vieni a veder nostra donna che giace.'	come and behold our lady who lies dead.'
Lo imaginar fallace	My false imagining
66 mi condusse a veder madonna morta;	led me to see my lady's lifeless form;
e quand'io l'avea scorta,	and as I looked at her,
vedea che donne la covrian d'un velo;	I saw those ladies wrap her in a veil;
ed avea seco umiltà verace,	and she had with her true humility,
70 che parea che dicesse: 'Io sono in pace.'	so that she seemed to say: 'I am at peace.'
Io divenia nel dolor sì umile,	Then I became so humble in my grief,
veggendo in lei tanta umiltà formata,	at seeing such humility in her
73 ch'io dicea: 'Morte, assai dolce ti tegno;	incarnate, that I said: 'Death, you are meek:
tu dei omai esser cosa gentile,	from now on you must be a noble being,
poi che tu se' ne la mia donna stata,	since in my lady you have made a home,
76 e dei aver pietate e non disdegno.	and you must show compassion, not disdain.
Vedi che sì desideroso vegno	You see I yearn so much to be with you
d'esser de' tuoi, ch'io ti somiglio in fede.	that I resemble you, if truth be told.
Vieni, ché 'l cor te chiede.'	Come now, my heart calls you.'
80 Poi mi partia, consumato ogne duolo;	Once the last rites were done I went away;
e quand'io era solo,	and when I was alone
dicea, guardando verso l'alto regno:	I said, while looking toward the realm above:
'Beato, anima bella, chi te vede!'	'Whoever sees you, lovely soul, is blessed!'
84 Voi mi chiamaste allor, vostra merzede."	Then, by your mercy, you called out to me."

METRE: canzone of six stanzas, each composed of fourteen verses (twelve hendecasyllables and two *settenari*), with rhyme scheme ABC ABC CDdEeCDD and without *congedo*. The *fronte* is six verses (3 + 3) and the *sirma* is eight verses.

41 Un dì si venne a me Malinconia

In the sonnet *Un dì si venne a me Malinconia*, Dante personifies his emotions – "Malinconia [Melancholy]" (1), "Dolore ed Ira [Sorrow and Distress]" (4), and "Amor [Love]" (8) – to express his "presentiment" of his lady's death. Her pending death will be announced by Love at the end of the sonnet, in a concise dialogue between Love and the narrator: "Ed io li dissi: 'Che hai tu, cattivello?' / E lui rispose: 'Io ho guai e pensero, / ché nostra donna muor, dolce fratello' [I said to him: 'What troubles you, poor man?' / And he replied: 'I mourn and feel deep pain / because our lady, brother, lies near death']" (12–14). The identity of the lady is not stated. This sonnet was not included in the *Vita Nuova*.

A parallel announcement by Love concerning a similarly unidentified "our lady" is in the canzone *Donna pietosa e di novella etate*: "Allor diceva Amor: 'Più nol ti celo; / vieni a veder nostra donna che giace' [Love said: 'No longer will I hide the truth: / come and behold our lady who lies dead']" (63–4). Contini rightly notes about *Un dì si venne a me Malinconia* that its "general contents are the same as those of the great canzone *Donna pietosa*," while in the sonnet "there is none of the tragic delirium that is in the canzone" (Contini, p. 78). In other words, Dante experimented with more than one approach for expressing presentiments of his lady's pending death. Whether or not these poems were written regarding Beatrice and whether before or after her death are different questions, to which we have no answers. The tragic and visionary approach of *Donna pietosa*, institutionalized by the prose of the *Vita Nuova*, represents the road that Dante chose to follow, not the only one that he ventured upon.

It is important to point out the originality of this theme. "The death of the lady (or lord) is not an unknown subject in the tradition of early Italian poetry," notes De Robertis (ed. comm., p. 388), but it is Dante who takes this subject and makes it an obligatory passage for Petrarch and his followers. A fundamental task of the *Vita Nuova* is its introduction of this theme into the courtly context; in fact, it would not be incorrect to read the *Vita Nuova* as a text dedicated to introducing the death of the lady – and the psychological and philosophical consequences of that death – into the lyrical tradition. In Guido Cavalcanti's poetry it is the poet who "dies," not his lady.

In the *Vita Nuova* the poet must learn death's lesson – that is, the lesson of the transience of life and of beloved earthly things, clearly stated in *Donna pietosa*: "Mentr'io pensava la mia frale vita, / e vedea 'l suo durar com'è leggiero [While I was thinking of my frail life, / and saw how my survival was unsure]" (29–30). It is a lesson that Dante imports into the system of courtly love via Augustine's *Confessions*, in which, after the death of a dear friend, Augustine learned to recognize the error of "loving a man that must die as though he were not to die [diligendo morituram ac si non moriturum]" (*Conf.* 4.8). In the *Vita Nuova* Dante is forced to reconceptualize love and in essence to put into practice the Augustinian lesson. He learns that he must redirect his desire in order to situate "all [his] bliss in that which cannot fail [him]": "tutta la mia beatitudine in quello che non mi puote venire meno" (*VN* XVIII.4 [10.6]). The "venire meno" – falling short, failing, and indeed dying – of the courtly lady functions within the economy of the *libello* as the existential pressure that triggers in the protagonist an understanding of the transience of even the noblest of mortal things.

Un dì si venne a me Malinconia shares the theme of mourning with *Donna pietosa* and with the group of sonnets (two in the *Vita Nuova* and two left out of it) that demonstrate Dante's interest in funeral rites and in social activities associated with death: *Voi che portate la sembianza umile, Se' tu colui c' hai trattato sovente, Onde venite voi così pensose?* and *Voi donne, che pietoso atto mostrate.* In *Un dì si venne* Love is presented as dressed for mourning: "guardai e vidi Amor che venia / vestito di nuovo d'un drappo nero, / e nel suo capo portava un cappello, / e certo lacrimava pur di vero [I looked and saw that Love was drawing near, / attired in brand-new clothing that was black, / and wearing on his head a hat as well, / and he was truly weeping real tears]" (8–11). The Barbi-Maggini commentary documents that "men in mourning wore black outfits, as the women wore brown (cf. Boccaccio, *Decam.*, 3.7), and a hood on their head," and that the expression *di nuovo* (brand-new, in the translation), meaning that "the outfit was specially made," is a technical expression that "also occurs in the Statutes" (Barbi-Maggini, pp. 273–4).

In two of the mourning sonnets we find the expression "nostra donna [our lady]," also present in *Un dì si venne*: in *Voi che portate* and *Voi donne* it is the women who appropriate the lady, referring to her as "nostra." The phrase "nostra donna" thus can indicate different points of view: when spoken by Love (a projection of the narrator) in *Donna pietosa* and in *Un dì si venne*, "nostra donna" includes the poet in the association, while the same phrase in the mouth of the women-companions instead suggests his exclusion from rituals of mourning.

Love is characterized as "dolce fratello [sweet brother]" in *Un dì si venne*, whose last verse continues the fellowship between the poet and his brother even after the lady's death: "ché nostra donna muor, dolce fratello [because our lady, brother, lies near death]" (14). The phrase "nostra donna" recalls the sonnet *Deh ragioniamo insieme un poco, Amore*, in which the journeying poet suggests to a benign Love that they while away the time by talking together about "our lady": "trattiam di nostra donna omai, signore [let's speak awhile about our lady, lord]" (4). *Deh ragioniamo*'s friendly Love hails from more joyful times, and is the forerunner of the Love, still brotherly but no longer smiling, that we find in *Un dì si venne*.

The sonnet *Cavalcando l'altr'ier*, included in *Vita Nuova* IX (4), has many features in common with *Un dì si venne*. Both are more narrative than lyrical, and in both the lover encounters a melancholy Love walking along a road: in *Cavalcando l'altr'ier* Love is "meschino [destitute]" (5), while in *Un dì si venne a me Malinconia*

Love is a "cattivello [poor man]" (12). Interestingly, the poet encounters Love again in *Io mi senti' svegliar dentro a lo core*, the sonnet that follows *Donna pietosa* in *Vita Nuova* XXIV (15), but there Love is "allegro [cheerful]" (4).

41 (B LXXII; C 25; FB 41; DR 66)

Un dì si venne a me Malinconia
e disse: "I' voglio un poco star con teco";
e parve a me che la menasse seco
4   Dolore ed Ira per suo compagnia.
Ed io le dissi: "Pàrtiti, va' via";
ed ella mi rispose come un greco;
e ragionando a grand'agio con meco,
8   guardai e vidi Amor che venia
    vestito di nuovo d'un drappo nero,
e nel suo capo portava un cappello,
11   e certo lacrimava pur di vero.
    Ed io li dissi: "Che hai tu, cattivello?"
    E lui rispose: "Io ho guai e pensero,
14   ché nostra donna muor, dolce fratello."

Once Melancholy came to me and said
"I plan to stay with you a little while";
and it appeared to me she'd brought along
both Sorrow and Distress for company.
I said to her, "Away with you, be gone!"
But like a Greek she answered haughtily,
and while she spoke to me with perfect ease,
I looked and saw that Love was drawing near,
    attired in brand-new clothing that was black,
and wearing on his head a hat as well,
and he was truly weeping real tears.
I said to him: "What troubles you, poor man?"
And he replied: "I mourn and feel deep pain
because our lady, brother, lies near death."

METRE: sonnet ABBA ABBA CDC DCD.

42 Io mi senti' svegliar dentro a lo core

The sonnet *Io mi senti' svegliar dentro a lo core*, placed by Dante in chapter XXIV (15) of the *Vita Nuova*, is among the most obvious examples of texts whose original sense is modified almost beyond recognition by the prose of the *libello*. The sonnet celebrates Love and the beloved ladies who are named in it: calling the ladies by name is without a doubt the most original aspect of the poem. The content takes the form of a two-part procession: first arrives Love and then in a second installment arrive the two ladies who are celebrated and named by Love. In the first part, which takes place in the octave, the poet sees Love coming from far off, as in *Un dì si venne a me Malinconia*, but instead of a sad Love full of presentiments about the death of *madonna*, this Love is happy and triumphant: "e poi vidi venir da lungi Amore / allegro sì, che appena il conoscia, / dicendo: 'Or pensa pur di farmi onore' [then I saw Love approaching from afar / (I barely recognized him for his cheer) / who said, while smiling after every word: / 'Now only think how you might honour me']" (3–5). Then, in the sestet, which corresponds to the second phase of the procession, the poet witnesses the arrival of the two ladies:

> io vidi monna Vanna e monna Bice
> venire inver lo loco là 'v'io era,
> l'una appresso de l'altra maraviglia;
> e sì come la mente mi ridice,
> Amor mi disse: "Quell'è Primavera,
> e quell'ha nome Amor, sì mi somiglia."
> (Io mi senti' svegliar, 9–14)

> [and saw the ladies Joan and Beatrice
> draw near the place where I was standing then,
> one marvel followed by a second one.
> And as my memory now recollects,
> Love said: "This one is Spring, the other's name
> is Love, because she so resembles me.]

The names "monna Vanna" and "monna Bice" are the source of much of the interest in *Io mi senti' svegliar*. For De Robertis, "it is curious that, as a nickname, the name of Guido's lady shows up only through Dante's testimony" (*VN*, p. 168), and in fact *Guido, i' vorrei* too refers to "monna Vanna" as the lady of Guido Cavalcanti (De Robertis is referring to "Vanna" as a nickname for "Giovanna"). In *Guido, i' vorrei*,

Beatrice's name does not appear and Dante's lady is indicated instead with the para-phrase "quella ch'è sul numer de le trenta [(she) who's number thirty]" (10). Thus, *Io mi senti' svegliar* offers a rare opportunity, always of interest, of seeing Dante's lady named outside the prose of the *Vita Nuova*; it offers, moreover, the only use of the name "Bice" in all of Dante's lyrics ("Bice" is used again only in *Par.* 7.14). The expression "monna Bice" is a *hapax* in Dante's oeuvre. The word "monna" indicates a married woman and is not associated with Beatrice's name in the *Commedia*, where the residue of personal and social identity present in the *Vita Nuova* has diminished further still.

The prose in chapter XXIV (15) of the *Vita Nuova* takes the modest sonnet *Io mi senti' svegliar* and hypes it almost beyond recognition. According to the prose, the *senhal* or lyrical code-name of monna Vanna, which is "Primavera" ("Spring"; see "piacente primavera" in Cavalcanti's *ballata*, *Fresca rosa novella*), corresponds to *prima verrà* or "s/he will come first." The name of Giovanna Primavera therefore corresponds to that of the Giovanni (John) who "will come first," which is to say, to that John who will come before Christ: "E se anche vogli considerare lo primo nome suo, tanto è quanto dire 'prima verrà', però che lo nome Giovanna è da quello Giovanni lo quale precedette la verace luce, dicendo: 'Ego vox clamantis in deserto: parate viam Domini' [And if you also consider her given name, you will see that it is practically the same as saying *prima verrà*, since her name, Giovanna or Joanna, is derived from that John who preceded the true Light, saying, 'I am the voice of one crying in the wilderness. Make straight the way of the Lord']" (*VN* XXIV.4 [15.4]). The simple, sweet arrival in the sonnet of "monna Vanna e monna Bice," in that order, "l'una appresso de l'altra maraviglia [one marvel followed by a second one]" (11), becomes, in the prose of the *Vita Nuova*, the arrival of John the Baptist who prepares the way of Christ.

Dante here shows that he is a young glossator who, while perhaps a bit heavy-handed, is always astute in singling out in the prose the salient and workable details of a sonnet. Most interesting in *Io mi senti' svegliar* is the naming of names, which is developed as a theme in the prose through use of the word "nome" (name): "Quell'è Primavera, / e quell'ha **nome** Amor, sì mi somiglia [This one is Spring, the other's name / is Love, because she so resembles me]" (13–14). Establishing naming as a theme of the sonnet permits the author of the *libello* to focus in the prose on the basic principle "nomina sunt consequentia rerum [names are the consequence of the things named]," announced earlier, in *Vita Nuova* XIII (6): "con ciò sia cosa che li **nomi** seguitino le **nominate** cose, sì come è scritto: '**Nomina** sunt consequentia rerum' [given that names follow from the things they name, as it is written: 'Nomina sunt consequentia rerum']" (*VN* XIII.4 [6.4]).

The idea of affixing a name that "follows from the thing it names," precisely as theorized in *Vita Nuova* XIII (6), is faithfully executed in the prose treatment of "monna Vanna," where Dante uses the phrase *imporre il nome a qualcuno* (to give a name to someone). We learn that "per la sua bieltade, secondo che altri crede, imposto l'era **nome** Primavera [she was given the name Primavera because of her beauty, as others believe]" (*VN* XXIV.3 [15.3]). Love explains that he moved Guido, "lo imponitore del **nome**" – literally, "the giver of her name" – to give his lady this name in order to indicate the role of Giovanna in relation to Beatrice: "ché io mossi lo imponitore del **nome** a chiamarla così Primavera, cioè prima verrà lo die che Beatrice si mosterrà dopo la imaginazione del suo fedele [I moved the one who gave her that name to call her Primavera, that is, *prima verrà,* she will come first the day that Beatrice appears, after the imaginings of her faithful one]" (*VN* XXIV.4 [15.4]).

The strange game of temporal inversion on which the construction of the *Vita Nuova* is based – a game based on maintaining that the poems were written not before the prose, as in fact was the case, but afterwards, to fix the moment described by the prose – generates many disorienting moments, but few more disquieting than this. The "imponitore del nome," Guido Cavalcanti, is "unaware of the true meaning of the name that he himself gave" (Gorni, *VN*, p. 142), a name that, moreover, he did not really give her, since Vanna/Giovanna "is a name that never recurs in Guido's lyrics" (Gorni, *VN*, p. 142). In a further disquieting move, right after having presented the analogy between Giovanna and the Baptist and between Beatrice and Christ – an analogy that clearly suggests that in the poetic sphere too there will be a hierarchy and that the poet of "monna Vanna" preceded and prepared the way for the greater poet of "monna Bice" – Dante tells us that he wrote *Io mi senti' svegliar* "to my first friend," Guido Cavalcanti: "Onde io poi, ripensando, propuosi di scrivere per rima a lo mio primo amico [Whereupon, thinking things over, I planned to write a poem to my best friend]" (*VN* XXIV.6 [15.6]).

The true "imposer of names," on everyone and everything – Dante – here says that he wrote to his best friend as if Guido were still the one who reigned supreme, in both poetry and love, as if he were still "primo" in the sense of "most important," rather than "primo" in the (new, just imposed) sense of "eclipsed." Dante writes as if Guido were still the Guido of *Guido, i' vorrei,* the friend of the poetic season that includes the sonnet *Io mi senti' svegliar dentro a lo core,* instead of the Guido he has fashioned through the *Vita Nuova* prose. In the elaborate analogy between Giovanna and John and between Beatrice and Christ imposed on the sonnet by the prose, Guido has been demoted from "first" to "second"; his position is preparatory, proleptic, passé. It is the position of the one who, in *Purgatorio* 11, will be chased from the nest: "Così ha tolto l'uno a l'altro Guido / la gloria de la lingua; e forse è nato / chi l'uno e l'altro caccerà del nido [Thus has one Guido taken from the other the glory of our language, and perhaps he is born who will hunt one and the other from the nest]" (*Purg.* 11.97–9).

42 (B XXI; FB 42; *VN* XXIV.7–9 [15.7–9])

Io mi senti' svegliar dentro a lo core	I felt a spirit of love begin to stir
un spirito amoroso che dormia:	within my heart, where it was fast asleep;
e poi vidi venir da lungi Amore	then I saw Love approaching from afar

4   allegro sì, che appena il conoscia,
      dicendo: "Or pensa pur di farmi onore";
      e 'n ciascuna parola sua ridia.
      E poco stando meco il mio segnore,
8   guardando in quella parte onde venia,
          io vidi monna Vanna e monna Bice
      venire inver lo loco là 'v'io era,
11   l'una appresso de l'altra maraviglia;
      e sì come la mente mi ridice,
      Amor mi disse: "Quell'è Primavera,
14   e quell'ha nome Amor, sì mi somiglia."

METRE: sonnet ABAB ABAB CDE CDE.

(I barely recognized him for his cheer)
who said, while smiling after every word:
"Now only think how you might honour me."
And while my Lord remained with me a while,
I turned my eyes to see from where he'd come
    and saw the ladies Joan and Beatrice
draw near the place where I was standing then,
one marvel followed by a second one.
And as my memory now recollects,
Love said: "This one is Spring, the other's name
is Love, because she so resembles me."

43 Tanto gentile e tanto onesta pare
First Redaction

The sonnet *Tanto gentile e tanto onesta pare* is among the most celebrated and anthologized in Italian literature. It was inserted into chapter XXVI (17) of the *Vita Nuova*, where it exemplifies the resumption of the *stilo de la sua loda*, the style that Dante will later call the *dolce stil novo*, dedicated to the praise of *madonna*'s virtuous and miraculous effects. In this chapter of the *libello* Dante returns to the theme of praise – developed earlier, in the great canzone *Donne ch'avete* and in the sonnet *Negli occhi porta la mia donna Amore* – but then put aside in order to concentrate on the theme of death and existential entropy. Now Dante explicitly declares his wish to "resume the style I had praised her with": "Queste e più mirabili cose da lei procedeano virtuosamente: onde io pensando a ciò, volendo ripigliare lo stilo de la sua loda, propuosi di dicere parole, ne le quali io dessi ad intendere de le sue mirabili ed eccellenti operazioni [These and other marvelous things proceeded from her by means of her power; so that I, thinking about all this and wishing to resume the style I had praised her with, planned to compose a poem in which I would describe some of the wondrous and excellent effects she brought about]" (*VN* XXVI.4 [17.4]).

The version of *Tanto gentile* reproduced here, however, is the first redaction, not the version in the *Vita Nuova*, whose refinements of the earlier redaction contribute towards underscoring the gains of the new style. Whereas in the preliminary version Dante writes "credo che sia una cosa venuta / di cielo in terra a miracol mostrare [I believe she is a creature come / from heaven to earth to show a miracle]" (7–8), in the final version he substitutes "e par che" for "credo che," reusing the verb *parere* from the incipit and eliminating any possible element "of participation and personal appropriation" (De Robertis, *VN*, p. 182). Similarly, the verb *ferire* in "che fier [ferisce] per gli occhi" (that strikes through the eyes) (10), which for De Robertis constitutes a "clear residue of the language and representation of suffering love" (*VN*, p. 183), is eliminated in the final redaction and corrected into "che dà per li occhi" (that gives through the eyes).[100]

The feature that distinguishes *Tanto gentile* from the many other sonnets that harken back to the Guinizzellian model and that share the same essential theme of *madonna*'s nobility and virtue is above all its capacity to make manifest, its theatricality:

---

100 It is worth remembering, however, that *ferire* is used for *madonna*'s eyes in *Donne ch'avete*: "De li occhi suoi, come ch'ella li mova, / escono spirti d'amore inflammati, / che *feron* li occhi a qual che allor la guati [Her eyes, wherever she should turn her gaze, / send spirits forth, inflamed with love, / that pierce / the eyes of anyone who looks at her]" (51–3).

instead of *describing* the lady and her miraculous nobility, *Tanto gentile* manages to *show* her nobility in action, to make it visible. The theatricality of *Tanto gentile* is all the more difficult to grasp because it is not at all obvious or melodramatic; in fact, the sonnet is so rigorously limpid that Dante himself refuses to muddy it through glossing and subdivision: "Questo sonetto è sì piano ad intendere, per quello che narrato è dinanzi, che non abbisogna d'alcuna divisione [This sonnet is so simple, because of what is said before it, there is no need to divide it up]" (*VN* XXVI:8 [17.8]).

If we were to assign a more theological term to the poetics of *Tanto gentile*, we could say that it deploys a sacramental art, bearing in mind the technical sense of "sacrament" as a visible sign of inward grace. A synonym for sacramental art could be art of manifestation, of making the invisible visible, as in the divine manifestation described in Romans 1:19–20, in a passage cited by Dante in the *Monarchia* and the Fifth Epistle: "quia quod notum est Dei, **manifestum** est in illis. Deus enim illis **manifestavit**. Invisibilia enim ipsius, a creatura mundi, per ea quae facta sunt, intellecta, conspiciuntur [because that which is known of God is manifest in them. For God hath manifested it unto them. For the invisible things of him from the creation of the world are clearly seen, being understood by the things that are made]."[101] This art of "making manifest" is of special importance to a poet who theorizes making the invisible visible as early as the *Vita Nuova*,[102] and is of course critical for the *Commedia*. We can say of *Tanto gentile* that "the lady's miraculously sacramental presence sets a precedent for the *Commedia*."[103]

To better understand how Dante creates the epiphanic effect of *Tanto gentile*, it is useful to compare it to *Negli occhi porta la mia donna Amore*, a sonnet with which it shares *stil novo* motifs, lexicon, and the fundamental stilnovist situation of the lady who passes by, gives her salution, and so creates a new moral reality. The two sonnets have in common a subtle mesh of delicately transposed elements. Take, for example, the adjective *gentile*, which in the incipit of *Tanto gentile* is applied not to the reality altered by her, as in *Negli occhi porta*'s "si fa gentil ciò ch'ella mira [renders noble all she looks upon]" [2]), but rather to the lady herself ("Tanto gentile e tanto onesta pare [My lady shows such grace and dignity]"). Another example is the verb *mirare*, which plays etymologically with the noun *miracolo* (miracle): while in *Negli occhi porta* her gaze is directed at others, in *Tanto gentile* the gaze of others is directed at her. The verb *mirare* therefore is transferred to those who gaze at her and to the

---

101 In *Mon.* 2.2.8, Dante cites Romans 1:20: "Voluntas quidem Dei per se invisibilis est; et invisibilia Dei 'per ea que facta sunt intellecta conspiciuntur' [For the will of God in itself is indeed invisible; but the invisible things of God 'are clearly perceived by being understood through the things he has made']." The same passage from Romans is cited in *Epist.* 5.23.

102 The chapter before *Tanto gentile* addresses the problem of how a poet may write "d'Amore come se fosse una cosa per sé, e non solamente sustanzia intelligente, ma sì come fosse sustanzia corporale [about Love as if he were a thing-in-itself, and not only as an intelligent substance, but as if he were a corporeal substance]" (*VN* XXV.1 [16.1]).

103 Barolini, *The Undivine Comedy*, p. 150.

sweetness they feel – "Mostrasi sì piacente a chi la mira, / che fier per gli occhi una dolcezza al core [She shows such charm to who looks on her / that through his eyes a sweetness strikes his heart]" (*Tanto gentile*, 9–10) – a sweetness that in *Negli occhi porta* is instead elicited by her speech: "Ogni dolcezza, ogni pensiero umìle / nasce nel core a chi parlar la sente [All sweetness and all humble thoughts are born / within the heart of those who hear her speak]" (*Negli occhi porta*, 9–10).

Negli occhi porta is, like *Tanto gentile*, a sonnet whose "new style" is already perfected. The lady is no longer "likened" in the Guinizzellian manner ("Io voglio del ver la mia donna laudare / ed asembrarli la rosa e lo giglio [I want to truly praise my lady, / liken her to the rose and the lily]" [1–2]), but is fully metaphorized: in the conclusion of *Negli occhi porta* the lady's smile is not similar to a miracle but *is* a miracle ("tant'è novo miracolo e gentile" [14]). However, in *Negli occhi porta* Dante achieves descriptive results, not performative ones. In *Tanto gentile* the lady about whom the poet writes "Ella se ·n va, sentendosi laudare, / benignamente d'umiltà vestuta [She moves along attending words of praise, / benignly dressed in true humility]" (5–6) is offered directly to the reader's sight, with the result that the reader becomes the hypothetical spectator who is encountered in the opening of another praise-sonnet: "Vede perfettamente ogne salute / chi la mia donna fra le donne vede [Whoever sees my lady with her friends / conceives complete perfection perfectly]" (*Vede perfettamente*, 1–2).

Tanto gentile hinges on making manifest: the key word, *mostrare* (to show), occurs at the conclusion of the octave and is immediately repeated at the beginning of the sestet. The lady-miracle come from heaven to earth is a manifestation of the art of the divine maker: "credo che sia una cosa venuta / di cielo in terra a miracol **mostrare**. / **Mostrasi** sì piacente a chi la mira [I believe she is a creature come / from heaven to earth to show a miracle. / She shows such charm to him who looks at her]" (7–9). The art of "mostrare," of creating a virtual reality with words – the "visibile parlare [visible speech]" of *Purg.* 10.95 – is Dante's art par excellence. When in the *Commedia* Dante meditates on his own art by using ecphrasis, representation of representation, for example with respect to the acrostic that is literally an "artifice" made (according to the fiction) by God himself (*Purg.* 12.23), he turns to the same verb *mostrare* that he had used in a similar representative context in the early sonnet *Tanto gentile*.[104]

In *Tanto gentile* Dante starts right off with the appearance of the lady, in an incipit that is indebted to Cavalcanti's splendid opening, *Chi è questa che vèn, ch'ogn'om la mira*. Dante, however, tones down the dramatic quotient, substituting for Guido's

---

104 See my "Representing What God Presented: The Arachnean Art of the Terrace of Pride," chap. 6 in Barolini, *The Undivine Comedy*: "The representational thrust of the reiterated 'mostrava' hardly needs underscoring; indeed, it should be noted that the words Dante chooses to build the *artificio* of *Purgatorio* 12 reflect the terrace's visual (*vedere*) and representational (*mostrare*) thematics" (p. 127).

question the simple purity of a declaration. The sonnet reveals an apparition, and the first rhyme word is critical: of *pare*, Contini writes that "*pare* is not the equivalent of 'sembra [it seems],' nor of 'appare [it appears],' but means 'to appear manifestly, to show oneself in one's manifestness.'"[105] The prose of the *Vita Nuova* glosses *pare* with the verb *mostrare* (a "perfect interpretation," according to De Robertis, ed. comm., p. 382): "Io dico ch'ella **si mostrava** sì gentile e sì piena di tutti i piaceri, che quelli che la miravano comprendeano in loro una dolcezza onesta e soave, tanto che ridicere non lo sapeano; né alcuno era lo quale potesse mirare lei, che nel principio nol convenisse sospirare [I tell you that she showed herself so gracious and so lovely that those who gazed on her sensed within themselves a pure and gentle sweetness they could find no words to describe; nor could anyone look at her without having to sigh at once]" (*VN* XXVI.3 [17.3]). What occurs in the opening of *Tanto gentile* is postponed to the ending of *Negli occhi porta*, where the manifestation of *madonna* – and the verb *pare* that verbalizes her manifestness – is the culmination of the sonnet: "Quel ch'ella par quand'un poco sorride / non si può dicer né tenere a mente, / tant'è novo miracolo e gentile [What she looks like when she begins to smile / cannot be told or held within the mind, / so rare and noble is this miracle]" (*Negli occhi porta*, 12–14).

The lady of *Tanto gentile* is a miracle in act – "maraviglia ne l'atto che procede / d'un'anima che 'nfin qua su risplende [a miracle / in act is seen proceeding from a soul / whose shining light extends as far as here]," in the words of *Donne ch'avete* (17–18) – and the sonnet wastes no time in making her visible, beginning with the verb *parere* in the incipit and then moving on to *mostrare*. *Parere* appears again in the final tercet (in the version of the *Vita Nuova* "pare" is also in line 7, where "credo che" becomes "e par che," bringing the occurrences to three), where there is also the paradigmatic verb *sospirare*, to sigh: "e par che della suo labbia si mova / un spirito soave pien d'amore / che va dicendo a l'anima: '**Sospira**!' [And from her countenance there clearly comes / a spirit that is sweet and full of love / which goes before the soul and whispers: 'Sigh']" (12–14). The verb *sospirare* is also used in *Negli occhi porta* ("e d'ogni suo difetto allor **sospira** [and then he sighs remembering his faults]" [6]), but it lacks the drama that the use of the imperative "Sospira!" confers at the end of *Tanto gentile*. The same less performative use of *sospirare* is found in the final lines of the praise-sonnet *Vede perfettamente ogne salute*, whose ending seems to be almost a gloss on that of *Tanto gentile*: "che nessun la si può recare a mente / che non **sospiri** in dolcezza d'amore [that no one's able to remember her / who does not sigh from sweetness filled with love]" (*Vede perfettamente*, 13–14).

---

105 "Un sonetto di Dante," in *Un'idea di Dante* (Turin: Einaudi, 1976), pp. 23–4. Barbi-Maggini gloss *pare* as follows: "she appears, she shows herself. Among many examples of *parere* for *apparire* (commonly used) we cite one of the most obvious in Dante's work, *Par.* 13.91: 'Ma perché paia ben ciò che non pare [But so that which does not appear may appear well].' At l.9 he will say 'mostrasi' with the same sense" (p. 110).

The limpid theatricality of *Tanto gentile* manifests perfectly in the final imperative, which is the literal expression in direct discourse of the spirit full of love that, moving from the countenance of *madonna*, communicates directly with the soul of the lover. The imperative encourages the lover to the mutual expression of his love, the cathartic demonstration of his passion through a corresponding sigh. The final imperative is the sigh with which the beloved commands her lover to sigh, the expression with which she commands her lover to express himself. The performative nature of the sonnet is enhanced by the fact that this speech act remains unanswered; to know how the drama finishes, how the lover responds, it is necessary to go behind the scenes – beyond the confines of our sonnet.

One may also recall that the lover's sigh – his "gettare sospiri [casting sighs]" – has clear erotic connotations in the courtly tradition,[106] as for example in Giacomo da Lentini: "Lo vostr'amor che m'ave / in mare tempestoso, / è sì como la nave / c'a la fortuna getta ogni pesanti, / e campan per lo getto / di loco periglioso; / similemente **eo getto / a voi, bella, li mei sospiri** e pianti [My love for you, which places me / upon a stormy sea, / is like a ship in peril / that must cast overboard its heavy bulk, / and by that act all hands / escape calamity; / just so I cast to you, / my fair, my sighs and cries of woe]" (*Madonna, dir vo voglio*, 49–56). The topos, with its erotic connotations, is echoed by Boccaccio: "Anichino **gittò un grandissimo sospiro** [Anichino heaved an enormous sigh]" (*Dec.* 7.7.14).[107]

The concluding imperative has the effect of opening the sonnet, dilating it like the confidence of the pilgrim, compared to an expanding rose in *Paradiso* 22: "così m'ha dilatata mia fidanza, / come 'l sol fa la rosa quando aperta [so (your affection) has expanded my confidence, as the sun does to the rose when opened]" (*Par.* 22.55–6). The expansiveness of *Tanto gentile* by means of the imperative "Sospira" recalls the expansiveness of the divine sigh in the moment of creation, the becoming manifest of the universe: the moment in which "eternal love opened into new loves" ("s'aperse in nuovi amor l'etterno amor") (*Par.* 29.18). The eternal love opens so "that his splendor might, shining back to Him, declare 'Subsisto'" ("perché suo splendore /

---

106 For *gettare sospiri* in a grieving context rather than an erotic one, but also with physical connotations, see below, the sonnet *Lasso, per forza di molti sospiri*.

107 Another example from the *Decameron* is at 3.5, where Boccaccio dramatizes the "ex-pression" of the love between Zima and the wife of Francesco Vergellesi through their *profondissimi sospiri, sospiretti*, and *sospiri*: "E quinci tacendo, alquante lacrime dietro a **profondissimi sospiri** mandate per gli occhi fuori ... La donna ... non poté per ciò **alcun sospiretto** nascondere ... Il Zima ... lei riguardando nel viso e veggendo alcun lampeggiare d'occhi di lei verso di lui alcuna volta, e oltre a ciò **raccogliendo i sospiri** li quali essa non con tutta la forza loro del petto lasciava uscire, alcuna buona speranza prese [And then going silent, he began to heave enormous sighs followed by some tears issuing from his eyes ... Although ... the lady was silent, she could not hide the little sighs ... Zima ... looking at her face and seeing her eyes flashing at him at times, and also gathering the sighs that she with all her strength could not but let out from her chest, found some hope]" (*Dec.* 3.5.16–18).

potesse, risplendendo, dir: 'Subsisto'") (*Par*. 29.14–15). The divine breath captured in the direct speech of "dir: 'Subsisto'" in *Paradiso* 29 is the poetic descendant of the breath of love "che va dicendo a l'anima: 'Sospira!'" in the last line of *Tanto gentile*.

43 (B XXII; FB 43; DR 64; *VN* XXVI.5–7 [17.5–7])
First Redaction

Tanto gentile e tanto onesta pare
la donna mia quand'ella altrui saluta,
ch'ogni lingua divien tremando muta
4   e gli occhi non l'ardiscon di guardare.
Ella se ·n va, sentendosi laudare,
benignamente d'umiltà vestuta:
credo che sia una cosa venuta
8   di cielo in terra a miracol mostrare.
Mostrasi sì piacente a chi la mira,
che fier per gli occhi una dolcezza al core
11   che 'ntender no·lla può chi no·lla prova;
e par che della suo labbia si mova
un spirito soave pien d'amore
14   che va dicendo a l'anima: "Sospira!"

My lady shows such grace and dignity
whenever greeting those who pass her way
that every tongue falls silent, quivering,
and eyes dare not direct their gaze at her.
She moves along, attending words of praise,
benignly dressed in true humility;
and I believe she is a creature come
from heaven to earth to show a miracle.
She shows such charm to him who looks on her
that through his eyes a sweetness strikes his heart,
which none can know who has not felt it first.
And from her countenance is seen to move
a spirit that is sweet and full of love
which goes before the soul and whispers: "Sigh."

VN 5. si va – 7. E par che – 8. Da c. – 10. Che dà per

METRE: sonnet ABBA ABBA CDE EDC.

44 Vede perfettamente ogne salute
First Redaction

The sonnet *Vede perfettamente ogne salute* accompanies and follows *Tanto gentile e tanto onesta pare* in chapter XXVI (17) of the *Vita Nuova*, where it too is featured as an example of the praise style. In the case of this sonnet, as with its companion piece, the redaction reproduced here is not that of the *Vita Nuova* but the earlier redaction as it appears in De Robertis. As compared to *Tanto gentile*, there are no interesting variants of an ideological nature between the first and second redactions of *Vede perfettamente*.

Contini and De Robertis consider *Vede perfettamente* to be chronologically prior to *Tanto gentile* on the basis of its "archaic" metrics; in his edition De Robertis prints the "three praise-sonnets" (ed. comm., p. 374) in the following order: *Vede perfettamente, Negli occhi porta, Tanto gentile*. I follow the order of the *Vita Nuova* for the texts collected there, preferring to follow a Dantean order when there is one.

In the brief prose bridge that separates *Vede perfettamente* from *Tanto gentile*, Dante explains that the perfection of his lady had praiseworthy effects on many other ladies, and that for this reason he wants to write a sonnet "which describes her effects on others": "lo quale narra di lei come la sua vertude adoperava ne l'altre" (*VN* XXVI.9 [17.9]). The ladies glimpsed in the opening of *Donne ch'avete intelletto d'amore* are able to comprehend the nature of this love, and they become in *Vede perfettamente* not only interlocutors but participants in the miraculous reality of "la mia donna" (2).

The sonnet begins and ends with the singularity of *madonna*, a singularity made more emphatic by the plurality of the companion ladies as her backdrop. To see her among her companions is to see complete perfection: "Vede perfettamente ogne salute / chi la mia donna fra le donne vede [Whoever sees my lady with her friends / conceives complete perfection perfectly]" (1–2). This English translation reverses the order of the Italian syntax, which literally declares that "He sees complete perfection perfectly / who sees my lady among her friends." Thus the Italian foregrounds the stunning vision of perfection in an absolute sense ("ogne salute") before moving to particularize perfection as the sight of "mia donna fra le donne"; the hyperbolic vision of the lady among other ladies as equal to perfection is secondary to the unmediated and absolute perfection of the sonnet's remarkable incipit.

From the stylistic point of view, the adverb "perfettamente" – the only occurrence in Dante's lyrics of an adverb that, because of its Aristotelian connotations, will be used as many as thirty times in the *Convivio* – is the most striking aspect of this sonnet. The same adverb will be used in an even more remarkable manner – and again only once – in the *Commedia*, where its single occurrence marks the end of the journey and the fulfilment of Dante's desire, its literal perfection (*perfectus* is the past participle of *perficere*, to finish, complete): "Acciò che tu assommi / perfettamente ... il tuo cammino [So that you may perfectly fulfil ... your journey]" (*Par.* 31.94–5). Taken out of context, the line "Vede perfettamente ogne salute" could well seem to be a line from *Paradiso*. And, indeed, the adverb "perfettamente" indicates the perfection of what the protagonist sees, but it can also indicate the perfection with which the protagonist sees: after all, this is a protagonist who one day, having arrived in paradise, will see perfectly.

After the opening, attention moves to the other ladies, explaining that "quelle che vanno con lei son tenute / di bella grazia a Dio render mercede [the ladies in her presence feel obliged / to render thanks to God for his good grace]" (3–4), because they have absorbed some of *madonna*'s miraculous endowments. In the same manner in which the lady of *Tanto gentile* is "d'umiltà vestuta [dressed in humility]" (6), so the plural ladies of *Vede perfettamente* are dressed in nobility, love, and loyalty: "vestute di gentilezza, d'amore e di fede" (7–8).

The first tercet continues the theme established in the octave, attributing to the plural companion ladies the same Guinizzellian miraculous effects possessed by *madonna*: "La sua vista face ogni cosa umìle, / e non fa sola lei parer piacente, / ma ciascuna per lei riceve onore [The sight of her makes every being kind: / her look not only makes her beautiful, / but through her every lady gains esteem]" (9–11). The second tercet returns to the theme of praising the singular lady, and incorporates many elements of *Tanto gentile* (including the first two words). In effect, the final tercet of *Vede perfettamente* offers a resume of *Tanto gentile*, and the last line is a less theatrical, less vivid version of the famous "Sospira": "Ed è negli atti suoi tanto gentile / che nessun la si può recare a mente / che non sospiri in dolcezza d'amore [And in her bearing she's so full of grace / that no one's able to remember her / who does not sigh from sweetness filled with love]" (12–14).

The originality of *Vede perfettamente*, besides its *Paradiso*-like incipit, lies above all in its delineation of a group of companions for the beloved. Critics have proposed the idea of a "chorus of praise" (De Robertis, *VN*, p. 185); for Contini "the choral background of the ladies on which she is singled out as queen, as the foundation of their honor and source of their beauty" is part of the stilnovist ideology whereby "the entire experience of the stilnovist poet is depersonalized, transferred to a universal order" (*Rime*, Introduction, p. xiv).

Foster-Boyde's commentary is more alert to the presence of a social reality in *Vede perfettamente*: a social reality that has been filtered and abstracted but is not entirely suppressed (p. 126). The English critics note that the women of that period, even in a sophisticated city like Florence, were less free than today and therefore depended on other women for most of their social life. Continuing along this line of historical contextualization, we note the attention paid to the interactions among women in the lines "sua biltate è di tanta virtute / che nulla invidia all'altre ne procede [her beauty is so powerful / in others envy's never born of it]" (5–6). These verses elicited the following essentializing comment from Barbi-Maggini: "The poet states this as a wondrous thing, since it is rare that envy is lacking between women with regard to their beauty" (p. 112).

As I have noted frequently in this commentary, Dante's lyrics preserve traces of lived experience in Duecento Florence, experience that is highly distilled but yet perceptible. In sonnets such as *Guido, i' vorrei che tu e Lapo ed io*, *Amore e monna Lagia e Guido ed io*, *Volgete gli occhi*, and *Sonar bracchetti* we can catch glimpses of the social life of long-ago *brigate* of male friends. The sonnet *Vede perfettamente* adds the distaff side to the "sociology of the *brigata*" that we are extrapolating from Dante's lyrics, offering the highly stylized vision of a *brigata* of women. A female *brigata* appears as well in the incipit to *Di donne io vidi una gentil schiera*. These women are attending to more pleasurable activities than those which unite the women in the sonnets *Voi che portate la sembianza umile* and *Se' tu colui c' hai trattato sovente*, which describe the rites of mourning. Mourning and healing are traditional female tasks, and a group of women is seen also in the canzone *Donna pietosa*, surrounding the sickbed of the poet.

In the *Decameron* Boccaccio describes two all-female *brigate*, both in contexts of recreation and pleasure: "la brigata delle donne di Catella [the *brigata* of ladies with Catella]," by whom Ricciardo Minutolo was received (*Dec.* 3.6.9); the "brigata di belle giovani donne e ornate [*brigata* of lovely adorned young ladies]" that enchants the son of Filippo Balducci. Just as in the *Vita Nuova*, these young ladies "da un paio di nozze venieno [were coming back from a couple of weddings]" (Introduction to Day 4, 20).

In *Vede perfettamente* we see Florentine women gathered together, not for a civic obligation such as funeral ceremonies or to assist the sick, but for their own delight and amusement.

44 (B XXIII; FB 44; DR 62; *VN* XXVI.10–13 [17.10–13])
First Redaction

Vede perfettamente ogne salute
chi la mia donna fra le donne vede:
quelle che vanno con lei son tenute
4 di bella grazia a Dio render mercede,
ché sua biltate è di tanta virtute
che nulla invidia all'altre ne procede,
anzi le face andar seco vestute
8 di gentilezza, d'amore e di fede.
La sua vista face ogni cosa umìle,
e non fa sola lei parer piacente,
11 ma ciascuna per lei riceve onore.
Ed è negli atti suoi tanto gentile

Whoever sees my lady with her friends
conceives complete perfection perfectly:
the ladies in her presence feel obliged
to render thanks to God for his good grace,
because her beauty is so powerful
in others envy's never born of it;
instead, it makes them bear her qualities
of love, nobility, and loyalty.
The sight of her makes every being kind:
her look not only makes her beautiful,
but through her every lady gains esteem.
And in her bearing she's so full of grace

che nessun la si può recare a mente
14 che non sospiri in dolcezza d'amore.

VN 5. E sua – 9. La vista sua fa o. – 10. sola sé p.

METRE: sonnet ABAB ABAB CDE CDE.

that no one's able to remember her
who does not sigh from sweetness filled with love.

45 Di donne io vidi una gentil schiera

While Contini labels *Di donne io vidi* "a true anthology of the most ordinary stilno-vist themes" (p. 71), I see it as rather more interesting. This sonnet is distinguished from other stilnovist poems by the temporal precision with which it situates itself on a specific date of the Florentine calendar. The action is immediately declared to have occurred on the most recent All Saints' Day: "Di donne io vidi una gentil schiera / quest'Ognisanti prossimo passato [I saw a band of lovely ladies meet / on All Saints' Day not very long ago]" (1–2). The specific reference to the feast of November 1, "in those days a more solemn holiday than in ours" (Barbi-Maggini, p. 263), evokes a feeling that we can still tap into: even today, in a time when civic life is so much more fragmented, there are still communal holidays that are difficult to ignore.

Such temporal precision is extraordinary in a love lyric of this period, which normally floats in a deliberately nebulous and stylized setting. The phrase "quest'Ognisanti prossimo passato," literally "this All Saint's Day that has just passed," boasts a strong deictic *questo* ("this") reinforced by the adjective *prossimo* ("near"). Recalling that a deictic, grammatically, is an element that situates what is said in a concrete spatio-temporal reality, we experience a *frisson* of immediacy and of lived, tangible history from the opening of this sonnet. Foster-Boyde observe that line 2 of *Di donne io vidi* indicates that the poet is writing only a week or two after the event he describes (p. 127); De Robertis even suggests that the sonnet can be dated "to All Saints' Day of 1289" (ed. comm., p. 368).

Perhaps it is no coincidence that a sonnet that so inscribes itself into Florentine life should invoke "a band of lovely ladies," given that the "schiera" – a group gathered together for social purposes, a *brigata* – cannot help but suggest collective experience. Such collective experiences are invoked in the prose of the *Vita Nuova*, and in the descriptions of *brigate* such as we find in Folgore da San Gimignano and Boccaccio.

The event described in *Di donne io vidi* is the arrival of the poet's beloved, flanked by Love, at the head of the female companions who are part of the "gentil schiera": "e una ne venia quasi 'mprimiera / veggendosi l'Amor dal destro lato [and one of them appeared to lead the rest, / Love standing close upon her right-hand side]" (3–4). At this point the sonnet begins to list the qualities and virtues of *madonna* that we know. From the eyes of this lady "gittava una lumiera / la qual parea un spirito 'nfiammato [radiated a light / that seemed just like a spirit made of fire]" (5–6); similarly in *Donne ch'avete*, "De li occhi suoi, come ch'ella li mova, / escono spirti d'amore inflammati [Her eyes, wherever she should turn her gaze, / send spirits forth, inflamed with love]" (51–2). Just as in *Io voglio del ver* by Guinizzelli, where the lady "abassa orgoglio a cui dona salute [curtails the pride of those she greets]" (10), in this sonnet she "d[on]ava salute / con [gli] atti suoi ... / e empiva 'l cor a ciascun di virtute [greeted anyone who was of worth ... / and filled the heart of each with inner strength]" (9–11). And as in *Tanto gentile e tanto onesta pare*, where *madonna* is "una cosa venuta / di cielo in terra a miracol mostrare [a creature come / from heaven to earth to show a miracle]" (7–8), in *Di donne io vidi* she "ven[n]e in terra per nostra salute [came for our salvation here on earth]" (13).

But if on the one hand the traits shared by *Di donne io vidi* and a "pure" praise-sonnet such as *Tanto gentile* are obvious, the points of divergence are notable as well. The differences begin with the reference to a historically situated event that occurred on "quest'Ognisanti prossimo passato": such an event requires a protagonist, who is placed in chronological relation to "this" holiday to which he alludes. And in fact the "I" of *Di donne io vidi* – not hidden but fully present as narrator and witness right from the start – is more the protagonist of this sonnet than are the ladies whom he describes. The narrator describes not only the event of *madonna*'s arrival with her "gentil schiera"; he describes as well an event of which he is the undoubted protagonist: the moment in which he dares to look at her. In *Tanto gentile* "the eyes dare not direct their gaze at her" ("gli occhi non l'ardiscon di guardare") (4). In *Di donne io vidi*, by contrast, the same verb *ardire* (to dare) signals the transgression of the lover's eyes, whose boldness is related in the first person, as though the narrator were staking claim to a kind of heroic action: "I became so bold I looked into / her face, and saw an angel figured there" ("io ebbi tanto ardir, [ch']in la sua ciera / guarda', e vidi un a[n]giol figurato") (7–8).

The octave of *Di donne io vidi* thus culminates not with the miraculous nature of *madonna*, as in *Tanto gentile*, but with the action of the male protagonist: his *ardire* (daring), which results in his *guardare* (looking), and therefore in his *vedere* (seeing). The protagonist sees a supernatural being, specifically "an angel figured there." In De Robertis' gloss, he sees "the image of an angel: as is seen flying over Fioretta in *Per una ghirlandetta*, 6–7, and as probably appears as the figure of Love in *madonna*'s face in *Donne ch'avete*, 55 (in short: 'I seemed to see an angel')" (ed. comm., p. 370).[108]

There are two uses of "vidi" (the dominant verb of the *Commedia*) in our sonnet: the "vidi" of the incipit and the "vidi" of the last line of the octave. This double presence of "vidi" signals an adventure of which the narrator is the hero, in which he passes from an entirely natural, real vision, whose quotidianness is reinforced by the chronological reference – "Di donne **io vidi** una gentil schiera / quest'Ognisanti prossimo passato" (1–2) – to a vision that is supernatural and beyond quotidian reality: "guarda', e **vidi** un a[n]giol figurato" (8). The supernatural vision of the angel stands out with greater intensity against the quotidian backdrop of Florentine life.

---

108 The angel that flies above Fioretta is described thus: "e sovr'a·llei vidi volare / un angiolel d'amore umìle [and over it (the garland) / I saw an angel full of gentle love]" (*Per una ghirlandetta*, 6–7).

At the end of the octave the narrator has completed a visual adventure that begins with the everyday "normal" viewing, grounded in historical reality, of the ladies in the incipit and culminates with the daring visionary feat that breaks the confines of normality in lines 7–8. Such boldness – "tanto ardire" of line 7 – will lead directly to the "bold" ("ardito") protagonist of *Paradiso* 33 who penetrates the *infinito valore* with his gaze: "E' mi ricorda ch'io fui più **ardito** / per questo a sostener, tanto ch'i' giunsi / l'aspetto mio col valore infinito [And I recall that I, because of this, was bolder in sustaining it, until I joined my sight with the infinite goodness]" (*Par.* 33.79–81). The emboldened gaze of the protagonist in *Di donne io vidi* is especially noteworthy because it is anchored in historical reality: the *Commedia* is distinguished from other visionary texts precisely in its being anchored in a dense network of local and historical references.

After the octave the sonnet falls back on the conventions of the praise style, listing the virtues of *madonna*. The list of her virtues in the sestet completes a circle that brings the reader back to the beginning of the sonnet: specifying that "every lady close to her is blessed" ("è beata chi·ll'è prossimana") (14), we return to the idea of the "gentil schiera" with which *Di donne io vidi* opens. Furthermore, the final word, "prossimana," echoes "prossimo" in the line "quest' Ognisanti prossimo passato" (2). The last verse of *Di donne io vidi* thus reminds the reader of the quotidian social life that gives our hero his context and that sets this sonnet apart from other sonnets of stilnovist love.

45 (B LXIX; C 22; FB 45; DR 60)

Di donne io vidi una gentil schiera	I saw a band of lovely ladies meet
quest'Ognisanti prossimo passato,	on All Saints' Day not very long ago,
e una ne venia quasi 'mprimiera	and one of them appeared to lead the rest,
4 veggendosi l'Amor dal destro lato.	Love standing close upon her right-hand side.
Degli occhi suoi gittava una lumiera	She radiated from her eyes a light
la qual parea un spirito 'nfiammato,	that seemed just like a spirit made of fire,
e io ebbi tanto ardir, [ch']in la sua ciera	and I became so bold I looked into
8 guarda', e vidi un a[n]giol figurato.	her face, and saw an angel figured there.
A chi era degno d[on]ava salute	She greeted anyone who was of worth
con [gli] atti suoi quella benigna e piana,	with humble gestures full of tenderness,
11 e empiva 'l cor a ciascun di virtute.	and filled the heart of each with inner strength.
Credo che de l[o] ciel fusse soprana,	I hold in heaven she was unsurpassed
e ven[n]e in terra per nostra salute:	and came for our salvation here on earth:
14 laond'è beata chi·ll'è prossimana.	so every lady close to her is blessed.

METRE: sonnet ABAB ABAB CDC DCD.

46 Sì lungiamente m'ha tenuto Amore

The poem *Sì lungiamente m'ha tenuto Amore* is placed by Dante in *Vita Nuova* XXVII (18). From the thematic point of view, *Sì lungiamente* returns to the effects that *madonna* has on the lover. If, in the preceding chapter, the poet illustrates the effects that she has on everyone ("propuosi di dicere parole, ne le quali io dessi ad intendere de le sue mirabili ed eccellenti operazioni [I planned to compose a poem in which I would describe some of the wondrous and excellent effects she brought about]" [*VN* XXVI.4 (17.4)]), in chapter XXVII (18) he wants to compensate for not having highlighted the effect she has on him "at the present time": "io non avea detto di quello che al presente tempo adoperava in me ... E però propuosi di dire parole, ne le quali io dicesse come me parea essere disposto a la sua operazione, e come operava in me la sua vertude [I had not mentioned the effects which her influence was bringing about in me ... And so I planned to write a poem in which I would say how I seemed to be susceptible to her influence, and how her power influenced me]" (*VN* XXVII.1–2 [18.1–2]).

Dante doesn't believe himself "capable of conveying this in the brief space of a sonnet" ("potere ciò narrare in brevitade di sonetto") (*VN* XXVII.2 [18.2]) and for this reason he writes a canzone. *Sì lungiamente* is a single-stanza canzone, the only one in the *Vita Nuova*, whose lone stanza is composed of fourteen lines like the stanzas of the three great canzoni of the *Vita Nuova*, the two ones before this (*Donne ch'avete* and *Donna pietosa*) and the one following (*Li occhi dolenti*).[109]

The poem that follows *Sì lungiamente* in the *Vita Nuova* is the canzone that mourns the death of Beatrice, *Li occhi dolenti*. In the narrative economy of the *libello* the positioning of *Sì lungiamente* and the link that Dante creates between it and Beatrice's death are its most notable features. The handling of *Sì lungiamente* in the *Vita Nuova* dramatizes the death of Beatrice, which is announced right after the canzone's conclusion, without any delay or digression: there are none of the usual "divisions" and textual glosses following it, no prose to fill the space between the end of the poem and the end of the chapter. Instead, from the last verse of *Sì lungiamente* we pass directly to the citation from Jeremiah's Lamentations with which Beatrice's death is announced, an event that Dante then links explicitly to the monostrophic canzone, offering the death of Beatrice as justification for the canzone's incompleteness: "Io era nel proponimento ancora di questa canzone, e compiuta n'avea questa soprascritta

---

109 The five canzoni in the *Vita Nuova* are *Donne ch'avete, Donna pietosa, Sì lungiamente, Li occhi dolenti,* and a two-stanza canzone, *Quantunque volte, lasso!, mi rimembra.*

stanzia, quando lo segnore de la giustizia chiamoe questa gentilissima ... [I was still engaged with this canzone, and had completed the above stanza, when the Lord of Justice called this most gracious of women ...]" (*VN* XXVIII.1 [19.1]). One might say, therefore, that Beatrice dies not so much *in mediis rebus* as *in mediis verbis*.

As always, it is necessary to keep in mind that the interpretative frame imposed by the *Vita Nuova* was added by Dante in a second editorial phase. In the case of *Sì lungiamente* it is important to extricate the canzone from the complex role that is assigned to it in the *libello*, where Dante underscores the trauma of Beatrice's death, blaming it for the supposed interruption of the single-stanza canzone. It is clear that the choice of a monostrophic canzone in this position of the *libello* is functional for the purposes of the diegesis and tied to the announcement of Beatrice's death. For our purposes, the canzone *Sì lungiamente*, which commentators agree is a complete treatment of the theme proposed in the first four lines, should be considered a finished single-stanza canzone, like the others that Dante wrote.[110]

The theme proposed in the first lines of *Sì lungiamente* is actually more interesting than that stated in the introductory prose of the *Vita Nuova*. Rather than illustrating the lady's virtuous effects on her lover, the canzone duly overturns the various modalities of painful love, the kind of Love that we expect to encounter when we read, "Sì lungiamente m'ha tenuto Amore / e costumato a la sua segnoria [So long a time has Love kept me in tow / and made his mastery of me the rule]" (1–2). The lexicon of these opening verses – the verb *tenere* that is a variant of *stringere*, the noun *segnoria*, and even the adverb *lungiamente*, which recalls the classic canzone of passionate love by Guido delle Colonne, *Amor che lungiamente m'hai menato* (cited twice by Dante in *De vulgari eloquentia*)[111] – indicates that we are before the masterful, imperious Love of the courtly tradition.

But everything is changed. The Love who in the past was experienced by the poet as "forte" – that is, harsh and agonizing – has now become "soave" (tender): "sì com'elli m'era forte in pria, / così mi sta soave ora nel core [even though he was at first severe, / he now reigns in my heart with tenderness]" (3–4). The antithetical adjectives – *forte* that transforms into *soave* – signal a conversion, in the truest sense of the word. A conversion is always a change in time from one condition to another, from a before to an after, and Dante here marks the transition from the state of "pria" (before) (3) to the state of "ora" (now) (4) with the same precision and temporal awareness used by St Augustine for his conversion in the *Confessions* or by Guido da Montefeltro for his failed conversion in canto 27 of *Inferno*. It is a brilliant move: the Dante who arranged the *Vita Nuova* chose for the liminal space that marks the turn

---

110   The other single-stanza canzoni by Dante are *Lo meo servente core* and *Madonna, quel signor che voi portate*.

111   *Amor che lungiamente m'hai menato* was still present to Dante when he wrote *Inferno* 5, with its echoes of the verb *menare*; see my "Dante and Cavalcanti (On Making Distinctions in Matters of Love)" in *Dante and the Origins of Italian Literary Culture*, esp. pp. 75–7.

towards Beatrice's death a text that already in itself delineates a turn from a before to an after. *Sì lungiamente* looks toward Dante's great theme of the *conversio* from the old life to the new.

On the other hand, the language of *Sì lungiamente* is not at all theologized and the conversion described here is from an *amore forte* to an *amore soave*. In the context of the poets whom Dante knows, *Sì lungiamente* recalls above all Guido Cavalcanti: not only the tragic Guido but also the sublime Guido of those (few) poems in which he sings of a quasi-mystical love-sweetness.[112] One thinks for example of Cavalcanti's *ballata Veggio negli occhi de la donna mia*, in which there are the following verses: "Là dove questa bella donna appare / s'ode una voce che le vèn davanti / e par che d'umiltà il su' nome canti / sì dolcemente, che, s'i' 'l vo' contare, / sento che 'l su' valor mi fa tremare [There where this beautiful woman appears / is heard a voice that comes before her, / and it seems to sing her name / so sweetly that, if I should tell of it, / I feel her power begin to make me tremble]" (13–17). The verses just cited from *Veggio negli occhi* are reflected in the humility and the sweetness of the woman in *Sì lungiamente*; line 12 in *Veggio negli occhi* declares that "La salute tua è apparita [Your salvation has appeared]," a phrasing that Dante picks up here in his "per darmi più salute [to accord me greater bliss]" (12).

Reading *Sì lungiamente* we seem to pass, within a single stanza, from the suffering love of Guido Cavalcanti to his sweet love, and moreover to complete this passage a full two times. The first cycle is in lines 5–8, where Dante completes in four verses the journey from the tragic Guido of the fleeing spirits and the weakened soul[113] to the tender Guido of *Veggio negli occhi de la donna mia*. The first three lines of the cycle seem to move directly towards tragic love – "Però quando mi tolle sì 'l valore, / che li spiriti par che fuggan via, / allor sente la frale anima mia [So when he takes my strength away from me, / which makes my spirits seem to flee in haste, / my feeble soul then feels]" (5–7) – but the movement towards tragedy is then dramatically interrupted by the strong enjambment between line 7 and line 8, and all of a sudden the reader is surprisingly plunged into "tanta dolcezza, che 'l viso ne smore [such sweet delight, the colour in my face begins to fade]" (8). The same itinerary between the two antithetical poles of *amore forte* and *amore soave*, and the same overturning of the reader's expectations, happens again in lines 9–12: the first three lines of the second cycle seem to promise Cavalcantian destructive love – "poi prende Amore in me tanta vertute, / che fa li miei spiriti gir parlando, / ed escon for chiamando [since Love asserts its power in me so much / it makes my spirits go about and speak, / and they rush forth to ask]" (9–11) – but the conclusive line goes in the

---

112 Dante is undoubtedly interested in and registers the existence of a Cavalcantian sweet love. The tendency of critics to forget this aspect of Cavalcanti's poetry results in various misinterpretations; see my "Dante and Cavalcanti (On Making Distinctions in Matters of Love)," in *Dante and the Origins of Italian Literary Culture*, p. 101.

113 De Robertis holds that "la frale anima mia [my feeble soul]") in line 7 of *Sì lungiamente* is an "updated variant ... of Cavalcanti's 'deboletta'" (*VN*, p. 189).

opposite direction, arriving not at a deadly lady but at "la donna mia, per darmi più salute [my Lady to accord me greater bliss]" (12).

Dante wrote many poems that are indebted to Guido Cavalcanti, to his tragic style and also to his altogether unique sweetness. But *Sì lungiamente* is the only poem in which Dante has placed these two Cavalcantian styles, so antithetical – one *forte* and the other *soave* – under a single yoke. Uniting a Guido *forte* and a Guido *soave*, Dante creates a new Guido, a Guido all his own, This canzone is undoubtedly a great tribute to Guido, but it also shows a Dante who has complete poetic control of his *imitatio*: he knows how to imitate his *primo amico*, while simultaneously creating something entirely original and new.

46 (B XXIV; FB 46; *VN* XXVII.3–5 [18.3–5])

Sì lungiamente m'ha tenuto Amore	So long a time has Love kept me in tow
e costumato a la sua segnoria,	and made his mastery of me the rule
che sì com'elli m'era forte in pria,	that even though he was at first severe,
4 così mi sta soave ora nel core.	he now reigns in my heart with tenderness.
Però quando mi tolle sì 'l valore,	So when he takes my strength away from me,
che li spiriti par che fuggan via,	which makes my spirits seem to flee in haste,
allor sente la frale anima mia	my feeble soul then feels such sweet delight
8 tanta dolcezza, che 'l viso ne smore,	the colour in my face begins to fade,
poi prende Amore in me tanta vertute,	for Love asserts its power in me so much
che fa li miei spiriti gir parlando,	it makes my spirits go about and speak,
11 ed escon for chiamando	and they rush forth to ask
la donna mia, per darmi più salute.	my Lady to accord me greater bliss.
Questo m'avvene ovunque ella mi vede,	This happens every time she looks on me,
14 e sì è cosa umil, che nol si crede.	and it's so sweet that it exceeds belief.

METRE: isolated canzone stanza of fourteen verses (thirteen hendecasyllables and one *settenario*), with rhyme scheme (featuring internal rhyme) ABBA ABBA (a5)CDdCEE. The *fronte* is eight verses (4 + 4) and the *sirma* is six verses.

47 Li occhi dolenti per pietà del core

Li occhi dolenti per pietà del core is the canzone in which Dante announces the death of Beatrice. Let me be clear: this is not the canzone that rehearses presentiments of the death of the beloved (*Donna pietosa*); this is the canzone that announces her death after it has in fact occurred. Placed in chapter XXXI (20) of the *Vita Nuova*, where it assumes the position of the fourth canzone of the *libello, Li occhi dolenti* is composed of five stanzas of fourteen lines each (the same stanza length of the earlier canzoni in the *Vita Nuova*), plus a congedo. In each stanza, one of the fourteen lines is a *settenario*, so that *Li occhi dolenti* occupies a metrical middle ground between *Donne ch'avete*, whose stanzas have only hendecasyllables, and *Donna pietosa*, whose stanzas contain two *settenari*.

"Li occhi dolenti [My eyes, distraught]" of the incipit are the poet-lover's, who is mourning the death of his lady; his tears are the mark of his bereavement: "Li occhi dolenti per pietà del core / hanno di lagrimar sofferta pena, / sì che per vinti son remasi omai [My eyes, distraught by pity for my heart, / have borne the suffering that weeping brings, / so that, exhausted, they concede defeat]" (1–3). Here the word *lagrimar* is used, later *piangere*, recalling the "sociological" and technical use of *piangere* in the four sonnets of mourning commented on earlier (*Voi che portate la sembianza umile, Se' tu colui c' hai trattato sovente, Onde venite voi così pensose?, Voi donne, che pietoso atto mostrate*).

It is important to emphasize that the convention of the death of the beloved – canonical after Petrarch – becomes important precisely due to its presence in Dante's lyrics. It is not an Occitan topos nor one of the earliest Italian poetry: it is a Dantean idea, linked to the *Vita Nuova*, where Dante brings together courtly love and the Augustinian doctrine (expressed in the *Confessions* after the death of a friend of young Augustine) according to which one ought not to love "a man that must die as though he were not to die [diligendo moriturum ac si non moriturum]" (*Conf.* 4.8). To impart this lesson, Augustine in the *Confessions* makes narrative use of death, as Dante will do in the *Vita Nuova*, where he applies to the system of courtly love the Augustinian idea just cited: it is necessary to learn from the death of the desired object to redirect one's desire, placing it only in "quello che non mi puote venire meno [that which cannot fail me]" (*VN* XVIII.4 [10.6]). It follows from this logic that one ought not to love mortal things, since they necessarily "will fail." It is precisely for this directional error that Beatrice reproaches Dante-pilgrim when they meet in the earthly paradise: "e se 'l sommo piacer sì ti fallio / per la mia morte, qual cosa mortale / dovea poi trarre te nel suo disio? [and if the highest pleasure so failed you with my death, what mortal thing should then have drawn you to desire it?]" (*Purg.* 31.52–4).

The death of the beloved, without all the Augustinian apparatus, is already in the canzone *Li occhi dolenti*. A canzone of "Beatrician mourning" (Gorni, p. 176), in other words a lament, *Li occhi dolenti* is – given the strict connection between *planctus* and praise – "primarily ... a praise-poem" (Foster-Boyde, p. 132). (For the traditional connection between lament/*planctus* and praise, see the introductory essay to the sonnet *Piangete, amanti, poi che piange Amore*.)

Li occhi dolenti, a lament-canzone, is explicitly presented as a complement and companion to the canzone *Donne ch'avete intelletto d'amore*, the praise-canzone par excellence. *Donne ch'avete* already features the desire to have madonna in heaven, a desire expressed unanimously by all the saints of paradise ("Lo cielo, che non have altro difetto / che d'aver lei, al suo segnor la chiede, / e ciascun santo ne grida merzede [Heaven, whose only imperfection is / the lack of her, implores its Lord to ask / for her, and all saints favour this request]" [*Donne ch'avete*, 19–21]), and then synthesized in the great verse "Madonna è disiata in sommo cielo [My lady is desired in highest heaven]" (*Donne ch'avete*, 29). In *Li occhi dolenti* the celestial desire to possess *madonna* is realized, with the result that the theme of the canzone is limpidly articulated in a verse that is effectively the "response" to *Donne ch'avete*'s "Madonna è disiata in sommo cielo": "Ita n'è Beatrice in l'alto cielo [Beatrice has gone to heaven on high]" (*Li occhi dolenti*, 15). Here the death of Beatrice is not only announced but simultaneously classified as an Assumption. Moreover, as De Robertis notes, Beatrice is "named for the first time with her whole name in the lyrics of the *Vita Nuova* (and similarly at l. 55)" (*VN*, p. 200): "with her whole name" because the nickname "Bice" occurs in *Io mi senti' svegliar dentro a lo core*, and "in the lyrics of the *Vita Nuova*" because "Beatrice" is named in the canzone *Lo doloroso amor*, a canzone excluded from the *Vita Nuova*.

In commenting on *Li occhi dolenti* in an edition of the *rime*, I can therefore comfortably refer to "Beatrice," and not limit myself to generic "madonna": for the first time, the name "Beatrice" is present in the canzone, not exclusively in the prose of the *Vita Nuova*. It is strange, from this perspective, that the second canzone of the *libello*, *Donna pietosa e di novella etate*, has aroused so much discussion about the possibility that it was written expressly for the *Vita Nuova* (on the strength of the overlaps between prose and poem), even though Beatrice is not named in it. The double presence in this canzone of the name "Beatrice" suggests that *Li occhi dolenti* is the ideal candidate for such a discussion.

The explicit references to *Donne ch'avete* begin right in the first stanza, a stanza that acts as proem, just as in *Donne ch'avete*. In the proem of *Donne ch'avete* the poet posits the theme of the speech-act: he addresses the ladies with the intention of "ragionar per isfogar la mente [to speak to alleviate my mind]" (4), and says: "tratterò del suo stato gentile ... donne e donzelle amorose, con vui, / ché non è cosa di parlarne altrui [I'll speak of her nobility ... dear ladies, maidens, who know love, / for this is something others should not hear]" (*Donne ch'avete*, 11, 13–14). The same thematization of speech is in *Li occhi dolenti*, as also the verb *sfogare*: now the poet wants to "sfogar lo dolore [vent my grief]" (4), instead of "isfogar la mente." Recalling that he had willingly addressed the *donne gentili* to speak about *madonna* while she was alive, the poet declares his wish to express his pain only to "a lady with a gentle heart":

> E perché me **ricorda** ch'io **parlai**
> de la mia donna, mentre che **vivia**,
> donne gentili, volentier con vui,
> non voi parlare altrui,
> se non a cor gentil che in donna sia;
> e **dicerò** di lei piangendo, pui
> che si n'è gita in ciel subitamente,
> e ha lasciato Amor meco dolente.
> (Li occhi dolenti, 7–14)

> [Since I remember how I used to speak
> about my lady willingly with you,
> my gentle ladies, while she was alive,
> I choose to speak to none
> except a lady with a gentle heart.
> And I shall speak of her while weeping, since
> she's gone away to heaven suddenly
> and left Love here with me in misery.]

The memory of past speech here enters as theme of *Li occhi dolenti*. Note in these lines the complex temporal game, which embraces past, present, and future in a weave of words and emotions. The poet remembers in the present – "me **ricorda** [I remember]" – of when he spoke to Beatrice in the past. The density of their past experience together is communicated by the interaction between the past definite tense, which corresponds to the lover, and the imperfect tense, which corresponds to the beloved: "io **parlai** / de la mia donna, mentre che **vivia** [I spoke of my lady, while she was alive]." He then declares that, even with all his suffering, he will speak about her in the future: "e **dicerò** di lei piangendo [And I shall speak of her while weeping]." This lady will be spoken about "piangendo," that is after her death, as an integral component of mourning her.

The nexus of *dire/parlare* and *piangere/lagrimare* evident in the line "e dicerò di lei piangendo [and I shall speak of her while weeping]" (12) will be important in the *Commedia*: one thinks, for example, of Ugolino's "parlare e lagrimar vedrai insieme [you will see speaking and weeping together]" (*Inf.* 33.9). Perhaps the link with the canto of Ugolino is not entirely coincidental. *Li occhi dolenti* is a meditation on the need to express suffering; as De Robertis comments, "it is the canzone of the manifestations of suffering (and once the eyes can no longer manifest it, words are necessary)" (*VN*, p. 198). Ugolino does not express his suffering to his sons, neither with tears nor with words: "Io non piangëa, sì dentro impetrai [I did not cry, I was so petrified within]" (*Inf.* 33.49). He does not obey the requirements for communion and expression that confirm our common humanity, and in *Li occhi dolenti* Dante denounces whoever does not mourn Beatrice as one who has a heart of stone, using the same metaphor that he will much later put into the mouth of Ugolino ("sì dentro impetrai"): "Chi no la piange, quando ne ragiona, / core ha di pietra sì malvagio e vile, / ch'entrar no i puote spirito benegno [Whoever speaks of her and fails to weep / betrays a heart of stone so vile and base / that no kind spirit penetrates inside]" (32–4).

The first stanza of *Li occhi dolenti* ends with the declaration that Beatrice has "gone away to heaven" (13–14) and then elaborates in the manner of *coblas capfinidas* at the beginning of the second stanza: "Ita n'è Beatrice in l'alto cielo, / nel reame ove li angeli hanno pace, / e sta con loro, e voi, donne ha lassate [Beatrice has gone to heaven on high, / the kingdom where the angels dwell in peace; / she lives with them, and leaves you ladies here]" (15–17). As we know from *Donne ch'avete*, the lady was "desired in highest heaven": Beatrice did not die from natural causes, as happens to other women ("no la ci tolse qualità di gelo / né di calore, come l'altre face [no property of heat or cold took her / away from us, as it has taken others]" [18–19]), but because of "sua gran benignitate [her great kind-heartedness]" (20), which caused her to be desired in paradise. While in *Donne ch'avete* the exceptional nature of *madonna* is a "meraviglia" (marvel) to the angels, now her light causes God himself to marvel, "fé maravigliar l'etterno sire" (23):

> ché luce de la sua umilitate
> passò li cieli con tanta vertute,
> che fé maravigliar l'etterno Sire,
> sì che dolce disire
> lo giunse di chiamar tanta salute.
> (Li occhi dolenti, 21–5)

> [because a ray of her humility
> traversed the heavens with such radiance
> it filled the Everlasting Lord with awe,
> so that a sweet desire
> moved Him to summon so much worthiness.]

The idea that Beatrice "filled the Everlasting Lord with awe" and then with "a sweet desire / ... to summon so much worthiness" is an indication that, as in *Donne ch'avete*, the young poet is not yet concerned with theological accuracy.

The distancing of Beatrice from the world and from her body – the "bella persona" of line 29, in the same locution used by Francesca in *Inferno* 5.101 – is reiterated at the beginning of the third stanza, where the phrase "piena di grazia" confirms that Beatrice is not like other women, but comparable to the Virgin, to whom the phrase was originally directed in the form of an angelic greeting: "Partissi de la sua bella persona / piena di grazia l'anima gentile, / ed èssi gloriosa in loco degno [Her tender, noble soul so full of grace / departed from her lovely human form / and lives in glory in a worthy place]" (29–31). Now Dante passes on to the effects of *madonna*'s singularity, a classic *stil novo* theme here varied by the unusual fact that the effects are described post mortem and by the emphasis on the base beings who are not capable of accepting the "spirito benegno" (34) of *madonna*. Far from the Guinizzellian "null'om pò mal pensar fin che la vede [no one can think evil thoughts when seeing her]" (*Io voglio del ver la mia donna laudare*, 14), Dante here portrays a world that contains not only those who have a heart "di pietra sì malvagio e vile [of stone so vile and base]" (33), but also those whose "cor villan [evil heart]" (35) is such that they cannot "imaginar di lei alquanto [figure forth an image of her]" (36): two categories – one more affective and the other more intellective – of people who are errant with respect to Beatrice's grace.

Contrary to what happens to hearts of stone and to minds lacking in imaginative capacity, for those who are instead capable of imagining her *as she was*, "quale ella fue" (42), in her ontological fullness – "chi vede nel pensero alcuna volta / quale ella fue, e com'ella n'è tolta [who see at times in thought / her essence and how she was torn from us]" (41–2) – the loss is unassuageable. Such a person literally "strips his soul of all consolation": "d'onne consolar l'anima spoglia" (40). The poet of *Li occhi dolenti* belongs to the category of those who cannot be consoled. Perhaps one might say that *ça va sans dire*, but Dante wants to say it, thus thematizing the failure of *consolatio*, and the fourth stanza personalizes this theme, recounting the devastating effects of Beatrice's death on her poet: "Dannomi angoscia li sospiri forte, / quando 'l pensero ne la mente grave / mi reca quella che m'ha 'l cor diviso [My sighing makes me grieve convulsively / when thinking brings back to my weary mind / the thought of her who's cleaved my heart in two]" (43–5). From one who generically "sees in thought" (41) both Beatrice's worth and the significance of her death there is a shift to the particular "pensero" that "brings back to my weary mind / the thought of her who's cleaved my heart in two" (45). This thought is so endowed with imaginative and life-giving power that it is able to bring his lady back to his mind, awakening in him "un disio tanto soave, / che mi tramuta lo color nel viso [so sweet a longing / that all the colour in my face is lost]" (47–8). The "dolce disire" (24) of God and the "disio tanto soave" (47) of the poet converge in the figure of Beatrice.

The imaginative – even visionary – power of the poet is an important theme of *Li occhi dolenti*, only a little less conspicuous than in the visionary canzone par excellence, *Donna pietosa*. In verses 49–51 – "E quando 'l maginar mi ven ben fiso, / giugnemi tanta pena d'ogne parte, / ch'io mi riscuoto per dolor ch'i' sento [And when my thought is wholly fixed on her, / from every side I'm so assailed by grief / that I'm brought back by all the pain I feel]" – Dante delineates a phenomenology of visionary seeing that will provide lexical solutions for the *Commedia* (and not only: Petrarch too will follow in using "fiso" in mystical and visionary contexts).[114] Dante

---

114 See *Rvf* 73, "Così vedess'io fiso [Might I gaze thus fixedly]" (70), in a context whose reach is explicitly metaphysical, as discussed in Barolini, "Petrarch as the Metaphysical Poet Who Is Not Dante: Metaphysical Markers at the Beginning of the *Rerum vulgarium fragmenta* (*Rvf* 1–21),"

will use "fiso" in the *Commedia* to indicate the intensity of seeing (for example, "Troppo fiso" in *Purg.* 32.9). Likewise, the formula "mi riscuoto" in line 51, glossed by De Robertis "I come back to myself, I come back to reality" (*VN*, p. 204), will be used in the *Commedia* for significant awakenings, with respect to the pilgrim as he negotiates a visionary transition ("Ruppemi l'alto sonno ne la testa / un greve truono, sì ch'io **mi riscossi** / come persona ch'è per forza desta [Heavy thunder broke the deep sleep in my head, so that I came back to myself like someone awakened by force]" [*Inf.* 4.1–3]) and with respect to Achilles in simile in the dream sequence of *Purgatorio* 9 ("Non altrimenti Achille **si riscosse**, / li occhi svegliati rivolgendo in giro [Not other than how Achilles came back to himself, his wakened eyes looking around]" [*Purg.* 9.34–5]).

The vivifying power of imagination pervades the end of the fourth stanza, where the verbs insistently in the present and the question addressed in direct speech by the lover to his dead lady give a strong sense of the presence and immediacy of Beatrice: "Poscia piangendo, sol nel mio lamento / **chiamo** Beatrice, e **dico**: 'Or se' tu morta?'; / e mentre ch'io la **chiamo**, me **conforta** [Then weeping, all alone in my lament, / I call to Beatrice: 'Are you now dead?' / And while I call on her she comforts me]" (54–6).

I have frequently noted the importance for Dante of direct discourse, which he uses to cross the boundaries between the imagined and the real, and in this case literally between life and death. The poet speaks directly, in the climactic expression of his suffering, to his lady, asking her, as if she were alive, "Are you now dead?": "Or se' tu morta?" (55). The conceptual paradox of this question is genial. Its form – not only direct discourse but the fact of its being a question, a locution that requires an interlocutor, as well as the literal and temporal meaning of the pleonastic particle "or" ("now") – battles and almost overwhelms its substance: it is not possible for Beatrice to be dead, if one can talk to her! The poet's question "makes her alive," in what we might call an "optical illusion" created by words.[115] And yet what it is that he asks her is if she is dead.

Verbal "optical illusions" are fundamental to sustaining the fiction that is not a fiction of the *Commedia*. The profound implications of the little question "Or se' tu morta?" in *Li occhi dolenti* come further into focus if we consider another apparently humble and straightforward question that begins with "or," at the culmination of *Paradiso*: "Segnor mio Iesù Cristo, Dio verace, / or fu sì fatta la sembianza vostra? [My Lord Jesus Christ, true God, was your appearance then really fashioned like

---

in *Petrarch and Dante*, ed. Zygmunt Baranski and Theodore Cachey (Notre Dame: University of Notre Dame Press, 2009), 195–225, esp. p. 217. For the visionary phenomenology in Dante, see the introductory essays to *Ciò che m'incontra* and *Donna pietosa*, and Barolini, *The Undivine Comedy*, above all chap. 7, "Nonfalse Errors and the True Dreams of the Evangelist."

115 For the idea of "optical illusions" within the *Commedia*, see *The Undivine Comedy*, and the examples on pp. 19 and 202.

this?]" (*Par.* 31.107–8). The childishly straightforward question "Or se' tu morta?" is only apparently a simple move; in Dante's hands it is a highly effective rhetorical way to create the illusion of crossing the boundary between life and death. As he works out in *Li occhi dolenti* a poetics in which he can obtain the reader's consent to the idea of a living man who speaks with a dead woman, Dante is laying the groundwork for the fundamental fiction of the *Commedia*, an otherworld journey in which a living man talks to the dead.

After the query "Are you now dead?" comes the extraordinary verse in which Beatrice comforts Dante: "e mentre ch'io la chiamo, me **conforta** [and while I call on her she comforts me]" (56). This is not the first appearance of *consolatio* in the poems collected in the *Vita Nuova*. The verb *confortare* also appears in the sonnet *Ciò che m'incontra* ("se l'alma sbigottita non **conforta** [if he does not console my troubled soul]" [10]), in the sonnet of mourning *Se' tu colui* ("e fa peccato chi mai ne **conforta** [to try to comfort us would be a sin]" [10]), and in the canzone *Donna pietosa* ("E quando un poco **confortato** fui [And after being somewhat comforted]" [27]).[116] *Donna pietosa* offers the verb *consolare* as well, "Deh, **consoliam** costui [Let's comfort him]" (23), and in *Donna pietosa* the ladies – who are indeed *pietose* – ask Dante, "Perché si ti **sconforte**? [Why are you so discomforted?]" (12), and then set about consoling him.[117]

But in *Li occhi dolenti* we see *consolatio* come to the fore in a new way: it is connected for the first time to the imaginative processes of the lover and to what he can do to obtain consolation for himself. *Consolatio* is now tied to the act of imagining his lady alive. We find in *Li occhi dolenti* not only the despondency aroused by the death of *madonna* but Dante's response: his move towards a poetics that brings the dead to life. While the death of Beatrice leaves the soul despondent, in a condition of fundamental deprivation, stripped of all consolation, "d'onne **consolar** ... spoglia" (40), the ability to imagine her alive to the point of talking to her opens the door to the possibilities of *consolatio*. And not to the *consolatio* provided by books or by abstractions like Lady Philosophy, but to the *consolatio* provided by Beatrice herself, as emphasized by the timely repetition of her name: "chiamo **Beatrice**, e dico: 'Or se' tu morta?'; / e mentre ch'io la chiamo, me **conforta** [I call to Beatrice: 'Are you now dead?' / And while I call on her she comforts me]" (54–6).

---

116 *Confortare* is found in the following lyrics not collected in the *Vita Nuova*: *Lo meo servente core*; *Madonna, quel signor*; *Onde venite voi*; and *Io son venuto*. *Sconfortare* appears only in *Donna pietosa*. The noun *conforto* appears in the canzoni *La dispietata mente*; *E' m'incresce di me*; *Io sento sì d'Amor la gran possanza*; and *Amor, che movi tua vertù dal cielo*.

117 In the lyrics included in the *Vita Nuova* the verb *consolare* occurs in *Donna pietosa*, *Li occhi dolenti*, and *Gentil pensero*; in the other lyrics it occurs in *Ne le man vostre* ("per tal ch'i' mora **consolato** in pace [so I might die consoled in peace]" [13]) and in the great canzone of exile, *Tre donne* ("**consolarsi** e dolersi [consoling themselves and grieving]" [74]). In the verse cited from *Tre donne* we can see how Dante takes both the fundamental terms of *Li occhi dolenti* – suffering and consolation – and transfers them from a personal and emotional context to a context of universal justice.

In the *Convivio*, the philosophical treatise written between the end of the *Vita Nuova* and the beginning of the *Commedia*, Dante, modelling himself on the protagonist of the *Consolatio Philosophiae* of Boethius, consoles himself for Beatrice's death with a personified abstraction, Lady Philosophy. In *Li occhi dolenti*, Beatrice is dead – but she is no abstraction. The consolation that Dante imagines is offered to him by Beatrice in *Li occhi dolenti* anticipates the *Commedia* in its historicity. Following Dante, the idea of *consolatio* provided directly by the dead beloved, as if she were alive, will be the basis of the second part of Petrarch's *Rerum vulgarium fragmenta*, where, for instance, the poet sees his dead lady "calcare i fior' com'una donna viva [treading the flowers like a living woman]" (*Rvf* 281.13)

The fifth stanza of *Li occhi dolenti* focuses on the "debased ['nvilita]" (66) life of the protagonist after the death of his lady. Once again we note the passage from the general to the particular, in this case the passage from those whose hearts are "vile and base" ("malvagio e vile") (33) in the third stanza to the debased life of the lover in the fifth. The antithesis between *gentile* and *vile*, which occurs throughout *stil novo* poetry, will develop into the far-reaching ethical and social discourse on the nature of true nobility in the fourth book of the *Convivio*. The *gentile/vile* antithesis also connects *Li occhi dolenti* to the famous sonnet by Cavalcanti to Dante, *I' vegno 'l giorno a·tte 'nfinite volte*, where Guido accuses his friend of being "steeped in shameful thoughts" ("pensar troppo vilmente") (2) and complains that "molto mi dol della gentil tua mente / e d'assai tue vertù che·tti son tolte [it pains me deeply that your noble mind / and many virtues have been stripped away]" (3–4).

I' vegno 'l giorno a·tte 'nfinite volte is a sonnet that was probably written in the period after Beatrice's death, and that could be defined as an "anti-consolatory" poem, in that it aims more to shake up the mourner and to rouse him from his mental lethargy than to console him.[118] One can usefully compare *I' vegno 'l giorno* to the fifth stanza of *Li occhi dolenti*. Cavalcanti is treating the same material but from a reversed and external perspective, from the viewpoint of an intimate friend who no longer sympathizes, whose sympathy has changed into scorn for the self-damaging behaviour that he peremptorily defines as "la **vil** tua vita [your debased life]" (9). Cavalcanti is referring, I believe, to the dejected, depressed condition described in the fifth stanza of *Li occhi dolenti*, where the life of the lover is acknowledged to be "sì **'nvilita** [so debased]." *I' vegno 'l giorno a·tte* concludes with the same adjective, *invilita*, that we find in the canzone: "Se 'l presente sonetto spesso leggi, / lo spirito noioso che·tti caccia / si partirà dall'anima **invilita** [If you reread this sonnet several times, / the loathsome spirit persecuting you / will be dispelled from your degraded soul]" (*I' vegno 'l giorno*, 12–14). The fifth stanza of *Li occhi dolenti* would seem to exemplify the "pensar troppo **vilmente**" of which Cavalcanti accuses his friend.

---

118 For *I' vegno 'l giorno a·tte 'infinite volte* as an "anti-consolatory" poem, in antithesis to Cino da Pistoia's canonic *consolatoria*, see the introductory essays to *Guido, i' vorrei* and *Videro gli occhi miei*.

But everything changes in the last two verses of the fifth stanza, in which a consolatory, anti-depressive option reopens. Here Dante imagines that his lady sees him and hopes (an anti-depressant emotion by definition) that she may offer him comfort even after death: "Ma qual ch'io sia la mia donna il si vede, / e io ne spero **ancor** da lei merzede [But what I have become my lady knows, / and I still hope to gain her clemency]" (69–70). This simple move – the idea that the beloved dies and that then from paradise she sees the sadness of her lover and helps him, and above all that her death is not an obstacle to such help – is the necessary precondition of the *Commedia*. The plot of the second canto of *Inferno*, where Beatrice comes to assist Dante, is prepared *in nuce* in *Li occhi dolenti*.

The *congedo* closes the circle and returns to the beginning, reprising the idea of weeping, the physical sign of mourning: "Pietosa mia canzone, or va piangendo [My somber song, I bid you now weep tears, and go]" (71). Sending the canzone to find "le donne e le donzelle / a cui le tue sorelle / erano usate di portar letizia [the ladies and the girls / to whom your sister poems / were sent as messengers of happiness]" (72–4), we note the difference between this canzone, "figliuola di tristizia [daughter of despondency]" (75), and the other *rime*, the happy "sister poems."[119]

The theme of *consolatio* is the final note of *Li occhi dolenti*. In the last line the poet assigns to his canzone the label "disconsolata," making it the emblem and spokesperson for the state of being inconsolable: "e tu, che se' figliuola di tristizia, / vatten **disconsolata** a star con elle [and you, the daughter of despondency, / go off in misery to stay with them]" (75–6).[120] It is not surprising that *Li occhi dolenti*, the first poem *in morte* and the quasi-official canzone of mourning for Beatrice, should end "disconsolata." However, the great importance of *Li occhi dolenti* actually lies in the *consolatio* that, despite everything, it manages to find. This *consolatio* is provided not by others (Dante's friend Cino da Pistoia, for instance),[121] but, characteristically for Dante, by

---

119 For the metaphor of blood relations between lyrics, see the essay on *Sonetto, se Meuccio*. The metaphor recurs with particular prominence in another series of lyrics connected to the theme of *consolatio*: the cycle that consists of the canzoni *Voi che 'ntendendo* and *Amor che nella mente*, the ballata *Voi che savete ragionar d'amore*, and the two sonnets *Parole mie che per lo mondo siete* and *O dolci rime che parlando andate*. For a discussion of this series of lyrics, see Barolini, *Dante's Poets*, pp. 27–9; for the term *consolare* in Dante's usage, see *Dante's Poets*, pp. 36–7.

120 *Disconsolato* is not a common adjective: *disconsolati* appears in the sonnet that follows *Li occhi dolenti* in the *Vita Nuova*, *Venite a 'ntender li sospiri miei*, and then two times in lyrics not anthologized in the *libello*, in the canzone *E'm'incresce di me*, where "la **sconsolata** [the disconsolate one]" (31) refers to the lover's soul, and in the canzone of exile *Tre donne*, where Love "salutò le germane **sconsolate** [greeted his disconsolate kin]" (58). Very interesting is the correlation between *Li occhi dolenti* and *Tre donne* that emerges from the presence in both of *consolare* and *disconsolato*.

121 Cino's *consolatoria* (canzone of consolation), *Avegna ched el m'aggia più per tempo*, is woven throughout with the word *conforto*: "per **confortar** la vostra grave vita [to console your unhappiness]" (3), "vi posso fare di **conforto** aita [I can help you find comfort]" (12), "che a l'egra mente prendiate **conforto** [that you take comfort for your ailing mind]" (38), "**Conforto** già, **conforto** l'Amor chiama [Comfort, indeed, Love calls for comfort]" (43), "dunque speme di **confortar** vi piaccia [therefore enjoy the hope of being comforted]" (56), "che vi **conforti** sì come vi piace [that He console you as you would wish]" (76, concluding line).

himself (the greatest example of self-consolation before the *Commedia* is the canzone of exile, *Tre donne*): this is the *consolatio* wrought by the poet's imagination.

47 (B XXV; FB 47; *VN* XXXI.8–17 [20.8–17])

Li occhi dolenti per pietà del core	My eyes, distraught by pity for my heart,
hanno di lagrimar sofferta pena,	have borne the suffering that weeping brings,
3 sì che per vinti son remasi omai.	so that, exhausted, they concede defeat.
Ora, s'i' voglio sfogar lo dolore,	And if I now should wish to vent my grief,
che a poco a poco a la morte mi mena,	which slowly though most surely leads to death,
6 convenemi parlar traendo guai.	I must lament with words while weeping tears.
E perché me ricorda ch'io parlai	Since I remember how I used to speak
de la mia donna, mentre che vivia,	about my lady willingly with you,
donne gentili, volentier con vui,	my gentle ladies, while she was alive,
10 non voi parlare altrui,	I choose to speak to none
se non a cor gentil che in donna sia;	except a lady with a gentle heart.
e dicerò di lei piangendo, pui	And I shall speak of her while weeping, since
che si n'è gita in ciel subitamente,	she's gone away to heaven suddenly
14 e ha lasciato Amor meco dolente.	and left Love here with me in misery.
Ita n'è Beatrice in l'alto cielo,	Beatrice has gone to heaven on high,
nel reame ove li angeli hanno pace,	the kingdom where the angels dwell in peace;
17 e sta con loro, e voi, donne ha lassate:	she lives with them, and leaves you ladies here:
no la ci tolse qualità di gelo	no property of heat or cold took her
né di calore, come l'altre face,	away from us, as it has taken others;
20 ma solo fue sua gran benignitate;	it was alone her great kind-heartedness,
ché luce de la sua umilitate	because a ray of her humility
passò li cieli con tanta vertute,	traversed the heavens with such radiance
che fé maravigliar l'etterno Sire,	it filled the Everlasting Lord with awe,
24 sì che dolce disire	so that a sweet desire
lo giunse di chiamar tanta salute;	moved Him to summon so much worthiness;
e fella di qua giù a sé venire,	he made her come to him from here below,
perché vedea ch'esta vita noiosa	because he knew this world of wretchedness
28 non era degna di sì gentil cosa.	was undeserving of so fine a being.
Partissi de la sua bella persona	Her tender, noble soul so full of grace
piena di grazia l'anima gentile,	departed from her lovely human form
31 ed èssi gloriosa in loco degno.	and lives in glory in a worthy place.
Chi no la piange, quando ne ragiona,	Whoever speaks of her and fails to weep
core ha di pietra sì malvagio e vile,	betrays a heart of stone so vile and base
34 ch'entrar no i puote spirito benegno.	that no kind spirit penetrates inside.
Non è di cor villan sì alto ingegno,	No evil heart could have sufficient wit
che possa imaginar di lei alquanto,	to figure forth an image of her worth,

e però no li ven di pianger doglia:
38 ma ven tristizia e voglia
di sospirare e di morir di pianto,
e d'onne consolar l'anima spoglia
chi vede nel pensero alcuna volta
42 quale ella fue, e com'ella n'è tolta.

    Dannomi angoscia li sospiri forte,
quando 'l pensero ne la mente grave
45 mi reca quella che m'ha 'l cor diviso:
e spesse fiate pensando a la morte,
venemene un disio tanto soave,
48 che mi tramuta lo color nel viso.
E quando 'l maginar mi ven ben fiso,
giugnemi tanta pena d'ogne parte,
ch'io mi riscuoto per dolor ch'i' sento;
52 e sì fatto divento,
che da le genti vergogna mi parte.
Poscia piangendo, sol nel mio lamento
chiamo Beatrice e dico: "Or se' tu morta?";
56 e mentre ch'io la chiamo, me conforta.

    Pianger di doglia e sospirar d'angoscia
mi strugge 'l core ovunque sol mi trovo,
59 sì che ne 'ncrescerebbe a chi m'audesse:
e quale è stata la mia vita, poscia
che la mia donna andò nel secol novo,
62 lingua non è che dicer lo sapesse:
e però, donne mie, pur ch'io volesse,
non vi saprei io dir ben quel ch'io sono,
sì mi fa travagliar l'acerba vita;
66 la quale è sì 'nvilita,
che ogn'om par che mi dica: "Io t'abbandono",
veggendo la mia labbia tramortita.
Ma qual ch'io sia, la mia donna il si vede,
70 e io ne spero ancor da lei merzede.

    Pietosa mia canzone, or va piangendo;
e ritruova le donne e le donzelle
73 a cui le tue sorelle
erano usate di portar letizia;
e tu, che se' figliuola di tristizia,
76 vatten disconsolata a star con elle.

and so it feels no grief for which to weep;
but anguish and desire
to sigh and then to die from weeping tears,
depriving their own soul of all relief,
arise in those who see at times in thought
her essence and how she was torn from us.

    My sighing makes me grieve convulsively
when thinking brings back to my weary mind
the thought of her who's cleaved my heart in two:
and many times while contemplating death,
so sweet a longing makes its way to me
that all the colour in my face is lost.
And when my thought is wholly fixed on her,
from every side I'm so assailed by grief
that I'm brought back by all the pain I feel;
and such do I become
that shame keeps me apart from everyone.
Then weeping, all alone in my lament,
I call to Beatrice: "Are you now dead?"
And while I call on her she comforts me.

    To weep for grief and sigh from suffering
destroys my heart whenever I'm alone,
so anyone who heard me would take pity;
and what my life's become now ever since
my lady passed into the other world,
there is no tongue that has the power to tell:
and so, my ladies, even if I wished,
I could not tell you what I have become,
so much life's bitterness distresses me;
for it is so debased
that those who see the pallor in my face
appear to tell me: "I abandon you."
But what I have become my lady knows,
and I still hope to gain her clemency.

    My somber song, I bid you now weep tears,
and go and find the ladies and the girls
to whom your sister poems
were sent as messengers of happiness;
and you, the daughter of despondency,
go off in misery to stay with them.

METRE: canzone of five stanzas, each composed of fourteen verses (thirteen hendecasyllables and one *settenario*),
with rhyme scheme ABC ABC CDEeDEFF and *congedo* XYyZZY. The *fronte* is six verses (3 + 3) and the *sirma* is
eight verses.

48 Venite a 'ntender li sospiri miei
First Redaction

The sonnet *Venite a 'ntender li sospiri miei* was placed in *Vita Nuova* XXXII (21), where it reprises the theme of mourning just treated in the great canzone that comes before it. In the sonnet the poet addresses himself to the "cor' gentili [gracious hearts]" (2), as in *Li occhi dolenti* he had addressed the "donne gentili [gentle ladies]" (9), and invites them, since pity requires it, to "'ntender li sospiri miei ... li quali sconsolati vanno via [listen to the sighs that issue forth in discontent]" (3). The adjective "sconsolati," here applied to the lover's sighs, echoes "disconsolata" in *Li occhi dolenti*, where it appears in the final verse with reference to the canzone itself ("vatten disconsolata a star con elle [go off in misery to stay with them]" [76]). This formal resumption of the end of *Li occhi dolenti* in the first quatrain of *Venite a 'ntender* indicates that the sonnet functions as a seal of the funereal canzone in the *Vita Nuova*'s overall economy.

The painful weeping of *Li occhi dolenti* is heard again in the obsessive repetition of *piangere* that closes the octave of *Venite a 'ntender*: "lasso!, di **pianger** sì la donna mia / che sfogassen lo cor **piangendo** lei [alas, by weeping for my lady in a way / that brings my heart relief by dint of tears]" (7–8). We note the lexical similarity of the apotheosis of *madonna* in the sonnet and in the canzone: "la qual se **n'è ita** / al loco degno della sua virtute [who has left this world behind / and gone where her perfection is esteemed]" (*Venite a 'ntender*, 10–11) echoes "**Ita n'è** Beatrice in l'alto cielo [Beatrice has gone to heaven on high]" (*Li occhi dolenti*, 15). The fundamental idea of *calling her* occurs in both texts: "**chiamar** sovente / la nostra donna [often calling on my love, / the lady]" in *Venite a 'ntender* (9–10) recalls "e mentre ch'io la **chiamo**, me conforta [and while I call on her she comforts me]" in *Li occhi dolenti* (56).

Of course, we do not know that the canzone was written before the sonnet; any discussion of the sonnet "echoing" the canzone can refer only to the experience of reading them in the order in which they are presented within the *Vita Nuova*. Outside the *Vita Nuova* we can speak only of similarities between them. Moreover, *Venite a 'ntender* refers to "la nostra donna" (our lady) (10), not to Beatrice. De Robertis accepts the explanation of the origin of *Venite a 'ntender* offered in the *Vita Nuova*: "it was probably composed, as Dante tells us, and we have no reason not to believe him, at the request of a friend of his and close relative of hers to whom it was given" (ed. comm., p. 392). But, as has often been noted in this commentary, the prose framework of the *Vita Nuova* adds many historical and sociological details that do not appear in the lyrics. In this case, for example, there is no trace in *Venite a 'ntender* of either the name "Beatrice" or of the friend mentioned by the prose, who is identified by commentators as Manetto Portinari, Beatrice's brother, on the basis of the assertion in the prose that this friend "fue tanto distretto di sanguinitade con questa gloriosa, che nullo più presso l'era [such a close blood relation of the glorious one that nobody was closer to her]" (*VN* XXXII.1 [21.1]).

The prose tells us that this friend, the brother of the glorious one, asked Dante for a poem "per una donna che s'era morta [about a woman who had died]," and not only that, but that "simulava sue parole, acciò che paresse che dicesse d'un'altra [he faked his words, so that it seemed that he was talking about another woman]" (*VN* XXXII.2 [21.2]). According to the prose, *Venite a 'ntender* is the composition given by Dante to Beatrice's brother as part of this complex game that recalls the many simulations of the first part of the *Vita Nuova*. But again, in the sonnet there is no trace of all of this.

As always, if a sonnet of the *Vita Nuova* exists in a version that pre-exists the version in the *libello*, this commentary follows the earlier redaction as it has been reproduced by De Robertis. In the case of *Venite a 'ntender*, the revisions that mark the passage from the first version to the version of the *Vita Nuova* are slight but consistent, in the sense that they connect the sonnet even more closely to *Li occhi dolenti*. In the first version we find "la nostra donna, la qual se n'è ita / al loco degno della sua virtute" (11), while in the version of the *Vita Nuova* it is "la mia donna gentil, che si n'è gita / al secol degno de la sua vertute" (10–11): the change from "nostra donna" to "la mia donna gentil" and the substitution of "secol" for "loco" reprise *Li occhi dolenti*, where "la mia donna andò nel secol novo [my lady passed into the other world]" (61).

48 (B XXVI; FB 48; DR 67; *VN* XXXII.5–6 [21.5–6])
First Redaction

Venite a 'ntender li sospiri miei,	Come listen to my sighs, O gracious hearts,
o cor' gentili, che pietà ·l disia,	the sighs of discontent that issue forth,
li quali sconsolati vanno via,	for this is something pity asks of you,
4 e s'e' non fosser, di dolor morrei,	and were it not for them, I'd die of grief;
però che gli occhi mi sarebbon rei	indeed, my eyes would have to compensate,
molte fïate più ch'io non vorria,	alas, more often than I would desire,
lasso!, di pianger sì la donna mia	by weeping for my lady in a way
8 che sfogassen lo cor piangendo lei.	that brings my heart relief by dint of tears.
Voi udirete lor chiamar sovente	You'll hear them often calling on my love,
la nostra donna, la qual se n'è ita	the lady who has left this world behind
11 al loco degno della sua virtute;	and gone where her perfection is esteemed,
e dispregiar talora questa vita	and hear them sometimes scorn this life
in persona dell'anima dolente,	by taking on the voice of my sad soul,
14 abandonata della sua salute.	which is abandoned by its true salvation.

VN 2. O(i) c. – 3. qual' disconsolati – 5. sarebber – 8. sfogasser – 10. La mia donna gentil, che si n'è gita – 11. Al secol degno

METRE: sonnet ABBA ABBA CDE DCE.

49 Quantunque volte, lasso!, mi rimembra

Quantunque volte, a canzone of two stanzas with thirteen lines each, was placed by Dante in *Vita Nuova* XXXIII (22), as the fifth and final canzone of the *libello*. The prose frame of the *Vita Nuova* emphasizes the relationship with Beatrice's brother, established in the previous chapter: *Venite a 'ntender*, the sonnet offered (conjecturally) to Manetto Portinari in the preceding chapter, is not a sufficient homage, and therefore "dissi due stanzie d'una canzone, l'una per costui veracemente, e l'altra per me, avvegna che paia l'una e l'altra per una persona detta, a chi non guarda sottilmente [I wrote two stanzas of a canzone, one actually for this man, and the other for me, although to one who doesn't consider things subtly both may seem written for one person]" (*VN* XXXIII.2 [22.2]). Presenting *Quantunque volte*, Dante explains that the first stanza is a lament for the death of Beatrice written from the point of view of the brother and that the second expresses instead the lover's point of view: "E così appare che in questa canzone si lamentano due persone, l'una de le quali si lamenta come frate, l'altra come servo [And thus it seems that two people are grieving in this canzone, one grieving as a brother, the other as a servant]" (*VN* XXXIII.4 [22.4]). The supposed "proof" of the change of perspective from brother ("frate") to lover ("servo," drawing on the courtly imagery of love-service) is the switch from "la donna" in the first stanza (3) to "la donna mia" in the second (18).

As we know, the prose of the *Vita Nuova* has its own objectives that are superimposed on the lyrics. Dante perhaps wanted to introduce Beatrice's brother and to resume the discussion of friendship, now hierarchically arranging his friends: "secondo li gradi de l'amistade, è amico a me immediatamente dopo lo primo [in degree of friendship, he is the friend of mine right after the first]" (*VN* XXXII.1 [21.1]). Creating a network of relations that includes a father, a sister, and a brother, he offers a glimpse of the elements of the Florentine family. He widens the network of friends and suggests the presence not only of the "primo amico," Guido Cavalcanti, but of a group of friends, a *brigata* of young Florentines: thanks to these two contrivances, Dante increases the historical density of the *libello*. (For the thematic of the male *brigata* in Dante's lyrics, see the introductory essays to *Deh ragioniamo, Sonar bracchetti, Volgete gli occhi, Guido, i' vorrei*, and *Amore e monna Lagia*.) On the other hand, as has been seen elsewhere, the canzone has its own poetic integrity that has little to do with the aims of the prose.

Whatever the objective with regard to Guido Cavalcanti, referred to again as "lo primo [amico]" in the introduction to *Venite a 'ntender* (*VN* XXXI.1 [21.1]), our canzone treats the theme of *madonna*'s death in a decidedly Cavalcantian manner. The first stanza of *Quantunque volte* is a testimony to Guido's influence, above all in the personification of the various faculties of the self, fragmented into "heart," "mind," and "soul." The self speaks to his soul in direct discourse. Every time that he recalls that he will never again see his lady on earth, "my grieving memory" (5) accumulates "such pain" (4) around the heart that he must ask: "Anima mia, ché non ten vai? / ché li tormenti che tu porterai / nel secol, che t'è già tanto noioso, / mi fan pensoso di paura forte [My soul, what keeps you here? / Because the pain that you will bear in life, / which you already find so anguishing, / oppresses me with deep anxiety]" (6–9). The result of the extremely Cavalcantian "paura forte [deep anxiety]" of line 9 is an intense desire for death, expressed again in direct discourse: "Ond'io chiamo la Morte, / come soave e dolce mio riposo; / e dico 'Vieni a me' con tanto amore, / che sono astioso di chiunque more [And so I call on Death, / the sweet and tender place of final rest, / and say 'Please come to me' with so much love / that I am envious of all who die]" (10–13).

Quantunque volte seems to mark a step backward with respect to *Li occhi dolenti* and *Venite a 'ntender*, as indicated by the use of the verb *chiamare*. Instead of calling on his dead lady and bringing her to life so that she comforts him, as in the paradigmatic verses of *Li occhi dolenti* – "e mentre ch'io la **chiamo**, me conforta [and while I call on her she comforts me]" (56) – *Quantunque volte*, more traditionally, calls on Death: "Ond'io **chiamo** la Morte [And so I call on Death]" (10). And it is to Death, not to his dead beloved, that the poet speaks directly, saying "Vieni a me [come to me]" (12).

The second stanza begins by reiterating the suffering of the lover and the invocation of Death: "E' si raccoglie ne li miei sospiri / un sono di pietate, / che va chiamando Morte tuttavia [A sound of pity gathers in my sighs / that calls on Death / and goes on calling unremittingly]" (14–16). But the meditation on the moment of death of *madonna* – "quando la donna mia / fu giunta da la sua crudelitate [(the day) my lady was beset / and overtaken by its cruelty]" (18–19) – seems to lend wings to the imaginative capacity of the lover, and the canzone turns to the moment in which *madonna*, "partendo sé da la nostra veduta [separated from our sight]" (21), is transformed into spirit such as beatifies even the angels: "divenne spiritual bellezza grande, / che per lo cielo spande / luce d'amor, che li angeli saluta [was turned into a spirit of great beauty / that spreads through paradise / a light of love which brings the angels bliss]" (22–4). A canzone of Cavalcantian stamp here shows itself capable of reaching a linguistic register that recalls *Paradiso*; "luce d'amor" in line 24 consistently elicits comparison to "luce intellettüal, piena d'amore [intellectual light, full of love]" (*Par.* 30.40).

The end of *Quantunque volte* is a mix of themes and lexemes already seen in *Donne ch'avete* and *Li occhi dolenti*, but compressed in such a way as to recall *Paradiso*, perhaps too because of the beautiful enjambment "spande / luce d'amor" (enjambment is a rhetorical feature of the third canticle).[122] The "spiritual bellezza"

---

122 On enjambment and the *Paradiso*, see "The Sacred Poem Is Forced to Jump: Closure and the Poetics of Enjambment," chap. 10 in Barolini, *The Undivine Comedy*.

of *madonna*, which spills the light of love that causes the angels bliss, is so "gentile" that it arouses wonder in the angelic intellects: "e lo intelletto loro alto, sottile / face maravigliar, sì v'è gentile [and makes their keen and lofty intellect / feel wonderment, so noble is she there]" (25–6).

49 (B XXVII; FB 49; *VN* XXXIII.5–8 [22.5–8])

	Quantunque volte, lasso!, mi rimembra	Alas, whenever I remember now
	ch'io non debbo gia mai	that I shall never see
3	veder la donna ond'io vo sì dolente,	the lady on account of whom I grieve,
	tanto dolore intorno 'l cor m'assembra	such pain my grieving memory accrues
	la dolorosa mente,	around my heart
6	ch'io dico: "Anima mia, ché non ten vai?	that I must ask: "My soul, what keeps you here?
	ché li tormenti che tu porterai	Because the pain that you will bear in life,
	nel secol, che t'è già tanto noioso,	which you already find so anguishing,
	mi fan pensoso di paura forte."	oppresses me with deep anxiety."
10	Ond'io chiamo la Morte,	And so I call on Death,
	come soave e dolce mio riposo;	the sweet and tender place of final rest,
	e dico "Vieni a me" con tanto amore,	and say "Please come to me" with so much love
13	che sono astioso di chiunque more.	that I am envious of all who die.
	E' si raccoglie ne li miei sospiri	A sound of pity gathers in my sighs
	un sono di pietate,	that calls on Death
16	che va chiamando Morte tuttavia:	and goes on calling unremittingly.
	a lei si volser tutti i miei disiri,	All my desires turned towards it the day
	quando la donna mia	my lady was beset
19	fu giunta da la sua crudelitate;	and overtaken by its cruelty,
	perché 'l piacere de la sua bieltate,	because the splendour of her loveliness,
	partendo sé da la nostra veduta,	when it was separated from our sight,
	divenne spirital bellezza grande,	was turned into a spirit of great beauty
23	che per lo cielo spande	that spreads through paradise
	luce d'amor, che li angeli saluta,	a light of love which brings the angels bliss,
	e lo intelletto loro alto, sottile	and makes their keen and lofty intellect
26	face maravigliar, sì v'è gentile.	feel wonderment, so noble is she there.

METRE: canzone of two stanzas, each composed of thirteen verses (ten hendecasyllables and three *settenari*), with rhyme scheme AbC AcB BDEeDFF and without *congedo*. The *fronte* is six verses (3 + 3) and the *sirma* is seven verses.

50 Era venuta nella mente mia
[Era venuta ne la mente mia]
First Redaction and Redaction of the *Vita Nuova*

The gloss proposed for *Quantunque volte* is valid as well for *Era venuta nella mente mia*: of this sonnet too we can say that theologized features have been grafted onto an originally quite Cavalcantian core. This sonnet exists in a pre–*Vita Nuova* redaction, and so, as customary, it is presented here in the early redaction. There are, however, further complications in the case of *Era venuta*, since in the *Vita Nuova* redaction Dante adds not only lexical touches but even what he calls a new "beginning" in the form of a new first quatrain. He does not substitute the new quatrain for the original; rather he adds it, so that the *Vita Nuova* redaction of the sonnet is uniquely presented in the *libello* with two different opening quatrains, labelled by the poet "First beginning" and "Second beginning."

This is therefore an instance of truly exceptional editorial intervention, exceptional even for an author who is never timid in his revisions. As a result we have here a foundational example of what we could call Dantean "auto-philology." With respect to the *Vita Nuova* version of *Era venuta* De Robertis writes that it presents "the integration of thematic variants ... of alternatives into a single solution" (*VN*, pp. 213–14). Given the exceptional nature of Dante's editorial intervention, and given Dante's desire to make the existence of variants obvious, to make manifest the archeology of the sonnet's composition, *Era venuta* is printed here both in its first redaction and in the redaction (with two beginnings) that was placed by Dante in *Vita Nuova* XXXIV (23).

The prose of the *Vita Nuova* situates the composition of *Era venuta* within a detailed scene: it is the day of the anniversary of Beatrice's death and the poet is drawing "uno angelo sopra certe tavolette [an angel on some boards]" (*VN* XXXIV.1 [23.1]), when he sees beside him some distinguished men (their identity is not specified, but the phrase "vidi lungo me uomini a li quali si convenia di fare onore [I saw beside me some men whose rank required that one greet them respectfully]" [*VN* XXXIV.1 (23.1)] leaves no doubt as to their social standing). The poet explains in a veiled way that he had been absorbed in contemplating his lady – dead, but undoubtedly present, because "meco [with me]": "e salutando loro dissi: 'Altri era testé meco, però pensava' [and greeting them I said, 'Someone else was just with me; that is why I was absorbed in thought']" (*VN* XXXIV.2 [23.2]). When the men leave the poet decides to write to them, "quasi per annovale [as a kind of anniversary memorial]" (*VN* XXX-IV.3 [23.3]); that is, to commemorate the anniversary of the death of *madonna*.[123]

---

123 This brilliant idea of the anniversary poem will be fundamental for Petrarch, who uses it in complex and innovative fashion throughout the *Rerum vulgarium fragmenta*.

What can be confirmed of this elaborate story? The first version of *Era venuta* is undoubtedly commemorative, and the fact that it commemorates precisely the first anniversary of the death of "quella donna gentil cui piange Amore [that noble lady because of whom Love weeps]" (*Era venuta*, first redaction, 2) is confirmed by the declaration of the final verses, directed to *madonna* herself: "O nobile intelletto, / oggi fa un anno che nel ciel salisti [This day, O noble intellect, / completes a year since you rose heavenward]" (*Era venuta*, first redaction, 13–14). Barbi-Maggini conclude "that therefore [the sonnet] must have been composed in June 1291" (p. 136). This date is deduced from the prose of the *Vita Nuova*, but the identity of *madonna* is not ascertainable on the basis of the sonnet.

The first version begins with a memory of *madonna*: "Era venuta nella mente mia / quella donna gentil cui piange Amore [That lady came into my memory, / the noble one because of whom Love weeps]" (*Era venuta*, first redaction, 1–2). Her memory is linked to a specific occasion ("entro quell'ora [precisely when]" [3]), in which "the power of her soul / forced you to see what I was doing then" ("lo suo valore / vi trasse a riguardar quel ch'e' facea") (*Era venuta*, first redaction, 3–4). In other words, the first version of *Era venuta* addresses people ("vi," you) whose sex and identity are not specified, but who have felt the presence of *madonna* ("lo suo valore" [3]) and are drawn to it, watching the activity (also unspecified) of the poet: "quel ch'e' facea [what I was doing then]" (4). At this point *Era venuta* falls back on typical Cavalcantian phrasing, with however a very important caveat: the "distrutto core [ravaged heart]" of line 6 is suffering over the real death of *madonna*, not, as in Cavalcanti, over the metaphorical "death" of the self because of his love for *madonna*. The Cavalcantian motifs include the vital spirits exiled from the self to whom they belong and Love's use of direct discourse to address them: "dicev' ai sospiri: 'Andate fore,' / per che ciascun dolente se ·n partia. / Parlando uscivan fori del mio petto [said to every sigh: 'Now leave at once,' / and so they all went off unhappily. / As they departed from my breast all spoke]" (*Era venuta*, first redaction, 7–9).

But *Era venuta* does not close in this Cavalcantian vein. Like *Quantunque volte*, the sonnet moves on to the redeeming power of *madonna* in paradise. Thus, the powerful presence of the Cavalcantian adverb of interior exile, *fuori* (as distilled in the persona of Guido invoked in *Amore e monna Lagia*'s "e Guido ancor, che·nn'è del tutto **fore**" [12]), is first applied in typical Cavalcantian fashion to the self's spirits, who are instructed to leave, "Andate **fore**" (7), and who do in fact depart, "uscivano **fori**" (9).[124] But there is redemptive resolution in a third use where *uscire fuori* (to go out) becomes an indicator of *madonna*'s arrival in heaven. In line 12 the verb "uscian fuor" indicates the action of the sighs that speak to the noble intellect of *madonna*, in her abode outside and distant from earthly suffering: "Ma quei che ne **uscian fuor** con

---

124 See also the discussion of *fuori* in the introductory essay to the Cavalcantian canzone *E' m'incresce di me*, in particular with respect to verses 29–31: "Innamorata se ne va piangendo / **fora** di questa vita / la sconsolata, che la caccia Amore [Still full of love my soul, disconsolate, / departs this life of ours / with tears of sorrow, driven out by Love]."

minor pena / venian dicendo: 'O nobile intelletto, / oggi fa un anno che nel ciel salisti' [But those that issued forth with lesser pain / remarked: 'This day, O noble intellect, / completes a year since you rose heavenward']" (*Era venuta*, first redaction, 12–14).

For the version of *Era venuta* that he placed in the *Vita Nuova*, Dante composed a new "First beginning" that highlights precisely *madonna*'s remarkable ascension to paradise, thus making a point of starting the new version of the poem with the redemptive language that the first version attained only in its conclusion. In the new quatrain, given in the *Vita Nuova* a title, *Primo cominciamento* [*First beginning*], there is no trace of the people who watch the poet, nor of the activity in which the poet is involved. The new quatrain moves from the memory of the "gentil donna" directly to the "excellence" ("valore") that renders her eligible to be "placed" ("posta") by God "within the heaven of the meek, where Mary is":

Primo cominciamento
Era venuta ne la mente mia
la gentil donna che per suo valore
fu posta da l'altissimo signore
nel ciel de l'umiltate, ov'è Maria.
           (*VN* redaction, 1–4)

[*First beginning*
That lady came into my memory,
the noble one who, for her excellence,
was placed by him who reigns on high
in the heaven of the meek, where Mary is.]

Thus, the new *Primo cominciamento* quatrain, which was not present in the pre–*Vita Nuova* version of *Era venuta*, emphasizes the feature of the sonnet that will be of most importance for Dante's future: God's direct intervention in *madonna*'s life and death and His personal placement of her in paradise.

The labels *Primo cominciamento* and *Secondo cominciamento*, used by Dante in the *Vita Nuova* version of *Era venuta*, have generated confusion and critical debates on the relative chronology of the two *cominciamenti*, debates that can now be set aside because they are based on Dante's story in the *Vita Nuova* prose and not on the material evidence offered by the pre–*Vita Nuova* redaction. We must keep clearly before our eyes the first redaction of *Era venuta*, a text that helps us keep at bay the gravitational field of the *libello*'s drive to control interpretation.

The first quatrain of the first redaction of *Era venuta* coincides (apart from small lexical variants)[125] with the *Secondo cominciamento* of the *Vita Nuova* redaction. In

---

125 For example, line 3 of the first redaction, "entro quell'ora che lo suo valore," becomes "entro 'n quel punto che lo suo valore" in the *Vita Nuova* redaction.

other words, in the *libello* Dante uses the label *Primo cominciamento* for the quatrain that we know was added later (the one cited above), and the label *Secondo cominciamento* for the quatrain that we know existed first (and we know this certainly, because it is the first quatrain of the first redaction, for whose earlier existence we have material proof). This means that the *Primo cominciamento* of the *Vita Nuova* in reality corresponds to a *secondary*, not a primary, moment of composition. The *Vita Nuova* labels seem almost intentionally deceitful and misleading.

In fact the labels *Primo cominciamento* and *Secondo cominciamento* enact microtextually, as a *mise en abîme*, the macrotextual deceit that governs the entire structure of the *Vita Nuova*. This deceit is essentially laid bare by the existence of poems in a pre–*Vita Nuova* redaction. Time after time the prose declares that a lyric was written in the circumstances described by the prose, as in our current chapter: "mi venne un pensero di dire parole, quasi per annovale, e scrivere a costoro li quali erano venuti a me; e dissi allora questo sonetto [the idea came to me of composing a poem, as a kind of anniversary memorial, addressed to those men who had visited me. And then I composed this sonnet]" (*VN* XXXIV.3 [23.3]). Instead we know that the poem already existed before the prose – and in the case of *Era venuta* and other poems that exist in a first redaction we know this incontrovertibly, because an earlier redaction exists materially. Thus, when Dante declares that a lyric was written in the circumstances described by the prose, he accomplishes a deliberate reversal of the actual chronology of the composition of the book.

This reversal is engineered in the most tangible and material of ways, as we see if we hold a copy of the *Vita Nuova* in our hands: the real chronological precedence of the lyrics to the prose – their real precedence in the history of the Dante's life, as witnessed by the material evidence of the manuscripts – is reversed, chapter by chapter, by the placing of the prose spatially and physically *before* the lyrics. In other words, the prose announces the composition of a poem that is then materially written or printed upon the page, and the material presence of the poem, which appears on the page always *after* the prose that announces it, functions as an apparent graphic confirmation of its posteriority – in time as well as in space.

The adjectives "primo" and "secondo" in the headings *Primo cominciamento* and *Secondo cominciamento* mirror not the chronology of the writing but the new logic of the new life, according to which the *Primo cominciamento* is primary because of the story it narrates: it tells the story of a "noble lady who, for her excellence, / was placed by him who reigns on high / in the heaven of the meek, where Mary is" (*Era venuta*, *VN* redaction, 2–4). The *Secondo cominciamento* is, for the same reasons, secondary: the story it tells, the original story, corresponding to the opening of the original sonnet, is less important. Without doubt the *Primo cominciamento* is primary because it affirms the glorious eternal life of *madonna*. But we note that the very concept of an anniversary is a way of keeping someone alive, of conferring life on a dead person – and that this concept is already present in the older version. The alteration of the *Vita Nuova* therefore does not constitute, in the case of *Era venuta*, a flagrant ideological alteration of this sonnet as it does elsewhere. The theologized message of *Era venuta* is already fully visible in the first redaction of the sonnet, and not only in the meaning of the concluding words – "O nobile intelletto, / oggi fa un anno che nel ciel salisti [This day, O noble intellect, / completes a year since you rose heavenward]" (*Era venuta*, first redaction, 13–14) – but in the fact that they are expressed in direct discourse to *madonna*, as if she were still alive.

50 (B XXX; FB 50; DR 68; *VN* XXXIV.7–11 [23.7–11])
Two Redactions

First Redaction

   Era venuta nella mente mia
quella donna gentil cui piange Amore,
entro quell'ora che lo suo valore
4 vi trasse a riguardar quel ch'e' facea.
Amor, che nella mente la sentia,
era svegliato nel distrutto core,
e dicev' ai sospiri: "Andate fore,"
8 per che ciascun dolente se ·n partia.
   Parlando uscivan fori del mio petto
con una voce che sovente mena
11 le lagrime dolenti agli occhi tristi.
Ma quei che ne uscian fuor con minor pena
venian dicendo: "O nobile intelletto,
14 oggi fa un anno che nel ciel salisti."

First Redaction

   That lady came into my memory,
the noble one because of whom Love weeps,
precisely when the power of her soul
forced you to see what I was doing then.
And Love, perceiving her within my mind,
was roused awake within my ravaged heart
and said to every sigh: "Now leave at once,"
and so they all went off unhappily.
   As they departed from my breast all spoke
together with a single voice that often fills
my saddened eyes with tears of agony.
But those that issued forth with lesser pain
remarked: "This day, O noble intellect,
completes a year since you rose heavenward."

Vita Nuova Redaction

Primo cominciamento

   Era venuta ne la mente mia
la gentil donna che per suo valore
fu posta da l'altissimo signore
4 nel ciel de l'umiltate, ov'è Maria.

Secondo cominciamento

   Era venuta ne la mente mia
quella donna gentil cui piange Amore,
entro 'n quel punto che lo suo valore
4 vi trasse a riguardar quel ch'eo facia.
Amor, che ne la mente la sentia,
s'era svegliato nel destrutto core,
e diceva a' sospiri: "Andate fore";

Vita Nuova Redaction

First Beginning

   That lady came into my memory,
the noble one who, for her excellence,
was placed by him who reigns on high
in the heaven of the meek, where Mary is.

Second Beginning

   That lady came into my memory,
the noble one because of whom Love weeps,
precisely when the power of her soul
forced you to see what I was doing then.
And Love, perceiving her within my mind,
was stirred awake inside my ravaged heart,
and to my sighs he said: "Go forth from here,"

8   per che ciascun dolente si partia.
   Piangendo uscivan for de lo mio petto
con una voce che sovente mena
11   le lagrime dogliose a li occhi tristi.
   Ma quei che n'uscian for con maggior pena,
venian dicendo: "Oi nobile intelletto,
14   oggi fa l'anno che nel ciel salisti."

at which they all departed mournfully.
   As they departed from my breast all wept
together with a single voice that often fills
my saddened eyes with tears of agony.
But those that issued forth with greater pain
remarked: "This day, O noble intellect,
completes a year since you rose heavenward."

METRE: sonnet ABBA ABBA CDE DCE.

51 Videro gli occhi miei quanta pietate
First Redaction

The sonnet *Videro gli occhi miei quanta pietate*, which is reproduced here in the version prior to the one in the *Vita Nuova*, was placed by Dante in chapter XXXV (24) of the *libello*. It is the first of the sonnets dedicated to the episode of the so-called *donna gentile* or *donna pietosa*, a label taken from the prose. (I will use the locution *donna gentile*, to distinguish this lady from the other *donna pietosa* of the canzone *Donna pietosa e di novella etate*.) The episode of the *donna gentile* covers chapters XXXV–XXXIX (24–8) of the *Vita Nuova* and includes the five sonnets *Videro gli occhi miei quanta pietate*, *Color d'amore e di pietà sembianti*, *L'amaro lagrimar che voi faceste*, *Gentil pensero che parla di vui*, and *Lasso, per forza di molti sospiri*. Of these five sonnets, three – *Videro gli occhi miei*, *Color d'amore*, and *Lasso, per forza* – exist in a first redaction that guarantees their original autonomy from the *Vita Nuova*.

It is more important than ever to insist on that original autonomy when considering the mass of critical discourse – and critical confusion – that has arisen around the *donna gentile* episode. Throughout this commentary I have consistently pointed to Dante's penchant for auto-exegesis, and to the ways in which the prose of the *Vita Nuova* sets about reshaping the lyrics to make them fit a new sense, that of the poet's "new life." The episode of the *donna gentile* unleashes multiple auto-exegetical possibilities, because Dante returns explicitly to the *donna gentile* episode in the *Convivio*, evoking it in order to offer an interpretation that is difficult to reconcile with the sense of the story that we read in the *libello*. According to the *Convivio* the episode of the *donna gentile* is no longer the story of a moment of erotic fickleness, of inconstancy and infidelity towards Beatrice, as we read in the *Vita Nuova*. Instead, the motivating force that pushed the poet toward the *donna gentile* was not a shameful *eros* but a virtuous desire ("non passione ma vertù" [*Conv.* 1.2.16]), and this because the *donna gentile* of the *Vita Nuova* was, according to the *Convivio*, not a woman of flesh and blood but Lady Philosophy, the same who consoled Boethius in the *Consolation of Philosophy*.

There is no trace of Lady Philosophy in the story of the *Vita Nuova*, and even less so in the sonnet *Videro gli occhi miei*, which is reproduced here in an early redaction that precedes the composition of the *Vita Nuova*.

Reading the redaction that precedes the redaction of the *Vita Nuova*, we are twice removed from the work of retroactive revision carried out in the *Convivio*. If I make reference now to the *Convivio* version of events it is to remind the reader that we are in a textual zone that will assume a particular archeological density in the arc of

Dante's poetic life.[126] For the moment our goal is to isolate the aspects of the episode that will later set in motion Dante's auto-revisionary impulses.

The story of the *donna gentile* is the most fleshed out version thus far encountered of a topos with great hold over Dante's imagination: the topos of the "new love." When Dante encounters Beatrice in the earthly paradise, she reproves him for having given himself to "altrui" (others) after her death: "Sì tosto come in su la soglia fui / di mia seconda etade e mutai vita, / questi si tolse a me, e diessi altrui [As soon as I was over the threshold of my second age and I changed life, he took himself from me and gave himself to others]" (*Purg.* 30.124–6). For Dante the core issue here is a moral question, connected to what in *De vulgari eloquentia* he will call the poetics of *directio voluntatis* (the category of poetics that he assigns to himself and uses for his moral canzoni): to what goal should the soul direct its desire? And is the soul capable, after having singled out a suitable goal, of remaining constant and not turning in a new direction?

Chapter XXXV (24) of the *Vita Nuova* recounts that "alquanto tempo [some time]"[127] after the anniversary of Beatrice's death, Dante is absorbed in "dolorosi pensamenti [painful thoughts]," so much that he finds himself in a condition "di terribile sbigottimento [of horrible turmoil]" (*VN* XXXV.1 [24.1]). The pronounced Cavalcantian lexicon of the prose picks up and amplifies Cavalcantian flourishes, already present in the sonnets, in order to describe the poet's mourning for Beatrice's death. While Dante finds himself in these circumstances, he sees at a window "una gentile donna giovane e bella molto [a gracious woman, young and very beautiful]," who "was watching me so compassionately, to judge by her look, that all compassion seemed gathered in her" ("mi riguardava sì pietosamente, quanto a la vista, che tutta la pietà parea in lei accolta") (*VN* XXXV.2 [24.2]). Impelled by her pity to feel

---

126 For the motives of Dante's revisionism, and for a discussion of the texts dedicated to the *donna gentile* in their entirety, see my *Dante's Poets*, chap. 1, above all the section titled "Textual History" (pp. 14–31).

127 The attempt to reconcile the temporal indications of the *Vita Nuova* concerning the *donna gentile* with those of the *Convivio* is a *vexata quaestio*: "alquanto tempo" seems to suggest a period of time not too long after the anniversary of Beatrice's death, 8 June 1291, so Barbi-Maggini suggest for the date of the composition of *Videro gli occhi miei* "some months after June 1291" (p. 137). In the *Convivio* Dante offers a complex astronomical periphrasis to calculate the time passed since Beatrice's death (8 June 1290) until the time when he first sees the *donna gentile*: "quando quella gentile donna [di] cui feci menzione nella fine della Vita Nuova, parve primamente, accompagnata d'Amore, alli occhi miei e prese luogo alcuno nella mia mente [when that gentle lady, of whom I made mention at the end of the *New Life*, first appeared before my eyes, accompanied by Love, and took a place within my mind]" (*Conv.* 2.2.1). The total of 1,168 days (three years and two months) passed since Beatrice's death according to the periphrasis of the *Convivio* brings us to a date after 21 August 1293, that is, to a date that is too late and implausible for the composition of the *donna gentile* poems for many reasons. For an exposition of the debate and the entire chronology of the poems for the *donna gentile*, see Foster-Boyde, 2:341–62.

pity for himself, the poet begins to cry and so, feeling ashamed, decides to leave, "temendo di non mostrare la mia vile vita [fearful of making a show of my base condition]" (*VN* XXXV.3 [24.3]). This last expression, "la mia vile vita," recalls *Li occhi dolenti*, where the poet describes his life as "sì 'nvilita [so debased]" (66) after Beatrice's death, and also the sonnet written to Dante by Guido Cavalcanti, *I' vegno 'l giorno a·tte*, where Guido refers to "la vil tua vita [your degraded life]" (9). The account of the *Vita Nuova* thus develops a pre-existing narrative of Beatrice's death and Dante's reaction to it, attested by Guido's sonnet (for which see the introductory essays to *Li occhi dolenti* and *Guido, i' vorrei*).

Videro gli occhi miei recounts an episode very similar to the one narrated by the prose, without the specific details (absent are the window, the new lady's beauty, the cause of his suffering, and so forth). The sonnet takes as its starting point the vision of the lady – "**Videro** gli occhi miei quanta pietate / era **apparita** in la vostra figura [My eyes were witness to the great compassion / that was evident upon your face]" (1–2) – which is immediately connected with a mutual glancing at each other: "quando **guardaste** gli atti e la statura / ch'io faccio per dolor molte fïate [when you observed the attitude and look / I show so frequently because of grief]" (3–4). The lady, characterized simply by her "pietate" (1) – feminine pity is a quality that Dante likes, as we recall from the canzone *Donna pietosa* – looks at him, mirroring and in this way legitimizing his mourning. What could be more seductive than that?

But the sense of legitimization felt by the poet, a feeling that is social in nature and that originates in the reciprocity that he experienced from the *donna gentile*, is swept away by another thought: this one, too, social and originating in reciprocity, but disquieting. Let us take note of the steps in this complex dance. In the first quatrain the poet sees the lady who is looking at him, thus obtaining a positive reciprocity that comforts him. In the second quatrain the poet realizes that the lady is thinking of him, and specifically of "la qualità de la mia vita oscura": "Allor m'accorsi che voi pensavate / la qualità de la mia vita oscura [And then I saw that you were pondering / the sorry circumstances of my life]" (5–6). From the thought of her thinking about his "vita oscura" he obtains a sense of negative reciprocity that shames him. The feeling provoked by this thought causes him "fear" of "showing" (rendering visible through his tears) his "viltate" (we remember Cavalcanti's identical reproof regarding "la vil tua vita"): "sì che mi giunse ne lo cor paura / di dimostrar con gli occhi mia viltate [and this aroused a fear within my heart / of showing my dejection through my eyes]" (7–8). The word "viltate," the last word rhyming with the "pietate" of the incipit, seals the sentimental distance traversed by the poet in the span of the octave: from the affective height of the beginning of the sonnet, where he sees and enjoys the lady's "pietate," he transitions to the depths of the realization of his own "viltate."

The sestet of *Videro gli occhi miei* replays the same conflictual dance between distance and nearness, shame and approval. The poet pulls back, so moved by the pity showing in the face of the *donna gentile* that he cannot hold back the tears and then the shame he feels for having wept and the resulting need to withdraw from her sight:

"E tolsimi d'inanzi a voi, sentendo / che si partian[128] le lagrime dal core, / ch'era somosso da la vostra vista [So I retreated from your presence then / as tears began to overflow my heart, / which was unsettled by the sight of you]" (9–11). But at the same time he reaffirms his nearness to the new lady, in fact the intimate nature of his relationship with her, insofar as "quella donna" is accompanied by "quello Amore" who, forcing him to tears and to grief, is but a projection of his own interiority: "Io dicea poscia nell'anima trista: / 'Ben è con quella donna quello Amore / lo qual mi face andar così piangendo' [And then I said within my anguished soul: / 'So with that lady dwells the very Love / who makes me go about expressing grief']" (12–14).

The *donna gentile* offers support and consolation. Beatrice too in the earthly paradise speaks of the support that she had offered in youth to Dante, always by means of visual interactions: "Alcun tempo il sostenni col mio volto: / mostrando li occhi giovanetti a lui [For some time I sustained him with my face: showing my youthful eyes to him]" (*Purg.* 30.121–2). But when she died Beatrice lost the capacity to direct his will, to guide him on the straight and narrow: "meco il menava in dritta parte vòlto [I led him with me turned in the right direction]" (*Purg.* 30.123). Her therapeutic and salvific powers could have no further effect on him after she died, because he "took himself" from her: "questi si tolse a me, e diessi altrui [he took himself from me and gave himself to others]" (*Purg.* 30.126). The words "questi si tolse a me" echo "E tolsimi d'inanzi a voi" in *Videro gli occhi miei*, and delineate the way of human emotional events, marked by the giving and the withdrawing of affection.

Often fidelity is withdrawn and reallocated in case of death, and in "normal" daily life we do not consider such a substitution sinful. In fact, we consider it healthy to accept the death of a beloved and to "move on." Ultimately Dante does not accept the normative rules of his society and so has himself be reprimanded by Beatrice in the earthly paradise for not having remained faithful to her after her death. According to the logic of their conversation in purgatory, only after her death did Beatrice become truly "useable" (in the Augustinian sense of the tension between *uti* and *frui*: one must use the things of this world, not take delight in them), capable of directing Dante's will beyond any mortal object towards the only correct goal, the transcendent object. All this is implicit in *Li occhi dolenti*, where Dante first comes up with the idea of having himself be consoled by his dead lady.

In the *donna gentile* sequence Dante has backed away from the radical consolatory move of *Li occhi dolenti* and of the *Divine Comedy*, in which the dead beloved returns to life and speaks and comforts the sufferer. In *Videro gli occhi miei* we find a more pragmatic reaction to loss, the reaction that prevails in the everyday human social consortium whose laws can be glimpsed behind the curtains of this sonnet: the

---

128 In the *Vita Nuova* Dante substitutes "partian" in "che si partian le lagrime dal core" (10) with "movean" ("che si movean le lagrime dal core"), achieving a result that is less pronouncedly Cavalcantian.

·process of mourning, often eased by others' sympathy, brings about resignation, and from the acceptance of the loss of the old love, one inevitably moves to the acceptance of a new. It is precisely this healthy and normative sequence of events, repeated over and over again in the course of human history, that Dante will ultimately refuse, not in his material life, in which he married and had children, but in his interior life, the one reflected in his writings. This refusal of normative consolation, in both its material form as the *donna gentile* of the *Vita Nuova* and in its allegorized form as Lady Philosophy in the *Convivio*, is the condition *sine qua non* of the *Commedia*, whose essential plot hinges on a far more radical form of self-consolation, whereby the old love is divinized.

Therefore, it is not a new lady but the original – and dead – lady who will help Dante when he finds himself lost at the beginning of the *Commedia*, in a condition defined by the adjective *oscura*: at the beginning of the poem he famously finds himself "per una selva oscura [in a dark wood]" (*Inf.* 1.2) and in the next canto we learn that it was Beatrice who sent Vergil to his aid and comfort. The adjective *oscura* is plausibly used for the first time in *Videro gli occhi miei*, which exists in a pre–*Vita Nuova* redaction; it occurs in another *Vita Nuova* sonnet, *Spesse fiate*, where it refers to the "dark qualities" that Love inflicts on him ("le oscure qualità ch'Amor mi dona" [*Spesse fiate*, 2]).[129] In *Videro gli occhi miei* Dante uses *oscura* to modify the noun *vita*; this early reference to a "dark life" will later be metaphorized into a "dark wood." *Mutatis mutandis*, the cause of the dismay in the first canto of the *Inferno* is the one already put forward in *Videro gli occhi miei*, where so many of the attributes of the beginning of the *Inferno* are present ("paura" in verse 7 and "viltate" in verse 8), and where first Dante experiences his life as *oscura*: "la qualità della mia vita oscura" (6).

51 (B XXXI; FB 51; DR 71; *VN* XXXV.5–8 [24.5–8])
First Redaction

Videro gli occhi miei quanta pietate	My eyes were witness to the great compassion
era apparita in la vostra figura	that was evident upon your face
quando guardaste gli atti e la statura	when you observed the attitude and look
4 ch'io faccio per dolor molte fïate.	I show so frequently because of grief.
Allor m'accorsi che voi pensavate	And then I saw that you were pondering

---

129 Only in *Spesse fiate* and *Videro gli occhi miei* do we find the adjective *oscura/o* in the *Vita Nuova* (it is interesting that both these early uses feature the noun "qualità"); the *Vita Nuova* prose features single uses of *oscuramente*, *oscurare*, and *oscuritate*. Dante will use the noun *oscuritate* in one canzone (*Amor, che movi*) and the adjective *oscura/o* in the two late canzoni *Doglia mi reca* and *Amor, da che convien*, neither time modifying *vita*.

la qualità de la mia vita oscura,
sì che mi giunse ne lo cor paura
8   di dimostrar con gli occhi mia viltate.
    E tolsimi d'inanzi a voi, sentendo
che si partian le lagrime dal core,
11   ch'era somosso da la vostra vista.
    Io dicea poscia nell'anima trista:
"Ben è con quella donna quello Amore
14   lo qual mi face andar così piangendo."

the sorry circumstances of my life,
and this aroused a fear within my heart
of showing my dejection through my eyes.
    So I retreated from your presence then
as tears began to overflow my heart,
which was unsettled by the sight of you.
And then I said within my anguished soul:
"So with that lady dwells the very Love
that makes me go about expressing grief."

VN 10. si movean

METRE: sonnet ABBA ABBA CDE EDC.

52 Color d'amore e di pietà sembianti
First Redaction

The sonnet *Color d'amore e di pietà sembianti*, which is reproduced here in the version that precedes the one in the *Vita Nuova*, was later placed by Dante in chapter XXXVI (25) of the *libello*, where it reprises the themes explored by *Videro gli occhi miei* of the preceding chapter. It belongs to the cycle of lyrics that in the *Vita Nuova* is dedicated to the encounter with the *donna gentile*. If considered in a wider context, these poems treat "new love" and the fickleness of the will. This theme will be amply developed in Dante's poetry, culminating in the encounter between Dante and Beatrice in the earthly paradise, where Beatrice reprimands Dante for having given himself to "altrui" (others) after her death (*Purg.* 30.124–6; see the introductory chapter to *Videro gli occhi miei*).

Color d'amore reprises the situation of *Videro gli occhi miei* and intensifies it: to the attractive qualities of the new lady, characterized by her seductive compassion in the opening line of *Videro gli occhi miei quanta pietate*, is added specifically her "colour of love." The original dialectic between compassion and self-pity has thus been transformed into a dialectic of desire expressed and reciprocated. Against the background that it shares with *Videro gli occhi miei*, the sonnet *Color d'amore* sketches an erotic drama. The poet's "dolorosi pianti [painful tears]" (4) and "la mia labbia dolente [my melancholy face]" (6) remain. But already from the first words "Color d'amore" it is clear that we are witnessing a drama that is less analytical and more erotic. The word "colore" is a clue to the difference: it is a word that belongs to the lexicon of vision, and thus remains within the visual theme of *Videro gli occhi miei*, but adds to it a new note of erotic expressiveness, a new, "colourful," intensity of feeling.

On Dante's use of the word "colore" to express the feelings that appear on the human face, here reaching its high point in the *rime*, see the introductory essay to *Donne ch'avete intelletto d'amore*. In contrast to the revelatory "Color d'amore" of our sonnet, I note the purposeful inexpressiveness of the phrase "Color di perle ha quasi [Her colour is like pearl]" in *Donne ch'avete* (47), which veils *madonna* in an exquisite and pure opacity.

The expression "color d'amore" draws on the traditional language of love poetry (Barbi-Maggini cite both Ovid and Horace),[130] as does the verb *prendere* in the

---

130 "Ovid, in the *Ars amandi* (1.729), very famous and much studied in the Middle Ages, had said: 'Palleat omnis amans; hic est *color* aptus amanti [May every lover be pale; this is the right color for lovers]'; and also Horace, *Carmina*, 3.10: 'nec tinctus viola pallor amantium [nor the violet pallor of lovers]' (from which Petrarch 224: 'S'un pallor di viola e d'amor tinto [If a pallor tinted with violet and with love]'" (Barbi-Maggini, pp. 138–9).

second line of *Color d'amore*, which we have noted as an infallible sign of passion (for example, in the opening line of *A ciascun'alma presa e gentil core*). Expressing himself in a complex sentence that encompasses verses 1–6 of the sonnet, the poet explains that never have love and pity so taken hold of a lady's face ("viso di donna" [3]), as happens to her face ("come lo vostro" [5]) every time she sees his suffering countenance ("la mia labbia dolente" [6]):

Color d'amore e di pietà sembianti
non preseno così mirabilmente
viso di donna, per veder sovente
occhi gentili e dolorosi pianti,
come lo vostro, qualora davanti
vedetevi la mia labbia dolente.
                    (*Color d'amore,* 1–6)

[The colour of love and look of sympathy
have never graced a lady's countenance
so wondrously, from often having looked
at eyes disposed to love and painful tears,
as they have yours whenever you regard
the semblance of my melancholy face.]

The masterly use of *colores rhetorici* heightens the intensity of *Color d'amore* (the wordplay is intentional, recalling that Dante himself uses the phrase "colore rettorico" twice in the *Vita Nuova*).[131] Of *colores rhetorici*, we note: the skillful syntax that prolongs a sentence that winds convolutedly from the first to the sixth line, heightening the reader's anticipation; the chiastic organization of nouns and epithets in the incipit and in line 4; the many enjambments, of which the most lovely, full of eros, is "così mirabilmente / viso di donna"; and the alliteration on the *v* of the visual, in "viso," "veder," "vostro," "vedetevi," which reminds us that visual stimuli have been the motor of this passion.

The two actors of this erotic drama divide up the sonnet between them. The first six lines of *Color d'amore* are dedicated to the feelings that she has for him; in fact the octave places the lady in the foreground and reveals her as the true protagonist of the action. She is the aggressor in this drama: she is more active, he is more pas-

---

131 Both uses occur in the chapter on making poetry: "onde, se alcuna figura o colore rettorico è conceduto a li poete, conceduto è a li rimatori [So, if some figure or rhetorical colour is allowed to lettered poets, it is also allowed to those who write rhymes in the vernacular]" (*VN* XXV.7 [16.7]); "però che grande vergogna sarebbe a colui che rimasse cose sotto vesta di figura o di colore rettorico, e poscia, domandato, non sapesse denudare le sue parole da cotale vesta [for it would be shameful for one who wrote poetry dressed up with figures or rhetorical colour not to know how to strip his words of such dress]" (*VN* XXV.10 [16.10]).

sive. (We find this same assortment of attibutes by gender in a way that is certainly less expected by the reader in the dynamic between Francesca – more active – and Paolo – more passive – in *Inferno* 5.)[132] Dante has imagined himself in a love-situation in which he is the one who receives the attention, and is more seduced than seducer.

This remarkable sex-role reversal recalls the last line of the sonnet *Amore e 'l cor gentil sono una cosa*, where Dante declares that a woman falls in love in the same way as a man: "E simil face in donna omo valente [The same is true of women as of men]" (14). In this way *Color d'amor* fulfils the theory of *Amore e 'l cor gentil*: Dante theorizes the woman's agency in love in *Amore e 'l cor gentil*; he imagines it concretely in *Color d'amore*.

The octave of *Color d'amore* is the dramatic expression of the final line of *Amore e 'l cor gentil*. The erotic parity between men and women, expressed in philosophical and conceptual form in *Amore e 'l cor gentil*, is transformed from theory to practice in *Color d'amore*, where the reader witnesses the woman's passion. She is "presa," taken hold of (cf. "preseno" in verse 2), by the "occhi gentili e dolorosi pianti" (4) of her lover, eyes that of course reveal a noble heart, capable of loving, like the "cor gentil" in the first line of *Amore e 'l cor gentil sono una cosa*. Just as the poet must be an "omo valente," as specified in the last line of *Amore e 'l cor gentil*, so the *donna gentile* is "savia" ("Questa è una donna gentile, bella, giovane e savia [This is a woman who is gracious, beautiful, young, and wise]" [*VN* XXXVIII.1 [27.1]), for *Amore e 'l cor gentil* establishes the correspondence between beauty and wisdom in women ("Bieltate appare in saggia donna pui" [9]).

The lover reacts to the stimuli coming from the new lady (her "color d'amore" and her "di pietà sembianti") only in the last two verses of the octave, where he experiences an inner conflict as he recalls a memory that breaks his heart: "sì che per voi mi vèn cosa alla mente / che teme forte non lo cor si schianti [so that because of you a thought occurs / that makes me greatly fear my heart will crack]" (7–8). What comes to his mind ("mi vèn cosa alla mente" recalls the incipit *Era venuta nella mente mia*) could be the memory of a dead beloved, and commentaries to the *Vita Nuova* do not hesitate to suggest that it is the memory of Beatrice. But there is no way to verify for the poem a gloss that is found only in the prose.

The sestet insists on the tormented will of the poet, whose "occhi destrutti [weary eyes]" (9) cannot keep themselves from gazing "per desiderio di pianger ch'egli hanno [because of their desire to shed more tears]" (11). But the desire to cry intensified by her pity – "e voi crescete sì lor volontate / che della voglia si consuman

---

132 On Francesca's gendered attributes, see my "Dante and Francesca da Rimini: Realpolitik, Romance, Gender," rpt. in *Dante and the Origins of Italian Literary Culture*, pp. 304–32. I had not yet realized the importance of the gender paradigm in *Color d'amore* when I wrote "Dante and Cavalcanti (On Making Distinctions in Matters of Love)" (also rpt. in *Dante and the Origins of Italian Literary Culture*).

tutti [and you increase this very wish of theirs, / so they're consumed completely by desire]" (12–13) – leads not to release but to an impasse: "ma lagrimar dinanzi a voi non sanno [yet in your presence they cannot lament]" (14). The reiteration in the final verses of his emphatic desire ("desiderio," "volontate," "voglia") does nothing but underscore that in *Color d'amore* the poet's desire finds no outlet. In this sonnet of female passion, the male poet remains in a condition of abject frustration.

52 (B XXXII; FB 52; DR 72; *VN* XXXVI.4–5 [25.4–5])
  First Redaction

Color d'amore e di pietà sembianti	The colour of love and look of sympathy
non preseno così mirabilmente	have never graced a lady's countenance
viso di donna, per veder sovente	so wondrously, from often having looked
4 occhi gentili e dolorosi pianti,	at eyes disposed to love and painful tears,
come lo vostro, qualora davanti	as they have yours whenever you regard
vedetevi la mia labbia dolente,	the semblance of my melancholy face,
sì che per voi mi vèn cosa alla mente	so that because of you a thought occurs
8 che teme forte non lo cor si schianti.	that makes me greatly fear my heart will crack.
Io non posso tener gli occhi destrutti	For I cannot prevent my weary eyes
che non riguardin voi molte fïate	from looking almost ceaselessly at you,
11 per desiderio di pianger ch'egli hanno;	because of their desire to shed more tears;
e voi crescete sì lor volontate	and you increase this very wish of theirs,
che della voglia si consuman tutti;	so they're consumed completely by desire;
14 ma lagrimar dinanzi a voi non sanno.	yet in your presence they cannot lament.

VN 2. preser mai c. – 4. gentili o d. – 8. Ch'io temo – 10. voi spesse f. – 12. cresceste (Gorni)

METRE: sonnet ABBA ABBA CDE DCE.

53 L'amaro lagrimar che voi faceste

L'amaro lagrimar does not exist in a redaction prior to the one in the *Vita Nuova* and so is not included in his edition of the *Rime* by De Robertis, with the result that I reproduce the poem as it is printed in De Robertis' *Vita Nuova*. Interestingly, however, De Robertis goes out of his way to note, with respect to this poem and its successor, that an earlier redaction is probable: "it may be that this poem [*L'amaro lagrimar*] and the following poem, *Gentil pensero*, had their own tradition prior to the book [*Vita Nuova*], without however there being any textual divergence" (ed. comm., p. 411).

In contrast with the poems contained in the first sections of the *Vita Nuova*, written according to typical courtly conventions, the poems of the cycle on the *donna gentile* are ideologically atypical, from the point of view of standard courtly love. Their irregularity derives from their theme: a conflict between the poet's dead original love and a new beloved.

Dante had already written poems that treat the subject matter of new love in a conventional manner. For example, *Ballata, i' voi* openly proclaims its provenance from the Occitan *escondig*, the poetic genre in which the lover defends himself from slander; the poet replies that, even if Love forced him to look at other women ("li fece altra guardare" [*Ballata, i' voi*, 23]), he has been true to his first love. The theme of the changeableness of the will is present also in *Cavalcando l'altr'ier.*

But the fickleness treated in *Ballata, i' voi* had not been provoked by the death of *madonna*. When the poet declares he has always remained faithful to *madonna*, of having "sì fermata fede [such steadfast faithfulness]" (*Ballata, i' voi*, 26), he is speaking about a faithfulness that is untested by death.

The case in the cycle of sonnets united in the *Vita Nuova* around the *donna gentile* is very different: here the ideologically innovative move is the introduction of the death of the original beloved. Even before situating these poems in the *Vita Nuova*, even before having contrived the *donna gentile* as she is described in the prose, Dante pushed the courtly game in a new, ideologically original direction by introducing the issue of fidelity to a dead beloved. This is the issue introduced in *Videro gli occhi miei* and *Color d'amore*, and resolved in *L'amaro lagrimar*: "resolved" in the sense that *L'amaro lagrimar* codifies clear rules according to which fidelity to the dead beloved is the lover's obligation.

Thirteen lines of *L'amaro lagrimar* take the form of a bitter reprimand in direct discourse to the eyes of the poet; the fourteenth line establishes that the speaker is the poet's heart: "Così dice 'l meo core, e poi sospira [So speaks my heart, and afterwards it sighs]" (14). The identity of the two interlocutors constitutes an appeal to the Cavalcantian technique of the fragmentation of the self (hence in the prose the Cavalcantian image of the "battaglia che io avea meco [battle I was having with myself]"(*VN* XXXVII.3 [26.3]), but everything has been transposed from an existential key to an ethical one: instead of the interior anguish of a frustrated lover, à la Cavalcanti, we read a scene of moral reproach similar to the one that takes place in the earthly paradise. The young Dante of *L'amaro lagrimar* has not yet created a complex virtual world in which his dead lady is perfectly capable of speaking for herself; he creates a drama on a more restricted stage in which there are only his heart and eyes as dramatis personae. But the sonnet presents already, in nucleus, the drama of *Purgatorio* 30–31, with the heart filling the role of severe moral critic that will later pass to Beatrice.

Although the drama of *Purgatorio* 30–31 is at the centre of a vast historical and theological panorama, its personal core reflects with strange accuracy the episode of the *donna gentile*, which ends when Beatrice appears to Dante in "una forte imaginazione [an intense vision]" (*VN* XXXIX.1 [28.1]). This vision is recalled in the encounter in the earthly paradise, when Beatrice says: "in sogno e altrimenti / lo rivocai [in dream and other ways I called him back]" (*Purg.* 30.134–5). But, while in the *Vita Nuova* the vision of Beatrice serves to bring Dante back to the "diritta via [straight path]," according to Beatrice in her purgatorial reprimand stronger methods were required, and therefore it was necessary to show him the realm of the damned:

> Né l'impetrare ispirazion mi valse,
> con le quali e in sogno e altrimenti
> lo rivocai: sì poco a lui ne calse!
>   Tanto giù cadde, che tutti argomenti
> a la salute sua eran già corti,
> fuor che mostrarli le perdute genti.
> (Purg. 30.133–8)

[Nor did praying for inspiration avail me, with which in dream and other ways I called him back: so little to him did it matter!

So far down did he fall, that all arguments for his salvation were already inadequate except for showing him the lost souls.]

Here Beatrice states that after her death Dante did not remain faithful to his memory of her, that he was deaf to her continual attempts to "call him back." What she accuses him of in this scene in the earthly paradise can be classified a form of oblivion, of forgetfulness – thus harkening back to the verb *obliare* used twice in precisely this way in *L'amaro lagrimar* (verses 5 and 13). In essence Beatrice reprimands Dante for having forgotten her, in a context in which it is taken for granted that such oblivion will lead to negative moral consequences.

The moral implications of forgetting *madonna* are specified for the first time in the sonnet *L'amaro lagrimar*, where the lover's duty not to forget is clearly enunciated in a moral contract that stipulates that not even her death makes such oblivion acceptable:

Voi non dovreste mai, se non per morte,
la vostra donna, ch'è morta, **obliare**.

[Unless you die, you should not ever be
forgetful of your lady who has died.]
     (*L'amaro lagrimar*, 12–13)

Here is an early variant of Beatrice's position in the earthly paradise, all the more interesting because one has the impression that Dante knows he is staking new ground. He words his precept in a way that forces the reader to come to terms with the new reality: semantic ambivalence leads to an immediate default understanding of verse 12 that is then corrected by what follows in verse 13. The stipulation that you should never forget your lady *se non per morte* (unless through death) is at first misleading, suggesting that her death will release him, and it is only the subsequent information that she is already dead – *la vostra donna, ch'è morta* – that brings clarity: the reference to the *morte* that releases is to *his* death, not hers. Thus, Dante overturns life as we know it, in which the death of the beloved releases us to "move on" (nowadays psychologists use the label "complicated grief" for the inability to move on).[133] In the world as Dante creates it only the lover's own death is sufficient to release him from his obligation to remember her.

The new moral precept distilled in verses 12–13 of *L'amaro lagrimar* is also noteworthy because it flies in the face of the courtly penchant to engage in afterlife hyperbole regarding the beloved's effects on the lover even after his death. We recall that in *Lo doloroso amor* the poet declares that his soul will be so intent on imagining

---

133 In earlier times there were no psychologists with labels, but there was little coddling of sentiment, and the imperative to move on was stronger and more pervasive than today. Here is the definition of "complicated grief" on the Mayo Clinic website (http://www.mayoclinic.com/health/complicated-grief/DS01023):

Losing a loved one is one of the most distressing and, unfortunately, common experiences people face. Most people experiencing normal grief and bereavement have a period of sorrow, numbness, and even guilt and anger. Gradually these feelings ease, and it's possible to accept loss and move forward.

For some people, feelings of loss are debilitating and don't improve even after time passes. This is known as complicated grief. In complicated grief, painful emotions are so long lasting and severe that you have trouble accepting the loss and resuming your own life.

If you have complicated grief, seek treatment. It can help you come to terms with your loss and reclaim a sense of acceptance and peace.

his lady that it will be immunized from the pains of hell (*Lo doloroso amor*, 38–40). And *Donne ch'avete* shows God reporting the speech of "someone who foresees / her loss and who will say in Hell: 'Lost souls, I have beheld the hope of all the blessed'" (*Donne ch'avete*, 27–8). All of this is part of the old narcissism and self-pity of the courtly lover, who imagines his torments in death and hyperbolically affirms that love will render them irrelevant: "sì·cche se 'n questo mo[n]do i' l'ho perduto, / Amor nell'altro me ·n darà tributo [and thus if I have lost it in this world, / Love in the other will repay me well]" [41–2]). All of this is swept away by the moral rigour and clarity of *L'amaro lagrimar*, which shows no interest in what will happen to the lover after *his* death. Rather, the focus is on his unremitting obligation to remember his lady even after *her* death.

L'amaro lagrimar reprises the situation of the lover's grieving and of the consequent pity of "altre persone [other persons]" (3). Rather than investigating the psychology or eroticism of the dynamic between his grief and the pity of others, as in *Videro gli occhi miei* and *Color d'amore*, this sonnet passes immediately to the moral danger of the forgetfulness that could result: "Ora mi par che voi **l'obliereste** [And now it seems that this you would forget]" (5). His grief ought not to lead the lover astray from the memory of her; the aim of weeping is not to solicit pity but to remind him of her: "membrandovi colei cui voi piangeste [by reminding you of her for whom you weep]" (8). Any other objective for his grief constitutes a moral error, a "vanità" that has literally "frightening" moral consequences (the verb *spaventare* means "to frighten"): "La vostra vanità mi fa pensare, / e spaventami sì, ch'io temo forte / del viso d'una donna che vi mira [Your lack of constancy distresses me / and is so shocking that I greatly dread / the face of her who often looks at you]" (9–11).

The octave begins "La vostra vanità," throwing the word *vanità*, a word that occurs only here in Dante's lyrics, into high relief. (The fact that *vanità* is a *hapax* gives *L'amaro lagrimar* an unacknowledged importance among Dante's lyric poems.)[134] The use of a word with such explicit moral connotations as *vanità* – levity, lack of moral constancy and moral grounding – is a clear indication of the special position of *L'amaro lagrimar* in the *Vita Nuova*. The term *vanità* is the index of the sonnet's special role: it is the only poetic text of this group that contains within itself the explicit moralism that is usually present only in the prose. For example, the prose that

---

134 Even the adjective *vano*, more common than the noun *vanità*, is late to appear with a strong moralistic sense, which is not present in *Sonar bracchetti* ("libero core e van d'intendimenti [free heart and empty of love]" [6]), *Donne ch'avete* ("E se non vuoli andar sì come vana [And if you do not wish to go in vain]" [64]), and *Donna pietosa* ("e ascoltando le parole vane [and hearing my wild words]" [5]). The moralism of the term is more pronounced in *Le dolci rime* ("è manifesto i lor diri esser vani [it is clear that what they say is empty]" [75]) and in the great moral canzone *Doglia mi reca*, where Dante uses not only the adjective *vano* ("chi con tardare e chi con vana vista [some by delaying and some by empty looks]" [119]) but also the verb *vaneggiare*, another *hapax* in the lyrics ("che 'nfinito vaneggia [stretches on to empty infinity]" [73]).

introduces the sonnet *Lasso, per forza* describes the experience of the *donna gentile* as "a wicked desire and vain temptation" – "desiderio malvagio e vana tentazione" (*VN* XXXIX.6 [28.6]) – but the "vana tentazione" of the prose is not in the sonnet *Lasso, per forza*. Only in *L'amaro lagrimar* is there language that is so clearly moralistic as "vostra vanità" (9), language that accurately reflects the strong position taken in this sonnet: not staying faithful to one's original beloved, even if she is dead, is a grave moral error.

Dante shows us in *L'amaro lagrimar* that he is already fully capable of bringing a radically new moral perspective into poetry that is only apparently governed by the courtly protocols that he inherited.

53 (B XXXIII; FB 53; *VN* XXXVII.6–8 [26.6–8])

"L'amaro lagrimar che voi faceste,
oi occhi miei, così lunga stagione,
facea lagrimar l'altre persone
4   de la pietate, come voi vedeste.
Ora mi par che voi l'obliereste,
s'io fosse dal mio lato sì fellone,
ch'i' non ven disturbasse ogne cagione,
8   membrandovi colei cui voi piangeste.
La vostra vanità mi fa pensare,
e spaventami sì, ch'io temo forte
11   del viso d'una donna che vi mira.
Voi non dovreste mai, se non per morte,
la vostra donna, ch'è morta, obliare."
14   Così dice 'l meo core, e poi sospira.

"The bitter weeping you have carried out,
O eyes, for such a prolonged interval,
has made the eyes of others weep as well
for pity's sake, as you yourselves have seen.
And now it seems that this you would forget
should I, for my part, be so recreant
as not to take away the cause of this,
by reminding you of her for whom you wept.
Your lack of constancy distresses me
and is so shocking that I greatly dread
the face of her who often looks at you.
Unless you die, you should not ever be
forgetful of your lady who has died."
So speaks my heart, and afterwards it sighs.

METRE: sonnet ABBA ABBA CDE DCE.

54 Gentil pensero che parla di vui

Like *L'amaro lagrimar*, the sonnet *Gentil pensero* is preserved only in the redaction in the *Vita Nuova*, although for both these poems De Robertis does not exclude
the possibility of a first redaction that has not reached us: "it may be that this poem
[*L'amaro lagrimar*] and the following poem, *Gentil pensero*, had their own tradition
prior to the book [*Vita Nuova*], without however there being any textual divergence"
(ed. comm., p. 411). Even without the existence of a pre–*Vita Nuova* redaction, *Gentil pensero* has a substantial part to play in reconstructing Dante's poetic autobiography. The first canzone of the *Convivio*, *Voi che 'ntendendo il terzo ciel movete*, is
essentially an extension of *Gentil pensero*; the second canzone of the *Convivio*, *Amor
che nella mente mi ragiona*, draws its incipit from the sonnet's third line ("e ragiona
d'amor sì dolcemente" [3]).[135]

The canzone *Voi che 'ntendendo* describes the same conflict between the old love
and the new love described in the *Vita Nuova*. The big difference is that, while the
Vita Nuova resolves the conflict in favour of Beatrice, the canzone resolves the situation in favour of the new lady. As a result of its divergent disposition, the canzone
does not accommodate the insults towards the new love that we find in the prose of
Vita Nuova XXXVIII (27). Even in the *Vita Nuova*, it is important to note that it is
really the prose that escalates the conflict between old and new loves and presents the
conflict in harsh and extreme language. The sonnet *Gentil pensero* is not at all conflictual – although the prose presents it as though it were. In reality, *Gentil pensero*
reports a highly civilized dialogue between the heart and the soul, not weighed down
by the heavy moralism added by the prose.

The prose of the *Vita Nuova* chapter in which *Gentil pensero* is located uses
Cavalcantian tropes to dramatize a "battaglia de' pensieri [battle of thoughts]" (*VN*
XXXVIII.4 [27.4]). However, although the mannerisms of speaking thoughts and
animated body parts reflect Guido's poetics, in its essence this battle is not at all Cavalcantian. Throughout the episode of the *donna gentile*, the Cavalcantian manner is
transposed from an existential key to an ethical key: from a genuinely Cavalcantian
situation, in which the lover is fragmented, dejected, and "dying" on account of his

---

135 For the connections among all the *rime* whose theme is a new love after Beatrice's death – those
placed in the *Vita Nuova*, those placed in the *Convivio*, those placed in the *Commedia*, and those
remaining outside of any macrotext – see Barolini, *Dante's Poets*, chap. 1, "Autocitation and Autobiography."

own existential conflict (see, for example, the introductory essay on *Cavalcando l'altr'ier*), to one in which the lover has to face an ethical conflict caused by the death of his beloved. The prose of *Vita Nuova* XXXVIII (27) describes the moral conflict beween the thought of the *donna gentile* and the thought that stays faithful to Beatrice, blow by blow, starting with the thought of the *gentile*: "Questa è una donna gentile, bella, giovane e savia, e apparita forse per volontade d'Amore, acciò che la mia vita si riposi [This is a woman who is gracious, beautiful, young, and wise, and perhaps she appeared by Love's will so that my life might find rest]" (*VN* XXXVIII.1 [27.1]). To this replies the thought faithful to Beatrice, abrasively defining the new thought in explicitly negative terms: "Deo, che pensero è questo, che in così vile modo vuole consolare me e non mi lascia quasi altro pensare? [God, what thought is this, which in such a base manner wants to console me and leaves me thinking about almost nothing else?]" (*VN* XXXVIII.2 [27.2]). Here the prose moralizes at the expense of the thought about the new lady, describing in harsh language the consolation that comes from her, which is said to operate on him "in così vile modo [in such a base manner]."

Another thought arises to defend the new love, calling it "uno spiramento d'Amore [a fresh breath of Love]" (*VN* XXXVIII.3 [27.3]), but the narrator curtly interrupts the debate to impose his bluntly moralistic and negative judgment. The thought of the new woman is "vilissimo": "e dico 'gentile' in quanto ragionava di gentile donna, ché per altro era vilissimo [and I say 'gracious' because it discussed the gracious woman, while in other ways it was entirely base]" (*VN* XXXVIII.4 [27.4]). Moreover, not trusting the interpretative capacities of the readers of the *Vita Nuova* and wanting to ensure that they interpret the sonnet correctly, Dante adjoins the allegorical key to reading it: the heart corresponds to appetite and the soul corresponds to reason.

Let me digress here briefly to note that Dante is aware of the contradiction between *Gentil pensero*, where the heart plays the "negative" role and must be reprimanded by the soul, and *L'amaro lagrimar*, where instead the heart plays the "positive" role and reprimands the eyes: "Vero è che nel precedente sonetto io fo la parte del cuore contra quella de li occhi, e ciò pare contrario di quello che io dico nel presente [It is true that in the previous sonnet I take the side of the heart against the eyes, which seems to contradict what I am saying here]" (*VN* XXXVIII.6 [27.6]). This overt acknowledgment of self-contradiction in the prose of the *Vita Nuova* is an indication of the authorial manipulations that render the textual terrain in the zone of the *donna gentile* particularly unstable: it suggests the ways in which Dante is plugging sonnets into the moralizing prose frame willy-nilly and his attempts to manage the reader's response, which include acknowledging the suture marks of the new construction. These signs of textual stress anticipate the more radical and irreconcilable contradictions between the *Vita Nuova* and *Convivio*. The fact that Dante is so overt about his self-contradictions already in the *Vita Nuova* throws further doubt on the current of critical thought that undertakes to believe what Dante says about the *donna gentile* in the *Convivio* – that she was really Lady Philosophy all along – and to make the *Vita Nuova* conform to the later work.[136]

As we were saying, in *Gentil pensero* the heart corresponds to appetite and the soul to reason. These equivalences, between heart and appetite and between soul and reason, make transparent the ethical parameters: this conflict pits appetite against reason. An identical ethical framework governs the circle of the lustful in Dante's hell, where the "carnal sinners" are those who allow appetite to dominate reason: "che la ragion sommettono al talento [who subordinate reason to desire]" (*Inf.* 5.39). The link to the *donna gentile* episode of the *Vita Nuova* is evident: although Francesca falls short in fidelity to a living husband, as someone who died for love she belongs to Dido's sphere ("la schiera ov'è Dido [the group where Dido is]" [*Inf.* 5.85]), and Dante writes of Dido that she failed to keep faith with a dead husband: "ruppe fede al cener di Sicheo [she broke faith with the ashes of Sicheus]" (*Inf.* 5.62). With these words *Inferno* 5 evokes the precise dynamic, although with an inversion of gender roles, of the *donna gentile* episode.

But there is no trace in the sonnet *Gentil pensero* of the ethical framework whereby the thought of the new lady represents the appetite (and is therefore a negative thought) and the thought of the dead lady represents reason (and is therefore positive). In the sonnet the dialogue between heart and soul unfolds in a highly civil manner, without insults and without one thought being presented as "good" and the other "bad." There is no clear ideological position taken, and neither thought is declared winner over the other.

The poet addresses himself to the new lady, "vui," in the incipit, explaining that "A gentle thought reminding me of you" comes frequently to dwell with him and causes his heart to yield:

Gentil pensero che parla di vui
vene a dimorar meco sovente
e ragiona d'amor sì dolcemente,
che face consentir lo core in lui.
    (*Gentil pensero*, 1–4)

[A gentle thought reminding me of you
comes frequently to dwell awhile with me
and talks of love with such great tenderness
that it compels the heart to yield consent.]

---

136 The bizarre invention of a different redaction of the *Vita Nuova*, whose ending conforms to the *Convivio*'s embrace of Lady Philosophy, is emblematic of the distortions generated by such acritical reasoning. For a meta-critical reading of this current of thought, see my "The Case of the Lost Original Ending of Dante's *Vita Nuova*: More Notes toward a Critical Philology," *Medioevo letterario d'Italia* 11 (2014).

The ethical problem is here presented in a subtle way, in the idea of "yielding consent": the thought of the new lady, discussing love so sweetly, compels the heart to consent to it ("face consentir"). The sonnet's nuanced treatment is effectively submerged by the heavy-handed vitriol of the prose, but a reading of the poem qua poem (and here we remember De Robertis' suggestion that *Gentil pensero* might well have existed in a pre–*Vita Nuova* redaction, like other *donna gentile* sonnets) should work to establish and patrol its independent parameters.

The soul reacts with a question that registers almost a sense of surprise with respect to the power of the new love. Asking who is this one who comes to console and drives away all other thoughts, the poet focuses on the theme of consolation and the spiritual compromises that consolation requires of us:

> L'anima dice al cor: "Chi è costui,
> che vene a consolar la nostra mente,
> ed è la sua vertù tanto possente,
> ch'altro penser non lascia star con nui?"
> >   (*Gentil pensero*, 5–8)

> [The soul says to the heart: "Who can this be
> who comes and offers solace for our mind,
> and does it have the strength to keep at bay
> all other thoughts that might remain with us?"]

The "gentle thought reminding me of you" of the incipit is thus endowed with such power of consolation as to take the place of every other thought. It erases the past. The result of this replacement of the old thoughts by the new is to forget the first love. We recall in this regard the crystal-clear ethical position staked by the verses of *L'amaro lagrimar*, where *oblio* of the first love is explicitly condemned: "Voi non dovreste mai, se non per morte, / la vostra donna, ch'è morta, obliare [Unless you die, you should not ever be / forgetful of your lady who has died]" (*L'amaro lagrimar*, 12–13).

The soul in *Gentil pensero* poses its question about the power of the thought of the new love without any of the aggression and scorn manifest in the analogous question in the prose. The difference between the soul's question as posed in the sonnet and the question as posed in the *Vita Nuova* prose – "Deo, che pensero è questo, che in così vile modo vuole consolare me e non mi lascia quasi altro pensare? [God, what thought is this, which in such a base manner wants to console me and leaves me thinking about almost nothing else?]" (*VN* XXXVIII.2 [27.2]) – is clear: the power of the consoling thought is not negatively judged in the sonnet. There is no moralizing scorn for the new thought in *Gentil pensero*, no heaping up of insults such as "in così vile modo vuole consolare me" in the passage above and the slightly later epithet "vilissimo" (VN XXXVIII.4 [27.4]). *Gentil pensero* does not even take the decisive position against the new thought that we saw in the previous sonnet, *L'amaro lagrimar*.

Gentil pensero never expresses a negative judgment with regard to the new love. The sestet is dedicated entirely to the heart's response to the soul's question. In the second quatrain of the octave the soul asks: "Chi è costui, / che vene a consolar la nostra mente? [Who can this be / who comes and offers solace for our mind?]" (5–6). The response, which runs from lines 9 to 14, corresponds to the section of the *Vita Nuova* narrative that describes the new love as authentic: "Tu vedi che questo è uno spiramento d'Amore, che ne reca li disiri d'amore dinanzi, ed è mosso da così gentil parte com'è quella de li occhi de la donna che tanto pietosa ci s'hae mostrata [You see that this is a fresh breath of Love, an inspiration that brings the desires of love before us, and arises from a place so gracious as the eyes of the woman who has shown such mercy towards us]" (*VN* XXXVIII.3 [27.3]). In the prose, the debate is interrupted at this point by the author's brusque condemnation of the new love. But in the sonnet the words that defend the new love are the final words of the poem. There is no condemnation of the "spiritel novo d'amore / che reca innanzi me li suoi desiri [newborn spirit full of love / that brings to me the sum of its desires]" (10–11). *Gentil pensero* dedicates its final lines to the *donna gentile* and finishes by praising her for her compassion.

The praise of the new love highlights the theme that underlies all of this: that of the volatility of the will. Dante after all gave an affirmative reply to Cino's question "utrum de passione in passionem possit anima transformari [whether the soul can move from one passion to another]" (*Ep.* 3.2; see the introductory essay on *Cavalcando l'altr'ier*). This is a topic that never ceased to preoccupy Dante. The last word on the new love described in *Gentil pensero* as "spiritel **novo** d'amore" (10) is not provided by the *Vita Nuova* or *Convivio*, but by *Purgatorio*, where Beatrice's reprimand judges affective novelty with great severity: "Non ti dovea gravar le penne in giuso, / ... o pargoletta / o altra **novità** con sì breve uso [No young girl or other novelty with such brief use should have weighed down your wings]" (*Purg.* 31.58–60).

54 (B XXXIV; FB 54; *VN* XXXVIII.8–10 [27.8–10])

Gentil pensero che parla di vui
sen vene a dimorar meco sovente,
e ragiona d'amor sì dolcemente,
4 che face consentir lo cor in lui.
L'anima dice al cor: "Chi è costui,
che vene a consolar la nostra mente,
ed è la sua vertù tanto possente,
8 ch'altro penser non lascia star con nui?"
Ei le risponde: "Oi anima pensosa,
questi è uno spiritel novo d'amore,

A gentle thought reminding me of you
comes frequently to dwell awhile with me
and talks of love with such great tenderness
that it compels the heart to yield consent.
The soul says to the heart: "Who can this be
who comes and offers solace for our mind,
and does it have the strength to keep at bay
all other thoughts that might remain with us?"
The heart replies to her: "O troubled soul,
this is a newborn spirit full of love

11 che reca innanzi me li suoi desiri;
    e la sua vita, e tutto 'l suo valore,
    mosse de li occhi di quella pietosa
14 che si turbava de' nostri martìri."

METRE: sonnet ABBA ABBA CDE DCE.

that brings to me the sum of its desires;
both its existence and the might it wields
came from the caring eyes of her
who felt such sorrow for our suffering."

55 Lasso, per forza di molti sospiri

First Redaction

The sonnet *Lasso, per forza di molti sospiri* was placed by Dante in *Vita Nuova* XXXIX (28), where it signals the end of the *donna gentile* episode. A vision of Beatrice, in which he sees her wearing the same crimson clothes in which she first appeared, puts the poet again on the *dritta via*. After the vision, Dante's heart repents the "desire by which it so basely had let itself be seized for a number of days against the constancy of reason" ("desiderio a cui sì vilmente s'avea lasciato possedere alquanti die contra la costanzia de la ragione") (*VN* XXXIX.2 [28.2]) and reconverts to Beatrice: "e discacciato questo cotale malvagio desiderio, sì si rivolsero tutti li miei pensamenti a la loro gentilissima Beatrice [and once this wicked desire had been driven off, all my thoughts turned back to their most gracious Beatrice]" (*VN* XXXIX.2 [28.2]).

The prose narrative of the *Vita Nuova* presents the sonnet *Lasso, per forza* as a seal and guarantee of the poet's (re)conversion to Beatrice,[137] a material sign that the love for the *donna gentile* – a "wicked desire and vain temptation" – is now completely "distrutto [wiped out]" (*VN* XXXIX.6 [28.6]). The adjective *vano* in the phrase "vana tentazione" is loaded with moralism (vain things are empty, lacking in foundation and content, and therefore not worthy of our attention), and is connected to the only explicitly moralistic sonnet of this group, *L'amaro lagrimar*, in which the noun *vanità* is used to condemn the poet's eyes: "La vostra vanità mi fa pensare, / e spaventami sì, ch'io temo forte / del viso d'una donna che vi mira [Your lack of constancy distresses me / and is so shocking that I greatly dread / the face of her who often looks at you]" (9–11). In the prose of chapter XXXIX (28), *vano* will be echoed by the verb based on it, *vaneggiare*, where it will be alliteratively associated with the verb *vergognare* (to feel shame), in a copula that will remain in Petrarch's memory:[138] "e dissi 'lasso' in quanto mi **vergognava** di ciò, che li miei occhi aveano così **vaneggiato** [and I said 'alas' because I was ashamed that my eyes had gone off on an empty digression]" (*VN* XXXIX.6 [28.6]).

The young Dante is depicted as suffering from a strong sense of shame, a sentiment that finds expression in his lyrics but most of all in his prose, in both the *Vita*

---

137 I use "(re)conversion" because, as we know from Beatrice in the earthly paradise, this conversion is not definitive. For Dante, life follows the form of the spiral: "the prefix *ri-* in the poem's first verb, 'ritrovai,' echoes the form of the spiral, in which no conversion is final" – finality takes the form of a circle (see Barolini, *The Undivine Comedy*, pp. 25–6).

138 See the first sonnet of the *Rerum vulgarium fragmenta*: "e del mio **vaneggiar vergogna** è il frutto [and of my empty desire shame is the fruit]" (*Rvf* 1.12).

Nuova and *Convivio*. In the *Vita Nuova* there are nine occurrences in which the protagonist experiences shame, of which six occur in the prose (and it is here that the use of the verb *vergognare* appears). The narrative frequently creates situations that provoke shame: the episode of the *gabbo*, the episode of the ladies who ask Dante to explain the nature of his love for Beatrice, the episode in which Dante is ashamed of having said the name of Beatrice while he was delirious, the episode of the *donna gentile*. Even the craft of writing poetry creates occasions for feeling ashamed in the world of the young Dante: "però che grande vergogna sarebbe a colui che rimasse cose sotto vesta di figura o di colore rettorico, e poscia, domandato, non sapesse denudare le sue parole da cotale vesta [for it would be shameful for one who wrote poetry dressed up with figures or rhetorical colour not to know how to strip his words of such dress]" (*VN* XXV.10 [16.10]).

Present in Dante's lyrics on nine occasions are either the noun *vergogna* or the adjective *vergognoso*. The feeling of shame refers to the writing self in five of the nine poems in which those words appear (*O voi che per la via*, *Sonar bracchetti*, *Donna pietosa*, *Li occhi dolenti*, and *Tre donne*, where it refers to Love),[139] but *Lasso, per forza* is not one of these. There is no shame in the sonnet *Lasso, per forza*. It is the prose of the *Vita Nuova* that interprets the word "lasso" in terms of shame, insisting that "I said *alas* because I was ashamed" ("dissi 'lasso' in quanto mi vergognava di ciò") (*VN* XXXIX.6 [28.6]).

As De Robertis notes, "The sonnet [*Lasso, per forza*] says nothing that was not said before the rising up of the 'vain temptation'; and in reality it could be placed among the other lyrics on the death of Beatrice, and is probably one of them" (*VN*, p. 235).[140] There is nothing, in other words, inherent to the sonnet itself that leads us to think in terms of the drama of temptation and seduction described by the prose of the *Vita Nuova*; it is a simple sonnet of lament and suffering. In this case, therefore, the manipulations of the prose are particularly explicit, as indicated by the fact that Dante himself provides the gloss to the opening exclamation "Lasso," telling us that it indicates shame. Recognizing that the reader of *Lasso, per forza* would not come to the idea of shame without his help, Dante openly sets about glossing not only the general sense of the sonnet but word by word.

If however we take the sonnet out of the *Vita Nuova* and read it apart from the machinations of the prose, the opening "Lasso" functions not as a sign of shame but as the expression of a suffering so elemental and primal that it remains in a preverbal state: a state of tears, of struggling to find a rational outlet in words. As the Barbi-Maggini commentary puts it: "The poem begins with a moan and continues in a tired

---

139 The lyrics in which a form of *vergogna* appears but without reference to the self are *Se Lippo amico*, *Per quella via*, *Io sento sì*, and *Le dolci rime*.

140 Similarly, in his commentary to the first redaction of *Lasso, per forza* De Robertis writes of the word *lasso*: "according to the explanation given in the prose, this is an expression of shame for his straying; in reality it refers to the suffering of his eyes" (ed. comm., p. 414).

tone, as of one who has exhausted himself by weeping and now speaks woefully" (p. 144).

The only possible link between this sonnet and the poems written for a new love later considered shameful is the observation that the poet's eyes "non hanno valore / di riguardar persona che gli miri [lack the strength / to glance at anyone who looks at them]" (3–4). The incapacity of the poet's eyes to "glance at anyone who looks at them," although a simple declaration of their extreme weariness and weakness, dovetails with the story of the *donna gentile*, whose charming pity was expressed and reciprocated through mutual glances. In the condition in which the lover finds himself in *Lasso, per forza*, the new love dramatized in *Videro gli occhi miei* and *Color d'amore* could not have occurred, since it was awakened by means of exchanged looks: the compassionate glance of the lady and the responding glance of the lover. *Lasso, per forza*'s denial of the lover's ability to participate in such a visual dance functions, in the context of the *Vita Nuova*, as an implicit reproof of the seduction through gaze in which the poet participated in the preceding chapters. The eyes that were so ready to let themselves be seduced in *Videro gli occhi miei* now "lament so much that Love / encircles them with crowns of suffering" ("piangon sì, ch'Amore / li cerchia di corona di martiri") (7–8).

There is an almost physical, primitive quality to the suffering in *Lasso, per forza*: from the violence of that "forza di molti sospiri [weight of many sighs]" (1) by which "gli occhi son vinti [my eyes are overcome]" (3), to the purple colour denoted by the "corona di martiri [crowns of suffering]" (8) that circle the eyes (and that for De Robertis evoke the "language of Christian martyrology" [*VN*, p. 236]). The sestet continues to create the sense of an intense internal pressure, suffocating and unbearable. Of the lines "Questi pensieri e li sospir' ch'io gitto / diventan nello cor tanto angosciosi [These thoughts, together with the sighs I heave, / become so harrowing within my heart]" (9–10), Barbi-Maggini write: "Inside the heart the thoughts and sighs that want to break through produce a sense of heavy anguish, of an even physical oppression" (p. 145). For the topos *gittare sospiri* (to heave sighs) in the courtly tradition, and for its obvious erotic connotations, see the introductory essay to *Tanto gentile*; here the topos is present in its suffering rather than erotic variant, but its physical nature is the same.

The last tercet of *Lasso, per forza* continues with the lover's thoughts and sighs, but introduces a new image, less primal, that of writing: "egli hanno in sé, gli dolorosi, / quel dolce nome di mia donna scritto / e de la morte sua molte parole [for they, the ones that suffer, have inscribed / within themselves my lady's tender name, / and many words relating to her death]" (12–14). These verses recall the canzone *Lo doloroso amor*, whose programmatic adjective, "doloroso," is echoed in the sighs that are so emphatically "dolorosi" (12), and which too contains the inscription of *madonna*'s name, there on the lover's heart, as here on his sighs: "Quel dolce nome che mi fa il cor agro, / tutte fiate ch'i' lo vedrò scritto / mi farà nuovo ogni dolor ch'i' sento [The sweet name that embitters so my heart / each time I see it written down someplace / will make the pain I feel renew itself]" (*Lo doloroso amor*, 15–17).

However, *Lo doloroso amor* contains the name "Beatrice"[141] ("Per quella moro c'ha nome Beatrice [I die for her whose name is Beatrice]" [14]), not present in *Lasso, per forza*. Most important, the death lamented in *Lo doloroso amor* is the Cavalcantian, metaphoric, "death" of the lover-poet, while the death lamented in *Lasso, per forza* is the Dantean death – historical, real – of *madonna*. Whatever her name, she is truly, corporeally, dead, and therefore the sonnet's sighs are spokesmen of "her" – not "my" – death: "e de la morte sua molte parole [and many words relating to her death]" (14).

55 (B XXXV; FB 55; DR 73; *VN* XXXIX.8–10 [28.8–10])
First Redaction

Lasso, per forza di molti sospiri	Alas, beneath the weight of many sighs
che nascon de' pensier' che son nel core	that spring from thoughts residing in my heart,
gli occhi son vinti, e non hanno valore	my eyes are overcome and lack the strength
4 di riguardar persona che gli miri;	to glance at anyone who looks at them;
e fatti son che paion duo disiri	they bear the image of my two desires,
di lagrimare e di mostrar dolore,	of shedding tears and manifesting pain,
e spesse volte piangon sì, ch'Amore	and often they lament so much that Love
8 li cerchia di corona di martiri.	encircles them with crowns of suffering.
Questi pensieri e li sospir' ch'io gitto	These thoughts, together with the sighs I heave,
diventan nello cor tanto angosciosi	become so harrowing within my heart
11 ch'Amor ne tramortisce, si glie ·n dole;	that Love, because he suffers so, must faint;
però ch'egli hanno in sé, gli dolorosi,	for they, the ones that suffer, have inscribed
quel dolce nome di mia donna scritto	within themselves my lady's tender name,
14 e de la morte sua molte parole.	and many words relating to her death.

VN 8. li 'ncerchia – 10. Diventan ne lo cor sì a. – 11. Amor vi tramortisce – 12. in lor li – 13. di madonna

METRE: sonnet ABBA ABBA CDE DCE.

---

141 See the introductory essay to *Lo doloroso amor* for the occurrences of the name "Beatrice" in Dante's *rime*.

56 Deh pellegrini che pensosi andate

First Redaction

This sonnet, reproduced here in the redaction prior to the one in the *Vita Nuova*, was placed by Dante in chapter XL (29) of the *libello*, where it signals the turn towards the book's conclusion. The prose explains that the poet, now reconsecrated to Beatrice, sees pilgrims passing through Florence, "pensosi [absorbed in thought]" but not in tears, and deduces that they are coming from far away – otherwise they would be sad and weeping over the death of Beatrice: "Poi dicea fra me medesimo: 'Io so che s'elli fossero di propinquo paese, in alcuna vista parrebbero turbati passando per lo mezzo de la dolorosa cittade' [Then I said to myself: 'I'm sure that if they were from a country nearby something in their bearing would appear disturbed as they passed through the middle of the suffering city']" (*VN* XL.3 [29.3]). Committed to transmitting the story of Beatrice, Dante imagines the words he would say to these pilgrims if he could communicate with them, words that would make them weep: "direi parole le quali farebbero piangere chiunque le intendesse [I would say things to them that would make anyone who heard them cry]" (*VN* XL.4 [29.4]). Unlike the situation that obtains with respect to *Lasso, per forza*, where the prose has the aim of rewriting the sonnet, the prose of chapter XL (29) elaborates what we read in *Deh pellegrini* but does not rewrite it. In this case the prose adds historical and sociological depth (the various types of pilgrims, etc.), but does not alter the basic situation described in the sonnet.

We may recall that in the sonnet of mourning, *Voi che portate la sembianza umile*, the poet communicates in the poem what he would have wanted to ask the grieving ladies if he had been allowed to speak to them. The situation is analogous to that of *Deh pellegrini*: in both sonnets the poet uses imagination and poetry to overcome the social distance that impedes communication. But the analogy also serves to underscore the contrast between a sonnet like *Voi che portate*, courtly and set in a local environment (the ladies are Florentine), and one like *Deh pellegrini*, which aims to leave the courtly world and the local environment behind.

In *Deh pellegrini* we see a young Dante who, although still a lyrical, courtly poet, is eager to project himself outside his early environment in order to interact and communicate in a less restrictive social context. He wants to find a wider public, and the pilgrims who, also according to the sonnet, come from far away – "da·ssì lontana gente" (3) – meet his demand for enlargement and expansion. We need only compare *Deh pellegrini che pensosi andate* with *O voi che per la via d'Amor passate* (also preserved in a redaction previous to that of the *Vita Nuova*, later placed in *Vita Nuova* VII [2]), to grasp the difference between those who pass along "the path of love [la via d'Amor]" and the pilgrims who proceed "through / the middle of our city wrought with grief" ("per lo suo mezzo la città dolente") (6). From the courtly "via d'Amore" we have reached the much more historicized "città dolente" – a phrase that Dante will reuse in the famous words on the gate of hell, "Per me si va ne la città dolente [Through me the way into the suffering city]" (*Inf.* 3.1).[142] The suffering Florence of *Deh pellegrini* is an image that also resonates with the words of the Lamentations of the prophet Jeremiah, cited in the *Vita Nuova*, about a different suffering city: "Quomodo sedet sola civitas plena populo! [How doth the city sit solitary that was full of people!]" (*VN* XXVIII.1 [19.1]).

A consideration of pilgrims in the *rime* permits us to track an analogous transition: from *Cavalcando l'altr'ier*, where the lover finds "Amore in mezzo de la via / in abito leggier di peregrino [Love before me in the road / attired in simple clothes that pilgrims wear]" (3–4), we move to *Deh pellegrini*, where real pilgrims – not figurations of Love dressed as pilgrims – are passing through Florence. The idea of pilgrimage is developed conceptually in the prose of *Vita Nuova* XL (29), where it is explained that "a *pilgrim* is anyone who is outside his homeland" ("è peregrino chiunque è fuori de la sua patria") (*VN* XL.6 [29.6]). The idea of pilgrimage comes from *Deh pellegrini*, the text in which Dante first seriously explores a concept that will come into its own in the *Commedia*, where it opens to its metaphorical possibilities: life is a pilgrimage towards the one true homeland, paradise. Thus, Sapia answers the question as to whether anyone in her group of souls is Italian by saying: "O frate mio, ciascuna è cittadina / d'una vera città; ma tu vuo' dire / che vivesse in Italia peregrina [My brother, each of us is citizen of one true city: what you meant to say was 'one who lived in Italy as pilgrim']" (*Purg.* 13.94–6).

It is impossible to overstate the importance for Dante of the metaphor of pilgrimage and of the "cammino della vita": "[i]l nuovo e mai non fatto cammino di questa vita [new and never travelled road of this life]" (*Conv.* 4.12.15).

This metaphor harkens back to *Deh pellegrini*, a text that (as the early redaction testifies) had been written before the *Vita Nuova*, and that already contains motifs typical of Dante's mature treatment of the metaphor of pilgrimage. The pilgrims of the sonnet are *pensosi* – pensive, absorbed in thought – as too will be pilgrims in a simile in *Purgatorio* that sketches their urgency: "Sì come i peregrin pensosi fanno, / giugnendo per cammin gente non nota, / che si volgono ad essa e non restanno [Just as pensive pilgrims do, who when they've overtaken along the way people they do not know, turn toward them but do not stop]" (*Purg.* 23.16–18). The melancholy of the sonnet, so evident in the opening lines, looks forward, as the commentaries note, to the celebrated verses that open canto 8 of *Purgatorio*, where the "novo peregrin [new pilgrim]" is pierced by the "squilla di lontano [far-off bells]" that mark the passing of the day. The *forse* in the wonderful verse "forse per cosa che non v'è presente [perhaps (thinking) of something that is not present]" (2) looks back at one of the rare occurrences of the word *pellegrino/peregrino* in the *Commedia* (while the

---

142 And then in *Inf.* 9.32: "cigne dintorno la città dolente [surrounds the suffering city]."

idea of pilgrimage pervades the *Commedia*, the word is not common): "E Virgilio rispuose: 'Voi credete / forse che siamo esperti d'esto loco; / ma noi siam peregrin come voi siete' [And Vergil responded: 'You perhaps believe that we are experts of this place; but we are pilgrims as you are']" (*Purg.* 2.61–3).[143]

The octave of *Deh pellegrini* slowly unfolds in a long sentence in the form of a question. The poet asks if it is because they come from far away ("venite voi da·ssì lontana gente" [3]) that the pilgrims don't weep when they pass through the suffering city, and that they give the appearance of not feeling the general affliction:

> che non piangete quando voi passate
> per lo suo mezzo la città dolente,
> come quelle persone che neente
> par che sentisser la sua gravitate?
> > (*Deh pellegrini*, 5–8)

> [that you should fail to weep as you pass through
> the middle of our city wrought with grief,
> like those who do not seem at all informed
> about the heavy grief that weighs her down?]

In the first tercet the poet invites the pilgrims to stop a while to hear the news of Florence's misfortune, certain that if they remain – "Se voi restate per volerlo audire [If you should wish to stop and learn the cause]" (9) – then they will find cause to weep and depart the city in tears: "che lagrimando n'uscirete poi [that you would leave ... weeping tears]" (11). Only in the last tercet, in a solemn ending, does the poet announce *madonna*'s death. Specifically, he announces that "she," the city, has lost her *beatrice*, literally the one who beatifies it (*beatrice* is the female version of *beatore*, from *beare*, to beatify): "ch'ell'ha perduto la sua beatrice, / e·lle parole ch'om di lei può dire / hanno virtù di far pianger altrui [for she has lost her blessed *beatrice*, / and words that can be used to speak of her / possess the power to make all people weep]" (12–14).

Here, finally, is the cause of the city's suffering, what makes it a "città dolente." Barbi-Maggini note that "the name of the lady reacquires its essential significance: she who made the homeland blessed" (p. 147); De Robertis notes that "the meaning of the name of the *gentilissima* is here stated for the only time" (*VN*, p. 241). In this sonnet addressed to foreigners to whom Dante wishes to communicate a message

---

143 It is no coincidence that all these citations are from *Purgatorio*, the canticle of journeying; for the application of this topos to the second realm, see Barolini, *The Undivine Comedy*, chap. 5, "Purgatory as Paradigm: Traveling the New and Never-Before-Traveled Path of This Life/Poem." Of the nine occasions in which forms of *pellegrino/peregrino* appear in the *Commedia*, six are in *Purgatorio*, three in *Paradiso*.

that he conceives as potentially universal, not local (let alone private), Dante refers to his lady in a way that brings out her public, indeed civic, function: she is the carrier of beatitude for all, the *beatrice*/beatifier of all, not only of the poet.

And it is precisely because this non-public woman possesses a public dimension that "·lle parole ch'om di lei può dire / hanno virtù di far pianger altrui [words that can be used to speak of her / possess the power to make all people weep]" (13–14). It is interesting that this last consideration reconnects *Deh pellegrini* to the old courtly genre of the Occitan *planh*. In the introductory essay to *Piangete, amanti* I discussed the theme of lamentation in Occitan poetry, and the tie between *planctus* and praise, so visible in the *planh* of Sordello cited there. Sordello laments – and praises – his dead lord, Blacatz; Dante laments and praises his dead lady, who is a *beatrice*. *Deh pellegrini* on the one hand continues the process of freeing Dante's poetry from its courtly matrix, and on the other reaffirms it in the final topos of combined praise and lament: a non-famous woman of whom there is no public record is nonetheless a figure of greater prominence than noble Blacatz, for her ability to bless and beatify has no boundaries – it is universal.

56 (B XXXVI; FB 56; DR 69; *VN* XL.9–10 [29.9–10])
First Redaction

Deh pellegrini che pensosi andate	You pilgrims who go forth absorbed in thought,
forse per cosa che non v'è presente,	perhaps by something in a distant place,
venite voi da·ssì lontana gente,	do you come from a land so far away –
4 com'alla vista voi ne dimostrate,	as your appearance seems to indicate –
che non piangete quando voi passate	that you should fail to weep as you pass through
per lo suo mezzo la città dolente,	the middle of our city wrought with grief,
come quelle persone che neente	like those who do not seem at all informed
8 par che sentisser la sua gravitate?	about the heavy grief that weighs her down?
Se voi restate per volerlo audire,	If you should wish to stop and learn the cause,
certo lo cor d'i sospiri mi dice	I'm sure from what my sighing heart relates
11 che lagrimando n'uscirete poi;	that you would leave our city weeping tears;
ch'ell'ha perduto la sua beatrice,	for she has lost her blessed *beatrice*,
e·lle parole ch'om di lei può dire	and words that can be used to speak of her
14 hanno virtù di far piangere altrui.	possess the power to make all people weep.

VN 1. peregrini – 2. forse di c. – 8. che 'ntendesser – 11. n'uscireste – 12. Ell'ha perduta

METRE: sonnet ABBA ABBA CDE DCE.

57 Oltra la spera che più larga gira

First Redaction

The extraordinary nature of this sonnet, placed by Dante in chapter XLI (30) of the *Vita Nuova* as its last poetic text, is evident from its first word: *Oltra la spera* is the only Dantean lyric to begin with the adverb *oltra* (a variant of *oltre*, beyond).[144] In *Paradiso* 26 Dante has Adam confess that his sin consisted in "il trapassar del segno [going beyond the boundary]" (*Par.* 26.117), and Dante's sublime "Ulyssean" adventure of going beyond – *trapassare*, or *andare oltre* – is already clearly glimpsed in the incipit of this sonnet.[145] De Robertis indicates that "Oltra" should be "joined with *passa: oltrepassa*" (ed. comm., p. 402). In other words, *oltra* is the youthful version of the verb *trapassare* that we will find in the mature Dante. Another point of reference is the extraordinary coinage "trasumanar [going beyond the human]" in *Paradiso* 1.70. This constellation – *oltrepassare, trapassare, trasumanare* – is at once existential/spiritual and linguistic/poetic (Dante's coinage of the word *trasumanar* testifies to the overlapping of the two spheres), and it is a Dantean trademark.

This sonnet exists in a pre-*Vita Nuova* redaction, and, as always, I reproduce the earlier version here.

In *Oltra la spera* Dante writes of spiritual matters very matter-of-factly, describing in the most straightforward language possible a voyage of his spirit. Better yet, the sonnet describes a pilgrimage of the spirit, as indicated by the metaphor "pellegrino spirito" in the eighth line of *Oltra la spera*: "lo pellegrino spirito la mira [the pilgrim spirit can then gaze on her]." For the metaphor of pilgrimage, see the sonnet *Deh pellegrini*, with which *Oltra la spera* establishes clear ties.[146]

In *Oltra la spera* the "sospiro ch'esce del mio core [the sigh that issues from my heart]" (2) goes in search of his lady, who is now dead and in paradise. Here Dante "goes beyond" the solution that he had designed in *Li occhi dolenti*, that of calling *madonna* and of thus finding consolation: "Poscia piangendo, sol nel mio lamento / chiamo Beatrice, e dico: 'Or se' tu morta?'; / e mentre ch'io la chiamo, me conforta

---

144 According to De Robertis, this opening has "remained without imitators (the only possible exception being Cecco d'Ascoli at the beginning of *L'acerba*: 'Oltre non segue più la nostra luce ...')" (ed. comm., p. 402).

145 See Barolini, *The Undivine Comedy*, p. 58, for *oltre* as the "adverbial correlative of *trapassare*" and passim for Dante's "Ulyssean" poetics, the poetics of the *trapassar del segno*.

146 Other points in common between the two sonnets are the use of the verb *passare* for the two journeys ("voi passate" [*Deh pellegrini*, 5]) and the use of the word *beatrice* in both ("ell'ha perduto la sua beatrice [for she has lost her blessed *beatrice*]" [*Deh pellegrini*, 12]). The redaction of *Deh pellegrini* prepared for the *Vita Nuova* establishes another connection in the use of the verb *intendere*, substituted for *sentire* ("che neente / par che **sentisser** la sua gravitate" becomes "che neente / par che **'ntendesser** la sua gravitate" [7–8]).

[Then weeping, all alone in my lament, / I call to Beatrice: 'Are you now dead?' / And while I call on her she comforts me]" (*Li occhi dolenti*, 54–6). Instead of calling her, now Dante's sigh goes to find her, like an emissary of the poet himself. The octave of *Oltra la spera* describes the voyage of the sigh and its arrival at the desired destination.[147] The sestet is dedicated to second-order problems connected with the completed voyage: the problem of understanding the vision, of recalling and communicating it.

Summarized in this way, *Oltra la spera* might be seen as a sketch for *Paradiso*, a text that aims both to recount an otherworld journey and to meditate on the problems of communication that arise from such a journey. However, in *Paradiso* Dante poses the great mystical problem of the presence or not of the body ("sive in corpore nescio sive extra corpus nescio, Deus scit," in the words of St Paul in 2 Cor. 12:2–4), and makes clear – remarkably – that he goes in the body.[148] This problem is not confronted in the early sonnet.

The prose of the *Vita Nuova* describes the genesis of *Oltra la spera* thus: "mandaro due donne gentili a me pregando che io mandasse loro di queste mie parole rimate; onde io, pensando la loro nobilitade, propuosi di mandare loro e di fare una cosa nuova [two gracious women sent me a request that I send them some of my rhymes; taking their nobility into account, I decided to send some poems to them and to compose something new]" (*VN* XLI.1 [30.1]).[149] *Oltra la spera* is here defined as

---

147 The same voyage, undertaken by a *pensero* rather than a *sospiro*, is recounted in the second stanza of the canzone *Voi che 'ntendendo il terzo ciel movete*:

> Suol esser vita dello cor dolente
> un soave penser che·sse ne già
> molte fïate a' piè del vostro Sire,
> ove una donna glorïar vedea,
> di cui parlav'a·mme sì dolcemente
> che l'anima dicea: "I' me ·n vo' gire." (14–19)

> [The life of my grieving heart was once / a tender thought that frequently would find / its way into the presence of your Lord, / where it would see a lady in glorious light / of whom it would speak to me so sweetly / that my soul would say: "I wish to go there."]

148 Paul's "sive in corpore nescio sive extra corpus nescio" becomes Dante's "S'i' era sol di me quel che creasti / novellamente, amor che 'l ciel governi, / tu 'l sai [If I was only the part of me that You created last, love that governs the heavens, You know]" (*Par.* 73–5). Dante here intimates the presence of the body in a veiled manner, following St Paul. He does not express doubt. As Sapegno notes in his commentary to *Paradiso*: "E non vuol esser dubbio, anzi attestazione solenne; come se dicesse: 'Dio lo sa che salivo con tutto me stesso, e non l'animo soltanto' [There is no doubt, but rather solemn affirmation, as though he were saying: 'God knows that I was ascending with all of my self, and not with the soul only']." See Barolini, *The Undivine Comedy*, p. 148 and the first section of chap. 7.

149 Dante creates for the *donne gentili* "a little poetic anthology, prior to the *Vita Nuova*, the first anthology of Dante's that we know of" (De Robertis, *VN*, p. 242), consisting of *Oltra la spera*, the "cosa nuova" just cited, "co lo precedente sonetto accompagnato, e con un altro che comincia: *Venite a 'ntender* [with the foregoing sonnet [*Deh pellegrini*] and with another sonnet that starts, *Venite a 'ntender*]" (*VN* XLI.1 [30.1]).

"una cosa nuova [something new]," and the novelty of this sonnet, commissioned by the ladies who seal the sonnet ("sì che lo 'ntendo ben, donne mie care [and this, dear ladies, I can understand]" [*Oltra la spera*, 14]), comes through in the gloss, which explains that the poet's thought goes to heaven where it sees the lady:

Ne la prima dico ove va lo mio pensero, nominandolo per lo nome d'alcuno suo effetto. Ne la seconda dico perché va là suso, cioè chi lo fa così andare. Ne la terza dico quello che vide, cioè una donna onorata là suso; e chiamolo allora "spirito peregrino," acciò che spiritualmente va là suso, e sì come peregrino lo quale è fuori de la sua patria, vi stae. (*VN* XLI.3–5 [30.3–5])

[In the first part I say where my thought goes, giving it the name of one of its effects. In the second I say why it goes above, that is, who makes it rise. In the third I tell what it sees, namely, a woman who is honoured above; and I call it "pilgrim-spirit" since it goes above in spirit, and since there it is like a pilgrim who is away from his homeland.]

The gloss continues by calling on Aristotle, in particular the *Metaphysics* ("e ciò dice lo Filosofo nel secondo de la Metafisica [as the Philosopher says in the second book of his *Metaphysics*]" [*VN* XLI.6 [30.6]). The two citations of Aristotle in the *Vita Nuova* constitute the first declarations of a love for classical philosophy that will last throughout Dante's career, as witnessed too by the precocious translation of Aristotle in verse in the canzone *Le dolci rime*.[150] The challenge launched by this gloss resides in its remarkable combination of radical simplicity of language about mystical experience on the one hand[151] with explicit intellectualism and erudition on the other. Language as simple and unveiled as "perché va là suso [why it goes above]" is easily ridiculed – and we should not forget that it was ridiculed. Dante was derided by his contemporaries for language of this sort, good-humouredly in the case of Cecco Angiolieri with regard to *Oltra la spera* (as we shall see below), or less kindly in the case of Cecco d'Ascoli, who considered heretical Dante's spiritualizing view regarding women: "Maria va cercando per Ravenna / chi crede che in donna sia intellecto [He who believes that there is intellect in women is looking for Mary in Ravenna]" (*Acerba* 4.9.4401–2).[152] At the same time, a citation of the "secondo de la

---

150 Aristotle is also named in *VN* XXV.2 (16.2). Dante's first citation of Aristotle in a poetic text occurs in the canzone on nobility, *Le dolci rime*: "Quest'è, secondo che l'Etica dice, / un abito eligente / lo qual dimora in mezzo solamente, / e tai parole pone [This is, as stated in the *Ethics*, / a chosen habit / which occupies the mean alone, / those are its very words]" (85–8). See Barolini, "Aristotle's *Mezzo*, Courtly *Misura*, and Dante's Canzone *Le dolci rime*: Humanism, Ethics, and Social Anxiety," in *Dante and the Greeks*, ed. Jan M. Ziolkowski (Washington: Dumbarton Oaks, 2014) 163–79.

151 De Robertis writes that "the adoption of the language of mystical ascent (*sale, grado*) is evident" (*VN*, p. 243); Gorni notes the "Pauline mystical experience" (*VN*, p. 229).

152 See Barolini, "*Sotto benda*: The Women of Dante's Canzone *Doglia mi reca* in the Light of Cecco d'Ascoli," *Dante Studies* 123 (2005): 83–8.

Metafisica [second book of the *Metaphysics*]" is a show of intellectual strength and a guarantee of intellectual rigour.

In the sonnet Aristotle is not cited by name, as is done in the prose, but one can feel his presence in the precision of "la spera che più larga gira [the sphere that makes the widest sweep]" (1), about which De Robertis writes, "This is the first 'physical' definition of Paradise in poetry" (*VN*, p. 245). Dante here refers to the celestial sphere with the widest rotation, the last physical heaven before leaving time and space: this is the ninth heaven or Primum Mobile, thus named because it is the motor – in the Aristotelian sense – of the universe. If one goes, like "the sigh that issues from my heart" (2), beyond the Prime Mover, "beyond the sphere that makes the widest sweep," it means that one penetrates into the Empyrean, into the mind of God, "in sua etternità di tempo fore [in his eternity outside of time]" (*Par.* 29.16).

And what is the force that "sù lo tira" (4), that "pulls it [the sigh] up"? It is a new, never-before-experienced, intellective power: an "intelligenza nova [a new intelligence]" (3). This "intelligenza" is infused by Love – thus literally constituting the "intelletto d'amore" of which the ladies partake in *Donne ch'avete* – through the experience of internalizing another's death (alluded to by the weeping of line 4): "intelligenza nova che l'Amore / piangendo mette in lui poi sù lo tira [a new intelligence that Love, in tears, / instils in it, then sends it up above]" (3–4).[153] Through suffering ("piangendo"), Love instils a new intelligence in the lover. The lesson of death has been learned; from this experience comes the "intelligenza nova" and its great power.

The second quatrain of *Oltra la spera* deals with the arrival of the sigh in paradise and the vision of "una donna che riceve onore [a lady held in high esteem]" (6). The voyage of the "pellegrino spirito [pilgrim spirit]" (8) is fulfilled in contemplation of the splendour that emanates from her: she "shines so brightly with reflected light / the pilgrim spirit can then gaze on her [luce sì che per lo suo splendore / lo pellegrino spirito la mira]" (7–8). We note the connection established here with the sonnet *Tanto gentile*: the action of gazing upon *madonna* in *Oltra la spera* ("la mira") recalls the lady who shows herself "sì piacente a chi la mira" (9) in *Tanto gentile*. From the lady's aspect in *Tanto gentile* moves "un spirito soave pien d'amore / che va dicendo a l'anima: 'Sospira!' [a spirit that is sweet and full of love / which goes before the soul and whispers: 'Sigh']" (13–14). In *Oltra la spera* we witness the completion of the voyage proposed in the conclusion of *Tanto gentile*. The imperative "Sigh" with which *Tanto gentile* ends is an invitation to desire (to "sigh for") *madonna*, and in *Oltra la spera* this desire is consummated "when it [the sigh] has reached the place of its desire": "quando [il sospiro] è giunto là dove disira" (5). The sigh "has reached" the place to which its desire tended, the destination for which it sighed. The *sospiro* has arrived at the end of its journey of desire: "così l'animo preso entra in disire, /

---

153 I would like to alert readers to a printing error in line 4 of *Oltra la spera* in De Robertis' 2005 commentary edition of the *Rime*, which reads "piangendo mette **il** lui" instead of "piangendo mette **in** lui." The 2002 *editio maior* is correct.

ch'è moto spiritale, e mai non posa / fin che la cosa amata il fa gioire [so does the soul, when seized, enter into desire, a motion of the spirit, never resting till the beloved thing has given it joy]" (*Purg.* 18.31–3).[154]

The sestet of *Oltra la spera* returns to another theme of *Tanto gentile*, that of the "dolcezza al core / che 'ntender no·lla può chi no·lla prova [a sweetness (in the) heart / which none can know who has not felt it first]" (*Tanto gentile*, 10–11). Announced in lines 9–10 of *Oltra la spera* – "Vedela tal, che quando il mi ridice / io no·llo 'ntendo [It sees her such that when it tells me this / I cannot understand the subtle words]" – the theme of understanding and of retelling dominates the final phase of the sonnet. The sigh obtains such a vision of Beatrice ("Vedela tal" [9]) that when it tries to retell ("quando il mi ridice" [9]) what it saw "to my sad heart, which makes it speak" ("al cor dolente che lo fa parlare") (11), it meets with incomprehension. Notwithstanding the obligation to communicate ("lo fa parlare [which makes it speak]") and the lexicon dominated by the verb *parlare*, which occurs in three successive verses, at the end of the first tercet communication is frustrated by failure to comprehend what the sigh is saying: "io no·llo 'ntendo, sì parla sottile [I cannot understand the subtle words]" (10).

But *Oltra la spera* is a sonnet marked by the triumphant energy of its opening, and the poet does not remain blocked. The last tercet marks a triumphant turn towards understanding. We note the epistemological vigour of "So io" – "I know" – at the outset of the last tercet:

So io che parla di quella gentile,
perché sovente ricorda Beatrice,
sì che lo 'ntendo ben, donne mie care.
          (*Oltra la spera,* 12–14)

[I know it speaks about that noble one,
because it often mentions Beatrice,
and this, dear ladies, I can understand.]

The poet knows that the sigh is speaking about Beatrice, whose name is recorded here, "remembered" in the text of the sonnet ("perché sovente ricorda Beatrice") just as it is written in the poet's memory. The importance of memory in this history of love for a dead lady cannot be overstated, and has been thematized in lines such as "Era venuta nella mente mia / quella donna gentil cui piange Amore [That lady came into my memory, / the noble one because of whom Love weeps]" (*Era venuta*, 1–2). The name functions here as a sign of epistemological conquest, of intellectual possession.

---

154 On desire in Dante's thought, and on the *longue durée* of Dante's meditation as distilled by these
    verses, see the introductory essay to *Savete giudicar*.

Oltra la spera confronts an exquisitely Dantean problem: not only that of going beyond, but also that of how to bring back and to utilize the knowledge acquired through such "oltraggio" (the noun, based on *oltre*, which Dante uses for his final vision in *Par*. 33.57: "e cede la memoria a tanto oltraggio [and memory fails at such a going beyond]"). In the end the functionality and utility of such knowledge is affirmed: "sì che lo 'ntendo ben, donne mie care [and this, dear ladies, I can understand]" (14). There is no contradiction between "io no·llo 'ntendo [I cannot understand]" of verse 10 and "sì che lo 'ntendo ben [I can understand]" of verse 14, as Cecco Angiolieri pedantically suggested.[155] There is rather the dynamic of the sonnet, which transitions from the mystical experience that remains inaccessible to consciousness (one senses the Pauline "nescio [I know not]" in "io no·llo 'ntendo") to that which is grasped and understood.

The robust affirmation of understanding that concludes *Oltra la spera* anticipates the passage of *Paradiso* 4 where Dante affirms that "nostro intelletto [our intellect]" arrives at truth, and that it rests in the truth like a beast in its lair: "Posasi in esso, come fera in lustra, / tosto che giunto l'ha; e giugner puollo [Mind rests in truth, like a beast in its lair, as soon as it reaches it; and mind *can* reach it]" (*Par*. 4.127–8). In *Paradiso*'s heroic affirmation "tosto che **giunto** l'ha [as soon as it reaches it]," referring to the intellect, we hear the echo of the "new intelligence" of *Oltra la spera*, which "has reached the place of its desire": "è **giunto** là dove disira."

57 (B XXXVII; FB 57; DR 70; *VN* XLI.10–13 [30.10–13])
First Redaction

Oltra la spera che più larga gira	Beyond the sphere that makes the widest sweep
passa il sospiro ch'esce del mio core;	proceeds the sigh that issues from my heart:
intelligenza nova che l'Amore	a new intelligence that Love, in tears,
piangendo mette in lui poi sù lo tira.	instils in it, then sends it up above.
E quando è giunto là dove disira,	When it has reached the place of its desire,

(line number) 4

---

155 The objection is raised by Cecco Angiolieri in the sonnet *Dante Alleghier, Cecco, tu' servo amico*:

> Ch'al mio parer ne l'una muta dice
> che non intendi su' sottil parlare,
> di quel che vide la tua Beatrice;
> e poi hai detto a le tue donne care
> che ben lo intendi: e dunque contradice
> a sé medesmo questo tu' trovare. (9–14)

[For in my view in one tercet it says / that you don't understand the subtle speech / of him who saw your Beatrice; / and then you said to your dear ladies that / you understood it fine: and so it contradicts / itself, this poem of yours.]

vede una donna che riceve onore	it sees a lady held in high esteem
e luce sì che per lo suo splendore	who shines so brightly with reflected light
8 lo pellegrino spirito la mira.	the pilgrim spirit can then gaze on her.
Vedela tal, che quando il mi ridice	It sees her such that when it tells me this
io no·llo 'ntendo, sì parla sottile	I cannot understand the subtle words
11 al cor dolente che lo fa parlare.	addressed to my sad heart, which makes it speak.
So io che parla di quella gentile,	I know it speaks about that noble one,
perché sovente ricorda Beatrice,	because it often mentions Beatrice,
14 sì che lo 'ntendo ben, donne mie care.	and this, dear ladies, I can understand.

VN 1. Oltre l. – 4. pur su – 5. Quand'elli è – là ove (Gorni) – 8. peregrino – 13. però che spesso r.

METRE: sonnet ABBA ABBA CDE DCE.

58 Per quella via che la Bellezza corre
[Per quella via che·lla Bellezza corre]
Two Redactions

In his 2002 critical edition of the *Rime*, De Robertis intervenes in the reception of this sonnet, printing two redactions of it: one with the heading "versione **ar**" and the other with the heading "il medesimo in lezione Am Mc¹" ("the same in the Am Mc¹ reading") (vol. 3, pp. 350–1). In his introductory essay to the sonnet, De Robertis presents the two redactions as equally valid from a philological perspective: he states categorically that there are no reasons for considering one version preferable to the other. The philologist urges us to consistency, not choice. If we choose a version because of one variant we must remain faithful to that version for all the variants ("choosing *chiese* means excluding *giunse*" [vol. 3, p. 348]). He insists that it is not permissible to mix variants to achieve the preferred pastiche, as Barbi had done in his 1921 edition: "If we are in the presence of at least two redactions, not necessarily, I repeat, the author's, the choice must be consistent, contaminations are not allowed (the text of [Barbi's] *Dante '21* is clearly contaminated)" (vol. 3, p. 348).

In his 2005 commentary edition of the *Rime*, De Robertis intervenes still more markedly in the fortunes of this sonnet, including only the "versione **ar**" and leaving out entirely "the same in the Am Mc¹ reading" (ed. comm., p. 327). He thus privileges one version over the other. (This privileging was perhaps already subtly implied by the rubrics in the critical edition, whereby one is "the version" and the other is "the same as" but different from the first and privileged version.) Why, given the equal philological validity of the two redactions strenuously proclaimed by De Robertis himself in the critical edition, does only one version appear in the more accessible edition with commentary? This is not a trivial matter, for the two versions are markedly different. Version **ar** (*Per quella via che·lla Bellezza corre*) and version Am Mc¹ (whose incipit is almost identical: *Per quella via che la Bellezza corre*) differ in particular with respect to the name "Lisetta": in place of "Lisetta" in line 3, "vanne Lisetta baldanzosamente [Lisetta sallies forth audaciously]" (version Am Mc¹, 3), version **ar** attests the name (presumably allegorical) of "Licenza": "passa Licenza baldanzosamente [Licence goes along audaciously]" (version **ar**, 3).

The version of the sonnet clearly privileged by De Robertis, insofar as it is the only version present in his "popularizing" 2005 one-volume commentary edition of the *Rime*, is thus the "Licenza" version: the only lady's name present in De Robertis' commentary edition is the name "Licenza." The variant "Lisetta" vanishes: that name, burnished in the imaginations of centuries of readers, the name that has in fact become the shorthand way of referring to the sonnet, called traditionally "the Lisetta sonnet," is no longer there. Omitting "Lisetta," De Robertis intervenes not only in the philological accuracy of his transmission but in the *interpretation* of the sonnet.

By omitting the "Lisetta" version altogether, De Robertis effectively promotes an allegorical reading for *Per quella via*.

In this commentary I honour what De Robertis calls the equal philological validity of the two versions, **ar** and Am Mc[1], by including both of them. My interpretation will give precedence to the "Lisetta" version, but not by omitting the "Licenza" version.

The omission of Lisetta from De Robertis' commentary edition is the more notable in light of the long history of the name in the centuries-old commentary tradition on the *rime*. "Lisetta" is a name known to the author of the Ottimo Commento of 1333, who cites it in the context of Beatrice's reprimand of *Purgatorio* 31: "Non ti dovea gravar le penne in giuso, / ... o pargoletta / o altra novità con sì breve uso [No young girl or other novelty with such brief use should have weighed down your wings]" (*Purg.* 31.58–60). Ottimo writes: "And she says, that neither the young woman who is called *pargoletta* in the *Rime*, nor Lisetta, nor the other, the *montanina* [lady from the mountains], neither that one nor the other should weigh down his wings" (Ottimo Commento). And Aldobrandino Mezzabati of Padova, in his response sonnet to *Per quella via* (a response *per le rime*, using the same rhymes as Dante's), *Lisetta vòi de la vergogna sciorre* [Lisetta I want to release you from shame], writes in defence of the beautiful lady of *Per quella via che la Bellezza corre*, and he calls her by name: Lisetta.

Mezzabati, remembered by Dante in *De vulgari eloquentia* as the only poet from the Veneto who wrote in the *volgare illustre* (1.14.7), was *capitano del popolo* in Florence from May 1291 to May 1292, and at first Barbi had proposed this period for the date of *Per quella via*, identifying Lisetta with the *donna gentile* of the *Vita Nuova*. Barbi eventually suggested a late date for *Per quella via*, on the basis of a possible connection between Lisetta and a correspondence between Giovanni Quirini and other poets from the Veneto; following this line of thought, Barbi placed *Per quella via* as the final poem of his edition of the *Rime*. The suggestion that *Per quella via* and Aldobrandino's response belong to the Giovanni Quirini time frame did not, however, meet with critical consensus. In the Barbi-Pernicone edition (1969), Vincenzo Pernicone added a final note after Barbi's note, in which he reasserts the importance of the Florentine period of messer Aldobrandino for the dating of *Per quella via*: "more than justified is the tendency of most recent scholars to bring the sonnet back to the time in which messer Aldobrandino Mezzabati, who responded *per le rime* to Dante's sonnet, was *capitano del popolo* in Florence, from May 1291 to May 1292" (p. 658). Foster-Boyde go further (1967), moving the sonnet to a position that reflects a date circa the period of the *Vita Nuova*. No longer situated last, *Per quella via* is positioned by Foster-Boyde right after *Oltra la spera*, a placement followed here as well.

Per quella via narrates a seduction, or rather, a failed seduction. Over the course of fourteen lines, this wonderful sonnet presents a drama of extraordinary complexity in language of extraordinary freshness and vitality. There are three main thematic strands, on which I will focus my discussion: the moral drama, that of an explosive and powerful desire that is nevertheless repelled; the metaphorization of this moral drama as movement, as a journey; and the "social" issues, of gender in particular, that are superimposed on the ethical issues.

Per quella via recounts a love story, but not from a quotidian point of view: the sonnet dramatizes the journey of falling in love in terms of the principles of scholastic philosophy. The best gloss is the great discourse on love in *Purgatorio* 18, which describes how the human soul, which was created already disposed to love, moves towards every thing that is pleasing (note the insistence on movement that pervades this discourse in *Purgatorio*), drawing an image from the pleasing object that is then "unfolded" in the soul: if the soul then turns towards that object, "quel piegare è l'amor [that turning-towards is love]" (*Purg.* 18.26). However, since not all things that please us are worthy, the human soul is endowed with a capacity of choice and rejection: "innata v'è la virtù che consiglia, / e de l'assenso de' tener la soglia [inborn in you is the power that counsels, and it must keep the threshold of assent]" (*Purg.* 18.62–3). The "power that counsels" is reason, which counsels the will on what it ought to want and not want, and which "keeps the threshold of assent." With extreme metaphorical concision, Dante declares that reason is the guardian that must give its assent before the door of the soul is opened, before the pleasing thing is admitted and accepted as a legitimate object of our inclination: of our love.

The image of the pleasing thing enters through the eyes, and it is at this point that the drama of *Per quella via* begins: down the path that beauty walks when she goes to the soul to solicit love, Lisetta boldly advances, trusting in the power of seduction with which she believes she can conquer the poet ("tôrre" = *togliere*, "to take away," translated here "to get the best of me" [4]). But, once the image of Lisetta has arrived at "quella torre / che s'apre quando l'anima consente [the tower's base, / which opens when the soul provides consent]" (5–6) – that is, once she has arrived at the point where the "consent" of the subject is required to let her enter (precisely as theorized in the discourse in *Purgatorio*, and with the same metaphor of a fortified building that requires leave to enter) – a voice impedes her, refusing her entry in strong but courteous terms and telling her to return whence she came and not to stay: "Volgiti, bella donna, e non ti porre! [Turn back, fair lady, you may not remain]" (8).[156]

The voice that blocks Lisetta in such a theatrical way, in direct discourse, also explains the cause of the refusal, a cause that is truly the crux of the situation. There is an *other*, who was there first, who already holds lordship over Dante, a lordship conceded to her by Love from the moment that she reached the mind of the poet: "ché donna dentro nella mente siede / la qual di signoria tolse la verga: / tosto che giunse, Amor sì glila diede [for here within a lady now resides / who seized the sceptre of authority: / as soon as she arrived, Love tendered it]" (9–11). We note that in the case of the first lady too there had been a journey, and an arrival ("tosto che giunse [as soon as she arrived]"), so that Dante provides an archeology of the soul on two levels: first the arrival of the original lady who, having arrived some time ago,

---

156 The specification that the voice speaks "cortesemente" is in the Lisetta version of the sonnet (verse 7); the adverb is instead "subitamente" in verse 7 of the Licenza version.

now resides in his mind, and then the exuberant arrival of Lisetta. In conclusion, the circle is closed: Lisetta, who arrives "[p]er quella via che la Bellezza corre [(a)long the path that Beauty quickly moves]" (1), leaves "di quella parte dove Amor alberga [from that abode where Love sets up its home]" (13). Let go, turned away, finding herself "dismissed" ("acommiatar") (12), she is ashamed: "tutta dipinta di vergogna riede [she goes away completely steeped in shame]" (14). The final verb closes the circle: "riede," analogous to Latin *redit*, means "she goes back" (De Robertis, ed. comm., p. 328). The command "Volgiti" ("Turn back") has thus been executed: Lisetta, who was thinking of conquering, is conquered.

From the ethical point of view, the issue raised here is discussed frequently in this commentary: it concerns the morality of choice in the affective domain, the ethics of finding a new love, whether to replace a living love (see *Cavalcando l'altr'ier*) or after the death of the first love (see the sonnets around the *donna gentile*: *Videro gli occhi miei, Color d'amore, L'amaro lagrimar*, and *Gentil pensero*). We cannot say with certainty that the lady who resides in the mind of the lover in *Per quella via* is dead, nor can we exclude that she may be. In any case, the identification of Lisetta with the *donna gentile* (a cause of major disputes, summarized by Pernicone in the article "Lisetta" in the *Enciclopedia dantesca*) is not the major issue; what is important is that Lisetta represents in Dante's life what the *donna gentile* represents, in that she is the other. Lisetta is a version of the seduction of the new, the seduction of alterity. She is an early embodiment of the ethical situation that Beatrice talks about when she says, "questi si tolse a me, e diessi altrui [he took himself from me and gave himself to others]" (*Purg.* 30.126).

Per quella via poses the ethics of a new love with particular vitality by means of the formidable dramatic qualities that Dante manages to compress into its fourteen lines. The dramatic qualities of the sonnet inhere in the predominant verbs of motion, and also in the three lines of direct discourse that are literally central, placed between the octave and the sestet. The plot of an arrival and a refusal of entry is conducted with energy and vigour by the verbs, not only those of motion ("corre" [1]), "va" [2], "vanne" [3], "giunse" [5], "Volgiti" [8], "giunse" [11], "acommiatar" [12], "riede" [14]), but also those of stasis, which refer to the lady already dwelling in the poet's mind: her journey to the mind of the poet already happened some time ago ("tosto che giunse, Amor sì glila diede [as soon as she arrived, Love tendered it]" [11]), and her dominion now is expressed in static verbs like "nella mente siede [resides in the mind]" (9) and "dove Amor alberga [where Love sets up its home]" (13). To Lisetta, such stasis is prohibited, for she is not allowed to stop and take up residence: "Volgiti, bella donna, e non ti porre! [Turn back, fair lady, you may not remain]" (8). The expression "non ti porre," literally "you may not put yourself here," bespeaks the stasis (in this case refused) of fulfilled desire.

In the pair "alberga"/"riede," where the first verb denotes the love associated with the original lady (*albergare* = to stay at the inn, here "sets up its home") and the second the love associated with the new, rejected lady ("she goes away"), we find condensed the metaphor that will be expressed in the great parable in the *Convivio*, in which the soul goes in search of the "albergo" ("inn") and does not find it:

E sì come peregrino che va per una via per la quale mai non fue, che ogni casa che
da lungi vede crede che sia l'albergo, e non trovando ciò essere, dirizza la credenza a
l'altra, e così di casa in casa, tanto che a l'albergo viene; così l'anima nostra, inconta-
nente che nel nuovo e mai non fatto cammino di questa vita entra, dirizza li occhi al
termine del suo sommo bene, e però, qualunque cosa vede che paia in sé avere alcuno
bene, crede che sia esso. (*Conv.* 4.12.15)

[And just as the pilgrim who walks along a road on which he has never travelled before
believes that every house which he sees from afar is an inn, and finding it not so fixes
his expectations on the next one, and so moves from house to house until he comes to
the inn, so our soul, as soon as it enters upon this new and never travelled road of life,
fixes its eyes on the goal of its supreme good, and therefore believes that everything it
sees which seems to possess some good in it is that supreme good.]

The soul is seduced by the other goods that it continually encounters along the path
of life, goods that provoke an erroneous and premature stasis (the "porre" denied
Lisetta in our sonnet), for they are not "the inn" of the one true and legitimate peace:

E perché la sua conoscenza prima è imperfetta, per non essere esperta né dottrinata, pic-
cioli beni le paiono grandi, e però da quelli comincia prima a desiderare. Onde vedemo
li parvuli desiderare massimamente un pomo; e poi, più procedendo, desiderare uno
augellino; e poi, più oltre, desiderare bel vestimento; e poi lo cavallo; e poi una donna;
e poi ricchezza non grande, e poi grande, e poi più. E questo incontra perché, in nulla di
queste cose truova quella che va cercando, e credela trovare più oltre. (*Conv.* 4.12.16)

[Because its knowledge is at first imperfect through lack of experience and instruction,
small goods appear great, and so from these it conceives its first desires. Thus we see
little children setting their desire first of all on an apple, and then growing older desiring
to possess a little bird, and then still later desiring to possess fine clothes, then a horse,
and then a woman, and then modest wealth, then greater riches, and then still more. This
comes about because in none of these things does one find what one is searching after,
but hopes to find it further on.]

In the case of the episode that is presented in *Per quella via*, the seduction fails, the
error is forestalled. But, as we see in the parable of the *Convivio*, which is a model
of the narrative structure of the *Commedia*, the encounters with desirable objects and
the choices that arise from such encounters never end.[157]

---

157 For the full explication of the parable and of its theological implications, see Barolini, "Medieval
   Multiculturalism and Dante's Theology of Hell," in *Dante and the Origins of Italian Literary Cul-
   ture*, pp. 102–21; for the connections between the parable of the *Convivio* and the *Commedia*, see
   Barolini, *The Undivine Comedy*, above all chap. 5.

Dante is a poet of ideas who loves to express his ideas in non-abstract form, and frequently in female form. The reading "Lisetta" is much more Dantean than the reading "Licenza" (even leaving aside that it is genial, and therefore had such success, while the other is pedestrian): Dante loves to incarnate his moral choices in the figures of women, whether they be called Beatrice, Violetta, Lisetta, *la petra*, or, looking forward to the earthly paradise, Matelda. *Per quella via* derives much of its poetic vitality from the non-abstract and exuberant female presence of Lisetta, the "bella donna"[158] who arrives on the scene adorned by the splendid adverb, used only here in all of Dante's oeuvre, "baldanzosamente" (3). And it is noteworthy that when Dante encounters the woman that we might consider the redeemed version of Lisetta (embodying seduction that can no longer se-duce but only con-duct, because the straight path can no longer be lost), this woman, Matelda, is also a "bella donna" ("Deh, bella donna, che a' raggi d'amore / ti scaldi [Oh, lovely lady, who in the rays of love warm yourself]" [*Purg.* 28.43–4]), and she too is adorned by an adverb that is a *hapax* in Dante's work, "donnescamente": "la bella donna mossesi, e a Stazio / donnescamente disse [the lovely lady moved, and to Statius said with womanly grace]" (*Purg.* 33.134–5).[159]

There is a reserve in the adverb used for Matelda, "donnescamente," that is not in the more exuberant "baldanzosamente" of Lisetta; and Lisetta remains in our memory above all for the joyous audacity of that entrance: "vanne Lisetta baldanzosamente [Lisetta sallies forth audaciously]" (3). But *baldanza* – a joyous resolve, a firm faith in oneself – is a two-edged sword, above all when we are dealing with feminine *baldanza*. The Barbi-Pernicone commentary is not mistaken, even if it uses terms that would be considered suspect today, when it glosses: "striking the pose of a woman excessively and impudently sure of herself" (p. 654). The negative shadow implicit in the bold arrival of Lisetta has become completely explicit by the time that she "goes away completely steeped in shame" ("tutta dipinta di vergogna riede") (14).

In other words, the figurative choice to embody the abstract discourse of seduction in a historicized form, that is, in a named female figure, carries consequences: Dante chooses to assign this figure an aggressive role and to suggest her moral complicity, such that she goes away feeling ashamed. But, one wonders, what responsi-

---

158 Despite his suppression of her in favour of the allegorical "Licenza," De Robertis writes that Lisetta is "la Bellezza incarnata in una presenza reale [Beauty incarnate in a real presence]" (ed. comm., p. 327).

159 The figure of Matelda is in many ways a lyrical figure, even if she is interwoven with classical and historical motifs, and the encounter with Matelda is not lacking in other reminiscences of Lisetta. She arrives as a literal embodiment of se-duction, that which takes you off the path (*disviare* in *Purg.* 28.38): "cosa che disvia / per maraviglia tutto altro pensare [a thing that for wonder pushes aside all other thoughts]" (*Purg.* 28.38–9). Moreover, her path is "painted" with the flowers that she gathers, in a verse – "ond' era pinta tutta la sua via [with which her pathway was all painted]" (*Purg.* 28.42) – that echoes and combines the first and last verses of *Per quella via*.

bility does the thing that pleases have if the subject errs, opening the door of the mind and accepting it? Or, in less abstract terms, why should Lisetta be ashamed? Isn't it Dante's fault if he is too pleased by her? Isn't it he who has the moral responsibility to remain faithful to the first beloved? The lady of the sonnet *Color d'amore* is aggressive too, but she is not considered guilty with regard to the possible moral failing of the poet. Given that Lisetta is rejected not for her intrinsic sinfulness but because of the sinfulness of a choice in favour of whoever is not the lady already seated in the mind, what is the possible justification of her "shame"?

We must then give credit to messer Aldobrandino for wanting to liberate Lisetta from the shame unjustly imposed upon her by Dante's sonnet, in his reply "Lisetta I want to release you from shame" (*Lisetta vòi de la vergogna sciorre*). But Dante's art lives precisely in the interstices between clarity of moral doctrine and the opacity of the lived: an opacity evoked and incarnated in the name "Lisetta." It is precisely the dynamic tension generated by the simple evocation of an ambiguous and complex real creature – let's call her "Lisetta" – that is lost in the "Licenza" version of the sonnet.

With the shame of Lisetta, we have moved from a philosophical and psychological analysis of desire to the area of cultural and social values associated with gender. Lisetta's shame belongs to a social reality in which the woman – the object of desire – is held responsible for the moral errors of those who desire her. In the introductory essay to *Lasso, per forza*, I discussed the strong sense of shame that Dante feels because of his own behaviour; in *Per quella via* he focuses instead on the shame imposed by society on the "bella donna" who is the object of masculine desire. There are instances of similes, above all in *Paradiso*, which reflect the same social values: instances of the pressure imposed by society on women, as carriers of their families' honour and therefore shame. We think, for example, of the following evocation of a "donna onesta" who becomes ashamed just at hearing of the fault of another woman: "E come donna onesta che permane / di sé sicura, e per l'altrui fallanza, / pur ascoltando, timida si fane [And like a woman who, although secure in her own honesty, will pale on even hearing about another woman's failing]" (*Par.* 27.31–3). This is clearly a theme that held a certain appeal for Dante.

Per quella via contains two words that appear only here in Dante's lyrics: not only "baldanzosamente," Lisetta's word, but also "verga," the sign of the mastery of the lady who resides in Dante's mind. These words can serve as emblems of the conflict dramatized in this sonnet, a conflict that does not run its course here but that will continue throughout the whole arc of Dante's career. Two of the canzoni of the *Convivio* (*Voi che 'ntendendo* and *Amor che nella mente*) return to this conflict, as does the prose of the *Convivio* and the *Commedia* itself (where the same two canzoni, bearers of this conflict, surface again as autocitations; see the introductory essay to *Donne ch'avete* for the autocitations of the *Commedia*). And in fact this volume ends with *Per quella via* because it is a text that signals with great force the variability and mutability of Dante's thought: the questions we have been dealing with in this volume are not now neatly resolved and concluded, as the reader might think if our journey ended with *Oltra la spera*. On the contrary, *Per quella via che la Bellezza corre* is the perfect emblem – in its theme, its lexicon, and its metaphorical fabric – of the long road, of the intricate twists and turns, that Dante still has to travel.

58 (B CXVII; C 54; FB 58; DR 47)
Two Redactions

[versione Am Mc¹]

   Per quella via che la Bellezza corre
quando a chiamare Amor va ne la mente
vanne Lisetta baldanzosamente,
4   come colei che mi si crede tôrre.
E quando giunse al piè di quella torre
che s'apre quando l'anima consente,
udissi voce dir cortesemente:
8   "Volgiti, bella donna, e non ti porre!
   ché donna dentro nella mente siede
la qual di signoria tolse la verga:
11 tosto che giunse, Amor sì glila diede."
Quando costei acommiatar si vede
di quella parte dove Amor alberga,
14 tutta dipinta di vergogna riede.

[versione ar]

   Per quella via che ·lla Bellezza corre
quando a destare Amor va nella mente
passa Licenza baldanzosamente,
4   come colei che mi si crede tôrre.
Quand' ella è giunta a piè di quella torre
che tace quando l'animo aconsente,
odesi boce dir subitamente:
8   "Lèvati, bella donna, e non ti porre!
   ché quella donna che disopra siede,
quando di signoria chiese la verga,
11 com'ella volse, tosto Amor glie ·l diede."
E quando quella acommiatar si vede
di quelle parti dove Amore alberga,
14 tutta dipinta di vergogna riede.

Redaction Am Mc¹

   Along the path that Beauty quickly moves
when entering the mind to call on Love,
Lisetta sallies forth audaciously,
like one who thinks to get the best of me.
And when she came up to the tower's base,
which opens when the soul provides consent,
a voice was heard to say with due respect:
"Turn back, fair lady, you may not remain,
   for here within a lady now resides
who seized the sceptre of authority:
as soon as she arrived, Love tendered it."
And when she sees herself dismissed in haste
from that abode where Love sets up its home,
she goes away completely steeped in shame.

Redaction ar

   Along the path that Beauty quickly moves
when entering the mind to waken Love,
Licence goes along audaciously,
like one who thinks to get the best of me.
And when she comes up to the tower's base,
which acquiesces when the soul consents,
a voice is heard to say quite suddenly:
"Be off, fair lady, you may not remain,
   for when that lady who now reigns within
sought out the sceptre of authority,
as was her wish, Love quickly tendered it."
And when she sees herself dismissed in haste
from that abode where Love sets up its home,
she goes away completely steeped in shame.

METRE: sonnet ABBA ABBA CDC CDC.

Alphabetic Index of First Lines

The number between parentheses after the incipit refers to the order followed in this volume. The next column indicates the placement of the poem in the *Vita Nuova*, if any, and any other relevant information. Page numbers are at the far right.

Index

as sleeping in lover's heart in, 191; *Negli occhi porta* and, 191; placement of, 188; "saggia donna" in, 124; in *Vita Nuova,* 188

Amore e monna Lagia e Guido ed io, **122–6**; attribution of, 122; *brigata* in, 124, 234, 256; Cavalcanti and, 122, 125, 126, 260; Contini on, 123–5; De Robertis and, 16, 26, 122–3; friendship in, 6, 124; quotidian flux of social life in, 124; in *rime dubbie,* 16, 26, 122–3

angels: in *Al cor gentil,* 183–4; in *Di donne io vidi,* 237; in *Donna pietosa,* 181; in *Donne ch'avete,* 180; *madonna* resembling, 183–4, 237; in *Per una ghirlandetta,* 129, 180, 237; in *Tanto gentile,* 183; women compared to, 166

Angiolieri, Cecco, 159, 296, 299; *Dante Alleghier, Cecco, tu' servo amico,* 47, 99

"Annabel Lee" (Poe), 181n89

ardire, in *Di donne io vidi,* 237

Arduini, Beatrice, 20n29

Aristotle: citations in *Vita Nuova,* 296–7; and friendship, 50; *Metaphysics,* 296–7; on moment vs. time, 83n31; *Nicomachean Ethics,* 4, 6, 55, 92, 113n45; in *Oltra la spera,* 297; *Physics,* 83n31, 117n56

Ars amandi (Ovid), 271

Asinelli tower, Bologna, 101

Augustine, St: *Confessions,* 219–20, 240, 243; description of ecstasy in *Purgatorio,* 151

Avegna ched el m'aggia più per tempo (Cino da Pistoia): as *consolatoria,* 114n49, 115n50, 251n121

Baglione, Cione, ser, 37n1, 40

baldanza, 72

"baldanzosamente," 307

Ballata, i' voi che tu ritrovi Amore, **138–42**; and Beatrice, 140–1; Cavalcantianism in, 135, 138, 144; courtly values in, 138–9, 275; as *escondig,* 138, 141, 275; Love

in, 138; *madonna* in, 138, 141, 275; and mediation, 140; *sdonneare* in, 139; in *Vita Nuova,* 138, 141

ballate: about, 127; number of Dante's, 127; and "sonetto" as technical term, 129; in *Vita Nuova,* 138

Barbi, Michele: about 1921 edition, 9; "Altre rime d'amore e di corrispondenza," 13; and *Amore e monna Lagia,* 122, 123; on *Ballata, i' voi,* 140–1; Contini following order of, 44; and *Convivio,* 16; De Robertis and, 10, 44; and *E' m'incresce di me,* 170; on *Guido, i' vorrei,* 119; and identity of women in poetry, 87; and interpretation, 17; and *Lo doloroso amor,* 161; on *Madonna, quel signor,* 87; Maggini and Pernicone as disciples of, 9; on *Morte villana,* 77; on *Ne le man vostre,* 159; and *No me poriano,* 100; numbers of poems in edition, 14; and *O voi che per la via,* 70; on *Onde venite,* 201; ordering of lyrics/canzoni, 13–14, 162; on *Per quella via,* 301, 302; on *Piangete, amanti,* 75; on the "tenzone del duol d'amore," 14, 43–4; and *Vita Nuova,* 16, 22, 23

Barbi-Maggini: about 1939 edition, 14; on *Deh pellegrini,* 292; on *Di donne io vidi,* 236; on encounter with Donati in *Purgatorio,* 198; on *Era venuta,* 260; on Florentine mourning customs, 196–7; on *Lasso, per forza,* 287–8; on mourning clothing, 220; *No me poriano* in, 100; on *Onde venite,* 202; on use of *parere,* 229n105; on *Vede perfettamente,* 233–4; and *Videro gli occhi,* 266n127

Barbi-Pernicone: about 1946 edition, 14; on *Per quella via,* 306

Bardi, Lippo Pasci de', 17, 25–6, 64, 113n46

Barolini, Teodolinda: *Dante and the Origins of Italian Literary Culture,* 7n5, 45n10, 140n72, 168n84, 179n88, 240n111; *Dante's Poets,* 64n21, 135n69;

304; in *Lo meo servente core*, 67; love for "distrutto," 286; pity in face of, 267–8; praise of, 284; reciprocity toward poet, 267–8; reconversion to Beatrice and, 286; in *Videro gli occhi*, 265–9. *See also* new love/new lady

donna gentile cycle: anthology for, 295n149; Cavalcantianism in, 280–1; and courtly love, 275; death of beloved and, 275, 304; existential vs. ethical conflict in, 280–1; shame in, 287; and topos of new love, 266

Donna me prega, per ch'eo voglio dire (Cavalcanti), 135, 179

Donna pietosa e di novella etate, **206–18**; angels in, 181; beatified lady in, 216; biblical elements in, 214–15; "colore" in, 185; and *Commedia*, 214, 215; *confortare* in, 249; *consolare* in, 249n117; date of composition, 209, 210–11; De Robertis on, 206–7; and death as lesson in transience of life/earthly things, 219–20; death of beloved in, 243; and *donna gentile* vs. *donna pietosa*, 265; *Donne ch'avete* compared to, 206; embedded speeches in, 213; *farneticare* in, 48, 60; feminine pity in, 267; Foster-Boyde on, 206; *Inferno* compared to, 213; length and construction of, 179, 239; *Li occhi dolenti* compared to, 243; mortality of poet in, 207, 214; mourning in, 220; and name Beatrice, 207, 244; "nostra donna" in, 220; painterly qualities of, 206; and *Paradiso*, 214–15; and *Purgatorio*, 215; and Rossetti's *Dante's Dream at the Time of the Death of Beatrice*, 206; *sconfortare* in, 249n116; shame in, 287; as theologized, 206; *Un dì si venne* compared to, 219; unidentified lady in, 219; *vanità* in, 278n134; visionary in, 206, 212–15, 247; in *Vita Nuova*, 206–7, 244; women tending poet's sickbed in, 234

Donne ch'avete intelletto d'amore, **177–87**; addressed to noble women, 58; afterlife in, 278; angels speaking in, 180; Beatrice in, 131, 244; Cavalcantianism of, 153; celestial scene in, 180–1; colours/"colore" in, 184–5, 271; in *Commedia*, 177; "cosa mortale"-"cosa nova" pairing in, 184–5; Dante's finding own voice in, 71; De Robertis on, 180, 198; in *De vulgari eloquentia*, 177, 179, 180; death of Beatrice in, 246; *Di donne io vidi* compared to, 236; *Donna pietosa* compared to, 206; *E' m'incresce di me* compared to, 178; as favourite of Dante, 177; God speaking in, 180, 181–2, 184; *gridare* in, 181; Guinizzellian heritage in, 167; "intelletto d'amore" in, 8, 179, 185, 297; *Io mi senti' svegliar* compared to, 178; *La dispietata mente* compared to, 178; ladies in, 170, 232; lady/*madonna* in, 88, 156, 174, 180–1, 185, 192, 226n100, 236, 237, 246; length and construction of, 179, 239; lexicon of speaking in, 179–80; *Li occhi dolenti* and, 243, 244–5; *Lo doloroso amor* and, 164, 178; love in, 184; metaphysical content, 178; as miracle in act, 229; narcissism in, 278; newness of, 178–9; among "nove rime," 188; placement of, 188; praise of lady/*madonna* in, 180, 181–5, 226; and *Purgatorio*, 20, 21, 177, 188; *Quantunque volte* compared to, 257; Rossetti and, 206; self-pity in, 278; Società Dantesca Italiana edition and, 16; speech-act in, 244–5; and *stil novo*, 79, 177; theology/theologization in, 164, 178, 181, 215; *vanità* in, 278n134; in *Vita Nuova*, 21, 177, 178, 188

donneare, 139

E di febbraio vi dono bella caccia (Folgore), 104–5

E' m'incresce di me sì duramente, **170–6**; Barbi and, 170; Beatrice in, 5, 170; *cacciare* in, 171–2; in *canzoni distese*, 11;

love in, 108, 110–11; lady painted in lover's heart in, 111; *madonna* in, 108, 111; Sicilian conventions and, 110, 111; *Sonar bracchetti* compared to, 110

weeping: and gender boundary crossing, 199; in *Li occhi dolenti*, 254; and moral danger of forgetfulness, 278; pilgrims and, 290, 292; in *Venite a 'ntender*, 254. *See also* mourning

will: Aristotle and, 55; intellect and, 8–9, 185; love vs., 55; reason and, 303; volatility of, 134, 138, 271, 275, 284